JUDICIAL TERRITORY

JUDICIAL TERRITORY

....

Law, Capital, and the Expansion of

American Empire

SHAINA POTTS

DUKE UNIVERSITY PRESS *Durham & London* 2024

© 2024 DUKE UNIVERSITY PRESS
All rights reserved
Printed and bound by CPI Group (UK) Ltd, Croydon, CR0 4YY
Project Editor: Bird Williams
Designed by A. Mattson Gallagher
Typeset in Garamond Premier Pro by
Westchester Publishing Services

Library of Congress Cataloging-in-Publication Data
Names: Potts, Shaina, [date] author.
Title: Judicial territory : law, capital, and the expansion of
American empire / Shaina Potts.
Description: Durham : Duke University Press, 2024. | Includes
bibliographical references and index.
Identifiers: LCCN 2023047394 (print)
LCCN 2023047395 (ebook)
ISBN 9781478030720 (paperback)
ISBN 9781478026488 (hardcover)
ISBN 9781478059714 (ebook)
ISBN 9781478094081 (ebook other)
Subjects: LCSH : Law—Political aspects—United States. |
Judicial power—United States. | Political questions and judicial
power—United States. | Mass media and judicial power—
United States. | United States—Foreign economic relations. |
BISAC: LAW / Legal History | SOCIAL SCIENCE /
Human Geography
Classification: LCC K487.P65 P676 2024 (print)
LCC K487.P65 (ebook)
DDC 347.73/12—dc23/eng/20240310
LC record available at https://lccn.loc.gov/2023047394
LC ebook record available at https://lccn.loc.gov/2023047395

Cover art: Jesús Perea, *Composición sobre mapa n48*.
Digital composition, 70 cm × 100 cm, edition of 20.
Courtesy of the artist.

For Margaret FitzSimmons (1947–2023)

CONTENTS

ACKNOWLEDGMENTS

This book has been a long time in the making. It was shaped by the insights, advice, and general support of a growing list of people along the way. I owe thanks, first of all, to my graduate committee at UC Berkeley, without whose formative input this project would never have materialized. To Richard Walker, for welcoming me to Berkeley Geography even before I was enrolled and for guiding me through my initial explorations of economic geography, finance, and political economy. To Michael Watts, for his incisive feedback at every stage and for always pushing me to connect the details to the bigger, more interesting questions. To Gillian Hart, for her insistence on theoretical rigor and for teaching me how important it is to identify the stakes. And to Jonathan Simon, for his generous guidance on legal history, theory, and context.

While I was at UC Berkeley, I also benefited from the wisdom and experience of Richard Buxbaum, who pointed me in the direction of many of the cases and legal questions that became central to this project. Conversations about space, debt, and contracts with Hannah Appel and about law and geography with Josh Barkan helped me sharpen my ideas and research questions early on. More broadly, my development as an economic geographer during and since graduate school has been influenced in many ways by conversations with and professional support from Jamie Peck and Brett Christophers. And the whole process would have been far less enjoyable without the support of many graduate school friends, including especially Julie Klinger, Zoe Friedman-Cohen, Sarah Knuth, John Elrick, Alberto Velazquez, Alicia Cowart, Jenny Greenburg, Ilaria Giglioli, John Stehlin, Gustavo Oliveira, Elizabeth Sibilia, Lauren Pearson, and Nick Anderman.

During development of the book, the project evolved more than I ever expected. I am grateful to the anonymous referees of my 2019 article in the *Annals of the American Association of Geographers*, in which I worked out earlier versions of some of the book's main arguments. I am especially indebted to the participants of my June 2021 Junior Faculty Manuscript

Workshop: John Agnew, Hannah Appel, Josh Barkan, Charmaine Chua, Helga Leitner, Adina Matisoff, Adam Moore, and Eric Sheppard. It is a rare gift to have eight scholars devote that much time and sustained attention to one's work. Their generous, thorough, and insightful feedback on the entire manuscript helped me sharpen my arguments and clarify the narrative and made the final book much stronger than it would have been.

I have also been lucky to have the support of numerous colleagues in UCLA Geography as I have worked on this manuscript. Beyond their participation in my book workshop, I am deeply grateful to Helga Leitner and Eric Sheppard for their careful feedback on multiple prospectus and chapter drafts, and for their wise advice about every stage of the publication process, as well as for their invaluable friendship. My colleagues Adam Moore, John Agnew, David Rigby, and Lieba Faier also provided useful comments and guidance at multiple points, while Kelly Kay and Juan Herrera have been a steady source of friendship and professional support since we joined the department together in 2017.

My editor at Duke University Press, Elizabeth Ault, has been enthusiastic about this book since the first time we spoke; I am very thankful for her guidance in shepherding it through publication. I owe sincere thanks, as well, to two anonymous reviewers for their engaged and constructive feedback, which significantly improved the final draft. Many thanks also to Clare Beer and John Schmidt for their diligent assistance with references and formatting.

Julie Klinger has been both a dear friend and a continued source of ideas, inspiration, and moral support. I cannot thank her enough for innumerable conversations about and close comments on many, many chapter drafts and especially for making this whole book-writing adventure more fun.

I would never even have begun this project if it had not been for my friend, mentor, and "surrogate aunt" Margaret FitzSimmons, to whom this book is dedicated. Margaret is the reason I became a geographer. Although she did not live to see the book's final publication, she followed the project closely from the start and offered unwavering support, advice, and wisdom throughout its development. I will be forever grateful for her penetrating intelligence, her expansive curiosity, and her consistent ability to reflect your own ideas back to you in a far more nuanced and articulate form. Most of all, I am grateful for her many years of love and friendship.

Finally, I am deeply appreciative of the enduring love and support of my mom, Laurel, my dad, Donald, and my brother, Stephen. And no words can adequately express my gratitude to my partner and best friend, Gabriel Page, for reading every iteration of every chapter, for talking through every thorny idea in far more detail than he ever could have wanted to, and, above all, for the joy that he, Lucian, and Willow have brought into my life.

Introduction

In February and November 2012, the District Court for the Southern District of New York ruled in favor of a handful of Wall Street hedge funds against the Republic of Argentina. Judge Thomas Griesa did not simply say that Argentina owed these hedge funds, widely referred to as "vulture funds," payment on the defaulted sovereign bonds they held—a common enough occurrence in such litigation. In a far more unusual move, he held that, unless it paid these funds first, Argentina was forbidden from paying any of its *other* creditors. He backed this up by prohibiting any financier *anywhere in the world* except in Argentina from helping the country make such payments.[1] In June 2014, the US Supreme Court allowed the decision to stand.[2] When Argentina defied the US court orders by refusing to pay the vulture funds, it was forced into a "technical" default on all its foreign loans, exacerbating an already deteriorating domestic economic situation and blocking the country from accessing new credit.[3] After a fraught election, in which the topic of vulture funds played a significant role, Argentina eventually settled with the funds for more than $10 billion. For those funds at the center of the case, this amounted to massive returns of at least 400 and possibly as much as 1,500 percent.[4]

The case sparked outrage from governments, activists, economists, and legal commentators around the world, with the most critical accusing the United States of legal and financial imperialism and extraterritorial overreach.[5] For those used to thinking about the world as composed of at least formally equal nation-states, such a blatant extension of the authority of one country over another seemed to breach the normal rules of territorial sovereignty.

Yet, the Argentina litigation is both more and less significant than these critics suggested. On the one hand, the transnational exercise of US judicial power beyond US borders is neither new nor unusual. US courts rule on transnational cases, including those involving foreign sovereign governments, all the time. On the other hand, it is precisely because this *is* so common that the case is even more important than most critics realized. Griesa's decisions were only possible because of a long history of gradually expanding US judicial authority over foreign state activities within and beyond US borders. Today, *many* significant economic decisions of other governments are subject to oversight by US law and courts.

It has not always been this way. A century ago, US courts nearly always refused to claim jurisdiction over foreign state officials, acts, or property even within US borders, let alone abroad. By the 1960s, however, this began to change. US courts were now willing to assert authority over what they understood as the "commercial" acts or property of foreign governments. This included things like operating state-owned enterprises or signing government-funded development contracts. Yet, other activities, like issuing public debts or expropriating US property, were still seen as sovereign acts, beyond US judicial reach. Moreover, even in commercial cases, courts required substantial spatial links between the matter at hand and the United States. By the 1990s, things had changed again. Courts readily extended authority over sovereign debt relations and other government acts that had previously been classified as sovereign and immune—and they required far fewer direct ties to the United States to do so.

What changed in the 2010s was not *that* US courts exercised authority over a foreign government, but how far they were willing to go to enforce their decisions. In the Argentina litigation, US courts ruled that the whole world, except for Argentina, was at least potentially subject to US legal authority. And where litigants and judges in previous decades had continually moved the boundary around what constituted protected sovereign activity, judges now questioned whether sovereigns should be treated differently from private corporations at all.[6] Finally, the case revealed a new and significant rupture between the views of the executive and the judiciary over the proper extent of US judicial reach. From the 1940s on, the executive branch had been a strong proponent of the extension of US judicial power over foreign sovereigns, and as late as the 1990s, US courts had, in turn, regularly referenced US foreign policy views in such cases.[7]

In the recent Argentina litigation, in contrast, the courts ruled in favor of the vulture funds in the face of direct opposition from the Obama Administration, dismissing the executive's "political" concerns not only with indifference, but with scorn.[8]

This book explores how we got from a world in which US domestic law and courts were largely confined within US borders to one in which they regularly operate beyond them; from a world in which US courts refused to adjudicate the acts of foreign sovereigns to one in which they freely pronounce judgment on and expect obedience from those sovereigns; and from a world in which foreign governments are considered to have special legal status to one in which they are increasingly treated just like private corporations.

The growing complexity of cross-border jurisdictional claims since the mid-twentieth century is well documented.[9] It is often interpreted as a natural and apolitical corollary of increasing economic integration. Law, according to this view, has become more flexible in the age of globalization, rendering the traditional identification of jurisdiction with the territorial boundaries of the nation-state obsolete. This book argues in contrast that the law has not become divorced from territoriality but rather remapped it; and that it has not simply followed globalization but actively produced it.

More specifically, the book traces the expansion of US judicial authority over the economic decisions of foreign sovereign governments within and beyond US borders to show how this has led to a re-territorialization of US and foreign state space via a judicial modality of American power. The extension of what I refer to as "judicial territory"—by which I mean that space within and beyond official US borders over which US courts exercise authority—has been a crucial, yet hitherto unacknowledged, pillar of post–World War II American empire and the liberal international order so closely connected to it. It has promoted private property rights and investments over all other considerations, and it has supported transnational capital by undermining national economic sovereignty, especially that of those Third World states attempting to pursue alternative development models.[10] Far from merely reflecting underlying economic changes, it has played a key role in constituting what we now think of as "the economy" and in forging a particular kind of (neoliberal) globalization. The increasing flexibility of law has not affected all states equally, nor has it merely followed the inevitable march of capital across borders.

On the contrary, law has helped make the whole world part of *US* economic space.

Although these arguments depend in large part on technical legal evidence, this book is not intended for a specialized legal audience. Rather, it aims to bring a history that has been almost entirely unexamined outside legal circles into broader social science conversations about territorial sovereignty, (neo)liberal capitalism, and US empire. The idea that law is too technical or complex for those without legal training to comprehend has itself been a source of great power for law and legal professionals.[11] Yet, law has never been separable from central concerns in human geography, political economy, anthropology, and other fields. Leaving law to the "experts" has too often left gaps in our understanding of important social processes. Moreover, it has allowed dominant narratives about law to depoliticize and normalize contemporary legal practices, obscuring critical questions about law, capital, and empire and about what sovereignty actually means in this nominally postcolonial world. Destabilizing the work of law today requires engaging with and exposing these standard narratives, not just to point out their flaws, but to show how they themselves are constitutive of both American power and global capitalism.

In the rest of this introduction, I first clarify the empirical scope of the project, defining transnational US commercial law and then briefly introducing the two main legal doctrines whose transformations have made the extension of US judicial reach over foreign governments possible. I then introduce my concept of judicial territory and explain why I use this term rather than jurisdiction or extraterritoriality. In the following pages, I clarify the book's main arguments. First, I sketch out a brief timeline of the role of judicial territory in promoting US empire and global capitalism since World War II. Next, I explain how this overarching historical argument emerges from a detailed analysis of the seemingly esoteric spatio-legal minutiae that enabled the transformation of foreign sovereign immunity and act of state rules. Specifically, I explain how the iterative redefinition of key legal dichotomies has been fundamental to extending US judicial territory over foreign government acts in and beyond US borders. This process has simultaneously effected a redefinition of territorial sovereignty and helped institutionalize a neoliberal understanding of the economy. Finally, I offer some comments on how I have approached reading and interpreting common law cases, before providing a brief outline of the structure of the book.

This book focuses on the extension of US judicial authority over economic relationships between private (usually US) companies and foreign sovereign governments. This is one subset of "transnational commercial law," which plays a key role in governing the global economy. It overlaps with but is distinct from (sub)national and international law.

International law, which many associate with global economic governance, is a common but fuzzy term. Sometimes called "public international law," it refers to rules and norms agreed on between and among sovereign states or other official international actors. This includes bi- and multilateral treaties, the rules of international institutions, and the more amorphous "customary" or "general" principles of international law. Together, these create a patchy if important set of rules governing state decisions, including economic policies.[12] Bilateral and multilateral trade treaties are especially significant for "legally locking in pro-business market reforms," though not in the equalizing way many standard accounts of "free market" globalization assume.[13] As geographer Matthew Sparke explains, "Contrary to flat-world visions, the so-called level playing field of so-called free trade actually relies upon a complex patchwork of bilateral, regional, and global agreements that re-regulate rather than deregulate trade."[14]

In addition to these properly inter- or supranational rules, some aspects of cross-border economic transactions are still governed by the national or subnational laws of the host states within which they occur. These laws can, of course, vary greatly among countries. Yet, since World War II, the "Americanization" of other legal systems, sometimes referred to as the global "harmonization" of law, has meant that countries around the world have increasingly reshaped their own domestic laws, particularly commercial laws, to mirror those of the United States.[15]

Transnational commercial law is less widely known beyond law and business circles than either national or international law. Yet, it is even more important for governing cross-border economic transactions between private companies or between companies and governments, with major effects on the global distribution of wealth and resources.[16] The precise definition of transnational commercial law remains elusive.[17] It consists of a wide variety of customary and codified rules. Sometimes overlapping with "private international law," this includes the important but often ambiguous "lex mercatoria, consisting of the unwritten customs and usages of merchants and general principles of commercial law."[18] It also includes the rules of international arbitration, in which contracting parties submit disputes to independent tribunals that are not technically subsumed within any one nation-state, though in practice they are dominated by Anglo-American training and jurists.[19]

One of the most important components of transnational law, however, is the transnational application of the *domestic* laws of economically powerful countries. Such laws are based in national legislatures and judiciaries, but they govern economic relationships occurring in whole or in part beyond those states' borders. This body of law, based most importantly in England and New York, is, as Pistor explains, "the backbone for global capitalism."[20] The courts of these jurisdictions, which are considered to be the most capital and creditor friendly in the world, claim authority over huge numbers of transnational economic transactions, while other states regularly recognize and enforce these foreign rules.[21]

In this book, I use the terms *transnational US law* or *transnational US commercial law* to refer to the national and subnational US laws used to govern economic relations that extend beyond official US borders. This law, of which New York state and federal US law are key components, itself takes several forms. It includes explicitly extraterritorial laws, such as US anti-trust statutes and other legislation whose transnational application usually depends on claims about a foreign act's "effects" on the United States.[22] Yet, it is also extended in much more sweeping ways. In some cases, courts base transnational jurisdictional claims on what are known as conflict of laws analyses of which of multiple jurisdictions has the most substantial claim over an activity. More straightforward is the use of governing law clauses, which allow contracting parties to select which jurisdiction will govern their own transaction. These have become nearly ubiquitous in major commercial contracts since the 1970s. New York and English law remain the favored choices in these clauses, especially for financial contracts, *even when those contracts have little or no connection to the United States or the United Kingdom.*[23] Together, conflict of laws analyses and governing law clauses extend US legal space over huge swathes of transnational economic relations between private parties. Bringing the economic acts of foreign *governments* under US judicial authority, however, has required an extra step. It has required rewriting the two US legal doctrines most closely concerned with defining the sovereignty of foreign states—foreign sovereign immunity and the act of state doctrine.

Since its founding, the United States has regularly intervened in the affairs of other sovereign countries. Yet, throughout the nineteenth and early twentieth centuries, such interventions were considered the domain of the executive branch and foreign policy, not of the judiciary. During this period, foreign sovereign governments were protected from US *courts* by two main common law doctrines. Foreign sovereign immunity rules ensured that even foreign government entities (e.g., diplomats or naval ships) *within* US borders would be immune from suit in US courts in most circumstances. Meanwhile, the act of state doctrine prevented US courts from questioning the validity of the acts of foreign governments in their *own* territories. This, for instance, prevented US citizens who had travelled abroad from using US courts to sue foreign governments for seizure of property or other mistreatment. Until the mid-twentieth century, strict or "absolute" versions of each doctrine dominated. After World War II, however, both underwent major transformations. Most importantly, both were gradually restricted to exclude what were understood to be the private, commercial acts of foreign governments—allowing US courts to assert authority over such acts in ways they would not have done previously.

The transformations of these doctrines have overlapping but distinct timelines. Support for the "restrictive" theory of foreign sovereign immunity began in the early twentieth century. Yet, the doctrine only really began to change in the 1950s, as a "commercial exception" was elaborated in State Department policy and US common law. This transition was strengthened with the passage of the Foreign Sovereign Immunities Act (FSIA) in 1976, which codified the commercial exception and introduced new, more flexible spatial rules for extending US jurisdiction not only within US borders but over foreign government acts with "direct effects" on the United States.[24] Since then, the range of government activities considered merely commercial and thus *not* immune from US judicial reach has continued to expand more gradually.[25]

The restriction of the act of state doctrine only began in the early 1960s, as attention shifted from the traditional territorial bases of the doctrine to maintaining a proper separation of powers within the US government. This paved the way for the gradual restriction of the doctrine with respect to acts that are seen as unlikely to interfere with the executive's US foreign policy interests. It eventually led to several specific exceptions to the act of state doctrine, including a contested but still significant common law exception for commercial activities. This has enabled US courts to claim authority in some cases even over foreign government economic acts carried out in that government's *own* territory.[26]

Neither foreign sovereign immunity nor the act of state doctrine are prominent in scholarship on transnational commercial law. Conversely, work on these doctrines tends to focus either on those issues still considered to be "political" matters and thus beyond US judicial reach or on the liminal cases in which the boundaries of judicial power remain actively contested. It rarely considers situations in which these doctrines no longer apply because the acts in question are *now* seen as merely private and commercial; the role of the transformation of these doctrines in *making* such cases "apolitical" is overlooked. Yet, it is only because such activity has been rendered merely economic that it can be seen as coming under US jurisdiction in the same way any other transnational commercial activity might. It was the restriction of these doctrines that enabled many foreign government acts today to be treated as private economic acts that can be adjudicated by US courts, rather than as foreign policy issues for the executive to handle. "The private cloak turns what would otherwise be significant inroads into, and infractions of, territorial sovereignty into unexceptional economic activity that leaves territorial sovereignty perfectly intact."[27]

In doing so, the restriction of foreign sovereign immunity and act of state rules has extended the power not just of any legal system, but of the most capital-friendly jurisdiction in the world. Conversely, even as judicial expansion bolsters US and global capitalism, transnational US law is dependent on US and especially New York economic power. Each step in the expansion of this law has been challenged by foreign governments. Yet, once judicial decisions are made, most foreign governments do obey them most of the time. This is true even though transnational law is not backed directly by the enforcement power of the police the way domestic law is. Rather, this obedience is due primarily to the importance of the US economy—foreign governments simply cannot afford to be locked out of US markets or legal services.[28] The transnational extension of US judicial power rests on US economic dominance.

I use the concept of judicial territory to refer to the entire space, within and beyond official US borders, over which US courts regularly exercise authority. This concept partially overlaps with common terms like *jurisdiction* and *extraterritoriality*. Yet, it captures empirical and theoretical dimensions of legal space missing from dominant understandings of those terms.

Legal scholars and jurists are well aware of the growing importance of transnational law. The common story is that while jurisdiction, territory, and sovereignty were coterminous in the Westphalian era, this spatial identity broke down in the second half of the twentieth century, as the territorial bases of law were supplemented or replaced by other jurisdictional criteria. Complicated cross-border supply chains, integrated financial markets, and the rise of cyberspace have indisputably led to complex jurisdictional questions. Prolific scholarship on these issues provides useful insights into the detailed operations of transnational law today.[29]

By and large, however, such accounts stop at noting or describing these tendencies toward jurisdictional complexity or flexibility, without considering how and why *particular* spatio-legal changes are produced. Indeed, such work often presents these transformations in aspatial and apolitical ways. Even as scholars acknowledge the dominance of New York and English courts in extending domestic laws transnationally, for example, they tend to overlook the significance of unequal power relations in shaping this particular geography. The importance of these courts is simply noted or described, while so-called political analyses of this importance are either rejected or deferred.[30] Existing differences among states, moreover, are often presented as transitory—that is, as in the process of becoming harmonized or homogenized and giving way, however gradually, to an emerging international consensus.[31] While all this work may register particular extensions of US legal reach over foreign governments, it fails to emphasize the uneven geographical and geopolitical dimensions of these processes.

Commercial law texts and treatises tend not to probe the conceptual or political implications of the transition from Westphalian to more complex bases for asserting jurisdiction at all.[32] Other legal scholars do discuss jurisdictional changes in more sophisticated ways, considering, for example, what they mean for the status of the nation-state, as well as for conceptions of sovereignty and the constitution of political subjectivity.[33] Yet, even here, the tendency is to talk about changes in the relationship between jurisdiction and "states" in general terms, rather than to emphasize the ways that *particular* states are positioned in relation to these changes.[34] Moreover, a normative focus in much of this work on what a more cosmopolitan, pluralist jurisdictional regime *could* look like tends to elide the continued highly unequal geopolitical economic context in which these jurisdictional changes are actually being made.

In contrast to much of this work, a small number of more critical legal scholars have theorized jurisdiction in ways that do center power and space, arguing, for example, that it is "a legal mechanism for organizing how political power is exercised, spatialized, and contested."[35] Mariana Valverde shows that while jurisdiction appears as a neutral legal technology, it is in fact crucial to organizing not only the who and what, but also the *how* of governance. Moreover, one function of jurisdiction has been to obscure the messiness of overlapping, often contradictory, and contested legal spaces.[36] Such analyses are helpful for analyzing the transnational extension of US judicial authority and showing how formal legal tools are both power-laden and depoliticizing.

Yet, in general, the tendency, even in more critical work on jurisdiction, to see the growing flexibility of law in terms of the extension of jurisdiction *beyond* territory, limits the explanatory potential of this concept for understanding the increasingly transnational character of US law in general and its extension over the economic activities of foreign governments in particular. This tendency reflects the widespread but simplistic assumption that territory is a nationally bounded spatial container within which the sovereign is supposed to operate. Transnational legal practices are then viewed as flexible, extraterritorial, or even de-territorializing, and, correspondingly, as making traditional Westphalian sovereignty and borders obsolete.[37] Yet, Westphalian territoriality has *always* been a myth, if a materially significant one. Powerful states have long exercised authority beyond their formal borders, and even domestically the power of states has always been fragmentary, contested, graduated, and incomplete.[38]

In contrast to most work on jurisdiction, the concepts of judicial territory and territoriality recenter space and power to offer a very different account of the history and operation of transnational law and its role in governing foreign state economic decisions—one that foregrounds not legal harmonization and leveling, or mere complexity, but rather the geopolitical and geographical *unevenness* of radical transformations in jurisdictional rules since the mid-twentieth century, as well as their implications for reconfiguring state borders and sovereignty.

Even the term *extraterritorial* does not fully capture such dynamics. That term applies generally to the "competence of a state to make, apply, and enforce rules of conduct in respect of persons, property or events beyond its territory."[39] Like the flexibilization of jurisdiction, the growth of extraterritoriality is often assumed to be "an inevitable—and either a desirable or innocuous—byproduct of globalization."[40] Legal scholars agree that the United States has been dominant in driving the expansion of extraterritoriality. Yet, while some criticize the outsize power of the United States in this domain, many others present this in essentially apolitical terms.[41] Moreover, across this literature, extraterritoriality is usually understood to apply only to limited cases of exceptional transnational reach in contrast to the supposed normal operations of domestic law. Focusing on US statutes and explicitly extraterritorial claims, this work neglects the much more widespread operation of ordinary transnational commercial law, which is seen as too mundane to merit the title of extraterritoriality. The term is rarely used in relation to governing law clauses,[42] or to cases brought under US jurisdiction via the restriction of act of state and foreign sovereign immunity rules. I therefore use the term *extraterritorial* in this book only when quoting others or to refer to explicitly extraterritorial rules or arguments.[43]

In addition to the empirical limits of the term, I also prefer territorial to extraterritorial because the latter suggests a static and identifiable national boundary that has been transgressed. This sits in some tension with conversations about flexible jurisdiction, instead reifying the idea that law still *is* normally contiguous with state borders. This reinforces a binary distinction between "inside" and "outside" that fails to capture the complex spatial logics of transnational cases in which defining the in/out boundary is precisely the question. While US courts sometimes assert explicit extraterritorial authority, we will see that they more often redefine the public/private distinction to justify the extension of US judicial power abroad or rewrite the definitions of home and foreign altogether to make transnational processes "domestic."[44]

The concepts of territory and territoriality also help capture other important characteristics of transnational US legal space missing from most discussions about either extraterritoriality or jurisdiction.[45] As political geographers have long emphasized, what makes something territorial is not the official demarcation of lines on a map, but the centrality of power to strategies for gaining spatial control. Territoriality—the struggle to establish the boundaries of and control over particular spaces—is a simultaneously material and discursive practice that structures and governs the management of boundaries, determining who can and cannot move in which ways, and whose authority applies in which spaces.[46] Territory, in turn, can be understood as an "effect" of territorial struggles.[47] Though territorial formations are usually relatively stable in the short term, they are never fixed. Rather, they are relational and processual.[48] They are best understood as referring to historically specific relationships among states, governance, resources, and people organized in space.[49] Furthermore, while not all territory is state space, and not all state space is territorial, territory remains fundamental to state power and constitutes both an object of governance and a political technology.[50]

Transnational US law as a whole is usefully understood as operating territorially in all these ways. Law always remains, at root, "an expression of state power,"[51] and it is an important but largely overlooked component of constituting the state itself as "an inescapably fluid and pluri-centred ensemble . . . an ongoing process of 'state work' and 'state effects' rather than a static thing."[52] This is particularly true for the extension of US judicial authority produced by the redefinition of foreign sovereign immunity and act of state rules. The subjection of foreign *governments* to governance by US courts directly implicates both US and foreign state space. More specifically, judicial expansion selectively distributes distinct modalities of US state power across space for strategic geopolitical and geoeconomic ends.[53]

Like all territorial struggles, moreover, the extension of US judicial reach has been based on repeated processes of border delineation and contestation. All common law develops through litigation, which is to say through disagreement and conflict. The cases through which US judicial power is extended over foreign governments frequently involve explicit debates over the proper contours of US and foreign territory and sovereignty—concepts that are still understood, in the legal cases documented here, as closely interlinked. Debates over the conceptual boundaries between public and private, political and legal, foreign and domestic are also key to judicial expansion—and, as I show throughout the book, are themselves entangled in more fundamental debates about territorial sovereignty. The centrality of struggle to transnational law is not captured in terms like jurisdictional flexibility or extraterritoriality alone.

Of course, the territorial formations produced in these processes have been neither homogeneous nor static. The map of judicial territory varies not only over time, but also by type of judicial power (e.g., judgment, discovery, injunction, attachment) and by subject matter (e.g., shipping, nationalizations, debt). Judicial territory is (like many legal and territorial formations) fragmented, overlapping, and differentiated, and its borders cannot be clearly drawn on any map.[54] Nevertheless, the history documented in this book makes the general contours clear: the United States has extended its own territorial claims over many transnational economic relations with foreign governments, encroaching on the territorial sovereignty of other, especially postcolonial, states. Its ability to do so cannot be explained simply by technical arguments about efficient, practical, or so-called necessary changes in jurisdictional rules. Rather, US judicial authority abroad is always dependent, at root, on US political and economic power, and on the strategic control of variegated legal space. Judicial territory and US power have evolved together.

JUDICIAL TERRITORY, US EMPIRE, AND THE POSTWAR INTERNATIONAL ORDER

The overarching argument of this book is that US judicial territory has been a potent tool of the linked projects of postwar American empire and the production of global capitalism. While the extension of US law over transnational relationships between two or more private companies remains far more common, litigation between private parties and foreign *governments* often has consequences for entire populations. This can be true for particular cases, as the example of the vulture funds that sued Argentina shows. But it is also true beyond individual cases insofar as US judicial decisions promote or hinder certain *kinds* of government economic activity altogether.

Histories of foreign sovereign immunity and act of state rules reflect the same aspatial and apolitical tendencies as broader conversations about jurisdiction and extraterritoriality. The restriction of each doctrine is usually explained as a natural response to changing economic conditions—in this case, not to "globalization" per se, but to the *growing* role of states in cross-border economic activity in the mid-twentieth century, which is seen as making it "necessary" to reduce states' "privileges" in global markets. Because these doctrines involve foreign governments directly, their political significance, where they still apply, is often noted. Yet, their transformations are presented overwhelmingly as technical, rather than political developments. The importance of geopolitical economic dynamics in spurring these changes is barely discussed. The Cold War, for example, is mentioned in histories of foreign sovereign immunity only in passing, while the relevance of Third World economic practices is rarely remarked at all.[55]

Yet, as I show in this book, the expansion of US judicial territory over the economic acts of foreign sovereign governments was motivated, first and foremost, by the desire of private corporations and US state actors to limit and tame what were seen as the interventionist economic practices of socialist and postcolonial states. Subjecting these states to US legal rules and courts has served both private and national US interests since World War II, though the substantive content of these cases and the details of how judicial territory operates have changed over time.

In short, as formal colonization and blatant interventions in other countries became illegitimate after World War II, the United States sought new ways to protect its economic interests and perpetuate access to foreign capital and resources. In this context, litigants, jurists, and politicians gradually learned to redefine foreign sovereign immunity and act of state rules for these purposes. Using this highly technical and seemingly mundane legal approach in place of more obvious interventions allowed the judiciary and the executive branch to cloak the pursuit of US geopolitical and geoeconomic goals (always entangled to a large degree with private corporate interests) in the guise of the "rule of law." This made it easier to project a judicial modality of US power while simultaneously professing commitment to a postimperial world composed of sovereign nation-states.

Yet, while all transnational law disrupts the idea that nation-states are at least formally fully sovereign within their own territories, this challenge is even more acute when governments themselves are subject to the authority of foreign judges. Expanding US judicial reach met with strong resistance, particularly from postcolonial states attempting to pursue economic programs that did not line up with American visions of the "rules-based" liberal capitalist international order. The clash between private US capital and these foreign governments produced the litigation that, piece by piece, created the conditions for the extension of US judicial territory.

In the 1940s through the 1960s, much of this litigation emerged from Third World countries' interventionist economic practices. These decades were characterized by what Gillian Hart calls "Cold War Era (CWE) national projects of accumulation and hegemony,"[56] which included social democratic and welfare policies in Europe and America, as well as large-scale planning and development projects throughout the Third World.[57] In this context, US courts, litigants, and the Department of State sought to protect US capital from both the Soviet Union and its satellites and from

Third World developmental states, while still allowing the United States to maintain a nominally anti-colonial position. Litigation in US courts during this period was particularly focused on figuring out how to deny immunity in relation to foreign state-owned enterprises, government development contracts, and official aid programs.

As US empire and the position of Third World states changed over the ensuing decades, the precise forms and functions of judicial territory changed as well. After the Cuban Revolution, expanding judicial reach became one of many tools used by the United States to contest Cuban expropriations of US property. This was linked to broader efforts to combat Third World support for a New International Economic Order (NIEO) that would challenge the US-dominated status quo by promoting not only formal but substantive economic equality. The ability to expropriate property held by multinational companies was a key component of NIEO plans.

Figuring out how to use US domestic law to respond to all these challenges was a fumbling and inconsistent process. At times there were disagreements between the executive and the judiciary. But from the late 1940s through the mid-1970s, both branches supported revising foreign sovereign immunity and act of state rules—literally changing the rules of national sovereignty—to bring the so-called commercial acts of foreign governments within US judicial oversight. This effort continued from the 1970s on, even as the global political economy and US power underwent major transformations.

By the late 1960s and early 1970s, the national development projects that had characterized the postwar decades were coming under increasing pressure, as was the international system of stable exchange rates and capital restrictions established after World War II. Although this was a moment of crisis for US power and legitimacy, the United States eventually emerged even stronger than it had been, on the basis of an expanded global role for the US dollar and US finance in a newly flexible and volatile international monetary system.[58] All this went hand in hand with the neoliberal counterrevolution of the 1970s and 1980s, which cemented the undoing of the Keynesian welfare state at home and dealt the death blow to Third World attempts to construct an alternative to either Soviet-style Communism or US-style capitalism abroad. Panitch and Gindin sum up the effects of all this as leading "to the realization by the end of the 20th century of a global financial order with New York as its operational centre, and with the American imperial state as its political carapace."[59]

The continued extension of US judicial territory during this period worked in tandem with these geopolitical economic changes. Alongside structural adjustment programs and debt restructurings managed by the International Monetary Fund (IMF), US law became an especially important tool for imposing neoliberal discipline on indebted countries in the context of the Third World debt crises of the 1980s, while simultaneously bolstering the interlinked power of Wall Street and US empire. The authority of US courts over foreign debtors solidified in the 1990s, just as the Clinton administration decisively embraced the dismantling of welfare states and the deregulation of finance at home and abroad.[60]

The legal terrain created in the last quarter of the twentieth century, in turn, set the terms for the further expansion of US judicial territory in the twenty-first century. The War on Terror brought the label of US empire back into common use and focused widespread attention on US military and executive power. Yet, US judicial power has also continued to expand during this period. At the same time, new tensions between the executive and judicial branches now raise questions about the relationship between judicial power and US empire going forward.

REASONING BY DICHOTOMY

The sweeping historical argument just laid out depends on other far more technical arguments about the spatio-legal operations of transnational US law. As I show throughout the book, a primary mechanism for extending US judicial territory has been the rewriting of key legal dichotomies.[61] Beginning in the 1940s, foreign government acts previously classified as "public" and "political" issues to be governed by the executive branch in the domain of foreign policy were reclassified as "private," "legal," and "commercial" matters to be governed by the judiciary. From the 1970s on, the foreign/domestic distinction was also redefined, with many acts previously seen as outside US borders being recoded as "in" or having "effects" on the United States. These legal minutiae are critical to understanding how judicial territory has not only operated as a US geopolitical economic instrument but has also reconfigured territorial sovereignty and helped construct "the" neoliberal economy in the process.

In focusing on these legal technicalities, I build on a rich body of critical work on dichotomies in Anglo-American law and liberalism,[62] while bringing the project of denaturalizing these distinctions to a domain and scale of law that has received little attention so far. In doing so, I also contribute more broadly to analyses of what Appel calls the "as ifs" of the liberal capitalist project—the constitutive fictions which allow capitalism to reproduce itself.[63] Producing and maintaining these fictions takes a lot of work. But acting as if public and private, political and legal, foreign and domestic are separable has been an important tool for perpetuating global capitalism in the face of its own actual messiness and of concerted resistance from those seeking alternatives. The point is not simply to show *that* these distinctions are artificial, or to offer so-called better or more accurate definitions. Rather, the point is to show *how* these dichotomies are continually redefined and with what geopolitical economic implications.

First and foremost, I show that these seemingly esoteric legal changes are inseparable from the deployment of US law as a geopolitical tool in the struggle between American-led capitalism and alternative economic approaches. The recategorization of key legal dichotomies in cases involving foreign governments has contributed to a shift in the modality of US empire operating abroad. By redefining certain activities as private and commercial, *rather* than public and political, US courts shifted responsibility for transnational economic issues from the executive to the judiciary. As we will see, this occurred for the most part with the explicit support of the executive and relieved that branch of responsibility for managing often messy diplomatic conflicts. It also increased and regularized the transnational extension of US state power by replacing ad hoc foreign policy decisions with more generalized legal rules.

This transfer of power from the executive to the judiciary resonates with the far more well-documented processes of "judicialization" and of the demise of the "political question doctrine" in the US domestic context. Both terms refer to the growing tendency of courts to weigh in on or even invalidate the decisions of the other branches in cases previously understood as political rather than legal matters.[64] Whether characterized as providing important checks on government power or as judicial supremacy, these processes, like the extension of US judicial territory abroad, raise questions about the rule of law, the separation of powers, and democratic accountability.[65] Yet, neither judicialization nor the political question doctrine are commonly analyzed in relation to transnational law or to economic questions.[66] Furthermore, the transfer of authority to the judiciary in transnational affairs involving foreign governments is unique in raising questions not only about politics, but about *geo*politics—and in complicating widespread assumptions about national territorial sovereignty.

By redefining key legal categories in order to claim authority over foreign government acts, US courts have promoted private corporate interests by formally restricting the economic autonomy of foreign governments within and beyond their own borders. This entails more than the de facto exercise of unequal power relations between corporations and countries, and between rich and poor states. It amounts to rewriting the *juridical* rules of territory and sovereignty in a process that took off just as the resolution of World War II led to international assertions about the sanctity of state borders and just as many postcolonial governments gained formal sovereign status for the first time. The fact that this re-territorialization of state space has occurred through the technical operations of law in ways that are illegible to all but a small number of legal and business experts has only made it more effective.

In addition to serving the geopolitical economic interests of US empire and rewriting the juridical terrain on which states interact in the postwar period, the reclassification of legal dichotomies at the heart of the extension of US judicial territory has simultaneously helped create the postwar international economic order of which the United States was the founder. It has done so by contributing to a neoliberal model of globalization in which state interventions in the economy in the name of society are devalued, even as state support for global markets becomes more entrenched than ever. Markets are never independent of state rules and institutions. Yet, the *attempt* to separate the economic from the political has been central to modern liberal market society.[67] Despite the ultimate futility of this endeavor, the politics/economics distinction is more than mere rhetoric— it is a powerful performative fiction.[68] Even as state and market remain constantly entangled, this fiction has been embodied in their "institutional separation" in rules and procedures, with significant material effects.[69] Transnational US common law has been an important, yet understudied component of this process. Through perpetuating a sharp public/private distinction and expanding the category of private, commercial activity, the extension of judicial territory has been key to managing the boundary between state and market, while expanding the domain of the latter. In doing so, it has helped institutionalize a neoliberal vision of the economy as a bounded sphere.[70]

Focusing on US judicial territory also shifts our usual understanding of the timeline of neoliberal change. While the emergence of neoliberal *ideas* in the early twentieth century is well documented, the neoliberal project is frequently seen as waiting in the wings until the crises of the 1970s.[71] Yet, attending to US judicial expansion shows that, even as social welfare programs became available to many in the United States and Europe after World War II, what we can now recognize as early neoliberal tendencies were already being implemented transnationally. Redefining foreign government acts from public and political to private, legal, and commercial was key to undermining economic practices of socialist and postcolonial states from the 1940s on. The depoliticization of the economy widely associated with the neoliberal turn of the 1970s was not on hold during the Bretton Woods era—it was actively wielded across the Third World in the fight between US-style capitalism and alternative economic approaches.[72]

It is also in light of this history that the relationship between judicial territory and globalization should be understood. It is not only that judicial territory has been extended more and more widely, if always incompletely and unevenly, since World War II. Even more importantly, by institutionalizing a sharp politics/economics distinction, undermining alternative economic models, supporting US financial power, and fostering the neoliberalization of Third World societies, the expansion of judicial territory has helped produce the particular form of American-led globalization that characterized the second half of the twentieth century and shaped the terrain on which the geopolitical economic shifts of the twenty-first century are playing out. Like the five hundred years of transnational economic integration that preceded it, this era of globalization has not been characterized primarily by homogenization or leveling, but rather by variegated processes of integration, differentiation, and uneven and combined development—that is, not only by the (re)production of differences of many kinds, but also by their exploitation in the service of capital accumulation.[73] This is the form of globalization that the increasingly global instrument of judicial territory has helped promote.

In short, the cases examined here matter not only for their effects on the countries involved, but also because of what they reveal about *how* law constitutes American empire, on the one hand, and sovereignty, territoriality, and neoliberal capitalism, on the other. Far more attention has been paid to the postwar US military-industrial complex, US military interventions since the end of the Cold War, and the growth of executive power associated with these processes. But alongside these obviously imperialist adventures and the blatant violations of foreign sovereignty they entail, the extension of judicial territory has been chugging along too, bolstering US power and global capitalism in ways that are arguably just as important, if much, much quieter.

Geopolitical and macroeconomic relations are always constituted through the mundane, daily practices of state and nonstate actors.[74] This includes legal practices. Law, in this sense, is a good example of what Agnew calls "low" or "hidden" geopolitics—terms that call attention to a wide range of practices not captured in most studies of official foreign-policymaking, but which are critical to constituting world politics and its complex imbrications with global economic relations.[75] That the geopolitical role of such practices has been largely unexamined is no accident, but part of how they actively obscure their geopolitical salience.

The iterative, mundane, and technocratic character of common law change makes it particularly difficult to determine the precise effects of any one case on a foreign country (the Argentine example at the start of this chapter is unusually clear in this regard). Moreover, the extension of US judicial authority never operates in isolation from other constraints on Third World states' behavior, including in the form of diplomatic pressure, aid conditionalities, economic threats, international treaties, and more. United States common law has operated alongside and in combination with these other geopolitical economic tools.

Yet, even where the direct consequences of litigation cannot be clearly measured, changes in the transnational operation of US law are significant far beyond the specific parties to any particular case. As law professor Tonya Putnam puts it in a discussion of US extraterritoriality:

> Because strategic behavior involves anticipating the costs of complying with various rules, and also the likelihood and magnitude of punishment for noncompliance . . . even a small number of decisions altering, (or clarifying) the reach of U.S. law, and concomitantly the jurisdiction of courts to decide related claims, can influence the character of transnational conduct in the issue area concerned.[76]

In other words, law, including transnational law, shapes the actions not only of those involved in litigation, but of all those who potentially could be. The "shadow of the law" is long.[77]

It is not only the text of the law, moreover, but *how* law works that matters. While never separable from wider social practices and ideologies, legal practices have their own specific modes, logics, and temporalities, which cannot be reduced to market, imperial, or other logics. Indeed, variations in legal practices across space and over time help explain important changes in capitalism itself.[78] Having some understanding of the legal modes and logics most relevant to the extension of judicial territory is, therefore, critical to the analysis in this book.

Common law, which developed in Britain and is now used in many former British colonies, refers to a system of law shaped by legal cases and past decisions (case precedent) over time. Civil law systems, in contrast, are determined primarily by authoritative texts, legal codes, and statutes. In practice the United States and many common law systems are now better understood as hybrids in which common law operates in combination with legislative power. The prevalence of common law within this complex whole nevertheless gives the system distinctive features. One fundamental characteristic of US common law is the tendency, described above, to reason by dichotomy.[79] This has been central to my own approach to reading and interpreting the cases discussed in this book, and I explore the centrality of dichotomies to law and liberalism more fully in chapter 2. Here, I identify other important characteristics of US common law that have informed my methodological choices and analyses.

Common law is necessarily produced through litigation or struggle. This struggle is shaped by litigants (in this book, mostly large-scale investors and Third World governments),[80] interested third parties, and lawyers, most of whom have been trained in elite US law schools.[81] Lawyers, in turn, draw heavily on case precedent and published legal authorities. Thus, neither judges nor litigants are isolated agents of common law change. This agential complexity is further compounded by temporal ambiguities. Though successive decisions may be debated and criticized, they typically only depart widely from earlier precedent when new ways of thinking have become acceptable *enough* for some judges to embrace them. Changes in what is or is not acceptable may, in turn, result from broader social shifts, developments in legal theory, personal interests and motivations, or some combination of the above. This means the origins of legal change cannot be ascertained from case documents alone.

Despite these ambiguities, case documents and judicial decisions can be understood as important points of articulation in broader socio-legal struggles. Moreover, the moment of formalization is materially significant; only when a legal interpretation is adopted by a judge can it officially determine the outcome of future cases. At the same time, previous decisions do not determine future cases in any easily predictable way. A case may not be cited in later cases at all, or it may hardly be cited for years and then suddenly become important. Furthermore, even commonly referenced cases are interpreted in different ways, both within the same case and over time. Case precedent thus conditions, rather than determines, possibilities for future legal change.

In this book, I do not do justice to the full agential and temporal complexity of the expansion of transnational US law. Instead, I attempt to map its primary coordinates. Rather than trying to identify every case involving foreign governments, or to find obscure or hidden cases, I thus focus on cases that have been especially important in driving changes in US foreign sovereign immunity and act of state rules, seeing these as turning points at which more nebulous shifts in interests and legal views coalesce. Within these cases, I focus primarily on final judicial decisions and, for some, on briefs submitted by litigating parties, the executive branch, and other important participants. These documents alone cannot capture all the dynamics shaping legal change, nor do they allow insight into the domestic politics of litigating governments. However, limiting attention to these documents allows for broader coverage and makes it possible to see the arc of judicial expansion as a whole.

The cases examined come from a variety of US states, but by far the most important courts for the expansion of US judicial territory have been the District Court for the Southern District of New York, the Second Circuit Court of Appeals (located in Manhattan), and the US Supreme Court. This is due largely to New York's economic dominance and the fact that so many transnational contracts are written under New York law—New York economic power has been central to the production of US judicial territory. As we will see, New York judges even sometimes justify decisions on the grounds of supporting New York commercial interests. Yet, New York courts do not represent New York power or interests alone. Cases involving foreign governments are heard in federal rather than state courts. These courts are located in particular states, but they are established under the authority of the Constitution, and they apply a *combination* of federal and state law.[82] This raises important questions about the intersection of US and New York legal power and interests, only some of which I address in this book.

Focusing on the most important cases in the history of foreign sovereign immunity and the act of state doctrine means that many of the cases I discuss have been analyzed at length by legal scholars and jurists. This secondary literature has been important for bolstering my own empirical understanding and for allowing me to see how these cases have been construed and deployed by legal professionals. However, I read these cases very differently from such scholars. Most importantly, I read them spatially and historically.

Critical legal scholars have long critiqued the reifications and abstractions of law. Yet, for a long time, this critique operated primarily through temporal analyses focused on historicizing and thus denaturalizing legal categories, but paid little attention to space. In the early 1990s, a small number of geographers, most notably Nicholas Blomley, David Delaney, and Richard Ford, founded the still small but now well-established field of legal geography.[83] More recently, there has been a spatial turn within legal studies as well.[84] Together, these scholars have shown that law is always spatially defined and that legal practices produce space. Moreover, both law and geography are simultaneously discursive and material. Legal ideas are not inscribed on material space. Rather, society is constituted in important ways through spatio-legal discursive practices.[85] Here, I take these lessons to heart, investigating the ways that transnational US law is co-constituted with the production and manipulation of key spatial distinctions and strategies.

Like traditional critical legal scholars, furthermore, I read the cases in this book historically, but in a way that is simultaneously geographically relational,[86] situating them with respect to a much broader geopolitical economic context than is usually done. Historical and relational contextualization is necessary both for denaturalizing common assumptions about law today and for refusing bounded understandings of legal acts, instead identifying links between and among people, places, and discourses at multiple spatio-temporal scales. It is also particularly important because of the ways in which common law actively *de*-contextualizes, tending to minimize or reject the significance of the broader social, political, and economic conditions in which legal cases are situated. Although, at first glance, the practice of case precedent seems to preserve the past, it does so selectively, privileging isolated components of past cases, while obscuring others. This continual erasure of its own contingent and historical development is part of law's "frozen politics."[87] Reading contextually is central to combatting both the historical amnesia produced in this process and, relatedly, the fiction of legal "closure," in which law is presented as an autonomous and technical domain, requiring legal expertise to understand. Examining how law both shapes and is shaped by other sociopolitical processes is critical to resisting this fiction, which is itself a key source of law's power.[88]

The complexities of common law change belie any simple idea of a decades-long unified strategy of judicial expansion. Nevertheless, that expansion has been remarkably continuous, if irregular, and it has been produced through the repeated deployment of a limited set of legal tactics. This tension between coherence and contingency can be partly resolved by distinguishing among the goals, mechanisms, and more or less unintended effects of common law decisions. Neither litigants, judges, nor the US executive set out to expand the spatial reach of US judicial power per se. They did, however, aim to protect US companies by containing or resisting anything that smelled vaguely of Communism or simply of non- or "more-than" capitalist developmental efforts,[89] and they explicitly sought to depoliticize conflicts with Third World governments and to bolster US financial and dollar power. Once the legal mechanism of redefining the public/private, political/legal, and foreign/domestic distinctions turned out to be useful for accomplishing these goals, litigants and judges learned to deploy this mechanism again and again. The effects of this included rewriting the rules of territorial sovereignty, bolstering American empire, and helping define the contours of "the economy" at the global scale. This book tracks these goals, mechanisms, and effects through a chronological examination of the expansion of US judicial territory and its role in mediating the relationship between private (mostly US) capital and Third World states.

Chapter 1 situates judicial territory in relation to broader conceptualizations of capitalism and imperialism and summarizes the changing role of law in this relationship over time. I suggest that different forms of law have been important to different imperial strategies. These legal forms, moreover, have distinct spatialities and have, in turn, helped constitute the variegated geographies of both empire and capitalism. By contrasting post–World War II us judicial territory with the territoriality of earlier imperial formations, I show that the messy irregularity of judicial territory today does not mark a simple rupture with obsolete Westphalian "national" geographies, but rather a continuation by new means of previous *imperial* ones.

The rest of the book examines key phases in the extension of US judicial territory. Chapters 2 and 3 investigate the period from the end of World War II through the mid-1970s, when judicial expansion was shaped most importantly by the threats of Cold War Communism, on the one hand, and anti-colonial economic practices, on the other. More specifically, chapter 2 focuses on the shift from an absolute to a restrictive theory of foreign sovereign immunity. I show that introducing a commercial exception to the doctrine required not only asserting *that* commercial acts were no longer immune, but first redefining all commercial acts as private for the first time and then gradually expanding the category of what counts as commercial. In the context of the Cold War, postcolonial economic practices, and growing Third World support for the NIEO, this expansion of the category of commercial activity was used to subject state-owned enterprises, government infrastructure contracts, and official aid programs to business-friendly governance by US laws and courts. This shifted responsibility for many fraught geopolitical issues from the executive to the judiciary, depoliticizing significant questions about how the economy should be governed, just as defining the proper relationship between political and economic sovereignty was becoming *the* most heated geopolitical question of the era. With the codification of the commercial exception in 1976, sovereign immunity was even further restricted by the weakening of explicitly spatial rules about how much of a connection between a foreign state's activity and the United States is required for investors to bring suit.

Chapter 2 takes a broad-brush approach to the emergence of the restrictive theory of foreign sovereign immunity, considering dozens of cases involving Communist and postcolonial governments in the postwar decades. The remaining chapters of the book are more focused, each considering only a few especially transformative cases. Chapter 3 examines how the act of state doctrine was weakened in response to Cuban nationalizations of US private property after the Cuban Revolution. The right to nationalize property and the question of whose laws should determine compensation were at the heart not only of US-Cuba hostilities, but of the NIEO and Third World efforts to regain control of national resources in the 1960s and 1970s. Although foreign nationalizations are still legally defined as public, sovereign acts, the Cuban nationalizations eventually spurred the adoption of a (partial) common law commercial exception to the act of state doctrine and the redefinition of what we could call nationalization-adjacent activities as private and commercial. Together with bilateral investment treaties (BITs) and international arbitration, these domestic US legal changes reduced the usefulness of nationalizations for all Third World states. The restriction of the act of state doctrine, which concerns the acts of foreign sovereigns in their *own* territory, was more heavily contested than was the restriction of foreign sovereign immunity. Its implications for redefining territorial sovereignty, I show, were correspondingly profound.

Bringing state-owned enterprises, government infrastructure contracts, official aid programs, and aspects of nationalizations within US judicial reach did not make them illegal, but it did make them less useful to foreign states by stripping them of the protections that had previously shielded most government acts from US courts and by subjecting them to the pro-business commercial rules of the United States. The upshot was that, just as many Third World countries gained formal sovereign status for the first time, this newfound sovereignty was undermined not just by growing US economic dominance and informal influence, but by the *juridical* extension of US power. As internal Third World tensions, structural crises in the Global North,[90] and the neoliberal counterrevolution of the 1970s put an end to the NIEO and other Third World developmental projects and led to the reconfiguration of US empire on new grounds, judicial territory was repurposed to meet new ends.

Chapter 4 shows how the form and function of US judicial territory shifted to address the Third World debt crises of the 1980s. In this context, both foreign sovereign immunity and act of state rules were further weakened to give US courts and private creditors more control over foreign sovereign debtors. The mechanisms for this new expansion of judicial territory included new rules for defining the foreign/domestic distinction in the context of intangible property, as well as the further reification of the public/private divide and the continued expansion of the category of private, commercial activity. Together, these changes undermined debtor governments' ability to manage national monetary and fiscal stability, strengthening private creditors and contract fundamentalism, while also helping institutionalize neoliberal market logics at the transnational scale. This occurred both through the direct application of transnational US domestic law and through the ways in which creditor litigation worked in tandem with IMF structural adjustment programs to impose neoliberal policies on debtors. The role of US courts in this process both depended on and further strengthened the growing power of New York finance and the US dollar.

Chapter 5 focuses on the creditor litigation against Argentina with which this introduction opened. It shows that the expansion of US judicial authority over more and more foreign government economic activities has continued in the twenty-first century, with US courts now claiming more authority than ever before—including, in some cases, over the entire world except the country being sued. In the process, courts have built on the case precedent discussed in previous chapters, while simultaneously breaking new ground by not only further expanding the categories of commercial and domestic, but even challenging their relevance altogether. This has led to significant tensions between the executive and the judiciary over the proper extent of US judicial reach for the first time. While US courts had long been respectful of and sometimes even directly deferred to the views of the executive in past moments of judicial expansion, in the Argentina litigation, the courts dismissed the executive's concerns altogether. When it comes to cases it understands as commercial, the judiciary no longer shows any interest in the executive's opinions or in the possible political implications of these cases.

These emerging tensions between the executive and the judiciary should not be overstated. Yet, they do raise important questions about the future of US judicial territory and its relationship to global capitalism, on the one hand, and US empire, on the other. The US has lost considerable legitimacy, if not yet its global dominance, in the past two decades. At the same time, the mutual interdependence of US economic and legal power is as relevant today as it was in the 1950s or 1970s. While the growing power of China and the expanding legal territories of jurisdictions like Singapore, Malaysia, and Hong Kong make the continued expansion of US judicial territory more fraught, in the conclusion I suggest that, as long as New York remains a global financial center, US courts and domestic law will remain globally important—even if they no longer serve the foreign policy interests of the US government as clearly as they once did.

CHAPTER ONE

Law, Capital, and the Geographies of Empire

In 1896, the US Supreme Court's now infamous "separate but equal" decision in *Plessy v. Ferguson* reinforced segregation and gave formal federal sanction to state-imposed Jim Crow laws around the country.[1] Five years later, *Downes v. Bidwell* held that the Constitution need not apply in full to recently annexed US territories or their inhabitants.[2] The main opinion in *Downes*, penned by Justice Brown, held that Puerto Rico was "a territory appurtenant and belonging to the United States, but not a part of the United States."[3] In a concurring opinion, Justice White suggested that the territory should be considered "foreign to the United States in a domestic sense."[4] This formulation echoed the 1831 case of *Cherokee Nation v. Georgia*, in which Chief Justice John Marshall held that "Indian tribes" were "domestic dependent nations," neither fully sovereign nor fully part of the United States.[5]

Plessy v. Ferguson was finally overturned by *Brown v. Board of Education* in 1954.[6] American Indians were recognized as full citizens of the United States in 1924, though tribal sovereignty of course remains partial and contested.[7] And while the United States has either fully incorporated or released some of its overseas territories and has granted US citizenship to the inhabitants of others, several remain less than equal members of the Union. *Downes* remains "good law," shaping life for millions in Puerto Rico, Guam, American Samoa, the US Virgin Islands, and the Northern Mariana Islands.[8]

All these examples showcase the role of US domestic law and courts in producing racialized and spatialized differences among people and places *within* what the United States sees as its official boundaries. Yet, the same

Court who oversaw *Plessy* in 1896 and *Downes* in 1901 issued another decision that illustrates a striking contrast between the application of US judicial power within and beyond official US borders at the turn of the century. In the 1897 case *Underhill v. Hernandez*, a US businessman sued a Venezuelan revolutionary military commander in US courts for alleged detainment and property seizure. The US Supreme Court, however, held that the US judiciary had no right to judge the actions of a foreign sovereign government in its own territory.[9] In what would become the most famous formulation of the traditional "act of state doctrine," Chief Justice Fuller declared that "Every sovereign State is bound to respect the independence of every other sovereign State, and the courts of one country will not sit in judgment on the acts of the government of another done within its own territory."[10] This was also the period of absolute foreign sovereign immunity, in which courts refused to allow litigation against foreign sovereign officials or properties within US borders, let alone beyond them.

Underhill is often seen as reflecting a commitment to the "positivist" norms of absolute Westphalian territoriality widely associated with the consolidation of the modern state form.[11] It remained essentially unchallenged until the 1960s. Yet, comparing *Underhill* with *Plessy*, *Downes*, and *Cherokee Nation* draws attention to the importance of judicial understandings of what counted as "in" or "outside" the United States at the time. To the extent that the Supreme Court embraced strict territorial sovereignty, as in *Underhill*, this was based on an *imperial* not a *national* understanding of US borders. While Venezuela was understood to be beyond US judicial reach, American Indian territories on the continent and overseas territories like Puerto Rico and the Philippines were not. The courts thus played an important role in legitimating and perpetuating imperial distinctions within official national *and* imperial US borders, whether in relation to the internal oppression of Black people in the United States or the formal conquest and colonization of American Indians and overseas territories. However, they simultaneously refused to act beyond these borders, at least in cases involving foreign governments or their officials.

Contrasting *Underhill* with these other cases highlights important spatial distinctions in the modalities of empire exercised by the United States. Even at the height of the so-called Westphalian era, the United States intervened in foreign affairs throughout the Western Hemisphere, whether through military, diplomatic, or economic coercion. These interventions went well beyond the territories that the United States had officially claimed or colonized, despite the Court's seeming commitment to territorial sovereignty in *Underhill*. Yet, these interventions were carried out by the *executive* branch, not the judiciary. The *Underhill* Court made this distinction between the sources of US power clear, suggesting that it was up to the US government to negotiate with Venezuela on Mr. Underhill's behalf, if it so wished.[12] This case did not so much reflect a commitment to absolute Westphalian sovereignty, then, but rather a certain view of the separation of powers within the US government. The question was not whether strict territoriality should prevent the United States from undermining the sovereignty of foreign states. Rather, it was whether the judiciary or the executive was the right branch to do so. In contrast to *Plessy*, *Downes*, and *Cherokee Nation*, in which US courts exercised authority within what were understood to be official US national and imperial borders, only the executive had the right to exercise US power beyond them.

This understanding of the relationship between law and transnational US power changed in the twentieth century. There is nothing new about the imbrication of law and empire. But different kinds of law have played different roles in shaping US imperial power over time. As formal colonization, gunboat diplomacy, and direct interference in other governments' decisions were delegitimized in the wake of World War II, the US judiciary simultaneously claimed more and more authority over the economic acts of foreign governments—including acts that occurred in the United States, in transnational or liminal spaces, and even within foreign sovereign territory. This meant that, just as the principles of self-determination and formal sovereign autonomy became the norm, this sovereignty was undermined by the juridical extension of the authority of US domestic laws and courts over other countries—in short, by the extension of US judicial territory.

The rest of the book examines specific transformations in US common law on which this expansion of judicial territory was built. This chapter instead provides a broad view of the changing relationship between law, capital, and US empire in order to make the case that judicial territory both initiated a new phase in the expansion of US empire after World War II and has remained continuous with previous imperial formations in many ways. More broadly, I suggest that law has long acted as a structuring link between capitalism and imperialism, with a particularly important role in defining the geographies of each.

In the following pages, I offer a conceptualization of empire, capitalism, and the relationship between them. I then turn more specifically to the role of law in that relationship, with a particular focus on US empire and capitalism, before and after World War II. Only then do I turn to judicial territory as an important modality of postwar US empire and situate this in relation to earlier forms and geographies of imperial power. I argue that the irregularity and dynamism of the boundaries of judicial territory today, and the way it has reconfigured practices of territorial sovereignty, do not signify a simple rupture with earlier national territorial practices. Rather, the extension of judicial territory has perpetuated, in new modes, previous highly irregular and ambiguous *imperial* spatial strategies. Finally, I conclude the chapter with a discussion of why judicial territory took on these functions when it did. Specifically, I consider the ways in which judicial territory is uniquely well suited to legitimate and obscure ongoing imperial relations of hierarchical governance and extraction in an anti-imperial climate.

CAPITAL AND EMPIRE

Empires predate capitalism by thousands of years, and no empire has been driven solely by capitalist logics. Conversely, capitalism has never fit seamlessly with any one state's geopolitical interests, and most capitalist states today are not empires. Yet, capitalism was forged in the crucible of empire, and for the past five hundred years or so, empires and capital, imperialist logics and capitalist logics have been closely entangled. This has remained true even as explicit empires have receded from the political map, and the modern nation-state has gradually become the dominant political form.

Empires can be conceptualized most generally as large state formations that are expansionary (seeking to increase control over new lands, people, and resources, with or without colonial domination), extractive (with a tendency to suck money and resources from the peripheries into the center), and hierarchical (characterized by unequal, often racialized distinctions, obligations, and privileges among subjects).[13] While empires, or in Stoler and McGranahan's insightful term "imperial formations,"[14] are necessarily tied to powerful states, this does not mean those states are monolithic or unified, nor that they wield absolute control over their many subjects.[15] Rather, as recent detailed historical research on particular empires has shown, imperial formations are always characterized by an array of state and nonstate actors, with interests that sometimes overlap and sometimes contradict one another. Indeed, it has often been imperial agents (e.g., settlers, merchants, and missionaries) on the edges of empires, who fight most fiercely for new bouts of expansion and extraction, drawing on imperial authority in some ways, even as they challenge or irritate their own imperial governments.[16]

From the fifteenth century on, European and, eventually, American imperial expansion were also inseparable from the development of capitalism. Capitalism began to coalesce as a powerful political economic formation in the fifteenth century and gradually increased in dominance over the next few hundred years. As Appel emphasizes, the capitalist "project" is always incomplete.[17] What's more, many aspects of life exceed or subvert capitalist logics.[18] Yet, capitalism is also now a worldwide, if always differentiated, phenomenon, leaving no place on earth untouched. While its particular features vary hugely over time and space, it is broadly characterized by the tendencies toward the separation of most people from producing the means of their own subsistence, the extraction of surplus value from those now dependent on laboring for others (whether as enslaved, indentured, or waged laborers), the dominance of the production of commodities (i.e., goods for sale rather than immediate use), the institutional promotion of property rights and private contract, and competition among capitalists.

Together, these characteristics make capitalism dependent on continual accumulation and growth—like imperialism, capitalism is inherently expansionary and extractive. It requires the constant input of new materials, land, and labor to fuel ever-increasing production, as well as the opening of new markets in which these goods can be sold.[19] Like imperialism, it is also always hierarchical, based on the production and exploitation of class-based, gendered, and racialized distinctions among workers, within and across political boundaries.[20]

The parallels between empire and capitalism are not accidental, but rather co-constitutive. While the desire for wealth and resources has always been a primary driver of imperial expansion, this took on particular characteristics with the development of capitalism. And while empires predate capitalism, capitalism has always existed in relation to imperial projects, and both the history and the geography of capitalism are inseparable from European imperial expansion and competition. The long dominant idea that capitalism was born in Europe, came into its own with the Industrial Revolution, and only then spread gradually from there to the rest of the world is a myth. Capitalism has been transnational from the start. It was always produced through the *interaction* between Europe and the rest of the world, as European imperial expansion spread to the Americas and the coasts of Africa and South Asia, and then eventually throughout Asia, Africa, and the Middle East.[21]

European imperial expansion was driven by many forces, including geopolitical logics of inter-imperial competition; domestic political unrest; the desire for status; the desire of imperial settlers and subjects for religious, political, social, and economic opportunity; and the racialized logics of civilizational expansion in which the line between cause and justification has always been fuzzy at best. Yet, the violent extraction of wealth, labor, and resources—necessary for the continued expansion of capitalism—was also a constant component.[22] It was these resources, cheaply produced through the exploitation of coerced labor in the colonies, that enabled European businesses and states to accumulate capital for investment at the rate they did and that provided the raw materials that made the industrial revolution possible. The colonies also provided luxury goods for the aristocracy and an emerging bourgeoisie, as well as cheap sugar, tea, and other products that enabled the rise of mass consumer culture in the industrialized world, while helping keep the wages of European workers relatively low.[23]

Even as they sent raw inputs to Europe, the colonies themselves provided new markets for European manufactured goods and outlets for European investment.[24] Meanwhile, European imperialism reconfigured diverse societies (though never totally) to make them more susceptible to capitalist logics, through everything from introducing European contract rules to turning peasants into wage laborers to fostering export-oriented monocropping.[25] The racialized civilizational discourses of empire legitimated all these interactions in Europeans' eyes.

If anything, the link between capitalism and empire became even stronger with the United States' separation from the British empire. While later accounts have too often accepted the idea that the United States had only a brief foray into imperialism around 1898, the US has always been both a nation-state and an empire. The first 150 years of American history were characterized by blatant imperial expansion and conquest, first on the continent and then overseas.[26] Of course, many Americans believed that their "empire of liberty," in Thomas Jefferson's famous words, was unique in bringing democracy and freedom to those places it conquered (if not immediately to the people who already lived there). Yet, American expansion, like that of the European empires, was always driven in significant part by the desire for land and resources that could feed the small-scale agrarian capitalist dreams of settlers, while also sustaining industrial capitalism in the Northeast and plantation agriculture in the South.

If anything was exceptional about US empire, it was the avidity with which Americans believed that the whole world's resources should be open to them, and that *freedom* and *markets* were near synonyms. As historian Thomas Bender has put it, "Almost unthinkingly—and to an extraordinary degree—Americans came to associate the meaning of America with an entitlement to unrestricted access to land and markets. Land, freedom, opportunity, abundance, seemed a natural sequence."[27] This stance spurred and legitimated both physical territorial conquest and more indirect forms of imperial coercion, as well as the push for the economic opening of the rest of the world to American capital: "There has been since Jefferson's presidency near American consensus that the whole globe should be open and available to American enterprise."[28]

The logics of empire and the logics of capital, in short, are impossible to disentangle, despite never being reducible to one another. What's more, if capitalism has always been distinct from, but linked with Western imperial expansion, then law has always been an important part of that linking. In the remainder of this chapter, I consider the changing roles of law in shaping the relationship between capitalism and imperialism before and since World War II, with a particular focus on the United States. Throughout, I emphasize the ways in which different forms of law have shaped distinct imperial modalities and *geographies* of empire, both at the same and at different points in time.

LAW, CAPITAL, AND EARLY US EMPIRE

As law and political economy scholar David Singh Grewal has written, "capitalism is fundamentally a legal ordering: the bargains at the heart of capitalism are products of law."[29] Law not only permits or prohibits particular activities (e.g., child labor or the sale of human organs), but also defines and underpins all property rights, mediates the distribution of value in so-called normal times and during crises, institutionalizes specific cultural norms in "market life," and transforms things into assets.[30] Law also plays a central role in the production of economic geographies. In addition to the inherently spatial character of all property relations, law defines and enacts the boundaries of markets for the sake of regulation, taxation, and competition.[31] More broadly, law not only links state power to a preexisting national territory, but also plays a key role "in *establishing* borders and *territorializing* space."[32] This includes its role in constituting (trans)national corporate sovereignty, as well as in producing seemingly disembedded spaces like the offshore and the enclave.[33]

Law has also been central to all imperial formations. Laws and legal practices define and structure the unequal status, obligations, and privileges of different groups within empires, as well as mediating relationships between insiders and outsiders, conquerors and conquered.[34] Jurists themselves, furthermore, have been important imperial agents, with their own interests and sometimes messy relations to central states, while other actors on the edges of empires have both relied on and subverted imperial laws for their own purposes.[35] Furthermore, despite a tendency to discuss the relationship between European and extra-European spaces in the colonial period in terms of a contrast between zones of law and of lawlessness, this representation was never accurate. Colonial encounters were shaped by the way imperial and local legal practices intersected and rubbed up against one another, often producing overlapping jurisdictional arrangements and hybrid legal forms.[36]

It is not only that law was constitutive of both capitalism and imperialism simultaneously. Rather, law facilitated processes of expansion, dispossession, and extraction that *connected* imperial and capitalist development. It also helps explain spatial variegation within each process. Echoing challenges to diffusionist accounts of capitalism, some legal scholars have challenged similar accounts of the spread of international law *from* Europe *to* the rest of the world. Instead, they have shown that the origins of contemporary international law lie in the colonial encounter *between* Europeans and non-Europeans.[37] More complicated than mere inclusion and exclusion, the phenomenon of unequal, hierarchical incorporation has long been a central characteristic of imperial formations. Differentiation according to the logics of white supremacy and biologically determinist understandings of race became especially pronounced in the Euro-American empires of the early capitalist period and reached a height in the high age of empire in the late nineteenth and early twentieth centuries.[38] Law played a key role in establishing and perpetuating these racial hierarchies.[39]

The international law that emerged during the colonial period made explicit distinctions between colonizer and colonized, and it structured and legitimated the dehumanization of non-Europeans and their formal subjection to the colonizer's authority. This was critical to justifying territorial expansion, the exploitation of indigenous labor, and the extraction of resources from non-white peoples on which both imperialism and capitalism depended.[40]

More specific legal practices operationalized these racialized logics within particular empires. In the US context, the central role of coercive, lopsided, and frequently violated treaties in facilitating indigenous dispossession in the eighteenth and nineteenth centuries is well known.[41] Bilateral legal agreements also structured the annexation of territory from other nation-states and empires, whether in treaties marking the cessation of violent conflicts (such as the Mexican-American War of 1848 or the Spanish-American War of 1898), or in agreements that facilitated the purchase of land from one state by another (as in the 1803 Louisiana Purchase in which the United States acquired 828,000 square miles from France or the 1868 purchase of Alaska from Russia).

Less well known are the more subtle domestic legal practices used to seize land from indigenous populations. As legal scholar K-Sue Park has shown, new approaches to mortgage, debt, and foreclosure were used to make land fully alienable in the New World in ways it was not yet in Europe. This made it possible for settlers to claim permanent ownership over land formerly held by American Indians. Only later were these colonial legal tools integrated into mainstream English and American property law.[42] Brenna Bhandar shows, more broadly, that many now standard forms of property law were first developed in the British colonies and based on racialized ideas about property, civilization, and whiteness. In short, "legal forms of property ownership and the modern racial subject are articulated and realized in conjunction with one another."[43] This history can fruitfully be read together with work on the peculiarly powerful position of lawyers in the United States and the close relationship between law, capital, and politics in the century and a half after the American Revolution.[44] The intensified American commitment to "free" markets and property rights was inseparable from ideas about racial superiority and the desire for new lands and resources.

With the closing of the so-called Western frontier in the late nineteenth century and the United States' turn from continental to overseas colonization, US domestic law likewise took on new imperial functions and geographies. As the United States annexed the Philippines and Puerto Rico, as well as Guam, American Samoa, and several other territories at the end of the nineteenth century, US courts struggled to define the relationship between these territories, their inhabitants, and the mainland. Westward expansion had always been a story of conquest and annexation, but Americans had squared this with their own anti-imperial revolutionary origins by requiring that all newly acquired continental territories eventually be added to the Union as equal states.[45]

Of course, this never included all *people* in those territories—indigenous, Black, Asian, and Mexican peoples, as well as women, had always been legally and practically excluded from full social and civil rights. Yet, the late nineteenth-century annexation of territories in which the *majority* of the population was non-white was different. Many Americans were uncomfortable with ever granting full citizenship to the people of these territories. At the same time, the idea of holding these territories in a permanently subordinate status threatened the supposedly exceptional moral character of the United States. Courts in the United States played a crucial role in settling these debates through a series of early-twentieth-century Supreme Court cases now known as the "Insular Cases." These cases, including the *Downes v. Bidwell* case discussed above, determined that the United States could hold on to its overseas "unincorporated territories" indefinitely *without* extending constitutional rights to the people living in them—and that it could relinquish these territories if and when it chose to.[46]

In addition to defining and structuring the spatio-legal relationship between the United States, its internal "others," and its formal colonies, law continued to play a critical role in facilitating the more informal expansion of US empire abroad. The United States had laid claim to a sphere of influence in the Americas as early as 1823 when President Monroe declared the Western Hemisphere off-limits to further European colonization. By the end of the century, it had exerted strong influence throughout the region and beyond, intervening dozens of times to protect its commercial interests abroad.[47] These practices intensified in the early twentieth century as US industrialists and financiers became increasingly entangled in the economies of supposedly independent states, leading to the heightened integration of financial and racial capitalism throughout the Western hemisphere.[48]

This was not merely a question of economic *influence*, but of coordinated engagement by US business elites and government officials. First, though not the norm, potential US military intervention was a powerful deterrent to those states that might threaten US economic interests or oppose US views on property law. This was borne out in over thirty-five direct military interventions and occupations in Latin American and Caribbean states in the first half of the twentieth century.[49] In other cases, the US government intervened directly in the *governance* of foreign states, arranging for direct US oversight of foreign finance ministries, central banks, tax collection, and fiscal policy. Such arrangements, Peter Hudson finds, sometimes even included explicit provisions for US military intervention in case of breach—"dollar diplomacy" and "gunboat diplomacy" were intersecting, not opposing strategies.[50]

Like the relationship between the US and its formal territories, the extension of US power *beyond* the formal boundaries of US empire was also shaped by law. But where the former was most impacted by domestic laws and judges, US interventions beyond those formal boundaries were instead shaped by the US's deployment of international law. So-called international law or the "law of nations," as it was then often known, had long been important in shaping interstate and inter-imperial relations. Yet, the term did not refer to any clear and codified body of rules. Rather, it was a much fuzzier concept used to refer to a growing body of treaties and agreements, as well as to what were understood by Western jurists to be the general rules agreed upon by "civilized" states. In the early twentieth century, the United States became increasingly active in forging this international legal arena.

Empire, in this period, was not anathema to international law but rather was "itself an international norm that was part of, not external to, the law."[51] In *Legalist Empire*, Benjamin Coates shows how a group of American lawyer-statesmen located mostly in the Department of State learned to use international law in support of American expansion, both to promote formal colonization following 1898 and to facilitate "new practices of informal empire by spreading legal regimes that protected the prerogatives of US capital while assuaging opposition from domestic and foreign opponents."[52] This continued the racializing practices of earlier European and American imperial expansion: "The rule of law was understood as the application of civilization to restrain irrational behavior."[53]

In sum, law was always an integral component of Western imperial practices and geographies, including in the United States. Central to the promotion of capitalist social relations and always shaped by and enacting ideas about racial hierarchies and civilization, the imperial and capitalist functions of law throughout this period are impossible to disentangle from one another. In the US case, law contributed to the dispossession of indigenous peoples, overseas colonization, and less formal but still blatant interventionism in the Western Hemisphere, all carried out simultaneously in the name of US geopolitical interests, freedom, and markets.

Yet, as the above examples show, different kinds of law had spatially distinct roles throughout this period. *Domestic* US law determined the internal differentiation and governance of populations *within* official US borders, whether national (i.e., within the incorporated states of the union) or imperial (on Indian reservations or in the overseas colonies). *International* law governed relationships with states understood to be formally outside the United States, including those Latin American and Caribbean countries that were officially independent but under more or less direct US dominance in practice. This distinction determined both the type of law in each sphere and its source. While domestic law was produced by Congress and the judiciary and iteratively interpreted and enforced by the courts, international law was the domain of the US *executive* branch, with power concentrated in the Department of State. Moreover, while often aiming to protect the interests of private US capital, this sort of international law did not directly govern cross-border relationships between private actors or between private actors and foreign governments; rather, it operated on the terrain of properly international relations *between* states.

US courts had no say over the content of this international law. Even as the US as a whole exercised extensive power beyond its official borders in the nineteenth and early twentieth centuries, *judicial* authority was strictly curtailed. As the *Underhill* case with which this chapter opened shows, US courts themselves refused to issue judgments that could be seen as interfering directly with the territorial sovereignty of foreign countries. For issues of that nature, the courts insisted, it was up to the *executive* to intervene, if it wanted to.[54]

Only when the form of US empire shifted after World War II did this division of power between the judicial and executive branches and between domestic and international law change. As formal sovereign equality became the global norm, the transnational extension of US *domestic* law, or what I call judicial territory, over other governments and state spaces became an increasingly important modality of transnational US power—one that depended on rewriting the rules of national territoriality and sovereignty themselves.

Yet, judicial territory is not the only form of law that has continued to mediate the relationship between capitalism and imperialism in the postwar period. Before turning specifically to judicial territory, I first sketch out the broader spatio-legal framework within which global capitalism and US power have developed since the 1940s. This is helpful both for contextualizing judicial territory as just one significant form of legal power among others in this period and for illuminating what is distinctive about it.

LAW, CAPITAL, AND US EMPIRE IN THE POSTCOLONIAL ERA

World War II sounded the death knell for the Western European and Japanese empires and led to the ascendence of two new superpowers and the Cold War conflict that would inflect the next half century of global economic, military, and political relations. While the Soviet Union cemented its hold over large parts of Central Asia and Eastern Europe, the United States became the world's most powerful capitalist economy, assuming the mantle of "leader of the free world," and coming, in Panitch and Gindin's words, to "superintend the making of global capitalism."[55] In the context of the waning legitimacy of imperialism and poised, by virtue of its unmatched economic strength, to reap the benefits of a less explicit empire of free trade in any case, the anti-imperialist narrative that had always been an important component of American identity became even more central to legitimizing US, military, economic, and political domination.[56] As McGranahan puts it, "In the era of decolonization, empire is a story of imperialism denied and disguised."[57]

This empire in disguise has had many dimensions. In addition to dozens of blatant military interventions in other countries, the United States has built the most extensive network of global military bases the world has ever seen. Meanwhile, it has continued to fuse its own geopolitical and geoeconomic goals through the construction of an emerging liberal international order focused on promoting procapitalist trade and financial practices (while doing far less to limit human rights abuses, military aggression, or environmental harms). Enrolling other states in this order has involved a mix of threats, persuasion, and incentives, from covert military interventions to the use of conditional foreign aid and loans.[58]

It was as the architect and primary beneficiary of this order that the United States presided over the era of globalization that began after World War II and accelerated with the neoliberal counterrevolution of the 1970s. In contrast to the previous high point of intensive cross-border economic integration in the late nineteenth and early twentieth centuries, this postwar phase of global integration has unfolded in a world of formally sovereign nation-states, overseen by a host of new international rules and institutions. Yet, like previous phases of globalization, this has not been primarily about leveling or homogenizing economic conditions within or across countries, but rather about simultaneous processes of integration, differentiation, and uneven development.[59] The United States has presided over a highly unequal transnational economy, in which the benefits of cheap labor and the flow of raw materials and capital from the periphery to the center (especially to the United States, but also to other parts of the rich world) has remained a fundamental pattern, notwithstanding the rise of the BRICs (Brazil, Russia, India, and China) and even as increased foreign direct investment and the functional integration of production across borders has reorganized global supply chains in complex ways.[60] Within this framework, law—national, international, and transnational—has remained central to the simultaneous maintenance and denial of US empire, while promoting not just the interests of particular capitalist states, but of global capitalism as a whole.

Neoliberal ideology is famously characterized by a powerful discourse about states *versus* markets and a commitment to so-called free market principles. Yet, in practice the period of intensified global economic integration we now refer to as neoliberal globalization has not meant the shrinking or retreat of the state, but rather its restructuring and reconfiguration.[61] Indeed, in contrast to the laissez-faire liberalism of the nineteenth and early twentieth centuries, the *neo*liberal period has coincided with a proliferation of laws and an expansion of the capacities of modern states.[62] As Panitch and Gindin explain: "As capitalism developed states in fact became more involved in economic life than ever, especially in the establishment and administration of the juridical, regulatory, and infrastructural framework in which private property, competition, and contracts came to operate."[63] This only intensified with the acceleration of neoliberal globalization from the 1970s on: "Far from the globalization of production and finance 'disembedding' markets from society, it was the ways in which capitalist 'laws of value' were embodied in 'rules of law' that made possible the further proliferation and spatial expansion of markets."[64]

Even as the role of law in constituting capitalism has intensified over time, its precise forms and functions have changed. Obviously racialized legal distinctions between colonizer and colonized became illegitimate by the mid-twentieth century. Yet, the use of law to differentiate between populations did not disappear. Rather, the terms *civilized* and *uncivilized* were replaced by more euphemistic claims about the "law of nations" or a "general consensus" among states—terms within which the views of non-Western countries have hardly ever been included. Jurists and investors today also continue to distinguish between those states seen as possessing the "rule of law" and "good governance" or not. These distinctions are regularly relied on to justify the use of US, English, or international law *rather* than the domestic laws of the states in which economic activities occur.[65] Indeed, the postwar period has been characterized not so much by the development of a more egalitarian "international" law, but rather by the spread of Anglo-American-style law at multiple scales.

This is evident in the outsized influence of the United States on the international institutions that emerged after World War II, including the United Nations, the IMF, the World Bank, and, eventually, the World

Trade Organization (WTO). The rules adopted by these institutions, as well as in proliferating multilateral and bilateral trade agreements, have been modeled to a large extent on US domestic commercial rules.[66] In this way, international law has continued to mediate the relationship between US empire and global capitalism. In addition to the US imprint on international rules and agreements, the second half of the twentieth century was marked by the Americanization of other *national* legal systems, often referred to more euphemistically as the "harmonization" of law or the spread of "constitutionalism." [67] United States law and lawyers, moreover, emerged as central players in all these processes, shaping increasingly technocratic national and international legal rules, and working in international law firms and tribunals to represent both US and foreign companies and other governments.[68]

In contrast to colonial era legal systems, in which the differential application of laws to colonizers and colonized was explicit, in this postwar framework, the *same* Anglo-American-style legal rules have applied (in theory, at least) to everyone. This has been important for the system's legitimacy. Invocations of universality underwrite the rhetorical power of the "rule of law," elevating it above so-called political pursuits. At times, this reliance on codified legal rules can even make the United States itself vulnerable to its own system. As Dezalay and Garth point out in an analysis of the general "legalization" of foreign policy and economic rules, "the price of legalization is some degree of autonomization, even if the rules and practices tend to favor the United States. Sometimes the United States will lose or be held accountable as a price for the legitimacy of the system."[69] Yet, in a highly unequal economic context, this very universalism has, *on the whole*, reinforced rather than mitigated material differences between high- and low-income countries, benefitting the US most of all. By applying so-called equal rules to a world characterized by hierarchy and inequality, the universalizing abstractions of law "deliberately ignore the phenomena of uneven development in favor of prescribing uniform global standards."[70] This perpetuates and reinforces colonial-era spatial patterns of inequality and extraction.

The United States, then, at least until recently, has been the biggest beneficiary of this postwar order. Yet, in contrast to the period of explicit inter-imperial rivalries among Western powers, US domination since World War II has also brought significant benefits to other wealthy countries and to transnational capital as a whole. It has thus been supported, by and large, not only by the United States, but by most other Western countries and by capitalists from around the world. Especially since the 1980s, it has also been supported by many political elites in the Global South, who often have both ideological sympathies with this system and who benefit materially even if their countries do not.[71]

This widespread, though by no means universal acceptance of the US-based international order, as well as the centrality of law to that order, have led many to see postwar US power primarily in terms of rules and cooperation, or at most in terms of hegemony, rather than in terms of blatant domination or empire. This term has often been used by American foreign policy apologists to foreground consent *rather* than coercion in ways that serve to disguise and justify the continued violence of American power in the world.[72] In more sophisticated analyses of hegemony, by contrast, the term is understood, drawing on Gramsci, as involving a complex *combination* of consent and coercion. From this perspective, American hegemony is understood to be based on a mix of military, political, economic, and cultural practices, and on the forging of a dominant if always incomplete "common sense" that serves the interests of the United States first and foremost, while also benefitting, at least to some extent, other states and/or their elites.[73]

The combination of coercion and consent—not mere domination—has been central to all empires as well.[74] Yet, this Gramscian-inflected concept of hegemony captures many aspects of postwar American power and of the spread of constitutionalism, market logics, and certain powerful discourses about freedom and liberalism that have gone along with it. To the extent that the expansion of transnational US law is articulated with these processes and, as I explore in the final section of this chapter, is itself a crucial tool for obscuring and legitimizing the imposition of US legal and market rules on other states, judicial territory too can usefully be seen as part of a US hegemonic project.

Yet, in my view, the concept of hegemony is better suited to analyzing the relationship between the United States and its Western allies than it is to capturing the continued radical inequality between the United States, on the one hand, and most of the postcolonial world, on the other. Specifically, the concept of hegemony is often associated with a "diffuse" and "networked geography of power."[75] Yet, this fails to capture key spatial dimensions of the relationship between North and South, including the ways the system continues to funnel raw resources and capital from the latter to the former, and the continued *expansion* of US power associated both with the proliferation of US military bases around the globe and with the growing reach of the US judiciary. Here, the concepts of empire and imperialism remain powerful.[76]

Of course, this leaves open the question of what *kind* of empire the US is today. Even among those who do see US power since World War II as imperial, many (especially those not focused primarily on the invasions of Afghanistan and Iraq) characterize this as informal empire in contrast to the "juridical" empires of the colonial era. This is meant to reference the fact that the US has not formally annexed new territories in over a century and the way that, despite massive imbalances in de facto sovereignty among states, the United States now operates in and supports a world of officially equal nation-states.[77]

There is significant truth to this. The end of formal colonization freed the United States from the need to spend money and resources directly governing new territories, while helping make all countries open to US influence and the penetration of US capital. The anti-imperialist discourse of self-determination has bolstered US legitimacy, while allowing the United States itself to make arguments from sovereignty when it wants to avoid international oversight.

Yet, this is not the whole story. The idea that we live in a world of even formally equal nation-states, in which no sovereign country can exercise direct governance over another, has been too easily accepted. It obscures the way that, alongside decolonization in the wake of World War II, another major transformation was underway as well—one that involved the formal, *legal* extension of US authority and the redefinition of territorial sovereignty itself.

Here, my framing of US judicial power as an imperial modality is meant to make visible important continuities with past imperial formations and their "repertoires of power"—specifically with their ambiguous geographical boundaries, their embrace of legal pluralism, and their production of overlapping, contested, and noncontiguous assertions of territoriality and sovereignty.[78]

JUDICIAL TERRITORY AND IMPERIAL POLITICAL GEOGRAPHIES

As direct interventions in the economic affairs of other states became illegitimate, the geography of US judicial authority changed. While courts had previously claimed authority within both the national and formally dependent territories of the United States, they had declined to exercise authority beyond these spaces. Instead, the executive branch, with the aid of State Department lawyers and international law, had determined US policy throughout the Caribbean and Latin America.

In the post–World War II period, this changed. Courts continued to operate within the fifty equal states, as well as in the remaining dependent territories. Yet, they gradually took on more and more authority beyond those boundaries as well. Contractual practices and changes in commercial law enabled the increasing extension of US judicial authority over private actors around the world.[79] At the same time, foreign sovereign immunity and act of state rules were rewritten to make it easier to bring foreign government actions of a so-called commercial character under US judicial power. This has resulted in a redistribution of different modalities of US state power across space. Specifically, it has implied a ceding of authority by the executive branch to the judiciary, as well as both the extension of the range of US domestic law and a new role for the judiciary in the interpretation and production of so-called international law. Together, these changes have enabled more and more foreign state economic activity to be subsumed within US judicial space. The rest of the book examines exactly how this was done. Here, I situate my analysis of judicial territory in relation to this chapter's broader discussion of the links between law, space, capitalism, and imperialism at different moments.

The gradual extension of this judicial territory enabled the United States to continue exercising substantial authority over the decisions of foreign governments in an age of avowed anti-imperialism and formal sovereign equality. This involved far more than economic or political *influence* on other countries. Just as many former colonies gained independence for the first time, US courts redefined traditional conceptions of sovereignty altogether to enable the extension of US judicial power (in certain matters) over formally sovereign governments.

This redefinition of sovereignty has been inseparable from a reconfiguration of national territoriality—or rather, of both national and imperial territorialities. With the extension of judicial power abroad, US domestic law has continued to foster the simultaneous development of both US empire and capitalism, and of their entwined geographies. In doing so, it has been marked both by substantial continuities with and distinctions from previous imperial formations. Seeing how requires stepping back to consider the geographies of earlier phases of imperial and capitalist expansion.

The subjection of much of the world to the linked processes of imperial expansion and capitalist development from the fifteenth through the nineteenth centuries did not homogenize either the colonizing or colonized world—rather, it produced an incredible variegation of both capitalist and imperial forms and practices.[80] This variegation was a product in part of the constant negotiation between colonizer and colonized, and of the many hybrid political and economic formations this produced.[81] It was also shaped by capitalism's tendency to uneven development—that is, by the ways that, far from leveling or erasing difference, capitalism itself both makes use of and produces differences of various kinds.

It was in this context of far-reaching but spatially complex and fractured empires and of a variegated but increasingly worldwide capitalism that the modern state, with its commitment to fixed territorial borders, gradually evolved. There has long been a tendency to see empires, with their associated practices of mapping and geographic knowledge accumulation, as helping to flatten and "rationalize" space "and to corral law into conventionally defined jurisdictions," paving the way for the eventual replacement of empires by modern, territorially defined nation-states.[82] Yet, there are at least two basic problems with this narrative. First, the period of state consolidation in Europe did not follow but rather coincided with the height of European empire. The high age of European nationalism and the high age of empire occurred at one and the same time.[83] As Jane Burbank and Frederick Cooper have argued, it is not only that "empire-states" and modern states existed simultaneously: more than this, the imperial practices of many states were central to their own "national" consolidation.[84] In other words, the Westphalian state system was coproduced with empire, not a replacement for it.

In addition, as Benton shows so well, imperial space was not regular or homogenizing at all. Rather, imperial territories were highly irregular and heterogeneous, characterized by a range of overlapping, partial, or shared governance arrangements. Neither the territorial limits of empires nor their sovereignty over imperial spaces were ever clearly bounded or defined. Despite maps like those of the British empire showing its imperial domains boldly marked in red, imperial borders on the ground were most often dynamic, fuzzy, overlapping, and ambiguous. Indeed, that fuzziness was sometimes strategic. As Stoler and McGranahan explain, "Sometimes empire-states were intent to establish their order by clarifying borders but as often they were not. Agents of imperial rule invested in, exploited, and demonstrated strong stakes in the proliferation of geopolitical ambiguities."[85]

These ambiguous spatial boundaries were inextricably tied to ambiguous and hybrid forms of authority and governance on the edges of empire. Burbank and Cooper emphasize the pervasiveness of messy territorial configurations and "shared out, layered, overlapping" sovereignties, in which imperial agents and local actors negotiated a wide range of (always unequal) governance arrangements.[86] As Benton shows in the context of Spanish and Portuguese colonization of the Americas, such complex imperial geographies were the norm. "Sovereignty," she argues, "did not have an even territorial or juridical dimension."[87] Rather, it was characterized by unevenness and contingency, by "fluid boundaries," "long, thin zones of imperfect control," and "anomalous enclaves."[88] What's more, as Benton explains, law played a central role in producing these complex configurations. Delegated legal authority and pluralist combinations of indigenous, colonial, and metropolitan law within empires contributed to the messy geographies of imperial territoriality and sovereignty. Conversely, legal theories of divided and layered sovereignty quickly emerged to account for this messiness.[89]

It was not that these irregular imperial formations gradually gave way to more and more regular ones and eventually to the territorially well-defined and internally spatially homogeneous nation-state; rather, among the empire-states of the imperial age, strategies for expanding the far-flung, irregular, and fuzzy boundaries of empire *coincided* with other strategies for territorial consolidation and demarcation. As Benton explains, "The impulse to territorial rule and the legal politics that transcended or splintered territory were parallel and not mutually exclusive processes."[90] Empires pursued multiple territorial strategies at once.

The same is true today. While the extension of judicial territory since World War II marks an important spatial shift in the modalities of US empire operating abroad, the irregularity of the boundaries of judicial territory does not signify a simple rupture either with earlier national territorial practices or with an imagined even and regularizing spread of imperial borders. Rather, judicial expansion can be seen as a perpetuation, in a different mode, of previous messy imperial spatial strategies. Like earlier imperial geographies, judicial territory too has dynamic, sometimes noncontiguous, and often ambiguous boundaries. Law here, as in previous periods, does not simply demarcate clear jurisdictional boundaries, but rather helps make claims to sovereignty in overlapping and contested transnational spaces. The result is not the Westphalian ideal of asserting smooth sovereignty within bounded nation-states, but rather a shifting patchwork of graduated and attenuated sovereignties with messy territorial borders—both those of the United States and of the countries over which its courts exercise authority.[91]

This complex geography of judicial territory in the postwar period complicates common narratives about the nation-state today. The legal redefinition of territory and sovereignty at the heart of the expansion of judicial territory means that this period cannot simply be characterized as shaped by juridically equal (even if substantively unequal) nation-states. Rather, territorial sovereignty remains *formally* fragmentary and overlapping, just as it was in the age of explicit empires.

Attending to these imperial continuities also complicates an equally widespread but somewhat contradictory idea about the *demise* of Westphalian sovereignty. A dominant narrative has been that, even as the end of World War II, the birth of the United Nations, and mass decolonization marked the formal triumph of the nation-state as the near-universal political form, the turn toward globalization in the post–World War II period began undermining the absolute Westphalian sovereignty of the nineteenth century. This assumption also undergirds the idea that the flexibilization of legal jurisdiction in the past half century represents the *divorce* of jurisdiction from state territory, as if territory—hopelessly confined to the official boundaries of states—no longer bears on this more "modern" form of jurisdiction.[92] Yet, such accounts assume some previous period of strict Westphalian territoriality that never existed. While state power and spatiality has certainly changed in the age of globalization, the discussion of imperial geographies above shows that powerful states always exercised authority beyond their official national (and even imperial) borders, and that zones of overlapping, graduated, and hybrid sovereignties were widespread, not anomalous deviations. Westphalian territoriality was *never* absolute. Conversely, globalization has not made political borders irrelevant. Rather, the juridical reach of some states has been extended, while that of others has been curtailed.

To recap, while postwar judicial territory is distinctive for the way it extends domestic common law and judicial authority vis-à-vis other modes of imperial power, its irregular and ambiguous borders are not unique among imperial geographies. Judicial territory, then, represents less a breakdown of Westphalian territorial sovereignty than it does a continuation of imperial spatial strategies in new forms. At the same time, judicial territory as a modality of imperial power is also distinct in important ways.

OBSCURING AND LEGITIMATING US EMPIRE

In short, although law has always been entwined with the United States and other empires, this relationship has shifted over time. Since before *Plessy v. Ferguson* and *Downes v. Bidwell*, US courts have played an important role in differentiating and governing populations within US national and imperial boundaries. Yet, only since World War II have they replaced the executive branch in governing important dimensions of transnational US interactions with foreign governments. Once formal colonization and imperial control were no longer seen as legitimate, judicial power became a more and more important tool of US geopolitical and geoeconomic strategy; one that enabled the United States to rewrite the rules of territorial sovereignty, undermining the national economic decisions of other governments. It has done so in a way that is not merely informal but juridical— instantiated in a truly transnational body of US law. In doing so, it has become an important part of the link between empire and capitalism.

By subjecting large amounts of transnational economic activity to US law, US judicial territory has helped ensure that much of the global economy is governed by rules that privilege contract and creditor rights and the interests of private capital. In combination with the outsized US influence on international law and the Americanization of other legal systems, judicial territory has thus bolstered the spread of market society and capitalist globalization everywhere. While not making economic activities like nationalizations or state-owned enterprises that threaten private investors' interests illegal, it has made them less useful to postcolonial governments. This has perpetuated the extraction of capital from formerly colonized nations and underwritten the uneven development that has long shaped relations between North and South. At the same time, even as it has helped perpetuate imperial inequalities, the distinctive characteristics of US common law have been perfectly suited to obscuring the imperial character of that law itself.

That judicial territory has taken on these imperial functions does not mean that it has been designed or masterminded by some central power in any coherent way. Rather, as in previous imperial formations, imperial expansion is always mediated by a combination of centralized and more capillary forms of agency.[93] While law is rooted in and enforced through state authority, the extension of judicial territory has been shaped by an array of interests. The executive and judicial branches have played dominant roles, but always alongside other players, most importantly private investors and their lawyers, who themselves can thus be understood as both agents *of* empire and as manipulating imperial forms to their own advantage.

This gives jurists, law schools, legal practices, and common law logics a unique importance in shaping judicial territory. Indeed, the prominence of these actors makes judicial territory as a modality of imperial power distinct from both prior imperial practices and other axes of US power today.

It also makes it especially well suited to promoting imperial processes of expansion and extraction, while simultaneously obscuring these processes and enabling the myth of formal equality to remain in place.

Judicial territory has done this in part in the same way as law more generally. The discourse of the rule of law has been central to papering over the constant tension between America's particular interests and its promotion of an international liberal order based on supposedly universal rules and values.[94] But judicial power is also distinct from other forms of law in several ways. While law and state power are closely connected, the question, as geographer Joshua Barkan has argued, is what kind of power specifically law entails, and why politics sometimes takes a legal form.[95] Here we can ask more specifically why politics sometimes takes the form of transnational, judicially produced common law. Or, what makes judicial territory distinctive—and useful—as a modality of imperial power?

Barkan, referencing Foucault, points out that as older forms of sovereign power gave way to governing "on the basis of economy and through the economy," law tended to replace ad hoc sovereign decisions with more standardized and generalizable tools of governance.[96] As we will see in the following chapters, judicial territory has done this in a very particular way by regularizing what were previously seen as ad hoc foreign policy decisions. Such decisions are traditionally made by the executive branch on a case-by-case basis. Moving such acts to the judicial domain, in contrast, subjects them to general rules and brings entire categories of foreign government activity under US authority. This regularizing function has been an explicit aim of the expansion of US judicial territory, which is often legitimized in the name of increasing predictability for market actors. It also means that the extension of judicial authority results not only in a different modality of US state power operating abroad, but also in an overall increase in the frequency with which that power is exercised; where the executive branch *may* decide to intervene in certain kinds of cases, the judiciary almost certainly *will* do so if asked.

Common law is also temporally distinctive. In comparison to not only executive policy decisions and military commands, but also to government legislation, common law changes in a gradual and accretionary way. Judges draw new distinctions to produce what are, for the most part, small legal changes that can be at least plausibly justified as in line with past case precedent. One effect is that common law change can lag behind other shifts in state strategies or power. This also makes common law even more entrenched and harder to dislodge, once made, than many other kinds of policies or legislation.[97]

Finally, while many forms of law contribute to legitimating and disguising US empire, common law does this in uniquely powerful ways. As noted above, both empire and hegemony are based on complex combinations of coercion and consent. The key question is not only how consent is manufactured but also how *dissent* is managed.[98] Anderson notes, moreover, that both coercion and consent have been harder to institutionalize at the international than the national scale.[99] Using judicial power to support US geopolitical economic goals, as we will see, has been a useful mechanism for helping overcome this difficulty, manufacturing consent and managing dissent *in the service of* the imperial aims of extraction and expansion.[100]

First, redefining hotly contested transnational affairs as private and legal, rather than public and political, literally depoliticizes these issues— recasting them as apolitical, natural, and technical matters and, in the process, reshaping not just American, but eventually the global common sense about what constitutes the proper spheres for states and markets, respectively. This resonates with broader (neo)liberal efforts to institutionalize the separation of politics and economics, with the concomitant depoliticization of important social relations.[101] The expansion of US common law helped transform this logic of technopolitical privatization into a *geopolitical* tool of empire at the transnational scale. The recoding of many foreign policy issues as merely legal has been an especially potent way for the United States to obscure its own imperial operations. This is an excellent example of what Susan Roberts, Anna Secor, and Matthew Sparke have called, in a very different context, "neoliberal geopolitics"—that is, of the way that neoliberalism has implied not the decline of the geopolitical, but rather that "contemporary neoliberal market-based logics are coming to rework the nature and practice of geopolitics."[102]

Second, the extension of judicial territory has not only helped forge widespread consent for US economic dominance, but also set the terms on which that dominance can be contested. Transferring transnational economic affairs to the judiciary has not eradicated dissent, but it has funneled it onto a juridical terrain. Only rarely do countries sued in US courts refuse to participate in litigation altogether. Much more often, foreign states hire US lawyers, go to trial in US courts, and defend themselves with US legal arguments. Almost all, furthermore, obey US court decisions once made, no matter how fiercely they resist during litigation. This has meant that, even as many countries protest each new step of the expansion of US judicial territory, they do so largely on the legal terrain established by previous US case precedent.

Third, one reason criticizing previous common law decisions is so rare is that common law practices of legal precedent and accretion themselves help obscure the contested origins of today's transnational US judicial power. Common law relies on case precedent. Although this makes common law explicitly historical, it also simultaneously erases historical context. Common law, forged in litigation, necessarily results from conflict and contestation. Yet, once made, decisions are transformed into precedent in ways that abstract from their original context. It is not only US judges and lawyers but also foreign governments themselves that facilitate this forgetting. While each new extension of US judicial territory is fiercely resisted, countries rarely contest the territorial advances of past decades, further contributing to disguising US imperial power today.

The effect of all of this is that, once extended, US judicial territory and common law power are almost never directly challenged. While serving to increase US authority over formally sovereign states in order to benefit private capital and perpetuate the unequal extraction of resources from South to North, the distinctive qualities of the common law have also ensured that these practices have remained invisible to most. These new legal structures simply fade into the rule of law to which all countries wishing to participate in today's international economic order must profess obedience. A primary goal of the rest of this book is to make this legal power more visible by exposing the largely hidden and technical spatio-legal practices through which this judicial modality of US empire has been produced.

CHAPTER TWO

The Politics of the Private

In August 1919, an Italian steamship called *The Pesaro*, loaded with, among other things, seventy-five cases of artificial silk, took off from Genoa. It transported the silk to New York City, where it delivered only seventy-four cases. One case, lost or damaged in transit, was not delivered. Claiming $250 in damages, the owner of said silk, Berizzi Brothers Company, sued *The Pesaro* in New York courts.[1] The case would have been straightforward except that *The Pesaro* was owned and operated by the Italian government. Since the early nineteenth century, it had been well established that foreign sovereign governments and their public ships were immune from suit in US courts. The question in this case was whether *The Pesaro* was truly a public vessel. The answer depended on how commercial activity like trading was mapped onto the public/private distinction.

The precise question of the public or private character of state-owned merchant ships had never before reached the Supreme Court. Berizzi and its lawyers argued that, although owned and operated by the Italian government, the ship was engaged in "a strictly commercial capacity" in carrying merchandise for sale, and that this did not "impress such a vessel with a public use."[2] The Italian government countered that what mattered was not whether an act was commercial or not, but rather whether it was done in the service of the people as a whole. "Obviously," its lawyers argued, "any interest designed to promote the welfare of people, not as individuals, but as members of the public, is a public, not a private interest."[3]

In 1926, the Supreme Court sided with the Italian government. In a unanimous opinion, the justices in *Berizzi Bros. Co. v. S.S. Pesaro* held that:

We think the principles [of foreign sovereign immunity] are applicable alike to all ships held and used by a government for a public purpose, and that when, for the purpose of advancing the trade of its people or providing revenue for its treasury, a government acquires, mans and operates ships in the carrying trade, they are public ships in the same sense that war ships are. *We know of no international usage which regards the maintenance and advancement of the economic welfare of a people in time of peace as any less a public purpose than the maintenance and training of a naval force.*[4]

The *Berizzi* Court refused a simple equation of private and commercial. Instead, they defined state engagement in economic activities as an important sovereign responsibility.

Fifty years later, US courts approached such issues very differently. The 1976 Foreign Sovereign Immunities Act (FSIA) rejected outright the idea that commercial acts could ever be public.[5] Instead, it codified a "commercial exception" to foreign sovereign immunity. This act, which still determines US foreign sovereign immunity rules today, is premised on the view that economic activities have nothing to do with the rights or duties of sovereignty—to the extent that states engage in such activities, they should be understood as participating in mere private, commercial transactions, and they should, accordingly, be treated just like any private corporation.

This chapter examines the shift from *Berizzi* to the FSIA. The restrictive approach to foreign sovereign immunity, which refuses immunity for commercial acts, was spurred first and foremost by the increasing participation of sovereign states in economic activities.[6] Initially, this concern was directed at both Western states, who had taken on a more active role in trade and other economic activities during World War I, and at the recently established Soviet Union. It was only after World War II, however, that the adoption of a commercial exception to foreign sovereign immunity really took off. By this time, foreign sovereign immunity cases in US courts rarely involved European governments. They often involved the Soviet Union and its satellites. Even more commonly, however, these cases centered around postcolonial states that had begun to nationalize large portions of their economies and make extensive use of state-owned enterprises (SOEs), government development contracts, and other state-based economic practices. It was these Third World economic activities above all that the commercial exception to foreign sovereign immunity aimed to bring within US judicial reach.

Yet, these dynamics are almost entirely absent from existing histories of the restrictive approach to foreign sovereign immunity. While the Soviet Union is often mentioned in passing as a spur to the restrictive theory, this is rarely given sustained attention. The suggestion is often simply that Soviet Communism made the adoption of such a theory inevitable. For example, Fox and Webb, authors of the most historically and spatially comprehensive study of foreign sovereign immunity laws, note in passing that the Soviet Union "had a profound effect on the evolution of State immunity," but explain the subsequent rise of the restrictive theory not as a strategic political economic decision, but rather as a "clearly necessary" response, as courts recognized that "a restrictive doctrine was required if justice was to be done."[7]

Even more marked than this superficial treatment of the Cold War's effect on foreign sovereign immunity rules is the near total absence of any reference to decolonization or anti-colonial economic practices in histories of sovereign immunity. Instead, the spread of the restrictive approach is narrated without geopolitical specificity as the gradual diffusion of a growing international consensus on the issue.[8] Similarly, the fact that, until recently, US courts have provided "over half of all the case-law on State immunity" is widely known, but rarely connected to US *power*. [9]

Instead, the diffusion of the restrictive approach to foreign sovereign immunity is explained as a natural response to changing economic conditions and to the growing importance of the rule of law and political rights. In 1951, in one of the most well-known early proposals for restricting foreign sovereign immunity, the famous international law scholar Hersch Lauterpacht argued that the absolute theory was based on "archaic" and "strained" ideas about the "dignity" of sovereign states.[10] The restrictive approach, in contrast, reflected both "modern developments in the economic sphere" and a growing challenge to state power on behalf of individual rights and the "incipient recognition of human freedoms."[11] Seamlessly blending these two narratives about modernization and rights, he argued that restricting foreign sovereign immunity would help redress both "inconvenience" and "injustice."[12] In thinly veiled civilizational language, he asserted that "enlightened governments" had already largely rejected the absolute theory due to their commitment to subjecting the state to the "rule of law."[13] Lauterpacht's article was cited repeatedly in legal proceedings and in policy documents throughout the mid-twentieth century, including in the hearings for the FSIA. It continues to be cited as an important source on foreign sovereign immunity even today. Framing the restrictive theory in this way as simultaneously a natural response to changing economic conditions and as promoting the rule of law remains common, as does the blurring of the line between commercial and other "rights."[14]

Yet, this way of understanding the rise of the restrictive theory of foreign sovereign immunity does not hold up to deeper scrutiny. In this chapter, I show that the adoption of the commercial exception to foreign sovereign immunity was far from a natural or inevitable response to either changing economic conditions or the love of liberty. Rather, it was part of a fumbling but concerted effort on the part of US corporations, jurists, politicians, and the Department of State to undermine socialist and post-colonial economic practices that challenged private US investors and US plans for a liberal capitalist international order. With the growing dominance of the US economy after World War II, foreign governments and US corporations increasingly interacted. The restriction of US foreign sovereign immunity rules, culminating in the FSIA, eventually succeeded in ensuring that many economic practices of foreign governments would be governed not by the laws of those governments, or even by international rules, but rather by a growing body of capital-friendly *US* law.

This did not occur all at once. The importance of precedent in common law meant that, even as attitudes toward foreign sovereign immunity began to shift within US law, business, and policy circles, neither the courts nor Congress simply asserted that commercial activities were no longer immune. Rather, the transition from *Berizzi* to the FSIA depended on gradual changes in US legal reasoning. Most importantly, creating the commercial exception required reclassifying more and more "public" and "political" activity as "private," "legal," and "commercial." From World War II to 1976, it was this process that enabled the gradual extension of US judicial power over more foreign government activities. The passage of the FSIA both codified these changes and redefined other, more explicitly spatial rules for determining jurisdiction over foreign governments.

Technical debates about these legal dichotomies did not occur in isolation. They were part of broader struggles within the West and among the West, the Soviet Union, and the Third World about the proper relationship between states and markets. The restriction of foreign sovereign immunity after World War II meant that economic matters were formally depoliticized in transnational US law just as both the Cold War and Third World anti-colonial struggles made the relationship between political and economic sovereignty one of *the* central questions of the twentieth century.

Doing this through technical changes in US common law helped obscure the reconfiguration of postwar US power in this period. Conflicts over foreign state-owned entities, nationalizations, and other matters would previously have been handled (or ignored) by the executive branch as foreign policy issues. Shifting these issues to the judiciary enabled the United States to constrain these practices while still presenting itself as a champion of national self-determination and the rule of law.

In the rest of this chapter, I first consider the centrality of the public/private, political/legal, and politics/economics distinctions in law and (neo)liberalism, as well as in Cold War and anti-colonial struggles over political and economic sovereignty. I then show how the shift from an absolute to a restrictive approach to US foreign sovereign immunity rules depended on rewriting these distinctions. I begin with the period of absolute sovereign immunity in the nineteenth and early twentieth centuries. I then turn to the period of the 1950s–1970s, during which the commercial exception to foreign sovereign immunity was introduced in US common law and the category of commercial was expanded to include many state-directed economic practices. I end with the passage of the FSIA, which codified the commercial exception while also regularizing and loosening more explicitly spatial rules for establishing US jurisdiction over foreign states. Throughout, I emphasize the influence of broader Cold War and anti-colonial struggles on these transformations. In the conclusion, I reflect on the (largely unplanned) implications for changing geopolitical economic relations, redefining territorial sovereignty, and forging a particular kind of globalization—one that privileges US capital and the rights of transnational corporations and that was set up *against* Third World attempts to produce alternative forms of economic interconnection.

DICHOTOMIES IN LAW AND LIBERALISM

Binaries have been central to the intertwined projects of liberalism, capitalism, and imperialism for the past five hundred years. The interlinked public/private and politics/economics distinctions have been especially important. In *The Great Transformation*, Polanyi wrote that a "self-regulating market demands nothing less than the institutional separation of society into an economic and a political sphere."[15] More recently, Panitch and Gindin, who emphasize not separation, but rather the "legal and organizational differentiation between state and economy," have labeled this "one of capitalism's defining characteristics."[16] Coronil ties these dichotomies more directly to the "joint unfolding of capitalism and imperialism," arguing that this "has always entailed not just the articulation but also the construction of 'economics' and 'politics' as separate domains or functions."[17]

The effort to clearly delineate state and market is never successful. It fails both because of the protective response from numerous social quarters and because this separation itself depends on continual state interventions.[18] Yet the *attempt* to establish separate spheres has been at the heart of liberal capitalism.[19] Indeed, Mann argues that the "stability of this regional separation—the clarity of the line that protects the economy from 'political' contamination—has been the central obsession of liberalism since at least the late eighteenth century."[20] The definitions of each category, however, have never been fixed, and the boundary between market and nonmarket is constantly contested.[21] Law has been one of the primary domains in which these debates have unfolded.

Sharp distinctions between public and private, politics and economics became increasingly common in US law in the nineteenth century, culminating in the Lochner era, during which US courts routinely struck down government attempts to regulate worker rights and other economic issues.[22] The very idea of such a separation, however, came under increasing critique in the first half of the twentieth century. It was not only the Russian Revolution that challenged these distinctions. During World War I, all the major Western powers participated in more extensive management of their economies than ever before, seizing foreign-owned property and engaging in centralized production, rationing, and resource allocation. With the Great Depression, the New Deal, and then World War II, which led to even more sustained government interventions in national economies, the lines between state and market became even more blurry. These practical developments were reflected in US legal theory. In the first half of the twentieth century, influential Legal Realists argued that the public/private, politics/economics, and law/politics distinctions were fuzzy and arbitrary, and that private contract was "nothing more than a choice to delegate public power to individuals based on social considerations."[23] The Realists' goal was not so much to jettison these distinctions altogether as to manage them in the service of particular social ends.

Yet, even as the Realist critique gained strength, early neoliberals on both sides of the Atlantic decried what they saw as the collapse of the politics/economics distinction. By the 1940s, there was a renewed attack on Legal

Realism and a defense of older "formalist" legal approaches, spurred largely by what jurists saw as the excesses of Nazism, fascism, and totalitarianism, as well as of the American New Deal.[24] Neoliberal critics doubled down on calls for a return to a sharp division between states and markets, even as some admitted that this was itself a *political* call.[25] Law was central to these early neoliberals' understandings of their own efforts. As historian Quinn Slobodian explains: "The ongoing depoliticization of the economic was a continual legal struggle, one that required continual innovation in the creation of institutions capable of safeguarding the space of competition."[26] The creation of a new body of international law was particularly important for those Slobodian refers to as the "globalist" neoliberals, located largely in Europe. In the 1970s, for example, Friedrich Hayek called for a "true international law" that would enable the "dethronement of politics" and limit the power of national governments.[27]

The triumph of these neoliberal attitudes in the 1970s and the proliferation of depoliticizing, technocratic practices of economic governance since is well documented. As neoliberals themselves were well aware, this never meant the retreat of the state, but rather its reconfiguration in support of markets.[28] Yet, both the discursive and the *institutional* separation of state and market gained ground in the neoliberal period.[29] In her foundational study of the financialization of the United States since the 1970s, Krippner shows that the depoliticization of the economy occurs through multiple avenues, including the bureaucratization of political decisions, the proliferation of economic "experts," and the naturalization of so-called market mechanisms that obscure and constrain the options of policymakers at the Federal Reserve and elsewhere.[30] She points out that this always depends on the movement of a *conceptual* boundary between politics and economics—one with real, material consequences.

In US domestic law, this crystallized in what Britton-Purdy et al. call the "twentieth century synthesis."[31] From the 1970s and 1980s on, the "law and economics" movement made market neutrality and efficiency central tenets of all "private" law subfields (contracts, property, corporate law, and so on). Jurists excised so-called political concerns from these areas and openly sought to use this law in the service of the market. Meanwhile, in domains understood as public, like constitutional law, so-called economic concerns came to be seen as irrelevant.[32] The result, in Britton-Purdy's pithy summation, is that "the economy has receded as a subject in fields now reconstituted as fundamentally political, and politics has receded as a subject in fields reconstituted as fundamentally economic."[33]

Yet what is missing from many accounts of the history of neoliberalism in and beyond law is the centrality of Third World anti-colonial practices in spurring the neoliberal counter-attack.[34] From the 1940s through the 1970s, even as the New Deal reshaped American society and Western European countries embraced social democracy, the West was locked in a concerted struggle with the rest of the world over how to define the boundary between states and markets, politics and economics. This struggle was strongly inflected by the Cold War and the ideological battle between capitalism and Communism. It was also central to Third World efforts to make formal postcolonial sovereignty more substantive.

As the European empires crumbled and the decolonization of African and Asian peoples accelerated after World War II, these newly independent states, together with Latin American countries, organized in opposition to their former colonizers and to the new threat of the bipolar Cold War order. Postcolonial leaders met in Bandung, Cairo, Havana, and elsewhere to formulate a "third" way, through which the hopes of postcolonial peoples for freedom and equality could be pursued independently of the major powers.[35] Central to this project was the debate over whether political sovereignty could have substantive meaning without economic sovereignty and at least relative economic equality. The Third World view that it could not was most forcefully articulated at the international scale in the attempt to forge a New International Economic Order (NIEO) from the mid-1960s to the mid-1970s.

Third World development efforts in the first two decades after World War II often had a strong emphasis on economic nationalism and industrialization, with a focus on state planning, subsidies, and tariffs, as well as investments in infrastructure and education. Although, as Getachew demonstrates, anti-colonial thinkers were always invested not only in national but also in world-making projects, many in this period saw at least partial delinking from the global economy as necessary for decreasing dependence on former colonizers.[36] By the mid-1960s, however, as the limits of national autarky became clearer, growing critiques of this strategy emerged within the Third World itself. In response, many Third World leaders began to focus less on independence from, and more on reconfiguring the international system. This was the basis for what became known as the NIEO.[37]

The NIEO was designed to redress the legacies of colonialism and the continuing transfer of wealth from South to North. It was based on the idea that national sovereignty required not only formal, juridical equality, but substantive economic equality as well. Overcoming the politics/economics distinction so deeply enshrined in liberal thought and institutions was central to this project. In formulating the NIEO, Third World leaders like Michael Manley of Jamaica and Julius Nyerere of Tanzania "engaged in a distinctive politicization of the economy that located economic inequality in an international and imperial division of labor."[38]

The NIEO was less radical in some ways than earlier postcolonial projects, combining a Marxist analysis of underdevelopment with calls for a reconfigured and redistributive but still generally liberal trade system.[39] Yet, Western states and investors found these calls threatening. Most egregiously from the West's perspective, the Declaration on the Establishment of a New International Economic Order and the Charter of Economic Rights and Duties of States (both adopted by the UN General Assembly in 1974) asserted the right of all states to permanent sovereignty over their own natural resources and economic activities. The Charter specified that this right, in turn, implied the right to nationalize or expropriate foreign-owned property, and to determine "appropriate compensation" for such property according to the domestic laws of the *host state*, not so-called international rules or standards. Both documents asserted the right of all states to regulate the activities of foreign corporations within their borders and made it clear that sovereign equality could be violated by "economic, political or any other type" of coercive measures.[40]

The mid-1960s to mid-1970s was a time of strength for the Third World, and the NIEO had some important successes.[41] Yet, by the late 1970s, the project was largely defunct. Declining global economic conditions, as well as splits within and between Third World states and contradictions inherent in the project of the NIEO itself weakened the Third World's position. At the same time, the West mounted concerted resistance.[42] The neoliberal counterrevolution of the 1970s, strengthened by a general crisis of Keynesianism in the West, lent weight to a barrage of free market critiques of the NIEO. These took practical shape in international institutional responses, including the push for more liberal trade rules at what would eventually become the World Trade Organization (WTO).[43] Meanwhile, the power of the UN General Assembly was undermined by Western jurists and politicians.[44] Finally, rising debt levels in the late 1970s paved the way for the debt crises of the 1980s, one effect of which was to subject Third World states to the dictates of international financial institutions, especially the International Monetary Fund (IMF) and the World Bank.

As geographer Geoff Mann has argued,

US power was built to a significant extent on the fact that an international economy emptied of its politics—an economy that posits poverty, dependence, and inequality as technical problems, which literally cannot exist in the abstract realm of formal political equality—is a massive resource distribution machine, channeling flows toward those with "legitimate" (i.e. apolitical) economic interests, and away from those whose claims are based on relative deprivation, powerlessness, or insecurity. More than in any other "truth," it is in the obvious necessity of the separation that liberal hegemony is reproduced.[45]

The growing dominance of international institutions that could be framed by Western powers as sites of technical, apolitical expertise, was a powerful mechanism for the depoliticization of substantive economic concerns, putting an end to the possibility that economic sovereignty would be widely seen as a precondition for political independence.[46]

These changes in international rules and institutions from the 1970s on were all critical components of the neoliberal turn and the full restoration of US power and liberal hegemony. Yet, the Third World threat to economic liberalism was met even earlier by a different strategy—one also based largely on policing the politics/economics divide. Starting in the 1950s, *transnational* law became a central site for the struggle over the proper relationship between states and markets—and an especially important one for sidestepping the international institutions on which the NIEO was focused altogether. This played out both in the development of transnational arbitration and in the extension of US judicial territory over foreign government economic acts.

Anghie, who focuses on the former, locates the origins of transnational law in the struggle between Western multinationals and newly postcolonial governments beginning in the 1950s. After decolonization, these governments attempted to assert sovereign rights to govern resources within their own borders—rights that had long been standard in Western legal regimes. Such rights, however, now threatened the interests of Western corporations, many of whom had been operating in these non-Western countries since the colonial period. New practices of arbitration before international tribunals were developed to undermine national claims to local resources. Under the old system, "host states" defined the terms for their own resources and contracts. Under colonialism, this meant the imperial state. After decolonization, this would have meant the postcolonial state. Yet, instead, international (Western) jurists argued for a new approach based on the view that it was now not local, but rather international law that should govern contracts between multinationals and host states. In practice, these jurists meant the laws of so-called civilized—in other words, Western—nations, particularly England. As a new body of law governing these transnational contracts took shape, any reference to "general principles" came to enable "the effortless transposition of Western concepts of law that provided for the comprehensive protection of private property."[47]

This body of arbitration law continued to develop through the period of the NIEO, and by the 1970s, it was a powerful tool for combatting Third World efforts to establish national economic autonomy. Anghie sums up the effects of all this on the reconfiguration of the public/private distinction and Third World sovereignty: "Rather than an expansion of public power over the private realm, transnational law was deployed for the purpose of achieving the reverse: of establishing that private law was not susceptible to amendment by the state."[48]

Even as this body of transnational *arbitration* was emerging, however, a new global power had become ascendant—the United States. Given the reach and scope of US capital and corporations after World War II, Third World states, often acting through state-owned enterprises or development contracts with foreign investors, came into increasing conflict not just with former European colonizers, but also with US capital and courts. As in international arbitration cases, the foreign states sued in US courts tried to wield established definitions of sovereignty to protect themselves. In response, US foreign sovereign immunity rules were rewritten altogether. As with arbitration, this transformation went beyond mere technical changes to alter the relationship between public and private power. As legal scholar Richard Buxbaum put it in the 1980s, the transformation of the "doctrine of foreign sovereign immunity, more than any other set of rules, illustrates the process by which private economic actors have 'domesticated' public international law."[49] Doing so allowed them to curtail Third World economic sovereignty and bring foreign governments in line with US commercial interests and expectations.

Implementing these changes, however, required more than just asserting *that* a commercial exception to foreign sovereign immunity existed. Expanding the authority of US courts over Third World governments required rewriting the dichotomies at the heart of liberal capitalism. A close examination of this process is useful not so much for focusing on the effects of particular cases, but for what it can show us about *how* judicial power operates and changes. By analyzing the shift from *Berizzi* and absolute foreign sovereign immunity to the codification of the restrictive approach in the FSIA, we can see how the transformation of foreign sovereign immunity rules was driven not by abstract forces like modernization, but rather by particular struggles with socialist and other postcolonial states that were attempting to structure their economies in ways that did not match the US vision of a postwar liberal capitalist order. At the same time, investigating the technical legal mechanisms through which these changes were effected also shows that the deployment of judicial power to respond to these anti- or more-than-capitalist efforts was gradual, piecemeal, and sometimes fumbling. Strategic legal logics took shape over years. Nevertheless, the general tendency toward depoliticization of foreign state economic practices has been strikingly coherent. In the process, US common law has become a geopolitical and geoeconomic support for US empire and a mechanism for the production of the economy as a supposedly separate sphere.

FROM PUBLIC *AND* COMMERCIAL TO PUBLIC *VERSUS* COMMERCIAL

Every statement about where the public/private or political/economic distinction is located is a statement about what the market is, and about what does or does not constitute acceptable government activity. Litigation on such issues in US courts did more than *reflect* broader debates about political versus economic sovereignty. As US dominance solidified after World War II, how these distinctions were drawn in US law became significant for *determining* what definitions of sovereignty would and would not be given material form. Two legal changes in foreign sovereign immunity rules were especially important. First, all government commercial activities were redefined as private and nonpolitical *for the first time* in transnational US law. Second, the definition of commercial was expanded.

Foreign sovereign immunity rules determine whether and under what conditions foreign sovereigns, their officials, or their property can be sued or seized in US courts. In the nineteenth and early twentieth centuries, those courts adhered to a theory of absolute sovereign immunity, in which suits against foreign sovereign governments were only rarely allowed. This theory was most famously articulated in the 1812 case *The Schooner Exchange*.[50] A privately owned American ship had set sail from Baltimore for San Sebastián, Spain in 1809. While underway, the ship was seized by order of Napoleon Bonaparte and outfitted as a French military vessel. In July 1811, at the height of the Napoleonic Wars, while the United States was still attempting to maintain neutrality vis-à-vis both France and Britain, the ship was forced into Philadelphia by bad weather. The former owners took advantage of the opportunity to file suit, demanding the return of their property. In his now classic defense of absolute foreign sovereign immunity, however, Chief Justice Marshall (the same Marshall who later defined Indian tribes as "domestic dependent nations") refused. He declared Napoleon's ship to be a public vessel of a foreign sovereign government that was, therefore, immune from US courts.

The absolute approach to foreign sovereign immunity is often characterized as having applied immunity to all government acts, public and private. The restrictive approach is then seen as having introduced a public/private distinction into foreign sovereign immunity rules for the first time.[51] In fact, what changed in the transition to the restrictive approach was not whether the public/private distinction mattered, but how each category was defined. More specifically, what changed was how economic or commercial acts were categorized. While it is true that commercial acts had already been commonly equated with private acts in *domestic* US law by the late nineteenth century, this only became the norm in foreign sovereign immunity cases much later.

Foreign sovereign immunity is and has always been premised on the idea that there is a domain of sovereign state activity that should not be subjected to the laws or courts of other governments. This domain is associated with what are understood to be the public or political acts of governments (also referred to as *jure imperii*, which literally means laws of the empire). In US law relating to transnational affairs, these terms are near synonyms, so that public implies political and vice versa. Public, political acts are considered to be under *executive* authority. Such activities may be addressed, if the executive chooses, by diplomatic attention, sanctions, or even military intervention, but not by US laws or judges. Private activity (*jure gestionis*, meaning literally laws of performance or management), in contrast, is categorized as legal *rather* than political, and thus as suited for adjudication by US courts. All these categories operate spatially in foreign sovereign immunity law by distributing US executive authority vis-à-vis judicial authority. In other words, they determine what modality of US power will be applied where and when. They work in tandem with more explicitly spatial jurisdictional considerations to define US judicial reach over foreign sovereign governments. Expanding US judicial territory in the first decades after World War II thus required redrawing these key conceptual boundaries.

Even in the period of absolute foreign sovereign immunity, courts debated whether immunity applied in each case. The public/private distinction was always the most significant factor. In *The Schooner Exchange*, Marshall distinguished between Napoleon's "public armed ship" (immune) and privately owned "merchant vessels" (not immune).[52] Later courts extended the category of public ships to include nonmilitary vessels operated for "public uses," such as small floating light boats or ships used for tax collection.[53] Throughout the nineteenth century, the commercial character of a foreign state-owned ship or other government entity was rarely addressed at all. The opposite of public was not commercial or economic. It was, rather, something closer to *personal*—referring, for example, to the individual possessions of a king or official in contrast to their state possessions.[54]

Whether all commercial activity, government-based or not, should be categorized as private only became a serious question after World War I. It first arose in relation to state-owned and -operated ships carrying merchandise for sale. The question of immunity for such vessels had not been addressed in the nineteenth century. Government-owned and -operated merchant ships had been definitively classified for immunity purposes *neither* as private *nor* as public.

In the 1910s and early 1920s, however, state-owned vessels from France, Britain, Italy, Portugal, and Canada, along with a few non-Western countries like Chile and Turkey, were embroiled in litigation in US courts. Those governments all claimed immunity. The ensuing litigation often revolved around the question of whether or not trade was necessarily a private activity. There was no natural or right way to decide this question, even within the framework of existing US case law. Deciding how to categorize state-owned vessels engaged in trade in relation to the public/private distinction depended, as always, on a struggle among investors, jurists, and foreign governments.

During the first two decades of the twentieth century, many private litigants and some lower court judges argued that even state-owned merchant vessels should be seen as private.[55] In 1921, the Department of State expressed support for this view as well.[56] Most judges, however, disagreed.[57] They concluded that it was up to the foreign sovereign government to decide what did and did not constitute proper governmental activity—and that it was up to the US executive branch, not the courts, to contest such decisions if it wished.[58] The debate reached the Supreme Court in the 1926 *Berizzi* case, with which this chapter opened. There, the Court asserted definitively that even state economic activities could be public acts, as long as they were designed to promote the "maintenance and advancement of the economic welfare of a people."[59]

Berizzi turned out to be against the tide of US legal history. Undoing a Supreme Court decision, however, is not easy. Later critics characterized *Berizzi* as anomalous in "extending" immunity to private entities like government merchant ships.[60] Yet, the crux of the Court's decision was that the Italian government's trading activity was both commercial *and* public—not private at all. Undoing *Berizzi* thus required two major steps: redefining all commercial activity as private, and expanding the definition of commercial.

In 1952, the Department of State's Acting Legal Adviser Jack B. Tate issued a statement expressing the Department's support for a commercial exception to foreign sovereign immunity.[61] The Tate Letter, drafted during the Truman administration, was a joint project of several lawyers at the Department of State, including both New Deal men like Tate and conservatives like Conrad Snow.[62] In it, the Department equated "commercial" and "private" government acts, and called for the adoption of a restrictive theory of foreign sovereign immunity under which such acts would no longer be immune from suit.

Like many others, Tate suggested that, under the absolute theory of foreign sovereign immunity, *all* sovereign acts—public and private—had been immune. Under the new theory, he wrote, "the immunity of the sovereign is recognized with regard to sovereign or public acts (*jure imperii*) of a state, but not with respect to private acts (*jure gestionis*)."[63] As we have seen, however, the idea that the restrictive theory introduced the public/private distinction into foreign sovereign immunity cases for the first time was false. What the Tate Letter did do was *extend* the definition of private to include all commercial activity.[64]

The Tate Letter was at odds with standing case precedent as established by *Berizzi* and affirmed in several later decisions.[65] Yet, it was quickly picked up by US courts in order to justify a commercial exception to foreign sovereign immunity that had not previously existed. That US courts accepted the executive's input on this judicial point reflected both their eagerness for this change and the growing role of the Department of State in foreign sovereign immunity cases. The Department of State had long been the arm of the executive branch most heavily involved in interpreting and shaping international law in the service of US foreign policy goals.[66] It could also play a more ambiguous role in (sub)national legal cases. While it had sometimes expressed opinions in nineteenth century immunity cases, by the 1940s, it had become standard procedure for governments to file their immunity claims through the Department. The Department, in turn, made "suggestions" about whether or not courts should uphold a claim.

This institutional change was accompanied by a shift in legal reasoning. Traditional foreign sovereign immunity cases had focused on the public or private character of an act or entity. Once the category was determined to be public, that issue was then defined as a political matter best suited for the executive branch. In the 1940s, the Supreme Court reversed this logic. Rather than defining something as public and, thus, political, the Court first determined whether or not an issue was *political*—while simultaneously redefining political to refer not to the nature of the act itself, but rather to whether it might negatively affect the *US executive branch or foreign policy*. Under this reasoning, issues that could be adjudicated without complication for the US executive could be safely treated as private and legal. Those that might "embarrass" the executive should be classified as political and *therefore* public.[67] Foreign sovereign immunity was no longer based primarily on the inherent sovereignty of foreign nations. Rather, it was based on protecting the policy interests of the United States.

As an expression of the executive branch's opinions, the Tate Letter could thus be read as proving that, in most cases, the executive would not mind if courts asserted jurisdiction over the commercial activities of foreign governments. Together, the growing role of the Department of State in foreign sovereign immunity cases and this subordination of the public/private to the political/legal distinction paved the way for the courts to use the 1952 Tate Letter to effectively overturn *Berizzi*.[68] This solidified a sharp political/economic distinction in US foreign sovereign immunity law.

In his letter, Tate tried to legitimize the embrace of the restrictive theory of foreign sovereign immunity by arguing that the United States was *following* other countries in making this transition. Naming a handful of primarily Western European states as examples, he suggested that, by embracing the commercial exception, the United States was simply falling into line with international law.[69] It was true that some Western states were already moving in this direction (although the United Kingdom had not yet done so). This was partly due to the rise of Western social democratic welfare states and the belief that this normalization of state intervention in the economy should be accompanied by a reduction in state privileges. Yet, at the time the Tate Letter was published, only around ten countries had actually embraced the restrictive approach.[70]

Asserting a supposed international consensus, however, allowed Tate to efface the importance of non-Western countries in shaping foreign sovereign immunity rules. Early critiques of the absolute theory did target the increased economic activity of Western states. By the time US foreign sovereign immunity rules actually began changing after World War II, however, it was not the activities of Western governments that concerned most private litigants. Rather, it was the spread of what were seen as anticapitalist economic practices in both the Soviet sphere and across postcolonial countries.

The Tate Letter itself made it clear that the Cold War was part of the reason for adopting the restrictive approach:

> Little support has been found except on the part of the Soviet Union and its satellites for continued full acceptance of the absolute theory of sovereign immunity. . . . The reasons which obviously motivate state trading [i.e., socialist] countries in adhering to the theory with perhaps increasing rigidity are most persuasive that the United States should change its policy.[71]

The commercial exception to foreign sovereign immunity, this passage implied, would reduce the advantages of Soviet enterprises in global commerce.[72] In the 1950s, of course, the United States was embroiled in the Cold War. Although many Department of State officials were New Deal men, their embrace of an expanded welfare state at home went hand in hand with a commitment to free trade abroad.[73]

Neither decolonization nor any Third World countries were mentioned in the Tate Letter. Yet, in practice, it was cases involving these countries, even more than the Soviet Union, that would shape the letter's application over the next two decades. Of the more than one hundred foreign sovereign immunity cases in which the Department of State was officially involved from 1952 through 1977, only about twenty involved other Western countries. Around ten involved the Soviet Union and its Eastern European satellites. At least sixteen involved Cuba, and more than sixty others involved Third World countries from Venezuela, to India, to Egypt, to Ghana.[74]

The Cold War, as well as increasing state interventions in Western economies, had driven changing attitudes toward foreign sovereign immunity by the 1940s and early 1950s. Yet, it was cases against Third World states that fueled the real transformation of US foreign sovereign immunity law from the 1950s through the mid-1970s. These cases raised a variety of economic issues that posed potential challenges to Western corporations and US-style liberal capitalism, from running state-owned enterprises, to government infrastructure contracts, to importing food aid. Yet, the Tate Letter alone did not simply solve the problem. Rather, once the Tate Letter created a commercial exception to foreign sovereign immunity, litigants and jurists spent the next two and a half decades arguing over what precisely counted as commercial. What resulted was the gradual recharacterization of many public and political acts previously seen as being in the domain of foreign policy and the executive branch as commercial and, therefore, private and legal.

EXPANDING THE COMMERCIAL

By characterizing all commercial activities as private, the Tate Letter greatly expanded potential US judicial territory, at a moment when the United States was in the midst of establishing the postwar international economic order and decolonization was accelerating in Asia and Africa. By increasing the number and kinds of cases in which US courts, rather than the executive branch, would exercise authority over foreign sovereign governments, this initiated a shift in the geography of the modalities of US power operating abroad. Yet, by itself, the Tate Letter did not complete this shift. First, while it supported the commercial exception to foreign sovereign immunity, it did not make this law. Instead, for the next twenty-five years, US courts applied the commercial exception to foreign sovereign immunity *unless* the Department of State said otherwise. While the Department of State itself usually applied the commercial exception to its own decisions, if the political stakes were high enough, it might recommend immunity even for commercial acts. In addition, while the Tate Letter advocated a restrictive approach for immunity from suit, immunity from *execution* (the seizure of property to satisfy monetary judgments) remained absolute. This meant that even when judgments against foreign sovereigns were obtained, it could be difficult to collect on them. Most importantly, while it reclassified all commercial activity as private, the Tate Letter did not clarify exactly what counted as commercial. The upshot was that, from 1952 until the FSIA was passed in 1976, defining the commercial became central to foreign sovereign immunity cases.

This lack of clarity about exactly when and how the commercial exception should be applied meant that foreign sovereign immunity litigation would be entangled in ongoing struggles over the relationship between states and markets in the context of the Cold War and postcolonial development. Examining the gradual redefinition of the commercial in the Tate Letter period can show us how it is that particular legal cases, shaped by the specific interests and backgrounds of various litigants, lawyers, and jurists, can, together, have broader implications for the distribution of US power and the construction of the postwar political economy.

All claims about the public/private distinction in relation to government acts imply beliefs about valid state behavior. In 1964, the Second Circuit Court of Appeals, a primary site for litigation involving foreign governments, recognized precisely this point:

> Functionally the criterion [for distinguishing between public and private] is *purely arbitrary* and necessarily involves the court in projecting personal notions about *the proper realm of state functioning.*[75]

That is what the court in this and other cases proceeded to do. While the Tate Letter itself was a clear statement of the executive's desire to limit immunity for foreign states' economic activities, there was no master plan for precisely how the public/private divide should be redefined. Instead, changes were driven by litigants and judges in courtrooms across the United States, as well as by case-by-case input from the Department of State. There were often disagreements. Yet, the overall pattern was remarkably consistent. Countries being sued argued that a range of state economic activities should be considered public. US litigants and courts repeatedly reclassified those activities as commercial and private. Doing so favored US capital in these cases, while narrowing the domain of public activity and reducing the national economic sovereignty of foreign states. The clearest examples involve state-owned enterprises, government contracts, and development aid.

By the early twentieth century, many states, including Western countries, had begun running and operating state-owned entities, from railroads to ships to oil companies. In Communist states, this became standard practice. From the 1940s on, many Latin American and newly independent states, whether socialist or not, also relied on state-owned enterprises to earn revenues that could be used to bolster economic development. Such enterprises enjoyed absolute immunity from litigation through the first decades of the twentieth century. This changed in the Tate period.

This was most obvious in the treatment of state-owned and -operated trading ships. As we have seen, *Berizzi* classified such ships as public and immune. However reluctantly, courts upheld this rule in the 1930s and 1940s.[76]

Under the Tate Letter, however, the Department of State and the courts refused to suggest immunity for government-owned and -operated merchant vessels belonging to Argentina (1952), Spain (1952), the Philippines (1960), Cuba (1964), Poland (1965), and Canada (1968).[77]

Similar changes occurred in the treatment of other types of state-owned enterprises. State-owned railways had been classified as public in cases involving Canada (1908), Mexico (1924), and Sweden (1930).[78] As late as 1952, the DC district court granted immunity for a state-owned oil company, because it was operated "in the British public interest."[79] In contrast, under the Tate Letter, immunity was denied to South African Airways (1955); a Venezuelan state-owned airline (1955); and Sudan Railways (1967).[80] In all these cases, the kinds of state-owned enterprises that had been considered public in the first half of the twentieth century were recharacterized via the Tate Letter as commercial and private—ignoring the arguments of the states involved in this litigation.

It was not only state-owned enterprises, but all government agencies engaged in so-called commercial activities that were denied suit under the restrictive theory. In practice, this included nearly any activity for which these agencies contracted with private parties. Projects designed to foster infrastructure and agricultural development—both essential components of many postcolonial development plans—were especially common foci of immunity litigation. For example, the Department of State declined to suggest immunity for governments involved in running a cattle improvement program (Venezuela, 1960); building low-cost housing (Cuba, 1962); financing a state-owned power plant (Argentina, 1962); constructing highways (Uruguay, 1972); and shipping fertilizer under a development contract (Pakistan, 1974).[81]

US courts did not distinguish between Soviet-sphere, postcolonial, and Western states in this litigation in any systematic way. As these examples show, the logic of the commercial exception was used to deprive apartheid South Africa, fascist Spain, and friendly Canada of immunity, as well as Cuba and many other low-income countries. Yet, neither was the centrality of Communist and Third World states in this litigation merely incidental. Common law only proceeds through litigation. These states made up the bulk of foreign sovereign immunity litigation in this period because their heightened use of state-owned enterprises and other developmental state activities brought them into conflict with US investors eager to expand their investments in and access to resources of the developing world.

Even transactions related to official development aid programs were classified as merely commercial during this time. Activities denied immunity under the Tate Letter included the Ivory Coast's purchase, with USAID funds, of a vessel intended for training fishermen (1967); the Vietnamese government's negotiation of cement contracts under another USAID program (1969); the construction of an aqueduct in Honduras with United States Foreign Assistance Funds (1969); and highway construction in Uruguay financed by the Inter-American Development Bank and the International Bank for Reconstruction and Development (1972).[82]

The changing treatment of food aid is especially striking. In 1922, the Supreme Court granted immunity (in its own courts) to a US-owned and -operated ship "loaded with foodstuffs for the relief of the civilian population of Europe."[83] The Court characterized the delivery of this food aid as public, even though the food was to be sold rather than donated to recipients. This characterization changed dramatically in the mid-twentieth century.

In the early 1950s, a private steamship owner sued Korea in US courts for damages sustained while unloading rice in a Korean harbor at the height of the Korean War. In defense, Korea argued that it had acquired the rice "not for sale, resale, barter or exchange—but for free distribution to its civilian population and military personnel in Korea."[84] Even under the Tate Letter, Korea argued, this was a "public and governmental" act involving "the safety and preservation of the nation and the well-being of its people."[85] Yet, in 1953, the year the Korean War ended, leaving the country physically and economically devastated, the Department of State rejected Korea's arguments and characterized its importation of food stuff as private and commercial.[86]

That case was ultimately dismissed on other grounds, but the private character of food aid was affirmed in several further cases. Under the 1954 Agricultural Trade Development and Assistance Act (commonly known as PL-480), the United States shipped surplus agricultural products to "friendly" nations for free or at very low rates.[87] This was both a form of strategic humanitarian aid ("food for peace"), and a way to manage agricultural surpluses hurting US farmers.[88] Yet, despite the importance of PL-480 grains in feeding undernourished populations, related activities were routinely classified as private and commercial, leading to the denial of immunity for Brazil, India, Spain, Greece, Pakistan, South Vietnam, and Bangladesh.[89]

One of these cases shaped the debate about the public/private divide well beyond food aid. In the 1964 case *Victory Transport*, Spain argued that it had purchased PL-480 wheat "not as a commercial transaction, but . . . in accordance with the public purpose of such aid."[90] The Second Circuit, however, rejected this view. In the process, it took the unusual step of enumerating what it saw as a *complete* list of "strictly political or public acts":

(1) internal administrative acts, such as expulsion of an alien.
(2) legislative acts, such as nationalization.
(3) acts concerning the armed forces.
(4) acts concerning diplomatic activity.
(5) public loans.[91]

These five categories, the court said, were areas "about which sovereigns have traditionally been quite sensitive," interference with which could thus potentially embarrass the US government.[92] The list, which excluded a huge amount of modern state activity, from the use of state-owned enterprises to infrastructure contracts to development aid, was used to define postcolonial development activities as commercial in numerous cases between 1964 and 1976. It continued to shape views on the public/private distinction even after the FSIA was passed.[93] (Nationalizations and public loans, still classified as public on this list, would be brought within US judicial territory by other methods, as I discuss in chapters 3 and 4, respectively).

The use of the commercial exception to extend US judicial territory over state-owned enterprises, government infrastructure contracts, and development aid during the Tate period did not make these activities illegal. It did, however, make them less advantageous to foreign countries by ensuring that they would be subjected not to those countries' own laws, or even international law, but rather to the business-friendly laws of the United States. More broadly, while courts had previously held that foreign states could determine what was and was not proper government activity, the repudiation of that view in the Tate period effectively denied foreign governments the right to define for themselves what constituted public action—and, conversely, what would be relegated to the *merely* economic. [94] Just as Third World states were struggling to introduce a new international economic order in which they could claim both formal and substantive economic sovereignty, US courts redefined the domain of sovereignty to exclude *all* commercial acts.

A few further comments about the *way* this redefinition of the public/private divide was carried out are also warranted. In a common law system built on case precedent, it is not only the outcome of cases that matter, but also the *reasoning* used to get there. Equating the commercial with the private and expanding the category of the commercial were key mechanisms for expanding US judicial authority over foreign sovereigns. Throughout the Tate period, these mechanisms were themselves made possible by focusing on the "nature" of an act and by a few particular strategies for defining that nature.

In the period of absolute sovereign immunity, courts had considered both the "nature" of the actor and the "purpose" of the act in drawing the public/private distinction.[95] In *Berizzi*, for example, the Court's determination depended not only on the fact that the *Pesaro* was owned and operated by the Italian government, but also on it being "held and used . . . for a public purpose."[96] By the early 1960s, however, the Department of State and US judges were attempting to jettison the purpose test altogether. Pointing out that "all governmental activity is presumably for the purpose of benefitting the state," the Department of State reasoned that the purpose test was incompatible with the development of the commercial exception.[97] Purpose had to be rejected, "else the restrictive theory of sovereign immunity would be meaningless."[98] Nor should the nature of the *actor* be relevant any longer—again, any act carried out by a sovereign or sovereign official could, on that logic, be deemed public. Instead, the nature of *the act* was to be the key criterion.[99] Yet, it turned out that defining this nature was far from clearcut. Two general techniques were used to define nature in a way that would support reclassifying government acts as commercial.

First, courts and the Department of State began to define any activity that *could* be performed by a private business as having a commercial nature. In one especially striking example, given the mass privatization of water in the neoliberal era, the Department rejected arguments by the Honduran government that constructing an aqueduct to improve the country's water supply was a public activity. The Department explained that: "While supply of water is often carried out by governmental agencies, this is not universally the case. In the United States, for example, a great many private companies are engaged in this enterprise. Moreover, the nature of the enterprise is essentially one of offering a product for sale to the public."[100] The sweeping privatization of many other sectors since the 1970s has made more and more activities liable to being reclassified as private in this way.

Second, defining the nature of an act turned out to depend on determining that act's relevant scope. Legal geographers have shown that boundary-drawing is one of law's key functions. Law determines domains of responsibility and establishes the geographical and substantive scope of markets.[101] Whether in criminal, constitutional, or civil cases, law also constantly defines where to draw the boundaries around "an" act or event. In foreign sovereign immunity cases during the Tate period, jurists supporting the commercial exception consistently defined the scope of government actions as narrowly as possible.[102] This included a growing tendency to characterize state economic activities in relation to the contract alone.

In *Victory Transport*, for example, the court determined that the relevant activity was not importing food aid to feed a hungry population. Rather, it was the fact that the shipment had been contracted to a private chartered vessel and that this charter contained an arbitration clause.[103] In another example, Cuba was sued for refusing to pay dollars rather than pesos on certificates of tax exemption. The court itself explained that Cuba's policy stemmed from regulations aiming to prevent capital flight, which "would have wiped out Cuba's dollar reserves."[104] Yet, the relevant issue was identified not as fiscal management or foreign exchange regulation, but as a simple breach of contract. Immunity was denied. The reduction of complex chains of events or relationships to the contract was repeated in other PL-480, USAID, and infrastructure development cases.[105] To be clear, there were contracts and contract breaches involved in all these cases. But in order to define each scenario as *merely* commercial, the broader context in which these contracts were enmeshed was systematically ignored. In one striking example, the fact that a Vietnamese cement contract was disrupted *because of the Tet Offensive* was deemed irrelevant.[106]

Defining the scope of an act as narrowly as possible and defining nature by analogy with things that *can* be done by private actors have remained important strategies for defending and expanding US judicial authority abroad. Although the FSIA codified the commercial exception, it did not end debates about how to define commercial activity. The cases and strategies discussed above continued to shape the application of foreign sovereign immunity under the FSIA into the twenty-first century. Nevertheless, the FSIA was the single largest step forward in the extension of US judicial territory, and it set the framework for all further extensions.

The Tate Letter allowed US courts to apply a commercial exception to foreign sovereign immunity cases for the first time. It inaugurated a twenty-year period in which jurists redefined the public/private distinction by expanding the category of the merely commercial to include state engagement in more and more economic activities, justifying this shift through a focus on the (narrowly defined) nature rather than the purpose of these acts. Yet, by the early 1970s, the transition to the restrictive theory remained incomplete.

The biggest limitation was that the Tate Letter left ultimate authority for determining whether or not immunity should be granted with the Department of State. This changed when Congress passed the FSIA in 1976.[107] By codifying the commercial exception to foreign sovereign immunity, the FSIA removed the Department of State from the equation altogether, ending the executive's ability to formally intervene in particular cases. This cemented a transfer of authority from the executive to the judiciary for dealing with many transnational economic relations with foreign governments. It also returned the political/legal distinction, which had been crucial to overcoming *Berizzi*, to a subordinate status in foreign sovereign immunity law.

This depoliticization of what had previously been potentially fraught geopolitical issues was an explicit goal of the FSIA. The bill was drafted by attorneys at the Department of State and Department of Justice in the late 1960s through the mid-1970s. These lawyers specialized in international investment law, and many would work in both government and private practice.[108] The primary goal of the FSIA was defined by its drafters as being "to facilitate and depoliticize litigation against foreign states and to minimize irritations in foreign relations arising out of such litigation."[109] This appeal to depoliticization was repeated throughout the FSIA hearings.[110]

Industry groups also argued that this would benefit private US investors. As one group of influential lawyers and businessmen who referred to themselves as the Rule of Law Committee explained, the FSIA would "benefit the American business community as a whole" by enabling "greater predictability" in commercial transactions, protecting investors from the vagaries of ad hoc foreign policy exigencies, and "placing private parties on the basis of nearer equality with governmental entities before the law in commercial disputes."[111] Similar arguments were made in the same hearing by the Maritime Law Association, as well as by the DC and American Bar Associations.

Department of State and Department of Justice attorneys, as well as the House Judiciary Committee, argued that depoliticizing these transnational cases would also benefit the US executive branch by freeing the Department of State from foreign pressure, relieving it of the need to expend time and resources on these matters, and deflecting responsibility for fraught or sensitive relations with foreign governments to the judicial branch.[112] But which relations precisely was this statute designed to depoliticize? As with earlier support for the restrictive approach, proponents of the FSIA cited the "extraordinary increase of trading activities conducted by foreign states in the United States since the end of World War II."[113] This concern was directed primarily at Communist countries and Third World anti-colonial governments.

This can be seen in scattered comments throughout the FSIA hearings. Just as Tate had in 1952, proponents stated that, by adopting the restrictive approach, the United States would merely be falling in line with an emerging international common sense. Yet, several speakers noted in passing that Communist countries were not included in this consensus. Third World politics too were indirectly referenced, as private and public sector supporters expressed concerns about increasing state interventions in the economy.[114]

The International Economic Policy Association, whose membership was composed of a "select group of major American firms with extensive overseas experience and interests," explained that the FSIA was especially important because of increasing state economic interventions in shipping and air travel, as well as in "the area of raw materials" like oil and agriculture. These were exactly the sort of areas on which anti-colonial claims about the rights to sovereignty over natural resources, central to the NIEO, were focused. The Association noted examples from Brazil, Iran, Algeria, Indonesia, and Venezuela, and urged the House to support the bill so that "state-owned firms are treated, as they should be, in the same way as are all private firms with whom they deal and compete."[115]

Food aid and USAID programs were also registered in the FSIA hearings. The Committee on Maritime Legislation noted that common law decisions had already helped reduce the immunity defense "in the context of massive Public Law 480 and U.S. military aid to foreign countries," and that the proposed FSIA "would unquestionably be of value to the Admiralty Bar" in connection with these issues.[116] A Judiciary House Report supporting the FSIA explained that the commercial exception would apply to contracts for goods or services "entered into in connection with an AID program."[117]

It was these sorts of activities, from state-owned enterprises to aid programs that the FSIA was designed to "depoliticize."[118] At a moment when Third World countries were struggling to address lingering colonial inequalities and the outsized power of transnational corporations, a primary goal of the FSIA was ensuring that governments who engaged in these practices would lose any advantage their sovereignty might have given them in international markets. By codifying the commercial exception, after two plus decades of juridical work ensuring that these kinds of activities would be counted as commercial, the FSIA brought all such activities under US judicial authority. The FSIA also codified the rule that the commercial character of an act should be defined by reference to its nature rather than its purpose. Unlike the court in *Victory Transport*, the FSIA did not attempt to provide an exhaustive list of either commercial or public acts. Instead, it left the continued redrawing of the public/private distinction to the courts, ensuring that struggles over this boundary as well as the case precedent established in the Tate period would remain central in future litigation.

The FSIA also went *further* than Tate period litigation did in a crucial way. By combining the commercial exception with new spatial rules for determining jurisdiction, it explicitly extended US judicial authority over foreign sovereign property and acts not only within US borders, but also beyond them. Nineteenth-century foreign sovereign immunity cases involved immunity for foreign sovereign property or officials who *entered* official US territory. While an act might occur beyond US borders, suit could only be brought if some property related to that act could be seized (or "attached") within them.[119] During the first half of the twentieth century, the spatial rules for foreign sovereign immunity became fuzzier, but as late as 1951, Lauterpacht, for instance, assumed that changes in foreign sovereign immunity rules would primarily affect the acts of foreign governments *within* the host state's territory. Changes restricting foreign sovereign immunity, he noted, would not contravene international law "so long as they are not intended to have extraterritorial effect."[120]

By 1976, the spatial common sense among US jurists was very different. The FSIA clarified, regularized, and loosened the spatial requirements for establishing jurisdiction over foreign sovereigns. Rather than focusing only on whether sovereign acts or property were located in or outside the United States, the FSIA articulated new spatial rules (or "nexus" requirements) for determining jurisdiction. In particular, foreign states would not be immune in any case:

in which the action is based upon a commercial activity carried on *in the United States* by the foreign state; or upon an act performed in the United States *in connection with a commercial activity of the foreign state elsewhere*; or upon *an act outside the territory of the United States* in connection with a commercial activity of the foreign state elsewhere and that act *causes a direct effect in the United States*.[121]

As we will see in chapter 4, these rules granted US courts potential authority over many transnational acts with looser links to physical US territory than before.[122] In the context of an interconnected and financialized global economy, within which US finance has been dominant, these changes became especially important.

CONFLICT OR CONSENSUS?

1976 marked a watershed moment in the expansion of transnational US judicial territory. It cemented the gradual transition away from the absolute to the restrictive approach to foreign sovereign immunity. This altered the modalities of US empire operating in particular domains, limiting the executive branch's authority over transnational issues involving foreign government economic activities and expanding the power of the judicial branch. Reclassifying all economic activity as having nothing to do with sovereignty at the height of the Cold War and of postcolonial struggles over the future of the global economic order was a primary goal of the commercial exception. The result was to privilege US capital by extending US jurisdiction and probusiness legal rules over many transnational economic relations with foreign governments. This perpetuated uneven postcolonial economic relations precisely by putting Third World states and massively powerful US corporations on an "equal" footing. Doing so through technical legal changes allowed the US to do this while still presenting itself as an anti-imperialist champion of national self-determination. The success of this strategy is reflected in the lack of attention given to the politics of changing foreign sovereign immunity rules since. The FSIA remains the basis on which US courts must make all jurisdictional claims over foreign sovereigns, and it laid the ground for a more gradual, but systematic expansion of US judicial territory in the following decades.

In most accounts, the transition to the restrictive approach to foreign sovereign immunity is portrayed as both modernizing and democratizing—

part of the process in which old-fashioned ideas about the dignity and rights of sovereigns gave way to the primacy of individual rights.[123] It is true that deference to sovereigns in US common law has declined.[124] The importance of valuing individual rights vis-à-vis the state and the potential significance of this for reducing the absolute power of rulers and governments over their own populations should be taken seriously. In practice, however, the reduction of sovereign privilege has been highly selective.

First, the commercial exception to foreign sovereign immunity has increased the *economic* rights of private actors vis-à-vis states. However, despite the tendency to conflate commercial and human rights in conversations *about* foreign sovereign immunity, sovereign immunity with regard to military actions, human rights, environmental issues, and criminal prosecution remains largely intact.[125] Moreover, as the cases discussed in this chapter show, it is rarely the economic rights of *individuals* that are upheld against foreign sovereign governments. Rather it is the rights of private *companies* that are promoted—usually corporations large enough to have significant overseas operations.

Moreover, seeing the adoption of restrictive foreign sovereign immunity rules as part of an emerging consensus, as is often done, obscures the struggles through which these changes were forged and naturalizes the definitions of private and public that emerged in the process. From the Tate Letter to the FSIA, the adoption of the commercial exception and the expansion of the category of commercial that accompanied it were not spurred by growing *agreement* on the proper relationship between states and markets. Rather, these changes were the result of socialist and anti-colonial efforts to resist sharp distinctions between politics and economics—and of US litigation that aimed to protect Western capital by overcoming that resistance. The resulting restriction of foreign sovereign immunity did not make it illegal for foreign states to engage directly in transnational economic practices. It did, however, ensure that, to the extent that they did so, they would lose the privileges that had long been associated with sovereignty and would instead be treated just like private corporations. Moreover, it ensured that their actions would be governed not by their own laws, or even by international law, but by domestic US laws and courts.

To the US proponents of the restrictive theory, collapsing the distinction between public and private in relation to all commercial acts was understood as making international markets fairer and more equitable. Yet, for postcolonial states, state-led development was seen as critical to redressing colonial legacies and resisting the power of major multinationals. The restriction of foreign sovereign immunity obstructed these efforts. It bolstered the position of private companies in transnational economic relations at a moment of *expanding* corporate power, when transnational companies, with the aid of the new field of transnational commercial law, were cementing their foothold across the Third World.

The transformation of foreign sovereign immunity, then, cannot be understood as a mere reflection of modernization or economic change. Rather, it was a tool for defining the economy in a particular way. By rewriting the public/private and political/economic distinctions in US law, it helped prevent one kind of globalization, in which governments might be understood to be privileged economic actors, from gaining ground, and it produced a form of globalization more supportive of private corporations instead.

These changes simultaneously implied a formal redefinition of the rules of territorial sovereignty for all states. In the 1950s–1970s, Third World states attempted to assert a definition of sovereignty based on substantive political *and* economic equality. Instead, changes in foreign sovereign immunity rules replaced traditional notions of absolute sovereignty with one from which commercial activity was expressly excluded, while simultaneously expanding the reach of US courts not only within but beyond US borders. These changes began during the Tate period and were solidified and extended with the passage of the FSIA, which not only cemented the commercial exception to foreign sovereign immunity, but also regularized and expanded the spatial conditions in which it could be deployed.

Even as the restrictive approach to foreign sovereign immunity has been adopted by most countries since the 1970s, moreover, the United States' nexus rules remain more flexible than those of any other country. Although this is recognized in legal scholarship on foreign sovereign immunity, it is, as usual, presented in depoliticized terms. Fox and Webb, for example, note that the United States has consistently embraced looser territorial rules for foreign sovereign immunity claims than any other state. Yet, they explain this as being about "US business interests *requiring* a more extensive reach for their national courts over transactions carried on abroad."[126]

This euphemistic phrasing obscures the importance of US state and corporate strategies and desires in shaping transnational US law. But it also highlights an important relationship between US economic power on the one hand and legal power on the other. US businesses do not "require" extensive US judicial power—they do, however, benefit immensely from it. Conversely, the expansion of US judicial territory has both depended on and further increased the economic power of the United States. The size and scope of the US economy means that all countries engaged in transnational commerce have links with the United States (something recognized at the FSIA hearings).[127] In combination with the flexible nexus requirements of the FSIA and the expansive definition of commercial in US law, the commercial exception has brought large amounts of transnational government economic activity within US judicial reach. This ensures that any state that wishes to maintain economic ties with US banks or businesses will have to subject this activity to US law.

In spite of hopes to the contrary on the part of many globalist legal scholars, moreover, US dominance in foreign sovereign immunity cases has still not been replaced by an international consensus on foreign sovereign immunity rules. It is true that the United States has not been alone in adopting these legal changes. Some Western states were already moving toward the commercial exception to foreign sovereign immunity by the 1950s and 1960s. Since the 1970s, more and more countries, including many formerly colonized states, have also adopted this approach—a testament in part to the defeat of the NIEO and the successful Americanization of other legal systems. Yet, even this has been both gradual and piecemeal. By 1952, when the Tate Letter was written and a year after Lauterpacht claimed as "fact" that a "majority" of states had already adopted the restrictive approach, only around ten countries had actually done so. By 1980, the number was about twenty. By 2010, around 75 out of 118 countries surveyed in a recent study had adopted the restrictive approach—a significant but still hardly overwhelming majority. Not only do Russia and China remain committed to absolute sovereign immunity, but so do over thirty other states, including Armenia, Bolivia, and Mozambique, to name a few.[128]

Perhaps more importantly, despite some efforts to replace national rules on foreign sovereign immunity with an international agreement, this has stalled due to continued substantive differences in how countries approach the issue. The United States has made no move to sign a 2004 UN convention on foreign sovereign immunity.[129] Why not? First, the convention requires stronger territorial links to establish jurisdiction over foreign sovereigns than does the FSIA. Second, it adopts a more limited definition of commercial activity.[130] In short, the convention cedes too much ground to foreign sovereignty for the United States' liking. The struggle over the proper relationship between states and markets, and between political and economic sovereignty, continues. Meanwhile, in the absence of an effective supervening international agreement, US laws and courts, not international rules, continue to govern a large proportion of the world's foreign sovereign immunity cases.

CHAPTER THREE

Revolution and Counterrevolution

On July 6, 1960, shortly after the Cuban Revolution brought Fidel Castro's socialist government to power, Cuba nationalized all American-owned sugar companies on Cuban soil. This was done in response to the US government's reduction of Cuban sugar imports into the United States, which Cuba saw as an act of "aggression, for political purposes."[1] The Cuban government continued producing and trading the nationalized sugar on its own behalf. This included signing new contracts with US-based commodity traders, who were eager to remain involved in the lucrative sugar trade. Under one such contract, Cuba loaded sugar onto the *S.S. Hornfels* in the Cuban port of Jucaro for shipment to Morocco. The ship set sail on August 12, 1960. When Cuba tried to collect payment from its US buyer in New York as contracted, however, the sugar's former American owners claimed the right to the proceeds. Rather than pay either party, the new owners handed over the payment to a court-appointed receiver named Peter Sabbatino while the legal claims were hashed out. Cuba immediately filed suit against Sabbatino and the buyers in the District Court for the Southern District of New York, claiming rightful ownership of the sugar and all proceeds from its sale. The case sparked disputes about nationalizations and US judicial authority that would embroil US courts, the executive branch, and Congress for more than a decade.

In *Banco Nacional de Cuba v. Sabbatino*, Cuba argued that, as a lawful, sovereign act in its own territory, its nationalization of American sugar was beyond the reach of US judicial authority.[2] Nationalizations had long been seen even in US law as public acts of foreign states in their own territory. As such, they had been protected from US judicial reach by the act of state doctrine. Yet, in the *Sabbatino* litigation, the District Court for the Southern District of New York and the Second Circuit Court of Appeals went against existing precedent to rule against Cuba.[3] In 1964, the US Supreme Court overturned these decisions, ruling in Cuba's favor.[4] Yet, while the Court upheld Cuban sovereignty in this case, it nevertheless loosened the act of state doctrine and the rules of territorial sovereignty in the process.

The story did not end there. Congress disliked the Supreme Court's ruling so much that it took the highly unusual step of passing legislation to undo a Supreme Court decision.[5] This, in turn, sparked a heated struggle among all three branches of the US government and between different courts over how best to tame Cuban nationalizations of US property while still protecting what the judiciary understood as the proper separation of powers. The ensuing litigation only eased in 1976, when a reconfigured Supreme Court created a partial commercial exception to the act of state doctrine.

This chapter examines how the authority of US domestic law and courts was remapped in the 1960s and 1970s in response to Cuban nationalizations of US property. Cuban act of state litigation has been extensively documented by legal scholars, and I make no effort to provide an exhaustive summary here. Instead, I focus on a few key decisions that show how efforts to rein in Cuban nationalizations through US judicial authority led to broader changes in the modality of US imperial power operating beyond US borders.

I first situate the act of state doctrine in relation to the history of nationalizations and expropriations in US law,[6] as well as to the broader context of the Cuban Revolution, the Cold War, and anti-colonial politics. I then show how, in spite of ruling in favor of Cuba in this particular case, the Supreme Court's redefinition of the act of state doctrine in *Sabbatino* nevertheless produced an important extension of US judicial territory not only beyond US borders, but directly into the territory of foreign sovereign governments. Next, I use the Cuban litigation struggles to examine the complex interaction of subnational, national, and international law within the exercise of transnational US legal power, and I show how racialized civilizational claims shape these dynamics. I then move on to discuss the development of a partial commercial exception to the act of state doctrine in the mid-1970s. Although less secure than the commercial exception to foreign sovereign immunity, this too contributed to the neoliberal bounding of "the economy" in the context of ongoing debates between the First and

Third Worlds about the proper relationship between states and markets. Finally, I step back to consider how US judicial territory worked in tandem with more explicitly international institutional changes to reign in Third World expropriations from the late 1970s on. In particular, I consider links between US domestic law, rising rates of international arbitration, and the introduction of bilateral investment treaties (BITs). All three developments served to depoliticize nationalizations, while relocating their governance from nationalizing states to trans- and international authorities.

The eventual outcome of all this for the act of state doctrine and US common law on nationalizations was more muddled than the transformation of foreign sovereign immunity. The act of state doctrine remains a common law doctrine—it has never been codified the way foreign sovereign immunity rules have been. Moreover, none of this has brought expropriations entirely within US judicial authority. Even today, most countries, including the United States, recognize the right of sovereign states to expropriate private property—provided "adequate" compensation is paid. Yet, changes to the act of state doctrine did help limit Cuban expropriations in particular cases and contributed, in combination with broader developments, to putting constraints on postcolonial expropriations more generally.

Furthermore, the transformation of the act of state doctrine highlights the coproduction of seemingly esoteric US legal debates and major geopolitical events. All significant changes to the doctrine in this period were driven by the Cuban Revolution and the attempts of litigants, judges, and politicians to respond to it. To the extent that it made nationalized property more vulnerable to US legal governance, the restriction of the act of state doctrine contributed to undermining one of the most important weapons of postcolonial struggles for political and economic sovereignty. In the process, these efforts led to rewriting the rules of territorial sovereignty even more strikingly than did the parallel restriction of foreign sovereign immunity.

THE NATIONALIZATION THREAT

The sugar nationalizations at the heart of *Sabbatino* were just one of the nationalizations carried out by the Castro government after the Cuban Revolution. On January 1, 1959, revolutionary forces had overthrown the dictator Fulgencio Batista and begun a radical transformation of Cuban society. Within two years, Cuba nationalized most foreign-owned property, as well as the property of wealthy Cubans, many of whom fled to the

United States. The 1959 Agrarian Reform Law reduced the size of all large landholdings in Cuba, including those of foreign-owned sugar and cattle-ranching companies. In summer 1960, this was followed by the nationalization of oil refineries and, shortly after, of all US-owned commercial, industrial, agrarian, and banking properties.[7]

The US response to the Cuban Revolution and these nationalizations was multipronged. The US government trained expatriate Cuban counter-revolutionaries, supported multiple invasion and assassination attempts (including the failed Bay of Pigs invasion in 1961), put diplomatic pressure on Cuba at the United Nations and other international organizations, and implemented severe and long-lasting economic sanctions that are still hurting Cuba today. All these dimensions of the US-Cuba conflict are well documented. What has gotten far less attention is the way domestic US law was used in the 1960s and 1970s to undermine Cuban nationalizations.

As with foreign sovereign immunity, most legal scholarship explains the act of state doctrine's restriction in *Sabbatino* as an apolitical response to growing economic interconnection, the increasing role of states in economic activity, and a democratizing shift toward individual over state rights.[8] Patterson adds that the "increasingly tight regulatory, commercial, and economic ties between western powers made adjudication of innocuous disputes seem less like a violation of sovereignty. Western regimes were drawing ever closer in shared democratic values and political interests."[9] Yet, this framing obscures the fact that most act of state cases from the 1960s on arose not between Western regimes, but rather between US investors and socialist or Third World states. Many of these cases involved the latter's expropriations of private US property. It was these *conflicts*, not growing consensus about the economy or democracy, that drove the most important act of state changes.

The Cuban expropriations led to dozens of legal cases concerning property title, restitution, taxation, and other questions in US courts. Some cases involved foreign sovereign immunity. This usually occurred when former owners of nationalized property attempted to seize Cuban assets in the United States in compensation for their losses. Most such efforts failed because, during the Tate Letter period, in which most of these cases occurred, immunity from this sort of seizure or "execution" remained absolute.[10] This only changed in 1976 when the FSIA limited immunity from execution for property "which has been taken in violation of international law or which has been exchanged for property taken in violation of international law"—a provision expressly targeted at expropriating states.[11]

International law, according to some of the FSIA's staunchest supporters, held that compensation for expropriation should be decided by "international law standards."[12]

In other words, shortly after Third World countries used the UN General Assembly to assert the rights of all states to determine compensation for expropriations according to the host state's *own* domestic laws, the FSIA undermined that effort by ensuring that any state who followed the General Assembly's rules would find its property vulnerable to seizure in US courts. As Mark Feldman, former Deputy Legal Adviser to the Department of State and one of the bill's drafters, explained in a recent retrospective account, "Throughout this period, foreign expropriation of American investment was a major foreign policy issue for the United States and a deep concern in Congress." He linked the origins of the FSIA to "intense diplomatic efforts by developing countries in the United Nations to establish a new international economic order including the right to nationalize foreign-owned natural resources without accountability under international law."[13] The desire to reign in such expropriations was an important motivating factor behind the FSIA.

Yet, while some nationalization cases involved foreign sovereign immunity, the act of state doctrine was far more important in this area—and more difficult to change. Foreign sovereign immunity rules determine whether and under what conditions foreign sovereigns or their officials can be sued in US courts, as well as when foreign sovereign property in the United States can be seized. The act of state doctrine, in contrast, determines whether US courts can assess the validity of a foreign sovereign *act* carried out *in that sovereign's home territory*. It deals not with jurisdiction but with justiciability—that is, with whether a question is suited for legal adjudication at all.[14] Act of state cases may involve foreign governments directly, as plaintiffs or defendants, or they may only involve third parties *affected by* a government's act (e.g., by property seizures or currency controls).

The traditional or absolute version of the doctrine held that courts simply could not adjudicate the public acts of foreign sovereigns in their own territories. The most famous articulation of this version comes from the 1897 case *Underhill v. Hernandez* in which the US Supreme Court held that "Every sovereign State is bound to respect the independence of every other sovereign State, and the courts of one country will not sit in judgment on the acts of the government of another done within its own territory."[15] Bringing Cuban nationalizations within US judicial reach required revising this rule.

Underhill is widely understood as a strict expression of Westphalian territorial sovereignty.[16] As discussed in chapter 1, however, it is more accurately seen in terms of the way the United States deployed distinct modalities of power in different contexts. In the late nineteenth and early twentieth centuries, blatant US intervention in the economic and political affairs of countries throughout the Western Hemisphere was ramping up. Yet *Underhill* illustrated the sharp boundaries between the domains of judicial and "political" or executive authority. While the judiciary claimed significant authority for governing populations within both the national and the imperial borders of the United States in cases like *Plessy v. Ferguson* and *Downes v. Bidwell*, in *Underhill* the Court refused to extend that authority beyond official US borders.[17]

The spatial logic of this classic version of the act of state doctrine was much simpler than foreign sovereign immunity had ever been. Because foreign sovereign immunity cases always involved the presence of sovereigns or their property *within* the United States, even absolute foreign sovereign immunity rules always complicated ideas of territorial sovereignty in significant ways. In the famous case of *The Schooner Exchange*, Chief Justice Marshall had grappled with this puzzle.[18] Granting immunity to a foreign sovereign ship or official, Marshall pointed out, meant that a foreign government was allowed to extend its own sovereignty into US space. Yet, this seemed to violate *American* territorial sovereignty. Marshall dealt with this by defining sovereign immunity not as an inherent trait of the foreign power, but rather as a concession granted by the host sovereign. Although "the jurisdiction of the nation within its own territory is necessarily exclusive and absolute," he argued, the host sovereign waives his *own* "exclusive territorial jurisdiction" for certain purposes.[19] In this way, US jurists reconciled the absolute doctrine of foreign sovereign immunity with the territorial sovereignty of both host and foreign nation.[20]

The act of state doctrine only ever applied to acts of a foreign government in that government's *own* territory. This made the territorial logic of the doctrine more straightforward. It also made restricting the act of state doctrine in the twentieth century even more difficult than restricting foreign sovereign immunity rules—and an even bigger challenge to traditional notions of territorial sovereignty. While the restriction of foreign sovereign immunity had begun in earnest by the late 1940s, no serious attempt to change the act of state doctrine took shape until the 1960s. It was the Cuban Revolution that sparked this effort.

The Cuban nationalizations posed a triple threat to the United States. First, they were a direct and serious blow to US economic interests in Cuba. Although nominally independent since the end of the Spanish-American War (or the Cuban War of Independence, as it is known in Cuba), Cuba had long been a de facto colony of the United States.[21] From 1903 to 1934, the Platt Amendment officially limited Cuba's control over its own finances and foreign policy and guaranteed the United States the right to intervene militarily in Cuba's affairs in the name of protecting Cuban "independence" or to protect private property rights.[22] Even once the Amendment was officially annulled, US political and economic influence over Cuba continued. Entanglement in the Cuban economy left US investors especially vulnerable to Cuban nationalizations after the Revolution. One 1975 study estimated that Cuba seized $1.6 billion worth of US corporate property and around $200 million from wealthy US individuals—more than the total value of US property seized by all other Communist countries combined up to that point.[23]

Second, the Cuban nationalizations also echoed earlier Soviet bloc nationalizations and posed a material and ideological threat to the United States in the context of the Cold War. From Cuba's perspective, nationalizations were necessary for the transformation from a capitalist to a socialist society. From the US perspective, they not only threatened individual investors, but potentially the whole international system of property titles, raising thorny questions about how to determine ownership of nationalized goods and resources traded internationally. The US was also gravely concerned about a Communist Revolution in its own backyard and worried that leftist ideas might spread to other Latin American societies.

Third, the United States was threatened by the link between Cuban nationalizations and broader Third World struggles for economic sovereignty. After decolonization, massive quantities of postcolonial resources remained in the hands of Western multinational companies, who had often acquired them during the colonial period. Expropriating such property was seen by many in the Third World as critical to casting off Western dominance, addressing the economic legacies of colonialism, and gaining control over national resources.

As early as 1960, in his first speech to the UN General Assembly, Castro made these connections explicit, denouncing American control of Cuban land, resources, banking, and utilities before the Revolution and declaring that the "problems we have described in conne[ction] with Cuba apply equally well to the whole of Latin America" and that the "problems of Latin America resemble those of the rest of the world, of Africa and of Asia." Detailing US retaliation for Cuban nationalizations and ridiculing, to applause from many of those assembled, the Department of State's demands for "prompt, effective, and fair compensation" as meaning "pay immediately, in dollars, the amount we ask for our land," Castro asserted "the right of the under-developed countries to nationalize their natural resources and the investments of the monopolies in their respective countries without compensation." He added, to further applause, that "if industrialized countries wish to do the same thing, we shall not oppose them."[24]

Like other Third World leaders and thinkers of the time, Castro associated this right with the critical link between political and economic sovereignty: "For there is one truth which we should all recognize as being of primary importance, namely, that there can be no political independence unless there is economic independence; that political independence without economic independence is an illusion. . . . Freedom does not consist in the possession of a flag, and a coat of arms and representation in the United Nations."[25] This link between substantive economic sovereignty and the right to nationalize property, with compensation to be determined according to the rules of the host state, would be a central pillar in what would soon become more concerted Third World efforts to establish a New International Economic Order (NIEO).[26]

In the first half of the twentieth century, most nationalizations had been confined to the Communist bloc.[27] In the 1960s and 1970s, soon after Cuba's sweeping nationalizations of foreign property, they became widespread across the Third World, in both socialist and more heterodox countries. One early study estimated that, not counting Cuba (whose nationalizations were so massive that they are excluded from quantitative studies of the topic), there were 1,705 foreign-owned firms seized in 563 acts of expropriation across 79 "Less Developed Countries" from 1960 to 1979.[28]

The United States and other Western states were staunchly opposed to these nationalizations. Yet, expropriations had been used intermittently by many countries, including in the West, for a long time, and a general right of states to expropriate property was recognized by the United States and others. Indeed, this right is still recognized today. Preventing Third World states from seizing foreign-owned property thus required changing the rules *surrounding* expropriations.

Much of this debate involved the question of compensation for expropriated property. Western, Communist, and Third World states disagreed vehemently about how much compensation, if any, was required in exchange for expropriations. Governments and jurists argued, variously, for full, partial, or no compensation.[29] The 1962 UN General Assembly Resolution on Permanent Sovereignty over Natural Resources asserted the rights of all states to their own natural resources and to nationalize those resources with "appropriate compensation" as determined by the host state.[30] The 1974 UN Charter of Economic Rights and Duties of States amended and strengthened this earlier resolution.[31] Among other things, it specified that compensation should be determined by the host state's own laws and that any conflicts should be settled in that state's own courts and tribunals. The United States and other Western countries did not agree.

The US executive branch's position on expropriations had been clarified in the 1930s by Secretary of State Cordell Hull. Appointed by Franklin Delano Roosevelt, Hull was an advocate for trade liberalization and low tariffs, as well as a fierce opponent of state expropriations. When Mexican President Lázaro Cárdenas nationalized Mexican oil in 1938, seizing property from the British and American companies that had controlled nearly all Mexican oil production up to that point, Hull was furious. In a series of letters between Hull and the Mexican Minister of Foreign Affairs Eduardo Hay, Hull criticized the Mexican government's most recent expropriation, as well as its earlier seizures of agrarian properties from American citizens in the 1910s and 1920s—seizures for which the two governments were still attempting to negotiate a settlement. Acknowledging the right of any country to expropriate private property within its own borders, Hull nevertheless claimed that under "international law" such expropriations must be accompanied by "adequate, effective and prompt compensation"—otherwise, he asserted, they were mere "confiscations."[32]

Hay rejected Hull's putative international law argument. He blamed the exaggerated demands of former American landowners for interfering with Mexican attempts to settle these claims, and he pointed out that Mexico's agrarian redistribution programs were at the heart of its political, social, and economic stability after the Mexican Revolution of the 1910s. "On the one hand," Hay wrote, "there are weighed the claims of justice and the improvement of a whole people, and on the other hand, the purely pecuniary interests of some individuals."[33] In a bombastic response, Hull excoriated Mexico's position on expropriations as contrary to democracy and the "universally recognized law of nations." He argued that being financially or economically unable to pay immediate compensation was no excuse. Such a position, he suggested, would "imperil the very foundations of modern civilization. Human progress would be fatally set back."[34]

The Hull Doctrine, as it has come to be known, is now defined as the idea that so-called prompt, adequate, and effective compensation is required for all government seizures of foreign owned property. It is now considered a primary basis for both US and international law on expropriations. Yet, when Hull pronounced the doctrine, there was no settled international law on the matter. Furthermore, there was no suggestion that US *courts* would step in to enforce such rules. Rather, the assumption was that the *executive* was responsible for dealing with foreign nationalizations when needed.

In practice, in the first half of the twentieth century, this meant that settling compensation claims took the form of negotiating lump sum settlements at far less than the full value of expropriated goods. This was true in US negotiations with Mexico, as well as in agreements signed with the Soviet Union, Hungary, Czechoslovakia, and post–World War II Germany. The Department of State not only handled these settlements outside the court system, but also criticized attempts to pursue compensation through ad hoc litigation for interfering with diplomatic efforts.[35] Only in the 1960s did opinions on the modality of US governance best suited for handling nationalization-related claims begin to change. In response to the mass nationalizations of the revolutionary Cuban government, US courts, Congress, and the executive branch began pushing for the expansion of US judicial authority in what had been understood as a foreign policy arena.

The bulk of the litigation involving Cuban nationalizations took place in federal courts in New York and Miami. Although judges in both cities were hostile to Cuba, one Cuban legal scholar later compared the general position of the two judiciaries: "In Miami, the judicial attitude was very virulent and admonitory. In New York, it was more sober."[36] Yet, despite the anti-Cuba stance of most Americans, including jurists, expanding US judicial authority over nationalizations was more difficult than revising foreign sovereign immunity rules in relation to state-owned enterprises, development aid, and government contracts. The biggest obstacle was that state expropriations had long been considered quintessentially public and political. In 1964, the Second Circuit had even included nationalizations in its brief list of "strictly political or public acts."[37] Moreover, these acts were understood to have occurred not in US territory, but within the nationalizing state.

Together, the public and foreign character of expropriations meant they were barred from US judicial consideration by the act of state doctrine. Indeed, expropriations were the most common source of act of state litigation in the first half of the twentieth century—and US courts had repeatedly upheld the act of state doctrine to bar judicial consideration in such cases. It is true that nationalizations had sparked litigation in US courts since the Russian Revolution. Yet, by and large, courts only proceeded when, for some reason, neither the act of state doctrine nor foreign sovereign immunity applied.[38] Through the 1950s, they refused, with one exception, to waive the act of state doctrine to rule against foreign governments where the validity of an expropriation in foreign territory was in question.[39] The Cuban Revolution changed this, leading to transformations in the act of state doctrine and the legal construction of territorial sovereignty, as well as to an important shift in the modality of US power used to respond to expropriations.

SABBATINO: FROM ABSOLUTE TERRITORIALITY TO THE SEPARATION OF POWERS APPROACH

The classic act of state doctrine articulated in *Underhill* depended on a sharp foreign/domestic distinction. Yet, as with early foreign sovereign immunity cases, this was always complicated by the public/private distinction. Most act of state doctrine cases involved seizures of tangible property whose location was beyond dispute. Therefore, early act of state analyses spent little time debating the foreign/domestic distinction. Instead, debate centered on whether the act in question was or was not public or "governmental."[40] While the word *political* appears in these early cases, it was usually as a simple synonym for *public* in reference to the character of the foreign state's act. The distinction between political and legal modalities of US governance was mostly implicit in the fact that only acts deemed private were suited for adjudication by US courts. If a public act was identified, plaintiffs were advised to seek recourse from the US executive.

Efforts to restrict the act of state doctrine after the Cuban Revolution began from these foundations. Most Cuban nationalizations targeted tangible things like factories, cigars, or sugar, so there was little question about where they were located. Instead, the first and most important reconfiguration of the act of state doctrine was achieved (in a move that paralleled earlier changes in foreign sovereign immunity) through shifting the primary focus of litigation from the public/private to the political/legal distinction.

This change was articulated in the 1964 *Sabbatino* decision with which this chapter opened. In that case, the Supreme Court, under Chief Justice Earl Warren, upheld the act of state doctrine in Cuba's favor but weakened it in the process. The Warren Court (1953–1969) is widely regarded as the most liberal in the Supreme Court's history. It emerged after the Legal Realist turn in US law and on the heels of the New Deal and the Progressive movement that challenged the laissez-faire liberalism of the nineteenth century and advocated an expanded role for government in regulating society and markets. Both fans and critics have characterized the Warren Court as "activist." It is perhaps best known for *Brown v. Board of Education*, which ended de jure segregation in US schools when Congress would not.[41]

This did not make the Court sympathetic to Cuba or other socialist states. Yet, the Court was less rabidly anti-Communist than the Burger Court that would replace it. It was more willing to uphold case precedent and longstanding legal principles, even in Cuba's favor, while also attempting to modernize the act of state doctrine. Indeed, Justice Harlan, who drafted the *Sabbatino* decision, was one of the Court's most conservative judges. According to Cuba's lawyer Victor Rabinowitz, he was a "capable spokesman for the commercial and banking interests of the country, and the fact that he upheld the act of state doctrine gave the result great weight. . . . Harlan's vote arose out of his respect for the integrity of the Court and for the doctrine of the separation of powers."[42]

While the Court characterized Cuba's nationalization as a public act in its own territory, it also criticized the strict territoriality of "historic notions of sovereign authority" in early act of state cases as obsolete.[43] It also shifted away from what had been a primary focus on the public versus private character of the foreign act. Instead, the Court now focused on the political/legal divide, while simultaneously redefining the term *political* to refer not to the character of the foreign government's act, but rather to its potential significance for *US foreign policy*. "The less important the implications of an issue are for our foreign relations, the weaker the justification" for applying the act of state doctrine to bar judicial inquiry—it was the potential threat of US adjudication to US foreign policy, not respect for foreign sovereignty, that gave the act of state doctrine continued validity.[44]

On these grounds, the Court elaborated what has since become known as the separation of powers approach to the act of state doctrine, holding that the doctrine "arises out of the basic relationships between branches of government in a system of separation of powers" and that its "continuing vitality depends on its capacity to reflect the proper distribution of functions between the judicial and political branches of the Government on matters bearing upon foreign affairs."[45] Where the traditional act of state doctrine had been grounded in the view that only the executive has the right to (attempt to) exercise power over a foreign government's acts in its own territory, *Sabbatino* instead presented authority over such acts as *potentially* divided between the judiciary and the executive.

It was from within this revised, more flexible framework that the Supreme Court upheld the act of state doctrine in Cuba's favor. While it declared strict norms of territorial sovereignty to be obsolete, the Court argued that "the *concept* of territorial sovereignty is so deep seated, any state may resent the refusal of the courts of another sovereign to accord validity to acts within its territorial borders."[46] In this case, because Cuba considered its expropriations to be important sovereign acts, challenging those expropriations could offend Cuba enough to raise problems for the US executive. Therefore, the act of state doctrine barred adjudication. In short, the Court downgraded territorial sovereignty from a fact of international relations to an old-fashioned, though admittedly powerful, "concept" whose violation could offend foreign states—and thus create political problems for the US executive.

The executive branch itself agreed with the *Sabbatino* Court and even filed an amicus brief on Cuba's behalf.[47] Signed by Solicitor General Archibald Cox and other members of the Department of Justice as well as by the Department of State's Assistant Legal Adviser for Economic Affairs, the brief expressed no sympathy for Castro's government. Nevertheless, the executive reminded the Court that the act of state doctrine was firmly established in US law and expressed concern about the possible effects changing this doctrine could have "upon the conduct of foreign relations."[48] In line with the executive's handling of previous nationalizations, the brief explained that the executive was already handling matters through the Cuban Assets Control Regulations program as well as by freezing Cuban assets in the United States; it "has acted and will continue to act to protect the interests of all Americans who have been affected by those Cuban nationalizations."[49] Moreover, allowing individual victims to pursue claims in court could interfere with these efforts; "the ability of the Executive to take such effective general action depends to a significant extent upon whether the act of state doctrine will be enforced."[50] Although the Supreme Court did not rest its opinion on this brief, it lent weight to the idea that the Court and the executive were in agreement about the proper distribution of authority between the two branches with respect to nationalizations.

Sabbatino is still considered the most recent articulation of the modern act of state doctrine.[51] Since *Sabbatino*, act of state cases have depended not only on the foreign/domestic and public/private distinctions, but also on how politically sensitive a case might be from the perspective of the US government. Where deemed safe for intervention, US courts can now potentially claim authority even over government acts in a state's own territory. Yet, *Sabbatino* was not the endpoint of the doctrinal changes to the act of state doctrine in the modern era, but rather the beginning. Further critical changes were sparked by dissatisfaction with the limits of the *Sabbatino* decision itself.

THE HICKENLOOPER AMENDMENT: CONTESTING *SABBATINO*

The *Sabbatino* decision should have ended this and similar nationalization cases in Cuba's favor. Instead, while the case was on remand to the lower courts for calculation of the exact amount owed to Cuba, Congress took the apparently unprecedented step of overturning a Supreme Court decision through legislation.[52] The history of this legislation is worth analyzing not only for its role in *Sabbatino*, but also because the surrounding debates demonstrate the intensity of struggles among all three branches of the US government over the proper boundaries of judicial territory and different modalities of US imperial power.

What is now known as the Hickenlooper Amendment was passed as a rider to Congress's 1964 amendment to the Foreign Assistance Act. It directly targeted the *Sabbatino* decision and sought to rewrite the act of state doctrine by statute:

> Notwithstanding any other provision of law, no court in the United States shall decline on the ground of the federal act of state doctrine to make a determination on the merits giving effect to the principles of international law in a case in which claim of title or other right to

property is asserted by any party including a foreign state (or a party claiming through such state) based upon (or traced through) a confiscation or other taking after January 1, 1959, by an act of that state in violation of the principles of international law, including the principles of compensation and the other standards set out in this subsection.[53]

January 1, 1959, as the bill's cosponsor Senator Hickenlooper himself noted, was "the date of the coming to power of the Castro regime in Cuba and the beginning of the greatest series of illegal takings of American property in recent history."[54] In addition to targeting Cuban expropriations, Congress sought to use the Amendment more broadly to "discourage illegal confiscations by foreign governments in violation of international law and thus to strengthen the flow of investment in commerce and protect American investments abroad."[55]

There was no attempt to hide the fact that the bill was intended to reverse a Supreme Court decision. The text accompanying the Amendment explained that the effect of the bill would be to achieve a reversal of the presumptions in *Sabbatino*. Under that decision, courts were required to avoid adjudication of foreign government acts where *the court* determined that such adjudication might interfere with US foreign relations. Under the Hickenlooper Amendment, "the Court would presume that it may proceed with an adjudication on the merits unless the President states officially that such an adjudication in the particular case would embarrass the conduct of foreign policy."[56]

Although the amendment nodded to executive authority in this way, it also claimed new ground for Congress in shaping US judicial territory. The *Sabbatino* Court had determined that expropriations were sensitive enough to be treated as political rather than merely legal issues and should thus be left to the executive branch. In a contortion of the usual logic of the political/legal divide, Congress now asserted that expropriations were *so* politically important that Congress had a right to assign them to the judiciary. As Senator Hickenlooper put it, it was "perfectly proper that the Congress of the United States should have the last word on this important policy question."[57]

The executive branch, which had already sided with Cuba in the *Sabbatino* case, disapproved of the Hickenlooper Amendment.[58] President Johnson did sign the bill into law, but the Departments of State and Justice suggested that, even if the Hickenlooper Amendment was now law, it should not apply retroactively to the already decided *Sabbatino* case.[59] In

1965, however, the District Court to which *Sabbatino* had been remanded ignored the executive on this point. Judge Bryan used the amendment to override the Supreme Court's decision.[60] The Second Circuit affirmed, and this time the Supreme Court denied Cuba's appeal. [61] Cuba lost the case after all. At the direct intervention of Congress, and against the wishes of both the Supreme Court and the executive branch, US judicial territory was expanded to invalidate a foreign government's expropriation of property within its own borders. Cuban legal scholar Olga Miranda Bravo, writing in a Cuban law journal in 1972, asserted that the Hickenlooper Amendment "revoked the principle of the act of state doctrine and, with the stroke of a pen, cast down the ephemeral triumph of justice [in *Sabbatino*]."[62]

This struggle over the treatment of Cuban expropriations in US law shows how fraught the contours of US judicial authority had become by the 1960s. Judicial territory, which the courts had been extending in foreign sovereign immunity cases since shortly after World War II, had become an important tool of US foreign policy vis-à-vis socialist and anti-colonial states. Its appeal rested not only in expanding US power over anti-colonial states per se, but in doing this through a legal modality that both regularized and depoliticized such expansion. The level of antipathy to Cuba within the United States and especially Congress in the early 1960s drove further shifts in transnational US law, even as these shifts raised tensions over the proper distribution of power within the US government.

SUBNATIONAL, NATIONAL, AND INTERNATIONAL LAW

The interplay between *Sabbatino* and the Hickenlooper Amendment also provides a window into the coproduction of subnational, national, and international law, and highlights the increasing role of Congress and the judiciary, rather than the executive, in not only influencing but actively determining the latter. The Hickenlooper Amendment did not merely assert that Congress could overturn a Supreme Court decision. It attempted to legitimize this move by making claims about what constituted "principles of compensation" under so-called international law. In 1961, Congress had defined this as "speedy compensation for such property in convertible foreign exchange, equivalent to the full value" of the property taken.[63] In making these pronouncements, Congress claimed to know what international law on the issue of compensation for expropriations was—a claim that ignored the opinions of Communist and postcolonial countries.

This move echoed arguments by the lower *Sabbatino* courts that had ruled against Cuba in 1961 and 1962 before being overturned by the Supreme Court.[64] In the first leg of the *Sabbatino* litigation, the District Court for the Southern District of New York's Judge Dimock conceded that traditional act of state rules did require deference to Cuba's nationalization of American sugar. Yet, he contended, surely "there is an end to the right of national sovereignty when the sovereign's acts impinge on international law."[65] He could not claim that nationalizations per se violated international law, as they had long been recognized as valid sovereign acts. Rather, Dimock routed his argument through the public/private divide. In contrast to other expropriations, he argued, Cuba's was "not reasonably related to a public purpose."[66] Rather, it was undertaken in "retaliation" for the US government's decision to reduce imports of Cuban sugar, and it was "discriminatory" because it "classifie[d] United States nationals separately from all other nationals."[67] Expropriations driven by such motivations, he concluded, were not properly public and were, thus, in violation of international law.

But what exactly counted as international? Dimock did not refer to any treaties or agreements. Rather, he made claims about "customary" or "general principles of" international law. This sort of customary law is only vaguely defined, and the sources considered in determining such law were and remain nearly all Western.[68] Dimock's decision referenced only American, European, and Japanese sources, including several cases from European courts regarding nationalizations in their own former colonies. He ignored the opinions of postcolonial states altogether.

The Second Circuit Court of Appeals made some effort to seem less parochial. Judge Waterman even noted that "many countries have acted upon the principle that, in order to carry out desired economic and social reforms of vast magnitude, they must have the right to seize private property without providing compensation for the taking."[69] Nevertheless, without further evidence, he concluded that "confiscation without compensation when the expropriation is an act of reprisal does not have significant support among disinterested international law commentators from any country."[70]

In these opinions, as in the Hickenlooper Amendment, universalizing claims about a supposed international consensus on nationalizations and compensation blatantly ignored the dramatic political struggles on just this question then unfolding between Third World states and former colonizers. The thinly veiled presentation of Western opinions as universal in international settings is a well-documented tactic of post–World War II imperial relations.[71] Here, we see how these claims about international law are also used to reshape *domestic* US law and extend US judicial territory.

The strategic invocation of international law in the lower *Sabbatino* decisions and the Hickenlooper Amendment also illustrates an important shift in the *agent* of international law. Through the early twentieth century, international law was seen as a political matter for the executive branch to handle—not as the responsibility of domestic courts at all. Attempting to skirt decades of precedent, Judge Dimock claimed to be the first judge to consider whether the act of state doctrine applied even when international law was violated. This was not true. Previous judges had considered precisely this question. They had found that while international law violations might give plaintiffs grounds for seeking assistance from the *executive* branch, this had nothing to do with the act of state doctrine.[72] What was new about Dimock's decision was his attempt to give the *judiciary* authority for dealing with international law.

This involved more than the mere application of international law to a domestic legal case—it involved a thinly disguised effort by a domestic court to *create* that law. The District Court for the Southern District of New York and the Second Circuit Court of Appeals attempted to use the claim that Cuba had violated international law to shift authority for responding to Cuba's nationalizations not from the United States to *international* organizations or tribunals, but from the political domain of US foreign policy to the US judicial domain. In other words, they invoked international law as cover for a US *domestic* court's challenge to a foreign state's territorial sovereignty. The Second Circuit admitted as much: "until the day of capable international adjudication among countries, the municipal [domestic] courts must be the custodians of the concepts of international law, and they must expound, apply and develop that law whenever they are called upon to do so."[73] After determining that something called international law superseded national sovereignty, the lower courts asserted the right of *subnational* (Western) courts to determine the content of that law.

This is made strikingly clear in the way that the Supreme Court in *Sabbatino* refuted these assertions. Reversing Dimock's and Waterman's decisions, Justice Harlan, writing for an eight-person majority, rejected the idea that international law simply superseded national sovereignty.[74] While not denying that a possible international law exception to the act of state doctrine could exist, he suggested that such an exception would only apply where there was in fact strong consensus on a topic.[75] In this case, however, no such consensus existed.

Unlike the lower courts, Harlan acknowledged differences of opinion between Western and non-Western countries and even cited Cuba's argument that it was serving "as an example for other countries to follow 'in their struggle to free themselves from the brutal claws of Imperialism.'"[76] More broadly, Harlan explained that Communist countries "commonly recognize no obligation on the part of the taking country" and that "representatives of the newly independent and underdeveloped countries have . . . argued that the traditionally articulated standards governing expropriation of property reflect 'imperialist' interests and are inappropriate to the circumstances of emergent states."[77] Indeed, this case unfolded just as these countries were attempting to change the rules on compensation for nationalizations through the UN General Assembly.[78]

Harlan's frank discussion of diverse views on nationalizations was not based on respect for Third World economic practices. Rather, in keeping with his new articulation of the separation of powers approach to the act of state doctrine, Harlan's primary concern was that judicial decisions not interfere with US foreign policy. The less of a consensus on an international issue existed, he reasoned, the more sensitive that topic would be for the countries involved and the more likely adjudication would therefore be to complicate US foreign relations. On nationalizations, Harlan wrote: "It is difficult to imagine the courts of this country embarking on adjudication in an area which touches more sensitively the practical and ideological goals of the various members of the community of nations."[79] Without denying that domestic courts *could* play a role in shaping international law, he therefore refrained from doing so in *Sabbatino*. The executive branch similarly rejected the international law violation argument in its own brief, pointing out that it had already been rejected by the Supreme Court in two earlier act of state cases.[80]

The Hickenlooper Amendment, however, directly contravened the Supreme Court and the executive on these points. It picked up the arguments of the lower *Sabbatino* courts, with Congress, rather than the courts, now in the position of unilaterally defining what constituted international law. Like Judges Dimock and Waterman, Congress claimed that there were general principles of international law regarding expropriations and compensation, blatantly ignoring the heated arguments about this issue then unfolding at the United Nations. It joined the lower courts in the push to shift responsibility for making international law from the executive branch to the judiciary.

The changing role of domestic courts in producing and applying international law, highlighted so clearly in the *Sabbatino* debates, has marked

US domestic law since the 1960s. Well beyond the act of state doctrine, it is now common sense among legal specialists that domestic courts are producers of international law. The implications for the post–World War II "international" legal order are profound. Just as more states gained access to formal sovereignty, international law was recast as a matter not just for negotiation between at least supposedly equal sovereign governments, but for direct production by national and even subnational jurists and litigants—at least those from a few powerful countries. Conversely, the decisions of powerful domestic courts are frequently invoked by international tribunals as evidence of the "customary" rules of international law.

DEVELOPING A (PARTIAL) COMMERCIAL EXCEPTION
TO THE ACT OF STATE DOCTRINE

The separation of powers approach outlined in *Sabbatino* is still considered the most recent definitive statement of the act of state doctrine. Yet neither *Sabbatino*, which was decided in Cuba's favor, nor the Hickenlooper Amendment, which overturned that decision, put an end to act of state debates with respect to Cuba in the 1960s and 1970s. While the Hickenlooper Amendment illuminates broader shifts in the relationship between domestic and international law, its effect on the Cuban nationalizations per se was limited. Although it was used to defeat Cuba in *Sabbatino*, many US judges were uncomfortable with what they saw as Congressional interference in legal matters. In response, later courts construed the amendment as narrowly as possible, often using small factual distinctions to hold that it did not apply.[81]

At the same time, personnel changes in the executive branch and the Supreme Court left both more determined than ever to rein in Cuban nationalizations. The Warren Court was superseded by the Burger Court in 1969. Under Chief Justice Warren Burger, who led the Court until 1986, and in the context of a broader neoliberal turn in American politics and legal circles, justices like Byron White, who had been the only justice to dissent from the *Sabbatino* decision, and new appointees like Justice Rehnquist found increasing support for their more conservative views.[82] Nevertheless, the Court could not simply ignore *Sabbatino* or the act of state doctrine.

All this left investors, courts, and the executive struggling to find a more satisfactory way to use US judicial authority to invalidate Cuban expropriations. Since nationalizations had long been defined in US law as not only foreign, but also quintessentially public, bringing such acts securely within US judicial territory depended on undoing this characterization. *Sabbatino* had not only not done this, but had even reaffirmed the political character of nationalizations, if only from the perspective of sensitivity for the United States. The Hickenlooper Amendment had tried to sidestep this question altogether by declaring that international law simply superseded the act of state doctrine. In the early 1970s, the executive branch, now under Nixon, similarly attempted to overcome the act of state doctrine by fiat.

In *First National City Bank v. Banco Nacional de Cuba*, the next Cuban nationalization case to go to the Supreme Court, the Department of State submitted a letter to the courts arguing that the issues involved in this "class of cases" were so *unimportant* to US policy that the act of state doctrine should not apply.[83] However, judges again chafed against what they saw as yet another violation of the separation of powers. The issue eventually split the Supreme Court four ways. In a plurality opinion, written by Justice Rehnquist, who had been appointed to the court that year, the Court held that the executive's letter did supersede the act of state doctrine and ruled against Cuba.[84] Two other judges concurred on different grounds, but strongly criticized executive intervention in the case, with one declaring that allowing the executive to determine the outcome in this way made the judiciary an "errand boy" for the executive branch.[85] Four judges (two of whom had been on the *Sabbatino* Court) dissented, arguing that relinquishing the power to define "the contours of a political question such as the act of state doctrine" to the executive "politicizes the judiciary" and "countenances an exchange of roles between the judiciary and the Executive, contrary to the firm insistence in *Sabbatino* on the separation of powers."[86]

It was not until the mid-1970s that the Supreme Court found a more satisfactory way to reconfigure the public/private and political/legal distinctions with respect to nationalizations. It did so not by denying that nationalizations were public acts, but rather by defining them as narrowly as possible and then declaring what could be called nationalization-*adjacent* activities to be private and commercial. This strategy in turn depended on both the redefinition of the political/legal distinction in *Sabbatino* and on claims about international law.

Alfred Dunhill of London, Inc. v. Cuba was a complicated case.[87] In 1960, Cuba had nationalized the businesses and assets of five Cuban-owned cigar manufacturers and appointed government "interventors" to take over and continue operating the businesses. As part of this continued operation, the interventors continued selling cigars to the companies' US and English importers. Those importers paid Cuba several times after the nationalization. Some of those payments were for cigars that had been shipped but not yet paid for when the nationalization occurred. The former owners of the cigars, however, having fled Cuba for the United States, sued the importers, claiming that the payments for at least the prenationalization shipments should have been made to them, not to Cuba.

In 1972, the District Court for the Southern District of New York held that Cuba was entitled to all payments for shipments made *after* the nationalization, but that it must return money mistakenly paid to it for the prenationalization shipments.[88] Cuba refused to do so, arguing that its nationalization had included not only the physical assets of the businesses, but their accounts as well. Even if it had not, Cuba argued, its later repudiation of these debts to the importers was itself an act of state. The District Court rejected this view, holding that the US importers were entitled to subtract what Cuba owed them for the prenationalization shipments from what they owed Cuba for postnationalization shipments. One of those importers, Alfred Dunhill of London, Inc., was owed more than it owed to Cuba. The court thus ordered Cuba to pay Dunhill the difference. The Second Circuit disagreed with this holding and reversed in favor of Cuba.[89] Dunhill appealed to the Supreme Court. The case again split the Court several ways.

In a majority opinion, penned by Justice White and joined by four others, the Court first defined the initial nationalization very narrowly, rejecting Cuba's argument that this had included the cigar manufacturers' accounts in addition to its physical goods.[90] The Court then argued that Cuba's repudiation of its debts to the importers was not an act of state, because the interventors appointed by the Cuban government to oversee the expropriated cigar operations lacked the authority to perform such an act. There was no evidence that the interventors had "governmental, as opposed to commercial, authority"—they were thus unable to perform a true act of state.[91] In other words, the Court questioned how public the act was by questioning the public versus private status of the *actor*. Under this reasoning, Cuba lost the case 5 to 4.

Justice White, who had written the sole dissent in the *Sabbatino* Supreme Court decision twelve years earlier, also took the opportunity to argue that there should be a commercial exception to the act of state doctrine. As in early foreign sovereign immunity cases, the opposite of public in classic act of state cases was not commercial, but rather personal or not social.[92] Yet, although the commercial exception strategy had been at the center of the restriction of foreign sovereign immunity since the early 1950s, during the first decade after the Cuban Revolution, no significant attempt was made to apply a similar exception to the act of state doctrine.[93] In *Dunhill*, White attempted to change this.

He argued that, even if the Cuban interventors did have the authority to carry out an act of state, "the concept of an act of state should not be extended to include the repudiation of a purely commercial obligation owed by a foreign sovereign."[94] In this case,

> Cuba's debt to Dunhill arose out of the conduct by Cuba's agents of a commercial business for profit . . . The debt would never have arisen if Cuba's agents *had not gone into the cigar business and sold to Dunhill*. This case is therefore no different from any case in which a buyer overpays for goods sold by a commercial business operated by a foreign government—a commonplace event in international commerce.[95]

White's argument depended on two moves. First, he drew a sharp distinction between the nationalization itself and activities related to it—in this case, running a business with the nationalized property. In other words, as in foreign sovereign immunity cases in which shipping or construction contracts were isolated from the broader context of food aid or development programs, here the category of commercial activity was expanded by *narrowing* the contours of "the act" of the sovereign as much as possible. The power to determine the legal boundaries of such acts—in other words, to define what does and does not count as relevant—is, once again, a significant part of judicial power.

Second, White then anchored his argument in the *Sabbatino* separation of powers logic, in which the character of an act had been made secondary to its political significance for the United States. In his dissenting opinion in *Sabbatino*, White had asserted that Cuba's nationalizations of US sugar amounted to "commercial property transactions which are contrary to the minimum standard of civilized conduct."[96] This time, White replaced this parochial civilizational argument with *Sabbatino's* own separation of powers logic. After categorizing Cuba's running of its cigar business as commercial, White went on to say that mere commercial matters are so mundane that they could not possibly offend foreign sovereigns enough to cause problems for US foreign policy: "Subjecting them in connection with such acts to the same rules of law that apply to private citizens is unlikely to touch very sharply on 'national nerves.'"[97] He went so far as to assert (quoting the State Department itself) that, at any rate, "in the commercial area the need for merchants 'to have their rights determined in courts' outweighs any injury to foreign policy."[98]

White received support for this argument from the executive branch (now under Ford).[99] He also attempted to legitimize this approach by making the sorts of international law claims made in the lower *Sabbatino* decisions and the Hickenlooper Amendment. He asserted (without evidence) that while international rules on expropriations might still be fuzzy, "more discernible rules of international law have emerged with regard to the commercial dealings of private parties in the international market."[100] This consensus, White suggested, was proof that no country could be offended by having to follow such rules.

This was, of course, a blatant dismissal of Cuba's own strenuous objections in the case, as well as of the views of all states who had emphasized the inseparability of political and economic sovereignty. In other words, White defined the commercial as *not* political at the height of the Cold War and of Third World efforts to establish the NIEO, when the question of the proper arrangement of economic relations was arguably *the* key global political issue. By blatantly ignoring the fact that many states *did* oppose the kinds of commercial rules he was talking about, White's assertions about consensus implicitly reaffirmed racialized assumptions about which states counted as civilized and which did not.

White's commercial exception argument opened the way for a potential expansion of US judicial territory over many acts of foreign governments within their own borders. (That Cuba's repudiation of its debts had occurred on Cuban soil was not questioned in this case.) Yet, his decision was only a plurality opinion and thus did not rise to the standard for setting well-established Supreme Court precedent. Only three other justices accepted White's commercial argument fully. Another concurred with the rejection of the act of state doctrine but not with the commercial exception argument.

Four justices, two of whom were the only remaining members of the *Sabbatino* Court, vehemently disagreed with both the idea of a commercial exception and with White's attempt to define government acts so narrowly. They argued that the repudiation of the cigar manufacturers' debts could not be separated from its broader "program of expropriating what [Cuba] viewed as part and parcel of the businesses."[101] These justices reiterated the importance of the act of state doctrine in preventing US courts from questioning the public acts of foreign governments in their own territory, and they repeated the *Sabbatino* Court's point that there was in fact no international consensus on the issue of nationalizations.

Despite this initial contestation, however, the commercial exception to the act of state doctrine proposed by White has been applied more and more widely, though not always consistently, since. It has been most firmly embraced by the New York courts, which hear the majority of act of state cases. Moreover, one recent study concluded that while debates about the exception continue, "courts seem to have gradually lowered the threshold for finding 'commercial activity.'"[102] Together, the increasing application of the commercial exception to the act of state doctrine and the expansion of the category of commercial accompanying it, have further extended US judicial territory even over foreign government acts within their own borders.

Though legally distinct, the commercial exception to the act of state doctrine was influenced by the much heartier embrace of the commercial exception to foreign sovereign immunity. Although the dissenting justices in *Dunhill* critiqued the conflation of act of state and foreign sovereign immunity logics, White himself cited the Tate Letter and the restrictive theory of sovereign immunity in his opinion.[103] *Dunhill*, which was decided a few months before the FSIA passed, has in turn been taken to provide clues as to how the FSIA's commercial exception should be interpreted.[104] The restrictions on expropriation-related activities in *Dunhill*, combined with the FSIA's new allowance for seizing property related to so-called illegal expropriations, created further difficulties for nationalizing states and made 1976 a watershed moment in the expansion of US judicial territory over the developmental efforts of other countries. Without calling nationalizations per se illegal, they severely limited what could be done with nationalized property—unless full compensation was paid. Together, this cast a kind of legal net around nationalizations and nationalized property, both within the United States and in foreign territory.

TAMING EXPROPRIATIONS: US LAW, BITS, AND INTERNATIONAL ARBITRATION

The transformation of the act of state doctrine was certainly not the only US response to increasing expropriations, and it is impossible to measure its direct impact on the rate of expropriations going forward. Cuba's nationalizations in the early 1960s were the most sweeping in the world, but the strategy was also deployed by many other Third World states for whom the ability to expropriate the property of former colonizers was central to reclaiming political and economic sovereignty. Not counting Cuba, the number of expropriations increased from an average of seventeen a year in the late 1960s, to peak at fifty-six per year from 1970 to 1975. After this they declined sharply, falling to an average of 21.8 per year in the second half of the 1970s and dropping to only a handful in the 1980s.[105] Multiple factors contributed to this decline.

For one thing, the nationalization of certain key sectors like oil had been largely completed by this time.[106] More broadly, the collapse of the NIEO in the face of global economic crises and neoliberal counterrevolution in the late 1970s constrained Third World policy choices and curtailed Third World efforts to win institutional recognition for economic as well as political sovereignty. Many Third World states became dependent on conditional Western loans and aid in the late 1970s and 1980s. This restricted their policy choices even further and made continued expropriations even less likely.

Changes to US rules on expropriation via the act of state doctrine and foreign sovereign immunity took place in this broader context and made life even more difficult for states considering expropriations, as did two other important institutional developments around the same time: the rise of bilateral investment treaties (BITs) and the expansion of international arbitration.

The effect of BITs on expropriations is much better known than that of US domestic law. A BIT is a formal agreement between two countries that establishes the terms on which the nationals and companies of one may invest in the other. BITs first emerged in some European countries after World War II in response to postcolonial challenges to Western capital, especially through import substitution industrialization policies and expropriations. The United States initiated its own BIT program in 1977 and released its first model BIT text in 1981. US-style BITs are now standard even in agreements in which the United States is not involved. BITs are routinely characterized by uneven power relations. Originally, most BITs were signed between wealthy and low-income countries, and many continue to reflect this pattern today.[107] The United States has existing or pending BITs with forty-seven countries, none of which are wealthy Western states.[108]

Expropriations are a central target of BITs. As a 2007 report for Congress on the topic explained, "When conceived, the primary goal of the U.S. BIT program was to bolster the U.S. position that . . . any expropriation must receive full compensation."[109] This remains an explicit goal. In the 1960s and early 1970s, US judges and Congress asserted that an international consensus on compensation for expropriations already existed, ignoring the position of Third World states on the topic. By getting individual states to promise by treaty that they would pay full compensation for any expropriation, BITs sidestepped this question of consensus altogether. As Sparke explains, the United States has continued to use bi- and multilateral investment treaties in this way, while simultaneously expanding them to include redress for "any laws or policies that are 'tantamount to national-ization or expropriation'"—a process that has involved redefining expro-priations to include any number of public health, environmental, and other rules that can be classified as "taking" profits from foreign investors.[110]

In the late 1970s and 1980s, new BITs also undermined the NIEO by specifying that any dispute relating to expropriations or other investment issues would be submitted to international arbitration—a requirement that stood in direct contrast to the 1974 UN General Assembly Charter's provisions for host country governance of expropriation-related disagree-ments. International arbitration had been a tool for subjecting Third World states to Western property rules since shortly after decolonization.[111] But the volume of arbitration rose dramatically from the late 1970s on and was increasingly based on New York or English law.[112] In 1977, a year after *Dunhill* and the FSIA, and the same year the United States launched its BIT program, an important international arbitral decision dismissed the General Assembly's entire 1974 Charter as nonbinding, characterizing its provisions on nationalizations as mere political posturing with no real legal status.[113] The establishment of the World Bank's own arbitration forum, the International Centre for Settlement of Investment Disputes (ICSID), provided another important site for using Anglo-American property rules to protect Western investors from the national development efforts of post-colonial states. ICSID was established in 1965, just a year after the *Sabba-tino* decision. It was heavily influenced by and designed to counter debates about expropriation then unfolding between Western and postcolonial states at the UN.[114] ICSID began seeing increasing caseloads in the 1980s.

The transnational extension of US domestic law, the rise of BITs, and the use of international arbitration all became more pronounced in the mid to late 1970s. All three changes contributed to institutionalizing West-ern views on expropriations and compensation, depoliticizing an issue that had been central to postcolonial claims about economic and political sov-ereignty by recasting it in technical legal terms. All three also contributed to shifting the legal geography of expropriation-related disputes away from Third World host states.[115] While changes in act of state and foreign sov-ereign immunity rules expanded US judicial territory over expropriations and their effects in and beyond a foreign state's borders, BITs and international arbitration shifted legal authority over expropriations to more properly international institutions and treaties—although these were themselves heavily shaped by US interests and Anglo-American legal norms.

Although they have remained one source of act of state litigation, US courts are no longer the primary locus of governance for many expropriation-related disputes.[116] International arbitration has taken on more significance in this arena. Yet, transnational US law continues to operate in tandem with BITs and international arbitration to promote US-style rules on nationalizations. For one thing, combined foreign sovereign immunity and act of state rules ensure that even a country that has not signed a BIT would find it very difficult to do much with nationalized property beyond its own borders, unless full compensation had been paid.

In addition, the interplay of US domestic law and BITs has made it easier for both courts and arbitrators to claim that there is in fact an international consensus on compensation for expropriations. The international law claim strategy used by the lower *Sabbatino* courts, the Hickenlooper Amendment, and in White's commercial exception argument was always specious in the face not only of opposition from Cuba but of Third World governments actively promoting the NIEO. This strategy, however, was given firmer ground by getting Third World countries to sign BITs. Indeed, BITs were pushed precisely to *address* the lack of international consensus on expropriations, and US views on expropriations (especially the famous Hull Doctrine and US domestic law on the takings clause) were enshrined in these BITs.[117] The proliferation of BITs since has in turn been cited by Western jurists as evidence that a true consensus now exists.[118]

CONCLUSION

Whatever its long-term effect on nationalizations, the transformation of the act of state doctrine in response to the Cuban Revolution led to a significant extension of US judicial territory. The classic act of state doctrine had barred adjudication of foreign governments' acts in their *own* territory. The restriction of the doctrine to expand US judicial authority changed this, especially where so-called commercial acts were concerned. The effect was that, just as many postcolonial states gained formal sovereign status for the first time in the 1950s to 1970s, the terms of that sovereignty changed to subject those states to increased oversight by US domestic courts. The

1964 adoption of the separation of powers approach, with its focus on US foreign policy interests rather than territorial sovereignty, was already a major step in this direction. Because *Sabbatino* failed to bring Cuba's nationalizations under US judicial authority, however, it was followed by numerous further efforts to weaken the act of state doctrine. Though none of the post-*Sabbatino* changes has been universally adopted, the Hickenlooper Amendment, the international law violation exception, and, especially, the commercial exception have all been used to get around the act of state doctrine in later cases. Other exceptions to the doctrine have since been added as well.[119]

The difficulty of bringing Cuba's nationalizations within US judicial reach provides striking evidence of the fact that the precise changes made were neither natural nor inevitable—rather they were the result of messy attempts by multiple parties to protect the interests of the US state and US capital from postrevolutionary Cuba, while also balancing the internal interests of various branches of the US government. What the reformers of the act of state doctrine and foreign sovereign immunity rules could not have predicted was that the new legal terrain developed in this process would be the basis for the next, very different phase of judicial expansion—this time, in the context of the Third World debt crises of the 1980s, which followed on the heels of the collapse of the NIEO, the neoliberal counter-revolution, and the reconfiguration of US empire to foreground American finance and dollar hegemony.

CHAPTER FOUR

Debt, Default, and
Judicial Discipline

The last quarter of the twentieth century was marked by broad transformations in the global political economy, often summarized through the terms *neoliberalization* and *financialization*.[1] Each of these processes, in turn, was intertwined with the crisis of American empire and its reconfiguration on the basis of New York finance and the US dollar. The continued expansion of US judicial territory during this period both reflected and helped constitute this new conjuncture. In this chapter, I focus on the role of US courts in disciplining foreign sovereign debtors during the 1980s and 1990s. I show how this process contributed to producing a neoliberal economy and a new legal geography for intangible financial property, while bolstering the power of the US dollar and Wall Street.

The defeat of the NIEO in the late 1970s coincided with growing domestic and international economic crises for both North and South. Along with CIA-backed coups against leftist governments and targeted US aid to anti-Communist (and often authoritarian) regimes, all this contributed to undermining the alternative economic strategies embraced by many Third World states in the postwar decades.[2] A massive debt crisis in the 1980s put the final nail in the coffin of the NIEO. Indebted governments participated (reluctantly or not) in IMF and World Bank structural adjustment programs that required them to reject the last vestiges of interventionist or socialist economic practices and to embrace the neoliberal worldview that had recently become prominent in the United States and the United Kingdom.

These structural adjustment programs compounded the already devastating debt crisis and led to a "lost decade" of development in much of Latin America and Africa. They have been widely criticized for initiating a new round of neocolonial domination, in which Third World sovereignty was curtailed by Western governments, international financial institutions, and transnational creditors.[3] Since then, the IMF and the World Bank have remained key to maintaining neoliberal discipline across much of the Global South. Scholars have also shown that they have been central to both the reconfiguration of US empire and to the imperialism of international law.[4] The role of US *domestic* law in underwriting both finance capital and American power, while imposing neoliberal discipline on indebted states, in contrast, has been largely overlooked.

Even as Third World debtors submitted to neoliberal adjustment programs, they attempted to resist the most rapacious private creditors—those who refused to participate even in IMF-mediated restructurings and instead sued debtor countries in US courts. At first, those courts ruled against these "holdout" creditors on the grounds that things like managing exchange restrictions or maintaining currency reserves were public, sovereign acts beyond US judicial reach. Under pressure from New York financiers and the US executive branch, however, the courts reversed course and claimed authority over transnational sovereign debt relations, thus further extending US judicial territory beyond official US borders.

In this chapter, I first provide an overview of the intersecting crises of global economic stability and American empire in the 1970s and explain how they triggered both a reconfiguration of US power and a massive debt crisis. Focusing on two of the most important legal cases arising out of the debt crisis, I then explain how US courts relied on, but went beyond, earlier precedent to further expand US judicial territory. This expansion most immediately benefited the private creditors suing sovereign debtors. Yet, the implications went much further. A close analysis of this litigation shows how neoliberal logics and financial power are both reflected in and institutionalized through US common law. US courts helped constitute the neoliberal counterrevolution by working in tandem with IMF structural adjustment programs to discipline debtor states, and by expanding the category of the commercial in ways that promoted contract fundamentalism and discouraged more interventionist state economic activity. Judicial authority over transnational debt relations supported the growing power of New York finance and the US dollar, while simultaneously depoliticizing fundamental questions about the role of governments in managing national monetary and fiscal stability.

THE 1970S: CRISIS AND RECONFIGURATION

By the 1970s, the United States was facing both external and internal crises. The growing industrial power of Germany and Japan, along with strong unions and an expanding welfare state at home, put pressure on American manufacturing and contributed to declining profits and economic stagnation. Major increases in the price of oil initiated by the Organization of the Petroleum Exporting Companies (OPEC) in 1973 and 1978 further exacerbated these tendencies and contributed to persistent inflation for oil importers in both North and South. Meanwhile, massive deficit spending on the protracted Vietnam War (itself damaging American legitimacy), combined with the growth of offshore Eurodollar markets, undermined the value of the US dollar. President Nixon's decision to delink the dollar from gold in August 1971 to address this problem radically altered the international monetary system, ushering in a system of floating exchange rates and high financial volatility.[5] When the usual Keynesian policy suggestions failed to contain either inflation or stagnation, the economic consensus that had been dominant since World War II began to collapse. Neoliberal economists stepped in to fill the gap.

These persistent economic and political crises led many to see the 1970s as a moment of real danger for the United States. In the end, however, the crises resulted not in a decline of American power, but in its transformation. The newly reconfigured American empire that emerged from these difficulties put dollar hegemony and Wall Street, rather than manufacturing, front and center.[6] The shift to floating exchange rates had the effect of making what were seen as the safe havens of Wall Street and the US dollar more appealing. This was even more true when, following Milton Friedman's monetarist theories, Federal Reserve Chair Paul Volcker famously increased the US interest rate from 11 percent to 20 percent between 1979 and 1981. The "Volcker shock" succeeded in stamping out US inflation, while simultaneously imposing harsh austerity on the US economy.[7] This cemented the undoing of the labor unions that had been so strong in the postwar period and helped restore the profitability of US manufacturing. High interest rates also attracted a flood of new money into Wall Street, bolstering the US dollar and catapulting finance into the driver's seat of both the global political economy and US empire.[8]

The crises of the 1970s and the transformations of US empire and global finance that emerged from them also finished off the NIEO and brought many of its promoters into the ambit of the US liberal capitalist international project.[9] Third World debt had been rising since the 1960s. The US bilateral and World Bank aid that comprised much of this debt were tied to Cold War security concerns and to undermining what were perceived as anti-capitalist practices in the Global South. This involved a two-pronged strategy. First, loans were made to anti-Communist US allies, however corrupt or authoritarian. Second, loan conditionalities were used to restrain the economic practices of countries that accepted aid.[10] When Third World debts spiked in the 1970s, additional strategies for using loans to push countries toward fully embracing US-style liberal capitalism were developed.

Economic stagnation in the wealthy world led to falling demand for Third World exports. The OPEC price hikes squeezed low-income oil-importers even further. Meanwhile, the money (or "petrodollars") OPEC states earned from these price hikes flooded New York and London banks; much of this money was "recycled" to developing countries. This meant that the sources of Third World debt shifted to include more commercial creditors. Low-income countries were eager for more loans in the face of economic recession, while Western banks awash in petrodollars, but faced with stagnation and limited investment opportunities in the North, were eager to lend.[11]

Total outstanding external debt for developing countries increased from around $70 billion in 1970 to around $540 billion in 1980 and $775 billion in 1986.[12] Of this, commercial loans rose from $36 billion in 1970 to $380 billion in 1980. These commercial loans were concentrated in Latin America and the Caribbean, as well as Nigeria and some of the larger Middle Eastern, Southeast Asian, and East European countries.[13] Loans were made in US dollars at low but variable interest rates. When Volcker increased the US federal funds rate to stamp out inflation, the interest on these loans thus shot up too. Currency depreciations fueled by growing crises in the context of the new system of floating exchange rates made these loans even more expensive. Countries capable of servicing their loans at lower interest rates in the 1970s were suddenly thrown into the red. Mexico was the first to threaten default in 1982. Dozens of others followed suit. It was this crisis that created the conditions for further extensions of US judicial territory via lawsuits by creditors against sovereign debtors.

STRUCTURAL ADJUSTMENT, RESTRUCTURING, AND HOLDOUT LITIGATION

In the early twentieth century, the internationalization of US finance capital throughout the Western Hemisphere facilitated the extraction of money and resources into American hands and underpinned a new phase in US imperial expansion. Together, private banks and the US government exerted control over the finances of other countries, sometimes even by determining those countries' central bank policies, managing local currencies, and mediating tax collection.[14] In the 1970s and 1980s, the transnational extension of US finance again became central to US imperial expansion. This time, however, control over foreign economies was mediated through the two key postwar international financial institutions (IFIs): the World Bank and the IMF.

The Volcker Shock was designed to tamp down inflation and worker power in the United States, not to create a debt crisis in the Third World. Had that crisis led to the collapse of the Western banking system, it would have been disastrous for the United States as well. Throughout the 1980s, US financiers and regulators thus struggled to improve the position of Wall Street in order to avoid this outcome. To ensure that debtors did not default outright, banks pursued case by case "restructurings," in which they agreed to lower the principal owed, extend the maturity of a debt, adjust interest rates, provide "rollover" loans, or some combination of the above. The US Treasury and the IMF were closely involved in negotiating these restructurings, and countries had to accept IMF bailout loans and the conditionalities attached to them before private creditors would sign restructuring deals. It was during this process that the United States also learned how useful debt crises in the South could be to its own interests. Such crises boosted the power of US finance by causing capital flight to Western banks and the US dollar, considered safe havens in times of crisis.[15]

In addition, the United States learned to use the IFIs to impose neoliberal adjustment on sovereign debtors to the benefit of US banks and US empire.[16] As outright debt relief was repeatedly denied throughout the 1980s, the IFIs extended "bailout" loans to debtor countries. These loans were low interest, but they were conditioned on debtors' rejection of the economic strategies many had pursued in the preceding decades. Under IMF and World Bank structural adjustment programs, countries were forced to implement what we now see as quintessential neoliberal policies, including privatizing state-owned companies and public sector industries like education and healthcare, liberalizing trade and financial markets, and pursuing currency depreciation and commodity exports to raise the dollars needed to pay off their debts. These policies opened debtor economies to penetration by Western investors and financiers. By further integrating these economies into global markets, liberalization also made these countries more dependent than ever on decisions in Washington, DC, and New York City.

Combined with the collapse of the NIEO and the defanging of the UN General Assembly, structural adjustment put increasing constraints on Third World efforts to forge an alternative economic order.[17] Demands for substantive economic equity were replaced by the neoliberal dictates of the IMF and the World Bank. The imposition of these neoliberal policies was accompanied by the internal reorganization of Third World social relations, as newly empowered technocratic elites, many of whom had trained in the West, gained strength within debtor governments. These elites, and Third World bourgeoisies more generally, have themselves often benefited from and helped maintain the neoliberal status quo established during this period.[18]

The interdependence of debt restructurings with private creditors, on the one hand, and structural adjustment programs, on the other, meant that even partial debt relief was contingent on neoliberal realignment throughout the 1980s. As the crisis neared its second decade, this arrangement remained at the heart of the only systematic debt relief program. The Brady Plan, which the US government rolled out in 1989 and strongly encouraged private banks to accept, offered more relief than previous restructurings. However, only debtors undergoing IMF structural adjustment were eligible. Indeed, the record of the conference proceedings at which the plan was rolled out reveals that the primary goal of the plan was not debt relief at all, but rather ensuring that Third World leaders would remain committed to neoliberal adjustment.[19] At the 1989 conference at which Treasury Secretary Nicholas Brady expressed support for what would become the Brady Plan, numerous speakers presented such adjustment as necessary for regaining economic growth.[20] Debt relief was a secondary policy intended to relieve the pain caused by this adjustment enough to ensure that governments would retain the will and ability to carry out IMF-mandated reforms. Participants were especially concerned about Latin America, where IMF-imposed austerity was already stoking mass unrest and street protests across the region.[21] As the editors of the published report on the conference proceedings noted, twelve elections were scheduled in Latin America over the next year and a half: "In these circumstances, negotiated debt reduction, apart from its economic value, could be useful political ammunition for leaders engaged in ongoing economic policy reform."[22]

It was at the intersection of structural adjustment and debt restructurings that US common law helped promote creditor interests, neoliberalism, and US power. During sovereign debt crises, most creditors eventually agree to restructuring deals with debtors. These deals allow creditors to emerge from crises with something rather than nothing. During the 1980s, however, a small number of creditors refused to participate in the restructurings overseen by the IMF and the US Treasury. Instead, these holdout creditors sued debtors for full recovery of the value of their loans plus interest in federal courts in New York.

Before the 1980s, this sort of holdout litigation against sovereign debtors was rare, in part because sovereigns were generally protected from such suits by foreign sovereign immunity rules or by the act of state doctrine. As the debt crisis unfolded, holdout litigation pushed US jurists to overcome these obstacles and extend US judicial authority over transnational sovereign debt relations for the first time. Two decisions—one against Costa Rica in 1985 and another against Argentina in 1992—were especially important. These decisions, which have influenced all sovereign debt litigation since, involved the further redefinition of the public/private and political/legal distinctions. This process was both shaped by and contributed to the broader ascendancy of neoliberal logics in law and policy, and it helped foster a neoliberal understanding of the economy as a separate sphere. At the same time, a new, more direct focus on remapping the foreign/domestic distinction with respect to intangible financial transactions gave courts greater flexibility in extending both judicial territory and the power of Western creditors over an increasingly financialized global economy.

Holdout litigation is often presented by sovereign debt policymakers, economists, and activists as a threat to orderly debt restructurings. Holdouts are widely depicted as predatory or exploitative, while creditors who agree to restructurings are seen as more responsible. Yet, during the 1980s and 1990s, the two strategies came to function hand in hand with each other and with structural adjustment programs to bolster the power of private financiers, promote the neoliberal disciplining of debtor societies, and underwrite a new phase of American empire.

Allied Bank Int'l v. Banco Credito Agricola de Cartago was one of the earliest holdout creditor cases to emerge from the debt crisis. A syndicate of thirty-nine banks represented by the New York–based Allied Bank International had issued loans to three Costa Rican state-owned banks in 1976. As the Third World debt crisis accelerated in the early 1980s, Costa Rica imposed foreign exchange restrictions that prevented its own banks from making payments on these loans. Allied sued the banks in the District Court for the Southern District of New York to recover the unpaid principal of $4.486 million plus interest. The District Court for the Southern District of New York and the Second Circuit both initially ruled in favor of Costa Rica—until the US executive branch persuaded the Second Circuit to reverse its decision.[23]

As TWAIL scholar James Gathii has argued in a detailed examination of this case, the final *Allied* decision cemented the primacy of the sanctity of loan contracts in US law, benefitting private creditors.[24] *Allied* also sheds light on the coproduction of law, finance, and US power in two ways. First, it established that the right of creditors to use US courts to enforce their contracts *outweighs* the US government's interest in promoting coordinated debt restructurings and structural adjustment programs. Gathii sees this as a contradiction within US policy that sounded the "death knell" for cooperative debt restructurings.[25] I suggest, however, that this new policy actually bolstered neoliberal adjustment and restructuring creditors by increasing the leverage of the latter in negotiating restructuring deals. Second, the court redefined the location or "situs" of a debt as being with the creditor rather than with the debtor—thus giving US courts authority over any debtor who has accepted loans from New York banks. Both dimensions of the case further extended US judicial territory over transnational sovereign debt relations, bolstering the intertwined power of US courts and of the New York financial sector on which US empire was more and more dependent.

CONTRACT RIGHTS VERSUS DEBT RESTRUCTURINGS

The first round of the *Allied* case was heard by Judge Thomas Griesa of the District Court for the Southern District of New York, who would later oversee the famous holdout litigation against Argentina in the 2000s. In 1983, he was not yet so committed to creditor rights. In *Allied*, Griesa drew on the Cuban cases of the 1960s and 1970s to rule in Costa Rica's favor.

Costa Rica's foreign exchange restrictions, Griesa held, were imposed "in response to a serious national economic crisis" and "were intended to serve a public, rather than a commercial, purpose."[26] The Costa Rican banks, therefore, had been prevented from paying their loans by a sovereign act of the Costa Rican government in its own territory. Echoing *Sabbatino*, Griesa argued that judicial intervention with this sovereign act would risk "embarrassment to the relations between" the United States and Costa Rica.[27] The act of state doctrine, therefore, prevented him from supporting Allied's claims.[28]

By the time the Second Circuit heard Allied's appeal, thirty-eight of the thirty-nine banks in the syndicate had dropped out of the lawsuit and agreed to restructure their loans with Costa Rica. The Fidelity Union Trust Company of New Jersey (Fidelity) was the only bank to refuse to participate in this restructuring, becoming the sole holdout creditor in the continuing litigation. In 1984, the Second Circuit upheld Griesa's decision in favor of Costa Rica but on different grounds.[29] Like Griesa, the court highlighted the public character of the exchange decrees, noting that Costa Rica was "clearly acting as a sovereign in preventing a national fiscal disaster."[30] In other words, maintaining economic stability in the midst of a crisis was understood, at this time, to be a proper function of sovereign governments. Rather than ruling on act of state grounds, however, the court based its decision on the fuzzier concept of comity—that is, on the political desirability of maintaining good will among nations, rather than on law per se. Both the legislative and executive branches had expressed support for Costa Rica's ongoing debt restructurings, which its exchange decrees were intended to support. The US itself was restructuring bilateral loans to the country. Therefore, the court concluded, allowing Fidelity's holdout litigation, which would interfere with these restructurings, would be against US policy interests.

This decision apparently "created shock waves throughout the U.S. international banking community."[31] Two months later, the Reagan administration took the highly unusual step of attempting to reverse an existing judicial decision. In an amicus brief submitted to the court, the executive explained that it had a strong interest in *Allied* because the case concerned the "legal framework applicable to the payment of billions of dollars of loans contracted by foreign governments and foreign private parties for which New York is the place of payment under the contract."[32] Signed by representatives of the Department of State, the Treasury, the Federal Reserve, and the Department of Justice, the brief argued that the Costa Rican decrees were not in fact consistent with US policy and that the act of state doctrine did not apply. While the United States did support Costa Rica's ongoing restructuring efforts, it did not condone *forcing* private creditors to restructure against their will. Instead, creditor participation must be entirely "voluntary."[33] Rather than criticizing Fidelity for not participating in the restructuring, the brief described Costa Rica's decrees as "unilateral" and a "cramdown."[34]

The government's support for holdout litigation despite its potential interference with IMF-led restructurings reflects an embrace of neoliberal views on voluntary creditor participation and the sanctity of contract rights. The executive also understood, however, that the possibility of holdout litigation would help *promote* "adjustment" (shorthand for liberalization and other free market policies) across the developing world. In its brief, the Reagan administration expressed support for

> (1) economic adjustment by borrowing countries . . . ; (2) an IMF adequately equipped to help borrowers design economic adjustment programs . . . ; (4) encouragement of private markets to provide prudent levels of financing to borrowers in countries implementing such economic programs.[35]

Far from supporting such adjustment, the administration argued, impeding holdout litigation would "encourage debtors to use the courts to establish their 'rights' to obtain concessions from their creditors, rather than addressing those problems through coordination, cooperation and needed economic adjustment measures."[36] In contrast, by *enforcing* holdout litigation, the courts would encourage sovereign debtors to participate in IMF restructurings and adjustments.[37]

New York financiers, not surprisingly, expressed similar views. The New York Clearing House Association, a major financial institution facilitating the settlement of interbank transactions, echoed both the concern for New York finance and the view that holdout litigation would promote economic adjustment. In its own amicus brief, the Clearing House argued that the Second Circuit's 1984 decision against holdouts would "reduce the bargaining power of lenders in debt restructuring negotiations by neutralizing the threat of swift judicial action in case of default."[38] The decision would also harm New York City, the Clearing House warned, because it would "force banks to reevaluate the desirability of participating in international syndicated dollar loans arranged and payable in New York City" and "undermine New York's role as the leading international financial center."[39] Other major New York financiers, even including some, like the Bank of America, that had participated in Costa Rica's restructuring, made similar arguments.[40] In other words, far beyond this particular case, holdout litigation was understood by financiers and the US government as an important tool for disciplining indebted governments and for bolstering both New York finance and the US dollar.

It is no surprise that such arguments found traction at a moment when the neoliberal counterrevolution had led to a renewed ideological commitment to market logics and contract rights. Such a commitment had, of course, been characteristic of the laissez-faire liberalism of the nineteenth and early twentieth centuries but was now associated with a more active emphasis on the role of law in promoting this.[41] At the same time, financial volatility and high interest rates had made Wall Street finance and dollar hegemony increasingly central to US global power.

In response to intense criticism from investors and the Reagan administration in this context, the Second Circuit revoked its initial ruling.[42] In a new 1985 opinion, the same three-judge panel adopted a radically different tone.[43] This time, the court hardly mentioned Costa Rica's economic crisis and no longer framed fiscal intervention as a sovereign's public responsibility. Instead, in a move that abstracted the case entirely from the broader context of the debt crisis, the court simply stated that "the defaults were due solely to actions of the Costa Rican government."[44]

Citing the executive's unwavering support for private contract rights and its explanation of the relationship between litigation and IMF restructurings, the court went on to explain that it had been mistaken about US policy. US support for bilateral and IMF-mediated restructurings were, in fact, perfectly consistent with upholding Fidelity's contract rights in this case. Indeed, refusing to allow holdout litigation would be detrimental to both debt restructuring efforts and US finance: "The Costa Rican government's unilateral attempt to repudiate private, commercial obligations is inconsistent with the orderly resolution of international debt problems. It is similarly contrary to the interests of the United States, a major source of private international credit."[45]

With the new *Allied* decision, "the international banking community breathed a noticeable sigh of relief. The 'sanctity of contracts' had been upheld."[46] *Allied* established that, under US common law, private contract rights supersede US support for IMF adjustment efforts. As the debt crisis unfolded, the case was cited in decisions in favor of holdout litigation against Jamaica, the Congo, Bolivia, Ecuador, and Peru, even when courts acknowledged the potentially damaging effects on both debtor countries and ongoing restructuring efforts.[47] A 1997 decision summed up the implications for the relationship between holdout litigation, IMF adjustment programs, and debt restructurings. A lower court had praised Peru's compliance with an IMF-mandated "reduction in the government deficit, with the consequent firing of thousands of public sector employees; and the privatization of many of the state-owned enterprises."[48] Nevertheless, the Second Circuit Court of Appeals concluded that, as evidenced by *Allied*, the US interest in protecting contracts and enforcing debts "limits" its interest in "IMF foreign debt resolution procedures under the Brady Plan."[49] Peru was ordered to pay its holdout creditors in full.[50]

Even today holdout litigation is commonly depicted as anathema to sovereign debt restructurings. In fact, *Allied* helped make the restructuring and holdout strategies interdependent. As two recent proponents put it, holdout litigation is important for "empowering creditors relative to debtors and minority creditors relative to the majority of the creditors."[51] The threat of expensive litigation, made possible by *Allied*, can increase the pressure on debtors to avoid restructuring at all.[52] If restructuring does become necessary, the holdout threat makes debtors willing to accept harsher terms from creditors. In short, by subjecting any country that resists even the worst restructuring terms to contract enforcement by US courts, judicial power works in tandem with Wall Street and the IMF to bolster the interests of Western creditors, increase neoliberal discipline on debtor states, and ensure that even more money is funneled from South to North.

MAPPING INTANGIBLE PROPERTY

The original *Allied* decision was reversed due to pressure from the financial sector and the executive branch. Yet, judges are generally reluctant to be seen as simply bowing to pressure from other branches of the government. Anxious to maintain some appearance of autonomy, the Second Circuit thus based its revised decision not solely on the US government's brief, but also on its own act of state analysis. Doing so both depended on and further strengthened growing New York financial power.

In order to accept the executive's view, the court held, it first had to determine whether the District Court had actually been correct in holding that the act of state doctrine barred US courts from invalidating Costa Rica's prevention of payments to the Allied syndicate. This in turn hinged on *where* that prevention had occurred. Most previous act of state cases had involved physical property, like sugar or cigars, whose location could not be easily questioned. Extending US judicial territory in those cases required manipulating the public/private and political/legal distinctions, as we saw in chapter 3, rather than questioning the physical geography of a sovereign's acts. The 1980s debt crises, in which intangible property took center stage, opened new possibilities for expanding US judicial territory more directly.

Although scholars of finance have long tended to emphasize the temporal, rather than the spatial, geographers have repeatedly shown that financial, temporal, and spatial relations are co-constituted—a critical insight for "bringing financial markets 'down to earth.'"[53] Law plays a key role in defining the geographies of seemingly intangible financial processes. Nowhere is this clearer than in the case of debt.

In its revised *Allied* decision, the Second Circuit got around the act of state doctrine by defining the location or situs of a debt as being with the creditor—overturning previous cases in which debts had been held to be located with the debtor. This allowed the court to characterize Costa Rica's default as occurring *within* the United States, thus making the act of state doctrine inapplicable and amounting to another significant extension of US judicial territory over transnational economic relations.[54]

All debts are relational, defined by a transaction between a debtor and (at least one) creditor—entities that are never located in precisely the same place. *Sovereign* debt is usually transnational, with the debtor government and its creditors located in different countries. The challenge for the *Allied* court was to assign this transnational relationship a definite legal geography. The question of the location of a debt had been discussed in some earlier nationalization cases involving the accounts of people or businesses from the nationalizing state, as, for instance, in *Dunhill*.[55] Such cases had spurred debates about whether nationalizations could "reach" debts *owed* by people inside the United States at the time of the nationalization. In other words, after a nationalization, should such debts still be seen as legally owed to their previous owners or to the nationalizing power? In cases against Iraq and Cuba in the 1960s and 1970s, US courts held that it was "well established that the situs of a debt is located with the debtor."[56] In these cases, this had meant the debts were located *in the United States* and thus beyond the reach of foreign nationalizations and act of state protections.

Had this rule been applied directly in the 1980s, Third World debts would have been legally located *outside* US borders. By the courts' own logic, creditors would therefore have been blocked by the act of state doctrine from using New York courts to recover on their loans. Indeed, in its first 1984 decision in *Allied*, the Second Circuit had suggested (without deciding) precisely this—that the debts in question were located in Costa Rica.[57] The second *Allied* decision, however, used the logic behind one Cuban nationalization case to reach the opposite result.[58]

The 1968 case *Tabacalera Severiano Jorge, S.A. v. Standard Cigar Co.* involved Cuban tobacco growers whose operations had been nationalized by the Cuban government.[59] The question was whether debts owed to those growers at the time of the nationalization by US tobacco importers had been nationalized as well. The Fifth Circuit Court of Appeals argued that the answer depended on where that debt was located. Like other courts, it held that the debt was located with the debtor—that is, in the United States, and thus beyond reach of the nationalization. The court's unique reasoning, however, would shape later debt cases.

Intangible property is notoriously difficult to locate. Situs decisions for such property have often been couched in the language of complicated and technical "contacts" analyses, considering, for example, where the contracting parties are domiciled, where the contract was signed, where payment is to be made, and so on.[60] In *Tabacalera*, in contrast, the court made the geography of a debt dependent on who had the *power* to enforce it. It rejected general assertions about debts being located either with debtors or creditors. Instead, it argued that the location depended on where payment could be made to "come to complete fruition."[61] Using this logic, the judges reasoned that the Cuban government did not have the ability to force American importers to pay it. "Whatever may be the ordinary concept of the situs of a debt," therefore, it "was simply *not within the power of Cuba* to accomplish this result."[62] *Because* Cuba did not have this power, the debt was located with the debtors—in the United States.

This analysis made the legal geography of debt directly dependent on relative power. In its 1985 *Allied* decision, the Second Circuit relied on this same logic to reach the opposite territorial result. In *Tabacalera*, the court had reasoned that, because Cuba's *debtors* were in the United States, Cuba could not force them *to pay*, and the debts were thus located in the United States. In *Allied*, the court argued that, since Costa Rica's *creditors* were in the United States, Costa Rica could not unilaterally *extinguish* its debts— thus, once again, the debts were located in the United States. Costa Rica simply did not have the power to bring its default to "complete fruition."[63]

In a bit of judicial boosterism, the Second Circuit also linked this analysis to the importance of New York finance. In support of its spatial determination, the court pointed out that:

The United States has an interest in maintaining New York's status as one of the foremost commercial centers in the world . . . [and] in ensuring that creditors entitled to payment in the United States in United States dollars under contracts subject to the jurisdiction of United States courts may assume that . . . their rights will be determined in accordance with recognized principles of contract law. In contrast, . . . [Costa Rica's] interest in the contracts at issue is essentially limited to the extent to which it can unilaterally alter the payment terms.[64]

In the final sentence, "interest" is a thinly disguised euphemism for power.

Legal commentators immediately recognized that this spatial analysis was not merely technical but strategic—it was designed to give US courts jurisdiction over transnational debtors. One scholar noted candidly that the application of the act of state doctrine to foreign debts "has been consistent only in that the American litigant, more often than not, has been the successful party. *Regardless of whether the United States citizen has been the debtor or the creditor, United States courts have determined the situs of the debt to be within United States territory.*"[65] Another pointed out that, while US law traditionally located debts with the debtor, this had recently changed because "that test would almost always place the loan in the foreign nation and would allow the act of state doctrine to be used by foreign nations as a mechanism to avoid payment of debts."[66] By remapping the geography of debt in this way, *Allied* undermined the power of sovereign debtors and supported New York creditors.

Moreover, since, under *Allied*'s reasoning, debts to foreign creditors can never be fully extinguished in the debtor's own jurisdiction (at least where that debtor is weaker than the United States), all foreign sovereign debts to US creditors could be legally located in the United States from then on.[67] Combined with the growing dominance of New York finance, this effectively removed the act of state defense from future sovereign debt cases and extended US judicial territory over Third World decisions about fiscal and monetary stability, even in the midst of severe economic crises. *Allied* has been cited over ninety times and remains the foundational case for interpreting the act of state doctrine in the context of sovereign debt.[68]

Critics of the Second Circuit's original ruling against Allied had suggested that it would allow judicial intervention into private markets and expand the power of sovereign debtors.[69] In fact, it was the second *Allied* decision, not the first, that extended US judicial authority over transnational markets. As Gathii puts it, "The extinction of any regard for the sovereign or regulatory functions of sovereigns in managing public functions such as refinancing sovereign debt results in an unbalanced projection of the authority of the United States over coequal sovereigns."[70] By deciding that US courts could enforce creditors' contracts against sovereign debtors—and that such contract "rights" were more important than either those states' fiscal responsibilities or US-backed restructurings and structural adjustment programs—the *Allied* case also strengthened private creditors, most of whom were based in New York City. That the court justified this not simply by citing US policy but also by remapping the legal geography of debt in relation to the act of state doctrine made *Allied* even more significant in the coming era of financialization and persistently rising debt levels. The court's reliance on previous nationalization cases to do so also illustrates the way past case precedent imposes its own forms on further US common law change in unforeseen ways, even as the political economic context shifts.

ARGENTINA: DEBT, DEFAULT, AND FOREIGN SOVEREIGN IMMUNITY

Allied settled key questions about how the act of state doctrine would be treated in the context of sovereign defaults. A few years later, in *Republic of Argentina v. Weltover*, the holdout creditors' case focused instead on foreign sovereign immunity. [71] In *Allied*, the exchange controls *preventing* Costa Rican banks from paying New York creditors had been characterized as public. It was defining the situs of the debt as in the United States that enabled New York courts to extend authority over those acts in spite of the act of state doctrine. In *Weltover*, the US Supreme Court defined *issuing* sovereign debt as a private, commercial act for the first time, while also weakening the spatial requirements for finding "direct effects" on the United States under the FSIA. As with *Allied*, *Weltover* led to a significant new extension of US judicial territory that bolstered the neoliberalization of debtor societies and reaffirmed the close connections between New York's financial and legal power. *Weltover* remains important for determining how direct effects and commercial activity are defined under the FSIA.[72]

MAKING PUBLIC DEBT PRIVATE

When the 1980s debt crises began, it was far from obvious that issuing sovereign debt would be treated as a mere commercial issue. In the influential 1964 case *Victory Transport* (discussed in chapter 2), the Second Circuit had listed "public loans" alongside nationalizations as one of a small number of "strictly political or public acts."[73] Indeed, this view shaped the initial drafts of the FSIA, which *excluded* public debts from the commercial exception to foreign sovereign immunity.[74] In addition to considering taking on debt to be part of a government's sovereign responsibilities, this exclusion had been justified on the grounds that maintaining immunity for sovereign debt would protect US financial interests. The FSIA's drafters worried that any sovereign would hesitate to issue debt in a country in which they could be sued for it.[75] Months before the FSIA's passage, however, the public debt section was removed. Some, like the District of Columbia Bar, wanted the bill to explicitly redefine public debt as commercial. The New York City Bar Association, in contrast, only wanted to specify that immunity would not apply to public debts undertaken "in connection with a specific commercial activity."[76] In the end, the topic of public debt was dropped from the bill altogether—leaving open the question of whether it counted as commercial for the purposes of the FSIA.[77]

This question reached the Supreme Court in 1992. Like *Allied*, *Weltover* was a holdout litigation case stemming from the Third World debt crisis. By the start of the 1980s, a deteriorating economic situation meant Argentine businesses were struggling to find the US dollars they needed to participate in foreign transactions. Hoping to shore up the private sector, Argentina promised to provide these dollars.[78] By 1982, however, the government's own foreign currency reserves were running out. Argentina issued new bonds in order to finance continued dollar payments.

These bonds, known as Bonods, were issued and payable in US dollars, with payment to be made in London, Frankfurt, Zurich, or New York. Argentina made its initial interest payments on the Bonods on time. When they began to mature in 1986, however, the crisis was still raging, and the country could not afford to pay. Argentina, like many countries, was in the process of restructuring more than $30 billion in other public and private sector debts under IMF and World Bank oversight—one of several restructurings it had participated in since the crisis began.[79] The Argentine Ministry of Economy also restructured the Bonods, apparently on its own, offering bondholders new debt instruments with longer maturities in exchange for their original contracts. Nearly all the Bonod holders agreed to the deal Argentina offered, including the US government's own Export Import Bank. Two Panamanian corporations and a Swiss bank, however, refused. Instead, they sued Argentina in the Southern District of New York for full payment on $1.3 million worth of Bonods. Argentina pled immunity under the FSIA. The District Court, the Second Circuit, and the Supreme Court rejected this claim and ruled in favor of the holdouts.[80]

Argentina's creditors argued that the country was not immune because the case fell within the third clause of the FSIA's commercial exception, which denies immunity for actions based on "an act outside the territory of the United States in connection with a commercial activity of the foreign state elsewhere and that act causes a direct effect in the United States."[81] The US executive branch, under George Bush, filed a brief supporting the holdouts. Illustrating its dual role as defender of both US and global capital, the executive justified its intervention by explaining that "this Court's interpretation of the FSIA has an obvious and substantial impact on the United States' conduct of foreign relations," and that the "international public debt market" is important for private finance, international financial institutions, and national economies around the world.[82]

The Supreme Court decided unanimously in favor of the plaintiffs. In a decision by a young Justice Antonin Scalia, who would go on to become an icon of judicial conservatism, the Court defined issuing sovereign debt as a commercial activity for the first time. Scalia noted that the FSIA had left the definition of commercial "largely undefined."[83] However, he argued, the Cuban nationalization case *Dunhill*, decided less than six months before the FSIA, offered clues to the legislature's understanding of the term. In *Dunhill*, Justice White had defined any "participation in the marketplace in the manner of a private citizen or corporation" as commercial.[84] Combining act of state and foreign sovereign immunity precedent, Scalia embraced this definition and argued that the FSIA's nature/purpose distinction helped clarify what "in the manner of" meant.

The US courts had been focusing on nature rather than purpose in order to expand the category of the commercial since the 1960s (see chapter 2). This approach had been codified in the FSIA, which mandated that only nature, not purpose, could be used to define commercial activity. In other words, *why* a government engaged in an activity was made legally irrelevant. In *Weltover*, Scalia applied this logic to extend the commercial exception to sovereign debt. "The question is not whether the foreign government is acting with a profit motive or instead with the aim of fulfilling uniquely sovereign objectives," he reasoned—what mattered was whether these were the "*type* of actions" a private party might pursue.[85] Scalia acknowledged that there was no easy way to draw this distinction. Yet, he argued, "however difficult it may be in some cases to separate 'purpose' (i.e., the *reason* why the foreign state engages in the activity) from 'nature' (i.e., the outward form of the conduct that the foreign state performs or agrees to perform) . . . the statute unmistakably commands that to be done."[86]

As always, this practice of drawing and redrawing sharp distinctions in the midst of fundamental ambiguity is an important source of legal power. In *Weltover*, Scalia determined that foreign exchange controls (like those considered in *Allied*) are public, because private actors cannot regulate currency. In contrast, corporations can and do issue debt all the time. Like corporate debt, Scalia wrote:

> The commercial character of the Bonods is confirmed by the fact that they are in almost all respects garden-variety debt instruments: They may be held by private parties; they are negotiable and may be traded on the international market (except in Argentina); and they promise a future stream of cash income.[87]

This was true, Scalia held, even if, as Argentina claimed, the Bonods were not issued in order to raise capital or finance government purchases, and even if Argentina received less than market value for them. Whatever its purpose, Argentina's bond issuance was a commercial activity, and restructuring those bonds was an act in connection with that activity. "It is irrelevant *why* Argentina participated in the bond market in the manner of a private actor; it matters only that it did so."[88]

This redefinition of public debt as commercial and thus not immune from suit cemented the ability of creditors to sue sovereign debtors. This further strengthened not only holdout creditors, but also restructuring creditors in the same ways as *Allied* had done—that is, by giving the latter more leverage in negotiations. *Weltover* also helped constitute the neoliberal counterrevolution in ways that went beyond debt. As with previous phases of judicial expansion, *Weltover* was another step in institutionalizing the sharp public/private distinction that, while always important for liberal capitalism, became even more rigid in the neoliberal era.

More specifically, by linking this distinction to nature, rather than purpose, *Weltover* cemented the shift within US common law toward a narrower and narrower conception of the scope of sovereign activity. By categorizing any act that could be construed as "like" a commercial act as, in fact, merely commercial, *Weltover* excised nearly all economic activities from the domain of sovereignty—in marked contrast to both previous case history and to the arguments of postcolonial governments. Fox and Webb go so far as to say that this case represented a "decisive shift from government control of finance to regulation by the market."[89] The role of US courts in constituting this shift provides a vivid illustration of the changing role of law in shaping the neoliberal economy—a change in line with the way neoliberal theorists themselves understood the function of law to be supporting markets.[90]

This neoliberalizing tendency was further supported by the decontextualization implied in the Court's understanding of the nature/purpose distinction. As discussed in chapter 2, any attempt to define the nature of an act requires defining that act's boundaries. Just as in the 1960s, expanding US judicial authority in this case depended on drawing those boundaries as narrowly as possible—here, by restricting the relevant act to the debt contract and excluding not only the broader context of the crisis in which it was embedded, but even all other directly linked government policies.

This strategic boundary drawing was unusually explicit in *Weltover*. Argentina argued that determining the nature of an act depended on understanding the broader "course of conduct" of which it was a part.[91] The Bonods were just one "component" of Argentina's "program to regulate and stabilize its limited supply of foreign exchange" in the even broader context of negotiating a severe economic crisis.[92] Regulating foreign exchange is a well-recognized sovereign function. The "act" in question, therefore, was public. Indeed, Argentina reasoned, "If a court insists on surgically removing foreign government acts from their context, and examining them microscopically in the absence of any meaningful background, they *will almost inevitably appear to be identical to conduct engaged in by private actors.*"[93]

In contrast, although Scalia himself referred to the subject of the case as "Argentina's default on certain bonds *issued as part of a plan to stabilize its currency*,"[94] the holdout creditors, the US executive, and the courts ultimately defined the act in question as the issuance of the Bonods, full stop. As the Second Circuit Court of Appeals put it, a court must "isolate the specific conduct . . . rather than focusing on 'the broad program or policy of which the individual transaction is a part.'"[95] Indeed, defining an act "overbroadly" (i.e., paying attention to context) would mean that government acts "*would almost inevitably be characterized as sovereign in nature, rather than commercial.*"[96]

In short, both sides agreed that defining acts narrowly makes it easier to characterize them as merely private and commercial.[97] This approach lends itself to defining both more developmental and more neoliberal approaches to governing markets as commercial. On the one hand, anything states do through "market-like" mechanisms (e.g., state-owned enterprises, development contracts, or debt issuance) can be classified as private and thus subjected to US judicial authority. At the same time, structural adjustment programs requiring privatization and market liberalization, as well as proliferating bi- and multilateral investment treaties, have meant that debtor governments have been pushed to refrain from more undeniably "state-like" behavior (e.g., foreign exchange restrictions and expropriations).[98] In short, states have been encouraged to behave as mere commercial actors—and denied the prerogatives of sovereignty when they do so.

That this approach to the nature/purpose distinction favored "developed" over "developing" nations was well understood.[99] One law professor concluded a few years later that *Weltover* would most affect "developing sovereign states, because of their greater need to intervene in their domestic economies" and because their "governments often act as private parties engaging in commercial development to encourage foreign investment."[100] Indeed, at the time, the United Nations International Law Commission, then in the process of drafting the Convention on Jurisdictional Immunities, was recommending that *both* nature and purpose be considered in defining commercial activity.[101] As one American lawyer explained, the goal of this "was to allow developing countries to protect themselves when they entered into contracts."[102] This remains a sticking point preventing the Convention's ratification to this day.[103]

DEFINING DIRECT EFFECTS

The recategorization of sovereign debt issuance as a commercial activity paved the way for a significant extension of US judicial territory over many indebted governments. Yet, on its own, it was not enough to bring Argentina within US judicial reach. This was because the Supreme Court understood Argentina's debt issuance and rescheduling to have occurred in Argentina and *outside* the United States. Suing Argentina under the FSIA therefore required the additional step of showing that this act had caused "a direct effect in the United States." In taking the position that it had done so, the Supreme Court interpreted the term *direct* more loosely than courts had before—in this case, holding that relatively tenuous connections with New York were enough. This meant that, even as government acts were defined as narrowly as possible for the sake of defining their nature, the Court simultaneously expanded the relevant spatial scope for identifying those acts' "effects."

Scalia argued that, despite some suggestions to the contrary in its legislative history, the FSIA did not require direct effects to be either "foreseeable" or "substantial"—only that they be "an immediate consequence" of the action in question.[104] In this case, although the plaintiffs were not American companies, they had collected interest in New York. The Bonods had also been issued in US dollars and had been handled by a New York financial agent. The Court thus had "little difficulty in concluding that Argentina's unilateral rescheduling of the maturity dates on the Bonods had a 'direct effect' in the United States."[105]

This was a weaker standard than had been adopted in previous FSIA analyses, and it gave courts greater flexibility for determining jurisdiction under the FSIA.[106] Given the at least indirect participation of New York financial institutions in nearly all Third World debt relations, the decision cemented the ability of litigating creditors to sue sovereign debtors in US courts.

More broadly, this definition of *direct* amounted to a rewriting of the foreign/domestic distinction. Fox and Webb suggest that the direct effects rules developed in *Weltover* "only" remove immunity given sufficient links to the United States, "as where bonds are denominated in US dollars, made subject to US law, or payable in New York or other US location."[107] Crucially, however, this rule applies whether or not the transaction in question has far *more* significant contacts with another jurisdiction. In *Weltover*, for instance, the Court did not argue that the case had *more* connections to New York than to Argentina, where, according to the Court itself, the acts actually occurred, or to Panama or Switzerland, where the holdout litigators were based. Such reasoning has made it possible to classify nearly any financial transaction that touches down in any way on Wall Street as within reach of US courts.

Given New York's prominence in global finance, this allows any major financier in the world to use US courts to pursue litigation. Conversely, it expands New York's linked judicial and financial power. Both the District Court and the Second Circuit had argued that ruling in favor of the holdouts in *Weltover* was justified in part on the grounds that it would benefit New York's financial status.[108] The Supreme Court was more careful to avoid the appearance of blatant boosterism, noting that the benefits to New York City should not be viewed as a *reason* for its effects analysis. Yet, the Court was nevertheless "happy to endorse the Second Circuit's recognition of 'New York's status as a world financial leader.'"[109]

As of November 2023, *Weltover* had been cited over seven hundred times, most often in the Second Circuit, Ninth Circuit, and DC federal courts.[110] Its effects on US judicial reach abroad were widely understood at the time. One Western commentator wrote approvingly that the case allowed US courts to assert "jurisdiction over non-U.S. defendants in a greater number of cases than they did prior to *Weltover*."[111] Another noted that "the *Weltover* decision seems to enlarge U.S. courts' jurisdiction over foreign sovereigns . . . by introducing a 'direct effect in the United States' requirement which can be seen as less than 'direct' and not exactly 'in' the United States.'"[112] Argentine scholars put things more bluntly. As two political economists from the University of Buenos Aires put it in 1998, the case had directly affected the sovereignty of Argentina, "rejecting the sovereign immunity of the Argentine state with respect to rescheduling bond payments on external public debt."[113] They saw this as just one example of an ongoing tendency in US foreign policy of working to "establish a criterion of extraterritoriality for US legislation that aspires to consecrate the supremacy of [US] national interest over international norms."[114]

Even within the West, reactions were more mixed than they had been to *Allied*. Some legal scholars criticized *Weltover* for having too lax a definition of direct effects.[115] One worried that this "could provoke foreign antipathy to American extraterritorial policing."[116] Another objected to the decision both for getting rid of the requirements of "substantiality" and "foreseeability" in assessing direct effects and for leaving "too much latitude in defining commercial activity."[117] In both ways, the Court "granted unprecedented access to U.S. courts for persons seeking to file suit against a sovereign state."[118] Today, the United States continues to push for more flexible jurisdictional rules than either Third World or most other wealthy countries—another obstacle to the adoption of international rules on foreign sovereign immunity.[119]

LAW, FINANCE, AND THE PRODUCTION OF "THE" NEOLIBERAL ECONOMY

In the postwar decades, Third World states tried to bolster their political and economic sovereignty in ways at odds with the liberal capitalist world order whose construction the United States was spearheading. With the collapse of the NIEO in the late 1970s and the debt crises of the 1980s, however, this changed. Even without US judicial pressure, Third World debtors submitted to neoliberal structural adjustment programs throughout the 1980s and 1990s. As debt burdens were eventually reduced through the Brady Plan and other IMF-led restructurings, the debt crisis receded, but not without altering power dynamics between North and South as well as within debtor countries.[120]

Courts in the United States influenced the crisis and its resolution by enabling holdout litigation against sovereign debtors. They did so by holding that contract rights trumped US support for debt restructurings; by redefining the situs of debt as with the creditor rather than the debtor; by characterizing public debt issuance as a commercial rather than sovereign activity; and by interpreting the direct effects clause of the FSIA very loosely. The direct impacts of *Allied*, *Weltover*, and other creditor litigation on particular countries' crises are difficult to measure. At the very least, where holdout creditors won cases, they were nearly always paid in full—diverting much needed resources from already cash-strapped debtors.

These cases also paved the way for a new class of boutique investors specializing in distressed debt and holdout litigation.[121] The litigation that led to this extension of US judicial territory presents a striking example of the way that investors "actively create an entire geography appropriate to their needs."[122] Today, such litigation is widely seen as a problem for sovereign debt governance.[123] Even within the IMF, many criticize holdout litigation for interfering with and delaying debt restructurings and leading to worse outcomes for debtors.[124] Yet, the possibility of holdout litigation is fundamental to today's sovereign debt restructuring paradigm.[125]

Since the 1970s, private creditors and creditor countries like the United States and the United Kingdom have staunchly opposed the creation of a binding international sovereign bankruptcy framework akin to domestic corporate bankruptcy systems. Instead, debt crises continue to be handled on an ad hoc basis, with each restructuring negotiated separately among debtors, a multitude of creditors and, often, the IMF. Proponents of establishing a formal international sovereign debt restructuring system argue that it would protect debtors from predatory financiers, make restructurings fairer and more predictable, and promote economic development and human rights. Opponents insist that it would be unfair to private creditors and give debtors too much power. They also argue that this would make it even harder for low-income countries to access needed financing.[126] Meanwhile, today's informal approach to sovereign debt restructuring increases creditors' ability to impose neoliberal discipline on debtor states, while masking these dynamics behind depoliticized discourses of technocratic market efficiency.[127]

Critically, under this informal system the possibility of holdout litigation is what ensures that restructurings are voluntary for creditors, even as debtor governments are all but forced into accepting agreements by economic necessity, as well as by pressure from the IMF and the US Treasury. Holdout litigation is not necessary for getting sovereign debtors to participate in debt restructurings. Furthermore, like Costa Rica and Argentina in the cases examined in this chapter, most debtors pay creditors according to the terms of those restructurings most of the time. Yet, the possibility of holdout litigation makes *creditors'* participation in these restructurings voluntary in practice, not just in theory. Without this possibility, a creditor who refused to participate in a restructuring would be left with nothing at all. The ability to sue gives creditors a choice between accepting a reduction in the value of their investments or pursuing costly but potentially extremely profitable litigation. All proposed formal sovereign debt restructuring mechanisms would limit holdout litigation and force private creditors to participate in restructurings. Resistance to this has led to the defeat of every serious attempt to create an international restructuring regime for sovereign debt since the 1980s.[128]

The litigation discussed in this chapter is also significant beyond the domain of debt. As in the first decades after World War II, the extensions of US judicial territory produced in *Allied* and *Weltover* were based on the further redefinition of key legal dichotomies and shaped by ongoing debates about what constitutes proper government activity. As in previous cases, the restriction of foreign sovereignty in the context of the debt crisis served the interests of both US capital and the executive branch, facilitating the continued extraction of capital into the United States and bolstering New York finance and the dollar power on which US empire increasingly depended.

Alongside structural adjustment programs, the extension of US judicial authority over sovereign debt relations also both reflected the ascendancy of neoliberal logics and helped constitute the neoliberal counterrevolution of the 1980s. By giving creditors even greater leverage in negotiating restructurings, legalizing holdout litigation led to deeper austerity for debt-burdened countries, itself ensuring a greater transfer of assets from South to North. More subtly, these legal changes reflected and helped institutionalize neoliberal conceptions of the economy. They did so by further entrenching a sharp public/private distinction; by linking this distinction definitively to nature rather than purpose; by defining that nature in narrow terms, ideally by reference to the contract alone; and by doing all this at a moment when governments were being pushed by structural adjustment programs to embrace the market-like behaviors that would be considered commercial under this framework.

Together, these changes contributed to redefining actions that Third World governments had seen as central to sovereign responsibility (e.g., maintaining fiscal stability, building reserves of foreign currencies, and managing exchange rates) as merely technical, commercial matters. This depoliticization of fundamental questions about development—a central theme in the neoliberal project as a whole—closes off public debate and makes dissent outside the narrow terrain of US courts more difficult. The fact that this is accomplished via specialized legal arguments also makes these changes difficult to see—and, correspondingly, harder to reverse.[129]

The extension of US judicial territory that emerged from the 1980s debt crises was also shaped by the growing importance of intangible property. From the 1950s through the 1970s, reterritorializing US judicial space vis-à-vis foreign sovereigns depended primarily on manipulating the public/private divide. A strong distinction between "here" and "there" remained an important component of act of state and foreign sovereign immunity analyses in these cases. The spatial ambiguity of debt and other intangible financial property, in contrast, gave courts greater leeway to question the legal location of sovereign acts. This opened new pathways for challenging the geography of both doctrines more directly. In the face of the spatial ambiguity of financial processes, litigants and judges *decide* how to map those processes for legal purposes. Despite the intangibility of finance, financialization and debt have not made space less important in US law—rather, they have meant that more time and effort are spent defining the geography of that law than ever before.[130] As I suggested in chapter 1, the messy, overlapping, and fuzzy legal geographies that result from this process represent less a breakdown of some previously neat Westphalian territoriality, than they do a continuation of a long history of complex imperial geographies.

In this iteration, the combined power of US law and finance has given US and especially New York judges more power than any others in this process. Conversely, the transnational reach of US law has both depended on New York's global financial importance and helped promote it. All cases against foreign sovereigns raise questions about why those sovereigns obey US courts at all. Domestically, judicial power rests, at root, on the ability of police to back up the law by force if needed. In contrast, US courts have no formal ability to force foreign sovereigns to obey them. Yet, those sovereigns nearly always do obey.[131] They do so because of the entwined economic and legal power of the United States.

Third World sovereigns are particularly dependent on New York finance and US dollars. This makes it very difficult for them to resist judgments by US courts once they are made. In *Allied* and *Weltover*, refusing to obey these rulings could very well have blocked Costa Rica and Argentina's access to New York and international credit markets—a possibility no Third World sovereign could seriously consider, especially in the middle of a devastating economic crisis.

CHAPTER FIVE

Sovereign Disobedience

In June 2014, the US Supreme Court backed two controversial rulings. In 2001, Argentina had defaulted on nearly $100 billion in sovereign debt. Over the next decade, 93 percent of the country's creditors agreed to restructure their bonds at a significant loss. A small number of specialized holdout creditors, however, instead sued Argentina in New York for the full face-value of the bonds they held, plus interest. As had been usual since *Allied*, the courts in NML *Capital v. Argentina*[1] ruled in favor of these holdouts. But unlike nearly all sovereign debtors since then, Argentina refused to pay. This resistance and the holdouts' struggle to overcome it created the terrain for a remapping of US legal space that went further than ever before.[2]

Argentina's refusal to obey the orders against it demonstrated that, although foreign sovereigns rarely disobey US courts, those courts remain unable to *make* them obey. Legally, there is nothing unusual about this. The "enforcement problem" has long been recognized as a component of sovereign debt litigation.[3] Yet, in this case, a small group of hedge fund holdout creditors, widely referred to as vulture funds, convinced Judge Griesa of the District Court for the Southern District of New York to find a way around it. First, Griesa adopted an unusual interpretation of a standard contract clause to prohibit Argentina from paying any *other* creditors, unless it paid the holdouts first. Second, he backed this up by prohibiting anyone anywhere in the world except Argentina from helping the country make such payments.[4] The Second Circuit Court affirmed.[5] In 2014, the Supreme Court declined to review the case, leaving it in force.[6] On the same day, the Supreme Court affirmed a related ruling that granted the holdouts the right to demand information (or "discovery") about all Argentine government assets, private or public, anywhere in the world except Argentina.[7]

This was a far cry from the legal geography of the early twentieth century, in which US courts had refused to question the acts of foreign sovereigns abroad and had only allowed litigation against sovereigns for acts *within* the United States in very limited cases. It was even far from the standards of the postwar period, in which the immunity of foreign states had been scaled back, as long as the act in question was deemed to be commercial. Even after the 1970s, litigation against foreign sovereigns depended on both the commercial exception and on showing that a commercial activity occurred in or had direct effects on the United States. In *NML Capital v. Argentina*, in contrast, US courts unilaterally claimed authority to govern Argentina's activities everywhere in the world *except* in Argentina—and even, in some situations, to do so whether the activities were commercial or not.

In some ways, the courts that made the Argentina decisions were very different from those deciding earlier cases involving foreign sovereigns. Although still staunchly procapitalist and in favor of free trade, many US jurists in the postwar decades were shaped by Legal Realism and New Deal politics. The Warren Court that wrote the *Sabbatino* decision in favor of Cuba is widely considered to be the most liberal in the Supreme Court's history. The shift to the Burger Court in 1969 began a transition toward the right among the US judiciary that only accelerated under the Rehnquist Court (1986–2005) and, even more dramatically, under the current Roberts Court.[8] This rightward shift has had major implications for issues ranging from campaign financing to environmental regulation to women's reproductive rights. Yet, as we will see below, this change does not explain the courts' support for the vulture funds suing Argentina—while conservatives like Justice Scalia clearly impacted the *tone* of the decisions, the outcome was supported by most of the Supreme Courts' liberal members as well.

Much more significant for understanding the courts' willingness to make such extreme decisions in this case has been the gradual neoliberalization of the judiciary as a whole. As discussed in previous chapters, while this is often dated to the 1970s and 1980s, the roots of this turn are visible at the transnational scale in bipartisan support for the logic of the commercial exception in the 1950s and 1960s. From the 1970s on, however, this commitment to market logics and the ever-sharper separation of politics from economics became more and more dominant. This was part of the context for the extension of judicial territory during the debt crises of the 1980s, which promoted neoliberalization through supporting the primacy of contract rights and through the abstraction of "the economy" from all surrounding context.

The neoliberalization of the courts had only grown stronger by the twenty-first century. Some legal scholars, referencing the high point of free market liberalism and anti-regulatory fervor at the start of the twentieth century, have referred to a new Lochner era under the Roberts Court.[9] This has been dramatically apparent in the reinterpretation of the First Amendment to give money and advertising the same protections as human speech, as in the infamous case of *Citizens United*.[10] It is true that the Court's conservative majority has been the most extreme in pushing these promarket views. Yet, this should not obscure the fact that the broader neoliberalization of US law, including the commitment to a sharp public/private distinction and the economization of many social questions, has been bipartisan. This is especially clear in the treatment of transnational economic relations with foreign governments. At this scale, the neoliberalization of the judiciary and the expansion of US judicial territory have gone hand in hand, continuing a process that began in the New Deal era, and has continued through the Reagan, Bush, and Clinton eras and into the twenty-first century.

In this chapter, I examine the vulture fund litigation against Argentina in the 2010s in the context of the long history of judicial expansion. I first explain how and why the case provoked such widespread public criticism and what is missing from common explanations for the courts' actions. I situate the case historically as standing at the conjuncture of over sixty years of expanding judicial territory, on the one hand, and the rise of a new class of specialized distressed debt investors with legal expertise on the other. I then examine both the pari passu and the discovery branches of the litigation, showing how, in each case, the courts built on but went beyond previous strategies for extending US judicial territory. In both cases, the redefinition of the public/private and foreign/domestic distinctions continued, if in more extreme ways. More unusual was the fact that the courts in these cases no longer saw any need to respect US foreign policy or the views of the US executive branch. Toward the end of the chapter, I consider the implications of the case for the resurgence of neoliberalism in Argentina, as well as for judicial territoriality more broadly. I end with a provisional discussion of what the split between the executive and the judiciary in this case signals for the future of US judicial territory.

It is likely that no contracts case has ever received as much public attention as *NML Capital v. Argentina*.[11] Dozens of third parties filed briefs in the case.[12] On Argentina's side, this included, among others, investors who had restructured their defaulted bonds with Argentina in 2005 and 2010, major US and European payment intermediaries like the Bank of New York Mellon and Euroclear, the IMF, and the governments of France and Mexico. Most strikingly, in contrast to most previous extensions of US judicial territory, the US executive branch under the Obama Administration weighed in on Argentina's behalf. On the vulture funds' side, amici included a variety of individual (or "retail") holders of Argentine bonds, law professors specializing in business law, other institutional investors, and the Washington Legal Foundation. The latter is a conservative free market law firm, lobbying group, and think tank, which law and political economy scholar Amy Kapczynski has linked directly to the recent "lochnerization" of the First Amendment.[13]

The Supreme Court's 2014 decisions in the case were condemned by activists, international organizations, government officials, economists, and financial journalists around the world as an outrageous victory for predatory investors and a shocking extension of US jurisdiction. Argentina received official expressions of support from across Latin America, including from the Economic Commission for Latin America and the Caribbean (CEPAL), PARLASUR (the parliamentary body of MERCOSUR, the Southern Common Market), the Bolivarian Alliance for the Peoples of Our America, and the Organization of American States (minus the United States), each of which criticized predatory holdout funds and the US court rulings and worried about negative effects on future restructurings.[14] Echoing longstanding postcolonial efforts to link political and economic sovereignty, Argentine Foreign Minister Héctor Timerman told a gathering of the Organization of American States that "we are talking about sovereignty . . . and thus we can see that this issue is much more than a simple economic calculation."[15] The rulings even sparked a (failed) attempt by the UN General Assembly to establish a binding sovereign debt restructuring mechanism that would make such holdout litigation illegal.[16] Criticism was not limited to the Global South. Veteran *Financial Times* writer Martin Wolf, for instance, called the rulings "extortion backed by the US judiciary."[17]

Some critics were motivated by sympathy for Argentina. Many more were concerned by what they saw as the dangerous systemic implications of the case for future sovereign debt restructurings. Despite widespread critiques of the legal bases for the rulings, most explanations for how and why they had been decided were unsatisfactory. Those most sympathetic to the courts suggested that Judge Griesa was so frustrated with Argentina's protracted resistance that he made a poor legal decision.[18] This, however, does not explain why both the Second Circuit and the Supreme Court failed to strike down Griesa's decisions. Harsher critics condemned Judge Griesa as a tool of the vulture funds, finance capitalism, and US economic imperialism.[19] This view is both partially accurate and incomplete. While Griesa's injunction did help the holdout creditors, it also undermined many other financiers by preventing payments to the exchange bondholders and interfering with the daily operations of influential banks and payment intermediaries.[20]

The long history of judicial expansion is missing from both explanations. Across the board, critics have framed the rulings as full of bad legal reasoning, improperly extraterritorial, and anomalous deviations from the rule of law. The Kirchner administration itself characterized Griesa and his rulings as "legal colonialism," "absurd trickery," "contrary to common sense," and "judicial malpractice."[21] In fact, they were not anomalous at all. Far from mere frustrated error or unprecedented example of judicial imperialism, the Argentina decisions together represent just one more step in a long history of gradually expanding US judicial territory. It is only in the context of judges' changing expectations about their own authority over foreign sovereign governments that the courts' intense frustration with Argentina and support for a handful of unpopular hedge funds makes sense.

At the same time, this case did represent a deviation from previous episodes of judicial expansion in two ways. First, rather than claiming new pieces of transnational space one bit at a time as in previous cases, here the courts asserted much more sweeping authority over the actions of both private financiers and a foreign government anywhere except in Argentina. Second, the case produced a new split within the US government over where the boundaries of US judicial territory should be drawn. From the 1940s through the end of the twentieth century, the expansion of US judicial authority had occurred with the support, and often even at the prodding of the US executive. By the time Griesa formulated his decisions against Argentina in the 2010s, this had changed. From the district court to the Supreme Court, the judges in this case not only ignored, but even scorned the Obama Administration's "political" concerns.

In addition to more than sixty years of case precedent involving the gradual restriction of foreign economic sovereignty and changing expectations about US judicial authority, *NML Capital v. Argentina* was also made possible by the rise of a new class of investors specializing in distressed debt trading. Neither the "exchange bondholders" who agreed to restructure their bonds after Argentina's default nor the holdout creditors who sued Argentina in New York were Argentina's original creditors. Things had changed since the 1980s debt crisis. That crisis primarily involved loans made to Third World governments by a relatively small number of Western banks. The gradual resolution of that crisis, however, altered the way sovereign debt markets operated. The Brady Plan and other restructuring deals converted troubled loans into bonds—discrete financial contracts denominated in relatively small amounts that are issued (i.e., sold) by a debtor, rather than being given or extended as a lump sum by one or more banks. By the 1990s, almost all new sovereign debt issuance took the form of bonds, rather than bank loans.

The shift from loans to bonds transformed sovereign debt markets.[22] Most importantly here, it changed the composition of a sovereign's creditors before and during crises. In the 1980s, the banks holding the loans when the crisis hit were the same banks that had signed the original loan contracts. This is no longer the case. The shift to bonds, which can be bought and traded in relatively small quantities, has allowed a much larger array of financial institutions to participate in sovereign debt markets. It has also meant that, when a crisis threatens, investors can offload their bonds onto other financiers—as long as someone is willing to buy them.

Beginning in the 1990s, a new class of boutique investors emerged to meet this need. These investors specialize in "distressed debt"—that is, they buy bonds before or during a crisis for well below face value. This makes it safer for more standard investors to participate in what would otherwise be very risky investments. This allows both mainstream investors and distressed debt specialists to go after "high yield" assets in a context of flagging profits outside the financial sector.[23]

Distressed debt investors are often applauded for "providing liquidity" to debt markets. Yet, they are willing to buy this debt, of course, only because they profit from it. They do so either by participating in sovereign debt restructurings in which even the haircuts they accept leave them with more than they spent on their bonds; *or* by suing sovereign debtors for the full value of those bonds plus interest.[24] Litigation is not simply a last resort for these creditors. The fact that it is easier for bondholders than for bank lenders to sue was understood from early on as an advantage of the shift from loans to bonds.[25] It was the extension of US judicial territory in the context of the 1980s debt crises that made this strategy effective. Once *Allied, Weltover*, and related cases had ensured that US courts would support holdout creditors against sovereign debtors, a small number of investors, many with legal training, began scouring markets for distressed bonds on which such litigation could be brought.

It was in this context that Elliott Management, one of the most famous vulture funds and parent company of the hedge fund NML Capital that would spearhead litigation against Argentina after 2001, began to specialize in sovereign debt. Elliott was founded by Paul Singer in 1977.[26] In 1995, Singer, himself a former lawyer, hired two other lawyers to assist him in purchasing secondary market sovereign debt. Jay Newman, who would go on to oversee the firm's later litigation against Argentina, had begun investing in "emerging market" debt soon after the debt crisis began in 1983. He pursued this work first for Lehman Brothers, then Dillon Reed, then Morgan Stanley. In 1993, he established his own offshore investment fund (the Percheron Fund), focusing on emerging market debts. In the same year, he began helping another offshore fund, Water Street Bank & Trust Limited, alongside lawyer Michael Straus. Straus already had a long history of suing sovereign debtors. He had been involved in over a dozen such suits in the United States. At the advice of Newman and Straus, Water Street purchased the debts of and brought suit in New York against the Ivory Coast, the Republic of Congo, Poland, the Polish People's Republic, Panama, and Ecuador. They also filed suit in London against Ecuador, Panama, and Poland. Straus was separately involved in lawsuits against Paraguay, Ecuador, and Zaire. Water Street disbanded in 1995.[27] Soon after, Straus and Newman formed another company in order to sue the Democratic Republic of the Congo.

Meanwhile, after being hired by Singer in 1995, Newman and Straus led Elliott in the purchase of and successful litigation on distressed Panamanian and Peruvian debt. *Elliott Assocs., L.P. v. Republic of Peru* was especially important for establishing the legality of the holdout creditor strategy. Peru had just negotiated a Brady agreement with most of its commercial creditors. Singer and Newman knew the terms of that deal when they purchased Peruvian bonds. Yet, in a deposition, Singer explained that those terms were unacceptable to him and that "Peru would either . . . pay us in full or be sued."[28] At the time, New York's "champerty doctrine" ostensibly barred investors from buying claims *in order* to sue. Based on Singer's deposition, as well as the litigation history of Singer, Newman, and Straus, the District Court for the Southern District of New York's Judge Sweet thus initially ruled against Elliott.[29]

The Second Circuit, however, reversed Sweet's decision, with an interpretation of champerty so narrow as to make the doctrine meaningless.[30] In short, the court ruled that Elliott's primary purpose had not been to sue, but rather to "obtain full payment"—if Peru had just paid up, Elliott would not have sued at all.[31] The court further noted that the champerty defense was inconsistent with precedent establishing that the United States' interest in enforcing debts outweighed its interest in promoting debt restructurings. Furthermore, the court argued, it would be contrary to the financial interests of New York City.[32] In 2004, the New York State legislature formally eliminated the champerty defense for any claim over $500,000.[33] Elliott allegedly lobbied the legislature to pass this bill.[34]

Together, the expansion of US judicial territory over sovereign debt relations in *Allied* and *Weltover*, along with the elimination of the champerty defense, made it possible for a new accumulation strategy based on litigation to emerge. Creditor litigation against sovereign debtors in default has become more and more common since. In perhaps the most thorough empirical study of sovereign debt litigation to date, Schumacher et al. identify 158 distinct lawsuits against thirty-four defaulting sovereigns between 1976 (the year the FSIA was passed) and 2010, with the number of suits rising from two per decade in the 1970s to twelve in the 1980s to sixty-one in the 1990s and eighty-three in the 2000s.[35]

Geographically, this litigation is concentrated in New York, with London a significant second. Of the suits in Schumacher et al.'s study, eighty-nine targeted Latin American or Caribbean countries (with fifty against Argentina alone following its 2001 default), fifty-four targeted African countries, thirteen targeted Asian countries, and two targeted European countries. While most countries sued are middle-income or emerging market debtors like Peru or Argentina (because these are the countries that have issued the most high-yield commercial debt), the world's poorest countries have also been hit. Of the 158 cases identified, forty-seven involved claims against the Heavily Indebted Poor Countries (HIPC). Claims against the most impoverished countries can often amount to significant percentages of those countries' GDPs.[36]

Although buying debt on the cheap in order to sue can be a long process, it frequently leads to huge payouts. While these funds do sometimes fail to collect, most holdouts have succeeded in getting paid most of the time. Sometimes they are paid through the formal satisfaction of court judgments. More often, the pressure of litigation eventually leads a debtor country to settle with the holdout creditor out of court. Holdout creditors' returns are often impossible to calculate, both because the amounts negotiated in settlements are often kept secret and because the price holdouts originally paid for the bonds they hold is usually unknown. Where estimates are possible, however, returns have been astronomical. For example, before its big win against Argentina, Elliott Management is estimated to have made a profit of between 60 and 300 percent suing Panama and around 400 percent suing Peru. Other hedge funds have made 33–40 percent off Vietnamese debt, 270 percent off Yemen's debt, and 400 percent off the Democratic Republic of the Congo.[37] It was vulture funds like those in these suits that would push US judicial territory further than ever before in litigation against Argentina in the 2000s.

NML CAPITAL V. ARGENTINA

When the Argentine government defaulted on over $80 billion of sovereign debt in December 2001, it was the largest sovereign default in history. It came on the heels of two-plus years of severe financial strain, rising unemployment, and desperate attempts to prevent Argentine banks from collapsing. Though Argentina defaulted "unilaterally"—that is, without the permission of the IMF or commercial creditors—the country did not simply write off its debts. Instead, Argentina paid off its remaining $9.8 billion debt to the IMF in 2005 and declared it and its monitoring programs unwelcome in the country. In the same year, private bondholders agreed to swap about 76 percent of defaulted bonds for new ones at a nominal loss of around 75 percent.[38] In 2010, most of Argentina's remaining debt was restructured under the same terms. The new bonds were issued under US, English, Japanese, and Argentine law and in dollars, euros, yen, and pesos, respectively. Argentina immediately began making payments on these "exchange bonds."[39]

The remaining 7 percent of Argentina's bondholders refused to participate in these exchanges. Instead, these holdouts sued Argentina for recovery on the defaulted bonds. Thousands of individual or retail investors, mainly Italian pensioners, pursued arbitration through the World Bank's International Center for the Settlement of Investment Disputes.[40] A group of hedge funds sued Argentina in federal New York courts. The most prominent holdout was the hedge fund NML Capital, an offshoot of Elliott Management. The fund first began purchasing discounted Argentine bonds shortly after the 2001 default and had filed suit against Argentina by 2005.[41] It continued purchasing discounted Argentine debt on secondary markets at least as late as 2007, even as it failed to collect any payments in ongoing litigation.[42] NML Capital was joined by several other vulture funds, including Aurelius Capital (run by Mark "The Terminator" Brodsky, a former employee of Elliott Management), Blue Angel Capital, and Olifant Fund, along with a handful of retail investors. I will refer to these plaintiffs collectively as NML et al.

NML et al. easily won judgments against Argentina. Despite decades of growing judicial authority over the economic decisions of foreign governments, however, there was still no formal way to force an unwilling sovereign to obey US courts. Argentina was unwilling. This does not mean that Argentina refused to participate in the litigation. Argentina spent millions hiring lawyers from Cleary Gottlieb Steen & Hamilton, a prestigious international law firm based in Manhattan that specializes in representing governments in complex business matters, with particular expertise in sovereign debt restructurings and litigation. Yet, despite participating in years of litigation, Argentina refused to obey the court orders against it.

Although formally difficult, enforcing US judgments against foreign sovereigns has rarely been an obstacle in practice.[43] Given the need for continued access to global markets and loans, very few sovereigns are willing to risk disobedience. Argentina's refusal was made possible by unique political economic conditions. By declaring default, Argentina gained respite from interest payments and found a breathing space from which to reconfigure its economic model. Under President Nestor Kirchner and then his wife President Cristina Fernandez de Kirchner, Argentina reversed the classic neoliberal policies it had implemented at the behest of the IMF in the 1990s. Instead, the government pursued an anti-austerity approach combining industrial subsidies, increased welfare payments, and other developmental policies. It also imposed capital controls and currency restrictions to combat capital flight and inflation. These policies, combined with growing Chinese demand for soy, fueled an impressive economic recovery and a large trade surplus from 2003 on, reflected in a rising GDP and decreasing unemployment and inequality.[44] It was this recovery and surplus that temporarily freed Argentina from needing access to new international loans. This removed the vulture funds' primary source of economic leverage over indebted countries. In addition, the Kirchners made the critique of US economic imperialism, the IMF, and neoliberalism central to their national narrative.[45] Refusing to pay the vulture funds was a popular component of this critique among the Kirchners' supporters.

Ironically, it was Argentina's refusal to pay the vulture funds that provided the terrain on which those funds and US courts grew even stronger. In two distinct but connected cases, the courts overturned the standard spatial logic of the FSIA, claiming US judicial authority over the entire world *except* Argentina; they rejected any characterization of the case as political, to the point of scornfully dismissing the US executive's foreign policy concerns; and they suggested that the public/private distinction should perhaps be jettisoned altogether. The result was a further increase in the power of private creditors over sovereign debtors and a more extreme extension of US judicial territory than ever before.

MAKING JUDGMENTS ENFORCEABLE: THE PARI PASSU ORDER AND INJUNCTION

Argentina's resistance to the holdouts in the early 2000s brought the continued salience of the enforcement problem to the fore. After being unable to collect on several early judgments against the country, in 2008–2009 NML et al. initiated a new suit in New York on more than $220 million in Argentine bonds.[46] This time, they pursued a new strategy designed to make judgments against sovereigns easier to enforce. First, they promoted an unusual interpretation of the pari passu clause in sovereign bond contracts to argue that Argentina could not pay the exchange bondholders without paying the holdouts first. Second, they connected this to an injunction preventing third-party financial intermediaries anywhere in the world except Argentina from helping the country pay those exchange bondholders. This amounted to an unprecedented extension of US judicial territory. It also pitted the holdouts and the courts against not only Argentina, but also numerous sophisticated New York and foreign financiers and the executive branch of the United States.

Pari passu clauses have been standard in corporate and sovereign bond contracts since at least the early 1900s. Yet, their meaning is notoriously elusive. Pari passu is usually translated from the Latin as "on equal footing." The exact text of the clause in the bonds in question in *NML Capital v. Argentina* reads: "Each series [of bonds] will rank *pari passu* with each other Series."[47] The question is what precisely this means.[48] NML et al. argued that it meant that Argentina could not continue paying the exchange bondholders unless it paid the holdouts in full first.[49]

This unusual interpretation of pari passu had been adopted by a Belgian court in 2000 on behalf of NML Capital's parent company Elliott Management in litigation against Peru.[50] That ruling had been criticized by many sovereign debt experts for being legally wrong and for giving a major advantage to holdout creditors, already considered a hindrance to orderly sovereign debt restructurings.[51] Griesa was well aware of these criticisms. When Argentina's creditors first made a similar argument in 2004, he had refused to rule on the issue at all.[52] In 2011, however, he changed his mind, accepting the holdouts' interpretation.[53] The Second Circuit upheld the decision in August 2013.[54] The Supreme Court declined to review the pari passu decision in 2014, thus leaving it in effect.[55] This was a major victory for holdout creditors, and it was this aspect of the case that provoked the most widespread public outrage. Yet, on its own, it was no more *enforceable* than any other order. To address this, Griesa and the vulture funds crafted a supplementary "injunction."[56]

Court judgments are legally binding decisions based on existing common and statutory law. Each judgment itself becomes law and implies at least potential generalizability to future cases. Injunctions, in contrast, are ad hoc remedies crafted to enforce judgments when a judge feels that "the equities" require it. Injunctions do not have legal status as precedent per se, though they can, of course, be copied. While not unheard of, injunctions have been rare in sovereign debt cases.[57] Indeed, a direct injunction on sovereign behavior is no more enforceable than any other court order. In this case, however, Griesa did not target Argentina directly. Instead, he forbade all *other* financiers from helping Argentina process payments to the exchange bondholders. Anyone who contravened this order would be held in contempt of court.

This injunction was unprecedented in scope. It purported to apply to "all parties involved, directly or indirectly, in advising upon, preparing, processing, or facilitating any payment on the Exchange Bonds."[58] It contained no explicit spatial limits. The injunction applied equally to financiers in New York, Luxembourg, or Belgium, and to not only New York, but also English law bonds. Griesa even prohibited Argentina from rerouting its payments to avoid US financial institutions altogether.[59] Only Argentine territory itself was beyond the injunction's reach.

The injunction was fiercely contested by Argentina and its lawyers, as well as by the exchange bondholders, the US executive branch, and major financial intermediaries. All these parties saw it as improperly interfering with the contract rights of the exchange bondholders, the normal processing of financial payments, and the proper scope of US judicial authority. More specifically, they argued that the injunction improperly seized funds it had no legal right to. At the start of a payment, they reasoned, those funds were sovereign property in Argentina and thus immune from seizure under the rules of the FSIA. By the time payments on the dollar-denominated, New York law bonds reached New York, they were already under the control of the Bank of New York Mellon and belonged to the exchange bondholders, not to Argentina. Payments on the euro-denominated, English law bonds, moreover, never "enter the U.S. or flow through U.S. entities" at all.[60] As Euroclear, one of two major European financial clearing houses, put it, this meant that, by forbidding payment on the euro exchange bonds, "the District Court purports to regulate and control the conduct of institutions and activities with little or no connection to the United States."[61]

Argentina reiterated all these arguments, while also putting more emphasis than other parties on the sanctity of territorial sovereignty. Its lawyers criticized Griesa's injunction for preventing Argentina from "making payments outside the United States" to the exchange bondholders unless it first paid the vulture funds "with funds also located outside the United States that are categorically immune from attachment and restraint under the Foreign Sovereign Immunities Act."[62] "A greater affront to sovereignty and sovereign immunity," Argentina concluded, "is harder [sic] to imagine."[63]

The courts rejected all these concerns. Their argument rested in part on the simple fact that they *needed* the injunction in order to enforce the pari passu order.[64] Euroclear again neatly captured the court's logic:

> The circular nature of the [Second Circuit] Court's reasoning is self-evident. The Court posits that it has jurisdiction over activities in foreign countries because otherwise the Court's order concerning those activities would be "for naught." The Court further holds that it can reach steps in the payment process that take place overseas because it is "necessary" to do so if the Order is to be enforced.[65]

While the public/private distinction was not as central in this case as in many earlier cases, it did play a significant rhetorical role. Argentina and many of its supporters emphasized the country's sovereign status. Griesa, in contrast, suggested repeatedly that Argentina should be treated just like any private actor: "No less than any other entity entering into a commercial transaction, there is a strong public interest in holding the Republic to its contractual obligations."[66]

More technically, the courts and the vulture funds acknowledged that they could not seize (or "attach") Argentine funds in Argentine territory, or directly from the exchange bondholders. However, they sidestepped these problems by asserting different geographies for distinct legal modalities. In effect, they argued that US *injunctive* power extends further than the power to enforce judgments or attach foreign property. The injunction, they said, did not attach funds at all. Rather, it "enjoined" behavior. Furthermore, although it happened to obstruct the actions of third party financiers, this was coincidental—it only directly enjoined Argentina.[67] Thus, there was no violation of the FSIA at all.[68] They dismissed Argentina's objection that this was a mere ruse to circumvent limitations on attachment under the FSIA.[69] As for applying the injunction even to European financial institutions, the courts simply asserted that this was as true for the euro bonds as for the rest.[70]

When the Supreme Court declined to review the case on June 16, 2014, leaving these decisions in force, Argentina defied the US judiciary by making its next payments on the exchange bonds anyways. The country transferred roughly $230 million to the account of BNYM New York and €225 million to the account of BNYM Luxembourg.[71] Not wanting to violate the injunctions, BNYM refused to pass the funds along. Argentina was forced into another default.[72]

The pari passu decision and the injunction that made it effective extended the reach of US courts further than ever before. They effectively brought not only Argentina's economic decisions, but most of the international payments system within potential US judicial territory. Although this was widely criticized in and out of the courtroom as improperly extraterritorial, the decisions, once made, were not challenged. Even the inclusion of European financial institutions did not provoke direct resistance. As of November 2023, this case had already been cited more than thirty times.[73] A more sweeping unilateral expansion of the judicial modality of US power is hard to imagine.

As with the extension of US judicial territory to impede foreign nationalizations in the 1960s and 1970s, or to discipline sovereign debtors in the 1980s and 1990s, the Argentina rulings worked, in the end, not because the United States has any formal authority beyond US borders, but because of its economic dominance—more specifically, because of the dominance of New York finance. Argentina allegedly did consider rerouting its payments to avoid US space altogether. If so, they were unable to find anyone to help them.[74] No significant financial institution was willing to contravene the orders once they had been affirmed. As the exchange bondholders pointed out, rerouting the payments would never work, because "no international bank would risk contempt."[75] The courts' unilateral extension of their own authority in *NML Capital v. Argentina* was possible because no major investor in- or outside the United States can risk losing access to New York's financial or legal space. Conversely, the continued extension of US judicial territory in this case further increased the power of private holdout creditors and of US courts.

HUNTING FOR ASSETS: THE DISCOVERY CASE

While the pari passu decision and injunction amounted to only one more, albeit major step in the expansion of US judicial territory, the case was unusual in that the judiciary and the executive were on opposing sides. In two 2012 briefs signed by attorneys from the Department of Justice, the Department of the Treasury, and the Department of State, the executive branch joined Argentina and the exchange bondholders in criticizing Griesa's injunction.[76] The briefs argued that it violated the FSIA by telling Argentina what to do with immune assets. This amounted to a "breathtaking assertion of extraterritorial jurisdiction. . . . Sovereign property located outside of the United States plainly falls outside the court's enforcement authority."[77]

In striking contrast to its support for judicial expansion in many other cases, here the executive reminded the courts "of the strongly held view of many foreign states that they are not subject to coercive orders of U.S. courts."[78] Moreover, recalling the courts' longstanding concern about not treading on the political side of the political/legal distinction in cases involving foreign governments, the executive expressed its view that, by violating a country's territorial sovereignty, this case could have negative foreign policy implications for the United States:

> The potential for affront is particularly heightened where, as here, the U.S. court purports to control the foreign state's conduct *within its own borders*. The breadth of the injunctions at issue here, which not only purport to exercise jurisdiction over foreign state property, but also have the effect of dictating to a sovereign state the implementation of its sovereign debt policy *within its own territory*, is particularly likely to raise foreign relations tensions.[79]

These decisions would have a "significant, detrimental impact on our foreign relations, as well as on the reciprocal treatment of the United States and its extensive property holdings."[80] One concern was that Griesa's orders could "encourage issuers to issue debt in non-U.S. currencies in order to avoid the U.S. payments system, causing a detrimental effect on the systemic role of the U.S. dollar."[81]

In the past, as we have seen, the courts had taken pains not to embarrass the US executive branch and had often looked to the executive itself to help them decide where the line between political and legal issues lay. This time, however, neither the District Court nor the Second Circuit spent much time at all addressing the executive's concerns—not even to reject them.

The tension between the executive and the judiciary was even more pronounced in the Argentina litigation that did reach the Supreme Court. On June 16, 2014, the same day it declined to review the pari passu decision, the Court issued a ruling in another arm of the case.[82] The Court granted the vulture funds the right to full discovery of "information about Argentina's worldwide assets," including not only commercial assets but also its public assets, such as military planes or diplomatic property.[83] In the process, the Court dismissed not only Argentina's but also the US executive's legal and political concerns about the case. The discovery case received much less public attention than the pari passu case. Yet, it not only effected another extension of US judicial territory, but also highlighted even more clearly the ways in which the judiciary broke down the spatial constraints of the FSIA and attempted to collapse the foreign/domestic, public/private, and political/legal distinctions altogether. It has already been cited almost three hundred times since 2014.[84]

Discovery refers to the practice by which litigating parties demand relevant information in the form of documents, depositions, and so on from their opponents or other actors. In debt cases, discovery is often granted to help creditors locate assets that can be attached to satisfy judgments a debtor has not paid. In sovereign debt cases, holdout creditors often attempt to locate and attach the government's assets abroad, as much to harass the government into paying as to collect on the debt itself. These attempts can be very dramatic. In 2012, for example, NML Capital managed to temporarily seize an off-duty Argentine naval vessel docked in Ghana, and in 2014, it attempted to seize the country's stake in Elon Musk's satellite launch company SpaceX. Attachments of sovereign property, however, remain notoriously difficult and, like these attempts by NML Capital, are often ultimately unsuccessful.

Under the FSIA, attachment is limited to selected "property in the United States of a foreign state . . . used for a commercial activity in the United States."[85] The usual practice has been to apply the same limits to discovery. NML Capital (this time on its own) sought to change this by seeking the right to demand information about Argentina's assets of any kind, public or private, located anywhere in the world. As with the pari passu order and injunction, NML attempted to evade the usual limits on extraterritorial authority by arguing that distinct modalities of judicial power have different geographies. Here, they argued that the FSIA's spatial limits only applied to attachment, not to discovery.[86]

Not surprisingly, Argentina and its lawyers objected to this move, arguing that it violated the FSIA's protections for immune sovereign property, that it improperly sought to make both public and private property subject to discovery, and that it constituted blatant extraterritorial overreach.[87] More surprisingly, the US executive branch objected just as vehemently. In two briefs signed by lawyers from the Department of State and the Department of Justice, the United States argued that granting such extensive discovery rights would not only be improperly extraterritorial, but would also undermine the immunity protections built into the FSIA.[88] US courts, the executive insisted, can only issue discovery with respect to assets over which they could legally order attachment. Since, under the FSIA, US courts can only attach commercial property located in the United States, they have no right to discovery about noncommercial assets in the United States or about any assets located outside the United States. Deciding otherwise would "circumvent the limitations imposed and protections afforded not only by the FSIA, but also by foreign law."[89] Moreover, such a ruling could cause foreign relations issues for the United States, both with Argentina and with other countries in which Argentina's assets were located.

Siding with the vulture funds on every point, the Supreme Court rejected the executive's analysis of the FSIA and dismissed its political concerns outright. In an almost comically literalist opinion, Justice Scalia explained that the text of the FSIA is "comprehensive."[90] The FSIA only mentions attachment. It does not say anything at all about discovery— thus, it does not limit it in any way. Furthermore, even if discovery should be limited to property that can be legally attached, the FSIA only says that the assets of a foreign sovereign *within* the United States must be commercial in order to be attached. It doesn't say anything at all about assets *outside* the United States, and therefore does not require them to be commercial.

Therefore, Scalia reasoned, the FSIA places *no* limits on attachment (or, by extension, discovery) outside the United States.

The US executive objected strongly to this astounding contortion of the FSIA's logic. It reminded the Court that, in 1976 when the FSIA was passed, the presumption was that the United States had no authority *of any kind* outside its own borders. The failure to mention the attachment of extraterritorial property simply reflected the fact that it would have been "unthinkable for a U.S. court . . . to presume to order the attachment of or execution against property of a foreign sovereign abroad."[91] The Supreme Court, however, ignored this point. In its view, only Argentina's own territory remained beyond the reach of US discovery powers—any other country in the world was fair game.

On paper, Scalia justified this analysis with his specious reading of the FSIA. Yet, the trial transcripts show that this move was rooted in a more fundamental desire by several justices, both liberal and conservative, to collapse the foreign/domestic distinction altogether. In an April 2014 hearing, for instance, Scalia repeatedly asked Argentina's lawyers why a US court ordering discovery outside the United States was any different from a New York court ordering discovery in Florida.[92] Justice Breyer, nominated by President Bill Clinton in 1994 and considered to be one of the Court's liberal members, picked up on this theme as well, saying: "Now, you agree that we can go do that in respect to property in California, Florida, and New Mexico. Well, in today's world we want the same information about France, Italy, and Turkey."[93]

Such statements collapse the legal distinction between domestic and foreign and show the justices bristling at the idea of any spatial restraints on their authority. Of course, there are still many cases in which US judges do recognize spatial limits on their authority. Nevertheless, comments like these suggest that, after decades of carefully justifying each new inch of judicial expansion, US judges now see the *possibility* of global reach as natural.

In addition to hacking away at the significance of the foreign/domestic divide in this way, the Court also accepted the vulture funds' attempts to collapse the public/private distinction that had been central to every prior extension of US judicial territory. NML sought discovery not only about Argentina's commercial assets—the only assets *in* the United States that a creditor could pursue—but about its public assets as well.

Both the US executive branch and Argentina's lawyers found this especially egregious.[94] During the trial, even the justices seemed to push back on this point. When asked why NML Capital should be allowed to seek information about Argentina's public assets, NML's lawyer Theodore Olson—the same man who had represented both George W. Bush in the disputed 2000 presidential election and Citizens United in the infamous case of the same name—responded that NML needed information about *all* Argentine assets to be able to tell whether something was actually being *used* for a public purpose. [95] Even "if it's an airline that says Argentine Air Force on the side of it, it still could be commercial property," he argued.[96] This answer perturbed the justices at the time. Even Scalia expressed skepticism.[97] The conservative Chief Justice Roberts observed, "That's pretty intrusive at a sovereign level to say you can find out how many jet fighters Argentina happens to have."[98] Yet, less than two months later, the Court granted NML full rights to discovery of "information about Argentina's worldwide assets generally."[99] Only Justice Ginsburg dissented, and only on this point; she wanted to limit discovery to property used in connection with commercial activities, whether "here or abroad."[100]

The inclusion of Argentina's public assets decentered the distinction that had long been at the heart of all litigation involving foreign sovereigns. Indeed, at moments, the justices seemed to wish to abolish the distinction between public and private, sovereign and nonsovereign altogether. For example, Justice Kagan (another liberal justice nominated by Barack Obama) asked, "What in the text would put a foreign government in a different position than . . . when the suit involved only private parties?" The Justices were apparently not persuaded by US Deputy Solicitor General Edwin Kneedler's point that "a foreign sovereign is not the same as a foreign private person."[101]

This desire to treat Argentina and its assets as they would treat any business entity was mirrored in the Court's conviction that the discovery case was a purely legal matter—not a political one. Just as in the pari passu case, this required dismissing the executive's own views on the case's political significance. The US executive noted that the case had already raised "significant foreign relations concerns" for the United States.[102] Both its briefs explained that immunity from the seizure of state property was intended precisely to prevent such foreign relations problems, and that upholding such broad discovery rights

> would invade substantially a foreign state's sovereignty in an especially
> sensitive area and would be inconsistent with the comity principles
> the FSIA embodies. It would risk reciprocal adverse treatment of the

United States in foreign courts. And it would more generally threaten harm to the United States' foreign relations on a variety of fronts.[103]

This decision would "strongly increase the possibility that U.S. courts would issue orders that constitute an affront to foreign states' coequal sovereignty."[104]

Scalia's utter lack of deference to the opinions of the US government in this case is striking. When Mr. Kneedler began his official statement at the hearing by explaining the executive's concerns about international comity and reciprocity, Scalia interrupted him, butting in with, "Wait, wait, wait, wait, wait, wait, wait, wait. I thought that the whole purpose of the Foreign Sovereign Immunities Act was to protect us from you, from the State Department and the government coming in and saying, Oh, you know, in this case, grant this one, deny that one." A few minutes later, Scalia came close to accusing Mr. Kneedler of lying about the concerns of other countries, again interrupting him midsentence to demand, "Why haven't they told us? They have to ask you to pass it along?"[105]

Scalia concluded the Court's published decision on a similarly scornful note:

> Nonetheless, Argentina and the United States urge us to consider the worrisome international-relations consequences of siding with the lower court. Discovery orders as sweeping as this one, the Government warns, will cause "a substantial invasion of [foreign states'] sovereignty," and will "[u]ndermin[e] international comity." Worse, such orders might provoke "reciprocal adverse treatment of the United States in foreign courts," and will "threaten harm to the United States' foreign relations more generally." These apprehensions are better directed to that branch of government [i.e. Congress] with authority to amend the [FSIA].[106]

This is the extent of the discussion of the United States' political concerns in that decision.

RETURNING TO THE NEOLIBERAL FOLD

The split between the US judiciary and the executive in this litigation raises important questions about the future of the relationship between judicial territory and US geopolitical economic interests. I return to these questions in the book's conclusion. In the rest of this chapter, I focus on the impact of these cases on Argentina and their broader implications for defining territorial sovereignty.

Like a long string of cases before it, NML *Capital v. Argentina* further restricted the economic sovereignty of a foreign government, subjecting it to US judicial authority, private creditors, and neoliberal market logics. The Supreme Court's 2014 decisions forced Argentina to choose between paying the vulture funds or defaulting once again on its external debts. Under President Cristina Kirchner, the government chose the latter, framing this refusal as part of the country's resistance to predatory vulture funds and financial imperialism.[107] Yet, the Argentine economy was much weaker than it had been when the government first refused to pay the holdouts. Collapsing international demand for exports, rising inflation, and decreasing real wages were already causing serious strain. The technical default caused by the US courts made it impossible for Argentina to access new loans to soften the economic pain. This was enough to affect the November 2015 presidential elections.

Vulture funds—and whether to pay them or not—were an important topic in both campaigns.[108] As Martín Guzmán, a heterodox Argentine economist, who has worked and written extensively on sovereign debt with Joseph Stiglitz, explains: "The [Kirchner] administration presented the saga as a case where the population and the politicians had to take one side, that of the 'Fatherland,' or that of the 'Vultures'—the slogan was 'Patria o Buitres,' or 'Fatherland or Vultures.' Anyone supporting full payment to the vultures would be against the Patria."[109] The opposition leader Mauricio Macri, in contrast, framed himself as a probusiness centrist, who was ready to take a different tack with Argentina's creditors. In the end, Kirchner lost the election.

The immediate effect was to shift Argentina from its "postneoliberal" approach back to overt neoliberalism.[110] President Macri immediately began dismantling the developmentalist regulations of the Kirchner era. Within months he settled with the vulture funds for far more than the original $1.6 billion originally sought by NML et al. As many had predicted, once NML et al. succeeded, a host of "me too" plaintiffs piled into the courts to sue Argentina as well.[111] In total, Argentina paid its institutional holdout creditors roughly $9.3 billion. Another $1.35 billion went to Italian retail investors who held out to the end.[112] NML Capital and its parent company Elliott alone received $2.4 billion in return for bonds with a face value of $617 million—more than a 400 percent profit on the bonds' original value. Since they purchased those bonds for far less than face value, the profit was actually much higher. Their real return has been estimated at from *ten to fifteen times* their original investment.[113] With this victory, Elliott's decade-long bet on Argentina "earned a place in history as one of the greatest hedge fund trades ever."[114]

Paying off the holdouts catapulted Argentina back into full participation in international debt markets. To make these payments, Macri's government quickly issued $16.5 billion in new international bonds—more than double what any developing country had raised in a single issue up to that point.[115] He also deregulated Argentina's financial markets, hoping to attract new investment into the country. Although the Obama administration had opposed the courts' decisions, it was pleased with the eventual results, noting that "the United States has a significant, and more general, policy interest in promoting open, market-based economies and sound macroeconomic policy in Latin America. Argentina's bold macroeconomic reforms set a positive example for other countries in the region."[116]

Yet, since 2016, Argentina's situation has only worsened. Macri's government reduced the country's current account deficit, but only at the cost of triggering a new recession and a drop in imports. By the end of his term, poverty and inflation had both risen, fueled in part by a 2018 currency crisis. In addition, Macri brought the IMF into the country once again. In exchange for the usual conditionalities, he accepted a $57 billion bailout loan—the largest ever in the IMF's history.[117]

This deteriorating economic situation contributed to Macri's defeat and the return of Kirchner's Peronist party in the very next presidential election in Fall 2019—just three months before the COVID-19 pandemic began. President Alberto Fernandez was faced with the unenviable situation of navigating the economic mess left over from the Macri administration while attempting to avoid austerity in the context of pandemic lockdowns and a global economic crisis. Like many other low- and middle-income countries, Argentina was soon facing yet another severe debt crisis. In May 2020, it defaulted for the ninth time in the country's history. Fernandez was soon negotiating new debt restructurings on $65 billion in debt held by private commercial creditors, $70 billion owed to multilateral institutions, and several billion further owed to wealthy governments. After a brief "market friendly" sally back into international debt markets under Macri, Argentina is now saddled with both further economic woes at home and significant new debt burdens stretching into the future.[118] The country's ongoing economic problems contributed to yet another wild political swing when the Peronists were ousted, yet again, by the election of the far-right libertarian Javier Milei as president in November 2023.

The role that US courts will play in the future of Argentina and other Third World debtors in the wake of the pandemic is not yet clear. Hold-out litigation has become the target of increasing criticism since the early 2000s. Contractual clauses intended to mitigate the threat of holdouts are becoming common but will likely be ineffective in many circumstances.[119] Debt activists routinely call for more radical changes, such as laws outlaw-ing holdout litigation altogether. Yet, neither courts nor governments have responded to these calls, and the effect of the possibility of such litigation on debtor states remains significant. Schumacher et al. "find that litigation and legal threats played a role in almost all recent debt distress cases and reportedly increased creditor bargaining power."[120] Even where holdout litigation does not materialize, it is worth remembering that the "shadow of the law" is long—all debt contracts and debt trading now occur with the results of the Argentina litigation in mind.[121]

REMAPPING JUDICIAL TERRITORY

Attempts to explain the courts' decisions in *NML Capital v. Argentina* as the misguided result of Griesa's frustration with a recalcitrant debtor may be partially accurate. But if so, then the extreme anger Argentina's behav-ior provoked, despite longstanding limits on the ability to enforce orders against foreign sovereigns, itself needs explanation. Harsher criticisms of the courts as serving the vulture funds and US financial imperialism are also partially correct. Yet, they have tended to overlook the fact that, in ruling for the vulture funds, the courts not only hurt Argentina but also went against the interests of many sophisticated investors and payment intermediaries, and of the US executive. It is possible that the courts are allies not just of finance, but of the most widely criticized and predatory financiers. Why this would be so, however, is not immediately clear.

Situating the case in relation to a long history of judicial expansion sug-gests a stronger explanation for both the courts' anger and their willingness to defend the vulture funds against the interests of other powerful actors. Decades of expanding judicial territory have altered the judiciary's expec-tations for its own authority; from the district to the federal level, judges have become accustomed to the gradual extension of their own power and learned to bristle at limits on that power—at least in so-called private, commercial cases.[122]

Far from aberrant or mistaken deviations from the normal rule of law, then, *NML Capital v. Argentina* can be seen as one more step in the history of judicial territory I have been tracing in this book. Yet, the courts in this case did also alter the logic of judicial expansion in some important ways. Most dramatically, they not only remapped the public/private, foreign/domestic, and political/legal distinctions yet again, but questioned their significance altogether.

With respect to the public/private divide, *NML Capital v. Argentina* effected another expansion of the categories of the private and commercial and a concomitant restriction of the domain of the public and political. Where previous judges had done this by changing the characterization of particular acts (e.g., debt issuance or operating state-owned enterprises), here judges questioned the very existence of a privileged sovereign domain. Of course, this does not mean that the public/private distinction is no longer important in US law. Central bank assets, for example, are still considered political enough to remain largely beyond the reach of US courts. Yet, by challenging whether a public and political domain beyond judicial reach exists at all, *NML Capital v. Argentina* contributed to the further depoliticization of economic relations in US legal practice.

The NML litigation also changed the parameters of the courts' more explicitly spatial reasoning. Until the 1970s, US judicial authority was extended primarily through the introduction and expansion of the commercial exception. After that, the FSIA and the growing importance of intangible financial property made the foreign/domestic distinction increasingly central. Until the end of the twentieth century, even as these spatial categories were manipulated, the general rule remained that US courts only had power over government acts defined as occurring within or having direct effects on the United States. In both the pari passu and discovery arms of the NML litigation, in contrast, the courts cast aside this restraint. They claimed to have authority (of certain kinds) over property and activities anywhere in the world except in the territory of the sovereign being sued. Here, the whole world *except* Argentina became part of US judicial space.

Does this sort of sweeping assertion of judicial authority signify a break with the territorial logics of the past? Does it validate arguments about a shift away from territoriality toward a widespread flexibilization of jurisdiction in contemporary law? It is true that in *NML Capital v. Argentina* US judges were less concerned about either US borders or about carefully justifying any extension beyond them than they had been in the past. This may signify a transition in the way US *claims* to authority over foreign sovereigns are made. Yet, that expansion remains territorial in important ways.

First, this case involved at most a partial move beyond existing spatio-legal logics. However inclined they may be to expand their own authority, US courts have not rejected all spatial limits. That is why, for example, they carefully justified both the injunction and discovery orders in this case by drawing distinctions between the geographies of different modalities of legal power. As we have seen in other examples throughout the book, the careful definition of spatial boundaries becomes not less, but more central in these moments.

Second, NML *Capital v. Argentina*, like other decisions involving foreign governments, was still fundamentally territorial insofar as it revolved around a *struggle over* the boundaries of US judicial authority. While the vulture funds and the courts dismissed Argentina's territorial claims as irrelevant, Argentina continued to make them. Every other major party in the case, from the US executive branch, to the exchange bondholders, to payment intermediaries caught up in Griesa's injunction also spent time debating where US judicial space ended and Argentine or European space began. While the private investors involved may not be especially concerned about territorial sovereignty in its own right, even they base their accumulation strategies on certain assumptions about the rules of territorial sovereignty—rules that were altered in this case, much to their frustration. For Argentina and even, within limits, the US executive branch, the desire to protect at least the principle of national sovereignty was more immediate. No matter how much ground governments have lost to US courts since the 1940s, the boundaries of US judicial power remain an important site of contestation over the contours of national economic sovereignty in the postcolonial era.

Finally, NML Capital upset so many around the world precisely because these decisions were unusually and unilaterally far-reaching. The pari passu and discovery decisions do not simply reflect a general tendency in the transformation of global law toward more transnational judicial authority over sovereign governments. Rather, they illustrate as forcefully as ever that US courts are uniquely positioned to limit the sovereignty of other countries. If Zimbabwean or, for that matter, Argentine courts claimed authority over US investors in the same way, they would be laughed at. The US judiciary's ability to make these claims remains dependent on the co-constitution of US economic and legal power. The Argentina decisions bolstered already powerful US hedge funds and, in the long run, perhaps all private creditors. These claims stand unchallenged because of the extensive reach of the US economy, specifically US finance, and because of the unwillingness of any major international investor to risk legal sanction by US courts. As with all forms of territorial control, the ability to hold or seize disputed ground depends on the power of the occupying force.

Conclusion

This book has examined the transnational extension of US judicial authority over the economic decisions of foreign sovereign governments. I have argued that, since World War II, the extension of this judicial territory has been a significant but largely overlooked modality of American empire. It has underwritten the unilateral expansion of US governance over other states, while supporting US (and global) investors and helping perpetuate the continued extraction of money and resources from South to North. At the same time, a key function of this modality of US power has been to obscure and legitimize these expansionary and extractive tendencies, cloaking them in esoteric legal details and the depoliticized language of the rule of law, while also funneling contestation from other states onto the terrain of US courts. In the process, US judicial territory has contributed to the production of both US power and the postwar international economic order and helped to forge the particular form of (neo)liberal globalization that became dominant in the late twentieth century.

This modality of US power goes beyond informal influence on either international institutions or the domestic affairs of other countries, and it goes beyond mere economic dominance, although it is bound up with all these things. The transnational extension of US judicial territory involves the institutionalized, juridical extension of the authority of US domestic law and courts over the affairs and into the territory of other, supposedly formally autonomous nation-states.

Cases dealing with foreign sovereign governments are only a subset of the broader transnational extension of US commercial law, which includes a far larger number of cross-border cases between two or more private corporations. This whole category of transnational US law is significant for the co-constitution of US power and the postwar international economic order. Yet, litigation involving foreign governments, made possible by the gradual weakening of US foreign sovereign immunity and act of state rules, is uniquely important in several ways.

Most immediately, it allows us to see that the development of transnational US commercial law was not simply driven by a general belief in the value of US-style commercial rules. Rather, it spread first and foremost in response to and through targeting the anti- or more-than-capitalist economic practices of Third World states, in ways that have shifted as both the form of US empire and the geopolitical economic context of North-South relations have changed.

In the first few decades after World War II, as Latin American and newly independent states experimented with an array of developmental, interventionist, or socialist economic practices designed to redress the imbalances of colonialism and give these states more leverage vis-à-vis powerful Western corporations, US investors, judges, and the executive branch (in the form, most importantly, of the Department of State) responded by restricting the long-standing theory of foreign sovereign immunity to remove protections for governments' so-called commercial acts. This involved a gradual effort over two-plus decades, from the publication of the Tate Letter in 1952 to the passage of the FSIA in 1976, to remove immunity protections for state-owned enterprises, as well as for acts related to government involvement in development contracts and foreign aid programs. Insofar as governments engaged in these activities, they would now be treated as mere private actors. The effect was that, just as many new states gained formal sovereignty for the first time, the legal definition of sovereignty itself was curtailed.

This struggle between postcolonial governments and US courts took on even more urgent dimensions in the wake of the Cuban Revolution and Cuba's mass nationalizations of US property. These expropriations were only the most dramatic of a much broader wave of Third World expropriations of Western property in the 1960s and 1970s. Even more than state-owned enterprises and government-negotiated development contracts, expropriations were at the heart of Third World attempts to wrest control of national resources from Western corporations and to address the uneven economic development that continued to define North-South dynamics. This issue was especially central to the most ambitious alternative world-making project of the era—the attempt to forge a New International Economic Order (NIEO) designed to redistribute wealth from

North to South. The proponents of the NIEO insisted that formal political sovereignty was meaningless without substantive economic sovereignty, and that the ability to expropriate foreign property under the host state's *own* laws was central to the latter.

In this context, the Cuban nationalizations were not only a blow to US investors and an affront to rabidly anti-Communist American judges and politicians, but also part of a broader threat to the postwar economic order the United States had worked so hard to produce. Extending US judicial territory over these nationalizations, which were understood to have occurred in Cuba's own territory and required the restriction of not only foreign sovereign immunity but also the act of state doctrine, was more difficult than curtailing sovereignty for state-owned enterprises and development contracts. It also created more tensions within the judiciary and among different branches of the US government. Yet, by the mid-1970s, the act of state doctrine had been effectively restricted through the weakening of the strict territorial bases of the doctrine in favor of a separation of powers approach and through the creation of a partial commercial exception through which nationalization-adjacent activities could be declared merely private. In combination with the rise of bilateral investment treaties (BITs) and a surge in international arbitration, these changes helped limit the usefulness of nationalizations for postcolonial states and ensured that the rules governing compensation would be those of the United States or US-influenced international law.

The effect of the combined restrictions of foreign sovereign immunity and act of state rules in the decades after World War II was to assert a strict separation between the political and the economic, just when the question of the relationship between political and economic sovereignty was *the* most significant geopolitical struggle of the era. It also established case precedent that would turn out to have important, if unforeseeable effects for the further extension of US judicial territory following the crises of the 1970s. These geopolitical and economic crises led, eventually, to a major reorganization of the global economy and American empire, from which the latter emerged with a stronger focus on the power of Wall Street and the US dollar and with an embrace of neoliberal policies and rationalities. At the same time, the neoliberal counterrevolution of the 1970s and the Third World debt crises of the 1980s signaled the end of the NIEO and of broader Third World efforts to reshape the global political economy. In the context of these debt crises, US judicial territory continued to expand, drawing on earlier case precedent to extend the logic of the commercial exception and redefining the geography of intangible property in order to refuse immunity for debtor governments' efforts to regulate foreign exchange and maintain fiscal stability. The effect was to bolster US dollar hegemony, contract fundamentalism, and the power of private creditors, helping ensure the continued extraction of money into the United States, while also working in tandem with better-known structural adjustment programs to facilitate the broader neoliberalization of the Global South.

Beyond its strategic role in mediating relations among the United States, private corporations, and Third World countries, the expansion of US judicial territory in the 1940s through the 1990s also set the stage for transnational economic governance in the twenty-first century, shaping the legal framework through which current sovereign debt crises, state-owned enterprises, and nationalizations are managed. The increased spatial reach of US judicial power has not made such practices illegal. But it has ensured that they will be governed not by the laws of the state's engaging in such activities, nor by strictly international law, but rather by US domestic law and the procapital, procreditor legal rules this entails. As always, the ability of US courts to claim such far-reaching authority remains dependent on the economic might of the United States and especially New York. US legal power and US economic power continue to support one another. Meanwhile, US courts have claimed more authority than ever before. In the context of the Argentine debt crisis and ensuing vulture fund litigation, they have asserted control, for certain purposes, over the entire world, except Argentina. Although this litigation created an unusual rift between the judiciary and the executive branch, as I discuss in more detail below, it has already shaped further litigation with foreign governments.

Cases involving foreign governments are also uniquely useful for illuminating the significance of transnational law to continued struggles over the legal content and spatial boundaries of territorial sovereignty. Together, the cases examined in this book show how the extension of US judicial territory led to rewriting long-standing rules of territorial sovereignty to extend a judicial modality of US state power over the transnational and even sometimes domestic activities of foreign governments. The result was that, just at the moment of decolonization and the supposed triumph of the nation-state form with its clearcut territorial borders and promises of formal autonomy, the extension of US judicial territory instead began producing new forms of messy, overlapping, and noncontiguous territorial formations and graduated sovereignties. At the same time, situating these changes in relation to earlier US and other imperial formations allows us to see that this represents less a break with some supposedly absolute West-phalian national territoriality, than it does a continuation of previous imperial geographies through new means.

Focusing on the nitty gritty legal mechanisms through which these spatial changes are produced, furthermore, allows us to avoid deterritorializing or even aspatial analyses of the flexibilization of jurisdiction. The complex spatial configuration of overlapping, dynamic, and ambiguous judicial authority today is not a necessary or natural corollary to the rise of cross-border flows in the age of globalization. Instead, focusing on the gradual, fumbling, but also relatively systematic tendency toward US judicial expansion allows us to see how struggles over the spatial boundaries of legal authority have become more, not less, pronounced since the 1950s. Precisely as the global economy has become increasingly integrated and complex, investors, courts, and governments have spent more and more time arguing over exactly how to (re)map judicial space. They have done so not simply in the name of general efficiency or practicality in a complex world, but *strategically*, in order to promote the interests of some state and non-state actors over others.

Exactly how these spatial struggles over the extent of US judicial reach have been carried out, moreover, sheds light on the immense effort it takes to sustain the "as ifs" of liberal capitalism—that is, the consequential fictions that enable the capitalist project to (re)produce itself.[1] In the case of judicial territory, this has centered most importantly on the redefinition and manipulation of key legal dichotomies. This has included recategorizing the foreign/domestic divide—or what counts as outside or inside the United States for the purposes of claiming judicial authority. Redrawing this boundary to expand the category of domestic US space has involved adopting looser rules for determining an act's connection to or effects on the United States, as well as redefining the location of intangible, transnational property.

No less spatial has been the recategorization of the interlocking public/private and political/legal distinctions, which together determine which *modality* of US governance (executive or judicial) will be deployed when and where. Narrowing the domain of the public and political, and expanding that of the private and legal, has been the primary mechanism by which transnational relations with foreign governments that would previously have been seen as foreign policy issues for the executive to handle have been turned into mere private, legal matters for the US judiciary to oversee. This has meant redefining conflicts that would previously have been dealt with through negotiations between at least formally equal sovereign states into allegedly mundane commercial matters for which foreign governments can be subjected to the decisions of the US judiciary.

Meanwhile, the restriction of the category of public activity and the expansion of the category of private, commercial activity has had even more far-ranging implications. By deploying a narrower and narrower view of the public, the extension of US judicial territory has established norms for what constitutes proper state activity, delegitimizing many economic practices of Third World states. The reification and constant expansion of the category of the commercial, premised in many cases on defining the nature of an act as narrowly as possible, has simultaneously promoted contract fundamentalism and contributed to constituting "the economy" in the neoliberal period. These shifting legal logics cannot be explained as mere reflections of the continuing globalization of the economy. Rather, they have helped forge globalization of a particular kind. This is a globalization in which nation-states have increasingly been reduced to the status of mere private companies for the purposes of economic decisions and transactions, and in which these so-called private interactions have been subjected to the legal governance of the most capital friendly jurisdiction in the world.

POSSIBLE FUTURES

There are other alternatives. In critiquing the displacement of Third World sovereignty through the extension of US judicial territory, my goal is not to recommend a return to absolute theories of foreign sovereign immunity and the act of state doctrine. Not only is this highly improbable, but there are also important reasons to be skeptical of total immunity for state actions, especially where things like torture, environmental destruction, or human rights violations are in question. That said, despite a tendency to suggest otherwise in many legal discussions of the subject, the vast majority of cases in which sovereign immunity or act of state rules have in fact been restricted do not involve such issues at all. Rather, it is the *economic* autonomy of states that has been compromised and the "rights" of private investors that have been upheld.

While a return to some idealized form of Westphalian national autonomy is neither possible nor desirable, the current distribution of economic governance among national, transnational, and international institutions is highly undemocratic. It actively promotes the interests of both transnational capitalists and procapitalist political elites and makes resistance to US-style capitalism through the adoption of alternative economic strategies more difficult.

A fairer approach would involve, at a minimum, a repoliticization of questions about foreign sovereign immunity and act of state rules and a reversal of at least some aspects of the commercial exception to return control over key governance issues (like maintaining fiscal stability or deciding how to deal with nationalized resources) to home governments. Such activities are far too important to be subordinated to an anemic if powerful ideology of contract rights above all else. Rather they should be returned to our understanding of the core functions of states and defined (again) as areas in which states *do* have prerogatives that set them apart from mere private actors.

More broadly, there is no reason why US or English or, for that matter, Chinese law should determine when national sovereignty is curtailed or under *which rules* state activities should be governed. This would ideally be decided, instead, by truly international rules—rules based not only on Western ideas about what constitutes good law, but rather on real, democratically produced, international consensus.

Of course, in the current moment, all of this remains highly improbable. Far more likely is that US judicial territory will remain powerful for a long time to come—even as we see, on the one hand, a possible rupture between US judicial territory and broader US geopolitical economic interests, and, on the other, the gradual extension of some other countries' legal territories.

Ironically, US judicial territory is expanding further than ever before at a moment when US empire is facing its biggest challenge in half a century. The initial transnational extension of US judicial territory emerged at a moment of transformation for the United States, as it went from being a regional empire to a global superpower. In the context of decolonization and US professions of anti-imperial sympathy, shifting responsibility for much transnational governance from the executive to the judicial branch became an important way to disguise continued US imperial behaviors behind the supposedly apolitical veil of the rule of law. Judicial territory not only survived the further reconfiguration of US empire in the 1970s and 1980s, but actively responded and contributed to it. As the base of US economic dominance shifted from manufacturing to finance, and US dollar hegemony became a fundamental fact of the global political economy,

US courts began to see bolstering the US dollar and New York finance as part of their mission.

In the twenty-first century, the imperial context has shifted once again. This time, the relationship between judicial territory and US empire is less clear cut. The United States is no longer the world's unquestioned superpower. China presents an increasing challenge to US economic dominance and may well become a military threat as well. Russia's 2022 invasion of Ukraine, more recently, has had the unintended effect of demonstrating that much of the Global South no longer feels compelled to support the United States in what they see as a Western geopolitical struggle.

In this already fraught context of relative US decline, disagreements between the executive and the judiciary over the appropriate borders of US judicial reach have emerged for the first time in decades. This was dramatically on display in the case of *NML Capital v. Argentina*, in which the judiciary not only declined to follow the executive's advice, but scoffed at the very idea that the executive should have any input in the matter at all. While the executive expressed major concerns about the possible foreign relations consequences of a case impinging on what it understood to be significant *political* questions, the judges, from the District Court to the Supreme Court, dismissed the executive's input as irrelevant to what they saw as a purely private, commercial matter.

These tensions between the executive and the judiciary should not be overstated. Despite signs of fracture in the NML litigation, there has yet to be a decisive rupture between the two branches over the boundaries of judicial territory. The executive remains wedded overall to the judicial power it helped develop. Nevertheless, this case is at odds with decades of prior judicial expansion. For most of its history, each step in the extension of US judicial territory depended on detailed analyses of the line between political and legal authority. Even as the modality of US power with responsibility for dealing with foreign sovereigns shifted more and more to the courts, this was justified not by rejecting, but by redrawing these boundaries, with courts constantly linking decisions to changing conceptions of the proper separation of powers. For the most part, this shift was supported by the executive and Congress as much as by the judiciary, and courts continued to show deference to the executive in cases dealing with foreign sovereigns until the end of the twentieth century. In the late 1990s, for example, US courts regularly pointed out that their sovereign debt decisions were in line with US foreign policy goals.[2] *NML Capital v. Argentina* shows how much things have changed.

This change cannot be explained by the Court's recent dramatic political shift to the right. Justice Scalia's derisive tone in the NML litigation may have been typical of him and his dislike of "big government" and the Obama Administration. Yet, unlike more recent cases on abortion, gun rights, environmental regulation, and a host of other important issues, support for the vulture funds suing Argentina did not break down along partisan lines.[3] Of the liberal justices on the Supreme Court for the discovery case, only Justice Ginsburg dissented. Even she did not object to the extension of judicial authority over most of the world per se, but only to including Argentina's *public* assets in the order. Justices Kagan, Sotomayor, and Breyer, the other liberals on the Court, did not dissent at all. What's more, during the trial, they displayed just as much eagerness as Roberts or Scalia to treat Argentina like any private debtor.[4]

The lack of consideration shown by judges of all political slants and at all levels, from the District Court through the Supreme Court, for the executive's opinions in this case can be seen as a sign both of the bipartisan embrace of neoliberal logics by the US judiciary and of just how successful the expansion of US judicial territory since World War II has been. After decades of chipping away at the categories of public and political and expanding those of commercial and legal, many significant geopolitical affairs have been recast as purely private. This has made US courts more and more comfortable claiming authority in transnational disputes that would previously have been left to the executive branch—even when the executive itself objects to judicial intrusion in what it understands to be political matters.

This is especially true because, while individual steps in this process were often calculated and strategic (with judges and other branches of government well aware not only that they were expanding US judicial authority, but also that this would bolster US and/or New York's economic status and increase the power of US investors and courts over other governments), the iterative step-by-step extension of US judicial territory also led to the simultaneous development of new legal techniques and logics. These have included the enlargement of the category of private, commercial activity and the concomitant restriction of the public sphere; the correlated expansion of the legal domain and the shrinking of the political domain; the rejection of the validity of a foreign sovereign's purposes in engaging in economic activities in favor of a focus on the nature of the act, narrowly defined; and the embrace of more and more tenuous or flexible bases for claiming spatial ties to the United States.

Over time, such techniques have become enshrined in US law, making it possible to detach them from the particular contexts in which they were developed. Thus, it no longer necessarily matters whether judges see their decisions as serving the economic or geopolitical interests of the United States or of New York City against the subversive economic practices of foreign states. It is enough for them to view the logics of commercial expansion or spatial flexibilization as normal or common sense. Such logics continue to support further extensions of US judicial territory, whether or not individual judges see that as a goal, and even, as in the Argentina litigation, when the executive branch is opposed to it.

Of course, all this may explain why US courts are now *willing* to ignore the executive branch, but it still leaves open the question of why the views of the judiciary and the executive have, in fact, diverged. At least two explanations are plausible. First, in the specific case of *NML Capital v. Argentina*, the executive may have been motivated by a concern not just for individual American capitalists but for global capitalism as a whole. The Obama Administration made no attempt to rein in the map of judicial territory as it stood in the early 2000s. It only wished to stop its further extension in this case, in part because of worries that these decisions could interfere with the international payments system or future debt restructurings.[5] Unlike private creditors, the US executive sees itself as having a responsibility for maintaining a relatively stable international financial system and a debt restructuring regime that has long served Western aims—something the executive, the IMF, and many economists feared the Argentina litigation would threaten by increasing the power of holdouts beyond acceptable parameters. This was arguably in line with the United States' broader role as both imperial power and "superintendent" of global capitalism.[6]

Another possible explanation for the split between the executive and the judiciary, however, goes beyond the particulars of the NML litigation. Most simply, the declining power of the United States relative to other countries, most importantly China, may have made the US executive branch more cautious about ruffling feathers by unilaterally extending judicial authority abroad. This has not meant any attempt to shrink the map of US judicial territory. New extensions, however, like new seizures of physical territory, are much more noticeable and, therefore, politically riskier. The executive branch may want to preserve the US role as world hegemon within an order that has used judicial territory as a tool for maintaining the international economic status quo. Yet, as the representative of a sovereign state, it does not want the extension of judicial power over sovereign governments to go too far. Certainly, it does not want its own behavior to be challenged by foreign judiciaries, many of whom have been adopting US-style legal rules for some time.

In this light, the emerging split between the views of the judiciary and the executive on the appropriate boundaries of US judicial reach raises pressing questions about the extent to which US judicial territory can be divorced from US geopolitical or economic interests, even as it remains dependent, at root, on US state authority and reconfigured US borders. In other words, can US judicial territory outlast US empire?

In the medium term, at least, I believe the answer is yes. Critical scholars of international political economy have already observed that the US-led liberal international order developed in the service of US interests might well outrun them.[7] This seems likely to be true of judicial territory as well. This is partly due to institutional inertia; although other legal systems have been rapidly Americanizing, New York remains the undeniable leader in commercial legal knowledge, resources, and lawyers. If nothing else, the sheer number of transnational contracts already written under New York law will ensure that New York remains an important legal space for a long time and will make maintaining New York's judicial territory of interest to many powerful parties. Moreover, though produced largely in the service of US capital, US judicial space has been useful not only for American but for many transnational capitalists. Both US and foreign investors have been able to use US law and courts to enforce contracts against foreign governments, as well as against one another. As long as New York's economic power, and thus its legal leverage, remains significant, this will remain true.

At the same time, we will also likely see a gradual shift away from the total dominance of US (and to a lesser extent English) judicial space and toward more use of legal territories anchored in East and Southeast Asian financial hotspots like Singapore, Malaysia, Hong Kong, and China.[8] Indeed, some of these countries are already actively competing with the US for legal authority, and more states are beginning to make extraterritorial claims along US lines.[9] Further, the New York Bar is well aware of growing competition from other jurisdictions especially via competition for governing law clauses in private contracts.[10] Escalating tensions between the US and China, as well as the struggle between the West and Russia over the imposition and avoidance of sanctions in the context of the latter's invasion of Ukraine will likely only accelerate efforts to make other legal territories viable.

How significant will such shifts be for American investors and for global capital as a whole? That will depend not only on where these legal territories are anchored, but on what their legal content is. As China becomes more economically and politically powerful, we may see interesting debates about how to treat explicitly hybrid state-market entities (as has already been the case in sovereign debt policy disputes in the context of the COVID-19 pandemic).[11] The lack of consensus on the United Nations Convention on Jurisdictional Immunities of States, due primarily to differences of opinion between the United States and countries in the Global South over the proper application of the nature/purpose distinction and the amount of spatial connection needed to claim jurisdiction, also suggests that immunity could be framed in slightly different ways in competing legal territories. [12]

Yet, both the widespread Americanization of other legal systems and the growing *utility* of essentially neoliberal rules for China and other well-positioned economies suggests that, by and large, the transnational legal territories of other countries will likely continue to (re)produce similar rules as those promoted by US judicial territory. Despite loud critiques of US hegemony and so-called Western values, China and the rest of the BRICs have, in some ways, become even more committed to neoliberal capitalism than the United States now is.[13] This makes it likely that these emerging legal territories will continue to reinforce strong, if slightly altered, public/private and political/legal distinctions, and thus that they will continue to enact an essentially (neo)liberal vision of the economy that favors the interests of powerful investors of all countries on the whole.[14]

That said, we may well see important shifts in the *geographic* centers of legal dominance. US courts have defined more and more activity as in the US, in order to both support the interests of private capital, which is often based in or has significant ties to, the United States, and to bolster the power of New York City and the judiciary itself. If and when other legal territories are able to compete successfully with US judicial territory, they will surely develop competing claims about the geographic center of transnational economic interactions—claims that will sometimes directly conflict with those of US courts. How these conflicts play out remains to be seen. Yet, what will undoubtedly remain true is that the ability to enforce these spatial legal claims will remain dependent on the economic power of the jurisdictions who make them.

Meanwhile, these new legal territories will continue to serve the interests of powerful transnational corporations and investors on the whole, although how individual capitalists will fare will vary depending on how they have designed their accumulation strategies vis-à-vis particular legal expectations. What remains predictable, however, is that shifts in the global center(s) of economic power and transnational legal space are unlikely to do much to promote the substantive economic sovereignty of most countries. Any transnational extension of nationally based legal authority, so long as it is hitched to essentially promarket legal rules and to foregrounding the spatial claims and interests of economically dominant states, will continue to subject weaker countries to foreign legal systems and hamper efforts to link formal political autonomy to substantive economic equality.

More broadly, the fact of overlapping, noncontiguous, and dynamic legal territories, whatever their particular content, means that transnational law will remain fundamental to defining the map of national territorial sovereignties for the foreseeable future. Indeed, as other legal territories become more successful in vying with US judicial territory for authority, this map will likely become even more complicated. If we want to understand how sovereignty works in today's world, we must remember that these legal configurations are not mere apolitical and spatially arbitrary reflections of economic practicality. Rather, they are strategically produced through struggles among politicians, investors, states, and others over particular legal boundaries. These struggles are characterized not by a lack of concern about space, but rather by the huge amount of ink and effort that goes into hashing out every spatial detail.

Continued attention to these operations is crucial for pushing back both against politically instrumentalist claims about the sanctity of Westphalian sovereignty, and against either triumphalist or fearmongering assertions about the obsolescence of the nation-state in the face of globalization. Understanding the complexity of state territoriality and sovereignty today, of which transnational law is a crucial but almost entirely overlooked part, allows us to avoid a binary view of states as either "having" sovereignty or not, and instead to see the authority of all states as only more or less overlapping with their official boundaries—with huge variation in the more and the less depending on the particular state in question.[15]

In short, whether anchored to New York or London or Singapore or Hong Kong, the practice of extending transnational law as a way to increase state power while retaining claims to international legitimacy shows no signs of flagging. The mundane operations of domestic law will continue to shape geopolitical economic struggles for a long time to come.

APPENDIX 1

SELECTED TIMELINE OF THE EXPANSION OF US JUDICIAL TERRITORY

Note: Contextual entries are italicized to distinguish them from events directly related to judicial expansion.

- 1812 THE SCHOONER EXCHANGE V. MCFADDON—The US Supreme Court affirms the doctrine of absolute foreign sovereign immunity, declaring a foreign state's "public armed ships" immune from suit in US courts and distinguishing these from foreign privately owned merchant vessels. The Court does not consider foreign state-owned and -operated merchant ships.

- 1897 UNDERHILL V. HERNANDEZ—The US Supreme Court affirms the absolute version of the act of state doctrine, declaring that "the courts of one country will not sit in judgment on the acts of the government of another done within its own territory." Under this version, the public/private distinction is central to act of state cases, but commercial is not yet equated with private activity. No serious changes to this version of the doctrine are implemented until the 1960s.

- 1914–1917 WORLD WAR I—*Western governments engage in more extensive management of their economies than ever before, including through seizing foreign-owned property and engaging in centralized production, rationing, and resource allocation. This leads many investors and some judges to advocate a commercial exception to foreign sovereign immunity.*

- 1917 RUSSIAN REVOLUTION—*Soviet nationalizations of foreign-owned property and engagement in extensive state-directed trade and other economic activities lead to heightened calls for a commercial exception to foreign sovereign immunity. Nevertheless, for the next few decades, most conflicts arising from Soviet nationalizations continue to be handled by the US executive branch.*

- 1926 BERIZZI BROS. CO. V. S.S. PESARO—The US Supreme Court affirms the doctrine of absolute foreign sovereign immunity, even for foreign state-owned merchant vessels. In the process, the Court rejects the equation of commercial with private activity, holding that "the maintenance and advancement of the economic welfare of a people" is a "public purpose."

- 1945 END OF WORLD WAR II—*Like World War I, World War II leads to extensive state involvement in economic management, even among Western countries. The end of the war also marks the beginning of the end of the European colonial empires and the ascendancy of the United States as global hegemon. This impels a United States outwardly committed to decolonization to find new ways to maintain the power of private Western investors in postcolonial countries. Shifting responsibility for handling economic conflicts with foreign governments from the executive to the judiciary soon becomes an important mechanism for doing this.*

- 1945–1960 DECOLONIZATION OF ASIA AND AFRICA—*With the embrace of a wide range of socialist and heterodox economic practices in Asia, Africa, and Latin America, Western countries and investors become increasingly hostile to what they see as foreign state interference in transnational economic relationships.*

- 1952 TATE LETTER—The Department of State expresses support for a commercial exception to foreign sovereign immunity, and for equating commercial and private government acts. This is the first significant step in the extension of US judicial territory over foreign government economic decisions. It also makes the executive's wishes central to particular foreign sovereign immunity decisions for the next two decades.

- 1959–1960 CUBAN REVOLUTION AND NATIONALIZATIONS—*Mass nationalizations of US-owned property in Cuba spur the first concerted efforts by all three branches of the US government to shift responsibility for dealing with foreign nationalizations from the executive to the judiciary. This involves both eventual further restrictions on foreign sovereign immunity and, more importantly, the first real restriction of the act of state doctrine.*

- 1962 UN GENERAL ASSEMBLY RESOLUTION ON PERMANENT SOVEREIGNTY OVER NATURAL RESOURCES—*This resolution marks an important moment in the rise of a Third World movement seeking to rewrite the rules of the international economic order. Among other things, it asserts the right of all states to nationalize their own natural resources, with "appropriate compensation" to be determined by the host state, rather than by foreign or international law.*

- 1964 VICTORY TRANSPORT, INC. V. COMISARIA GENERAL DE ABASTECIMIENTOS Y TRANSPORTES—The Second Circuit Court of Appeals embraces the commercial exception while acknowledging the essential arbitrariness of the public/private divide. It proceeds to enumerate what it says is a complete list of "strictly political or public acts," including nationalizations and public loans, highlighting some of the limits to US judicial territory at the time.

- 1964 BANCO NACIONAL DE CUBA V. SABBATINO—The US Supreme Court replaces the traditional act of state doctrine with the separation of powers approach, under which the doctrine is defined not by a strict commitment to territorial sovereignty, but rather by the US judiciary's responsibility not to embarrass or interfere with the US executive's foreign policy interests. While the Court upholds the act of state doctrine in this case, it also weakens it and paves the way for a significant extension of US judicial territory going forward.

- 1964 HICKENLOOPER AMENDMENT—The US Congress declares by statute that the act of state doctrine should not apply in any case involving a "confiscation or other taking . . . in violation of the principles of international law," unless the President of the United States expressly disagrees. The amendment openly targets the Cuban nationalizations and is used to overturn the Supreme Court's *Sabbatino* decision. US courts are uncomfortable with the amendment and tend to interpret it as narrowly as possible going forward. Yet, it sparks further struggles among all three branches to find another way to restrict the act of state doctrine in order to extend US judicial territory over foreign nationalizations.

- 1971 NIXON DELINKS THE US DOLLAR FROM GOLD—*This marks a key moment in the transition from stable exchange rates and relatively closed financial borders to a far more volatile and open international financial system. The latter contributes to creating the conditions for both neoliberalization and financialization and lays the groundwork for the eventual reconfiguration of a US empire now resting more squarely on the power of Wall Street and the US dollar.*

- 1974 UN GENERAL ASSEMBLY DECLARATION ON THE ESTAB-
LISHMENT OF A NEW INTERNATIONAL ECONOMIC ORDER AND
CHARTER OF ECONOMIC RIGHTS AND DUTIES OF STATES—*These
documents mark the high point of the Third World push for a New International Economic Order that would promote substantive economic as well
as political equality among states. This is seen as a major threat by Western
powers and transnational corporations.*

- 1976 ALFRED DUNHILL OF LONDON, INC. V. CUBA—The US
Supreme Court defines the act of nationalization as narrowly as possible,
holding that it does not apply to the accounts of nationalized businesses
and limiting the types of officials who can be considered properly public
actors for act of state purposes. In a plurality opinion, Justice White also
argues for a blanket commercial exception to the act of state doctrine and
defines various acts that we might term nationalization-adjacent as merely
commercial. Although not a majority opinion, this commercial exception
to the act of state doctrine has been applied more and more widely since,
constituting another significant extension of US judicial territory.

- 1976 FOREIGN SOVEREIGN IMMUNITIES ACT—The FSIA codifies
the commercial exception to foreign sovereign immunity, as well as the
rule that commercial activity is to be defined solely by reference to
the nature rather than the purpose of an act. It also puts an end to the
Department of State's explicit influence on sovereign immunity cases.
In addition, it loosens the spatial requirements for establishing US jurisdiction over foreign state commercial acts by extending that jurisdiction to acts carried out abroad but having a "direct effect" in the United
States. Together, the codification of the commercial exception and the
direct effects rule enable a major expansion of US judicial territory.

- 1979 VOLCKER SHOCK—*In order to combat rising inflation at home,
US Federal Reserve Chair Paul Volcker sharply increases US interest rates,
contributing to the reorganization of US power to foreground finance and
dollar hegemony, while also sparking a massive debt crisis across much of
the Third World.*

- 1980S–1990S THIRD WORLD DEBT CRISIS—*The crisis marks a definitive end to many heterodox economic practices of postcolonial states and
to Third World efforts to establish a new international economic order. It
ushers in the era of IMF and World Bank structural adjustment programs,
which impose neoliberalism on indebted countries. It also leads to the credi-*

tor litigation that creates the terrain for another major expansion of US judicial territory.

· 1985 ALLIED BANK INT'L V. BANCO CREDITO AGRICOLA DE CARTAGO—In response to pressure from the financial industry and the US executive branch, the Second Circuit Court of Appeals reverses its own initial decision in this case to hold that private creditors can use US courts to sue foreign sovereign debtors. In the process, the court redefines the legal location of a debt from being with the debtor (as in previous cases) to being with the creditor. Since most creditors use New York banks, this means that nearly all Third World sovereign debts can now be legally located in the United States, enabling the extension of US judicial territory over transnational sovereign debt relations.

· 1992 REPUBLIC OF ARGENTINA V. WELTOVER, INC.—In creditor litigation against Argentina, the US Supreme Court determines (contra *Victory Transport*) that issuing public debt is a private, commercial act and thus not eligible for immunity. It further extends US judicial territory over many foreign government economic acts by defining any act in which a commercial business might engage as commercial and by declaring that direct effects need be neither "foreseeable" nor "substantial."

· 2001 ARGENTINE DEBT CRISIS AND DEFAULT—*A massive economic collapse and default in Argentina, in combination with the development of the holdout litigation strategy, sets the stage for extensive creditor litigation against Argentina and for the most dramatic expansion of US judicial territory in the twenty-first century so far.*

· 2014 REPUBLIC OF ARGENTINA V. NML CAPITAL, LTD.—On the same day, the US Supreme Court allows the Southern District Court of New York's pari passu ruling against Argentina to stand and issues its own decision in the discovery arm of the same case. The former decision allows a US court to prohibit all financiers anywhere in the world except in Argentina from helping that government make certain transnational payments. The second decision similarly extends the ability of US courts to demand information about any and all Argentine assets, public and private, located anywhere in the world except in Argentina. Both represent a massive extension of US judicial territory and an inversion of the spatial logic of the FSIA as understood up to that point. These decisions go so far that they provoke an unusual rift between the judiciary and the US executive branch over the proper extent of US judicial reach.

APPENDIX 2

List of Cases and Auxiliary Case Documents

CASES CITED

Abaclat and others (formerly Giovanna A. Beccara and Others) v. Argentine Republic (ICSID Case No. ARB/07/5)

A.I. Credit Corp. v. Government of Jamaica, 666 F. Supp. 629 (S.D.N.Y. 1987)

Alfred Dunhill of London, Inc. v. Cuba, 425 U.S. 682 (1976)

Allied Bank Int'l v. Banco Credito Agricola de Cartago, 566 F. Supp. 1440 (S.D.N.Y. 1983)

Allied Bank Int'l v. Banco Credito Agricola de Cartago, 733 F.2d 23 (2d Cir. 1984)

Allied Bank Int'l v. Banco Credito Agricola de Cartago, 757 F.2d 516 (2d Cir. 1985)

Banco Nacional de Cuba v. Farr, 243 F. Supp 957 (S.D.N.Y. 1965)

Banco Nacional de Cuba v. Farr, 272 F. Supp 836 (S.D.N.Y. 1965)

Banco Nacional de Cuba v. Farr, 383 F.2d 166 (2d Cir. 1967)

Banco Nacional de Cuba v. First National City Bank of New York, 442 F.2d 530 (2d Cir. 1971)

Banco Nacional de Cuba v. Sabbatino, 193 F. Supp. 375 (S.D.N.Y. 1961)

Banco Nacional de Cuba v. Sabbatino, 307 F.2d 845 (2d Cir. 1962)

Banco Nacional de Cuba v. Sabbatino, 376 U.S. 398 (1964)

Banque de Gestion Privee-SIB v. La Republica de Paraguay, 787 F. Supp 53 (S.D.N.Y. 1992)

Berizzi Bros. Co. v. S.S. Pesaro, 271 U.S. 562 (1926)

Bernstein v. N.V. Nederlandsche-Amerikaansche Stoomvaart-Maatschappij, 210 F.2d 375 (2d Cir. 1954)

Briggs v. Light-Boat Upper Cedar Point, 93 Mass. 157 (1865)

Brown v. Board of Education, 347 U.S. 483 (1954)

Bush v. Gore, 531 U.S. 98 (2000)

Cargo & Tankship Management Corp. v. India Supply Mission, 336 F.2d 416 (2d Cir. 1964)

Cherokee Nation v. Georgia, 30 U.S. 1 (1831)

CIBC *Bank and Trust Co. (Cayman) Ltd. v. Banco Central do Brasil*, 886 F. Supp. 1105 (S.D.N.Y. 1995)

Citizens United v. Federal Election Commission, 558 U.S. 310 (2010)

Cole v. Heidtman (S.D.N.Y. 1968)

Commercial Bank of Kuwait v. Rafidain Bank, 15 F.3d 238 (2d Cir. 1994)

Dexter & Carpenter, Inc. v. Kunglig Jarnvagsstyrelsen, 43 F.2d 705 (2d Cir. 1930)

Dobbs v. Jackson Women's Health Organization, 597 U.S. ___ (2022)

Downes v. Bidwell, 182 U.S. 244 (1901)

Elliott Assocs., L.P. v. Republic of Panama, 975 F. Supp. 332 (S.D.N.Y. 1997)

Elliott Assocs., L.P. v. Republic of Peru, 12 F. Supp. 2d 328 (S.D.N.Y. 1998)

Elliott Assocs., L.P. v. Republic of Peru, 194 F.3d 363 (2d Cir. 1999)

Elliott Assocs., L.P. v. Republic of Peru, 194 F.R.D. 116 (S.D.N.Y. 2000)

Ex Parte Republic of Peru, 318 U.S. 578 (1943)

Ex Parte United States, 257 U.S. 419 (1922)

First National City Bank v. Banco Nacional de Cuba, 406 U.S. 759 (1972)

Flota Maritima Browning de Cuba, Sociadad Anonima v. Motor Vessel Ciudad de la Habana, 335 F.2d 619 (4th Cir. 1964)

Frazier v. Hanover Bank (Sup. Ct., N.Y. 1953)

French v. Banco Nacional de Cuba, 23 N.Y.2d 46 (N.Y. 1968)

Guaranty Trust Co. v. United States, 304 U.S. 126 (1938)

In re Grand Jury Investigation of Shipping Industry, 186 F. Supp. 298 (D.D.C. 1960)

In re Investigation of World Arrangements, etc., 13 F.R.D. 280 (D.D.C. 1952)

Lloyds Bank PLC v. Republic of Ecuador, 1998 U.S. Dist. LEXIS 3065 (S.D.N.Y. 1998)

Long v. The Tampico, 16 F. 491 (S.D.N.Y. 1883)

Mason v. Intercolonial Railroad of Canada, 197 Mass. 349 (1908)

Menendez v. Faber, Coe & Gregg, Inc., 345 F. Supp. 527 (S.D.N.Y. 1972)

Menendez v. Saks & Co., 485 F.2d 1355 (2d Cir. 1973)

Morrison, Inc. v. Servicio Autonomo Nacional de Acueductos y Alcantarillados, Civil No. 5092 (N.D. Ind. 1969)

National City Bank v. Republic of China, 348 U.S. 356 (1955)

National Union Fire Ins. Co. v. People's Republic of Congo, 729 F. Supp. 936 (S.D.N.Y. 1989)

New York & Cuba Mail S.S. Co. v. Republic of Korea, 132 F. Supp. 684 (S.D.N.Y. 1955)

New York State Rifle & Pistol Association, Inc. v. Bruen, 597 U.S. ___ (2022)

NML Capital, Ltd. v. Republic of Argentina, 2009 U.S. Dist. LEXIS 19046 (S.D.N.Y. 2009)

NML Capital, Ltd. v. Republic of Argentina, 2011 U.S. Dist. LEXIS 110811 (S.D.N.Y. 2011)

NML Capital, Ltd. v. Republic of Argentina, 699 F.3d 246 (2d. Cir 2012)

NML Capital, Ltd. v. Republic of Argentina, 727 F.3d 230 (2d. Cir 2013)

Ocean Transport Co. v. Government of Republic of Ivory Coast, 269 F. Supp. 703 (E.D. La. 1967)

Oetjen v. Central Leather Company, 246 U.S. 297 (1918)

Oliver American Trading Co. v. Mexico, 5 F.2d 659 (2d Cir. 1924)

Pan American Tankers Corp. v. Republic of Vietnam, 296 F. Supp. 361 (S.D.N.Y. 1969)

Petrol Shipping Corp. v. Kingdom of Greece, Ministry of Commerce, etc., 360 F.2d 103 (2d Cir. 1966)

Plessy v. Ferguson, 163 U.S. 537 (1896)

Pravin Banker Assocs., Ltd. v. Banco Popular del Peru, 109 F.3d 850 (2d Cir. 1997)

Pravin Banker Assocs., Ltd. v. Banco Popular del Peru, 165 B.R. 379 (S.D.N.Y. 1994)

Pruitt v. M/V Patignies (E.D. Mich. 1968)

Republic of Argentina v. NML Capital, Ltd., 573 U.S. 134

Republic of Argentina v. NML Capital, Ltd., 134 S. Ct. 2819 (2014)

Republic of Argentina v. Weltover, Inc., 504 U.S. 607 (1992)

Republic of Cuba v. Arcade Bldg. of Savannah, 104 Ga. App. 848 (Ga. Ct. App. 1961)

Republic of Cuba v. Dixie Paint & Varnish Co., 104 Ga. App. 854 (Ga. Ct. App. 1961)

Republic of Iraq v. First National City Bank, 353 F.2d 47 (2d Cir. 1965)

Republic of Iraq v. First National City Bank, 382 U.S. 1027 (1966)

Republic of Mexico v. Hoffman, 324 U.S. 30 (1945)

Ricaud v. American Metal Co., 246 U.S. 304 (1918)

S&S Mach. Co. v. Masinexportimport, 706 F.2d 411 (2d Cir. 1983)

Shapleigh et al. v. Mier, 299 U.S. 468 (1937)

State ex rel. National Institute of Agrarian Reform v. Dekle, 137 So. 2d 581 (Fla. Ct. App. 1962)

Stephen v. Zivnostenska Banka, Nat'l Corp., 12 N.Y.2d 781 (1962)

Tabacalera Severiano Jorge, S.A. v. Standard Cigar Co., 392 F.2d 706 (5th Cir. 1968)

The Anne, 16 U.S. 435 (1818)

The Carlo Poma, 259 F. 369 (2d Cir. 1919)

The Gul Djemal, 264 U.S. 90 (1924)

The Maipo, 252 F. 627 (S.D.N.Y. 1918)

The Maipo, 259 F. 367 (S.D.N.Y. 1919)

The Navemar, 90 F.2d 673 (2d Cir. 1937)

The Paquete Habana, 175 U.S. 677 (1900)

The Pesaro, 13 F.2d 468 (2d Cir. 1926)

The Pesaro, 277 F. 473 (S.D.N.Y. 1921)

The Roseric, 254 F. 154 (D.N.J. 1918)

The Sao Vicente, 260 U.S. 151 (1922)

The Schooner Exchange v. McFaddon, 11 U.S. 116 (1812)

Turkmani v. Republic of Bol., 193 F. Supp. 2d 165 (D.D.C. 2002)

Underhill v. Hernandez, 168 U.S. 250 (1897)

United States of Mexico v. Rask, 118 Cal. App. 21 (Cal. Ct. App. 1931)

United States v. Belmont, 301 U.S. 324 (1937)

United States v. Pink, 315 U.S. 203 (1942)

United States v. Wilder, 28 F. Cas. 601 (C.C.D. Mass. 1838)

Venore Transportation Co. v. President of India, 67 Civ. 2578, 68 Civ. 1134–1139 (S.D.N.Y. 1967 and 1968)

Victory Transport, Inc. v. Comisaria General de Abastecimientos y Transportes, 336 F.2d 354 (2d Cir. 1964)

W. S. Kirkpatrick & Co. v. Environmental Tectonics Corp., Int'l, 493 U.S. 400 (1990)

Weilamann v. Chase Manhattan Bank, 21 Misc. 2d 1086 (N.Y. App. Div. 1959)

Weltover, Inc. v. Republic of Argentina, 753 F. Supp. 1201 (S.D.N.Y. 1991)

Weltover, Inc. v. Republic of Argentina, 941 F.2d 145 (2d Cir. 1991)

West Virginia v. Environmental Protection Agency, 597 U.S. ___ (2022)

AUXILIARY CASE DOCUMENTS CITED

Amended February 23, 2012 Order, NML *Capital, Ltd. v. Republic of Argentina* (S.D.N.Y. Nov. 21, 2012) (No. 08 Civ. 6978 (TPG))

Brief for the "Pesaro" and for her Claimant, the Royal Italian Ambassador, *Berizzi Bros. Co. v. S.S. Pesaro* (U.S. 1925) (No. 334)

Brief for the Appellant, *Berizzi Bros. Co. v. S.S. Pesaro* (U.S. Apr. 10, 1926) (No. 334)

Brief for the United States as Amicus Curiae in Support of Petitioner, *Republic of Argentina v. NML Capital, Ltd.* (U.S. Mar. 3, 2014) (No. 12–842)

Brief for the United States as Amicus Curiae Supporting Respondents, *Republic of Argentina v. Weltover, Inc.* (U.S. Mar. 5, 1992) (No. 91–763)

Brief for the United States as Amicus Curiae, *Allied Bank Int'l v. Banco Credito Agricola De Cartago* (2d Cir. 1985) (No. 83–7714)

Brief for the United States as Amicus Curiae, *Banco Nacional de Cuba v. Sabbatino* (U.S. Sep. 10, 1963) (No. 16)

Brief for the United States as Amicus Curiae, *Republic of Argentina v. NML Capital, Ltd.* (U.S. Dec. 4, 2013) (No. 12–842)

Brief for the United States of America as Amicus Curiae in Support of Reversal, *NML Capital, Ltd. v. Republic of Argentina* (2d Cir. Apr. 4, 2012) (No. 12-105-cv(L))

Brief for the United States of America as Amicus Curiae in Support of the Republic of Argentina's Petition for Panel Rehearing and Rehearing En Banc, *NML Capital, Ltd. v. Republic of Argentina* (2d Cir. Dec. 28, 2012) (No. 12-105-cv(L))

Brief for the United States of America as Amicus Curiae, *Aurelius Capital Master, Ltd., et al., v. Republic of Argentina* (2d Cir. Mar. 23, 2016) (No. 16–628(L))

Brief of Amicus Curiae Euroclear Bank SA/NV in Support of Petitioner, *Republic of Argentina v. NML Capital, Ltd.* (U.S. Mar. 24, 2014) (No. 13–990)

Brief of Defendant-Appellant the Republic of Argentina, *NML Capital Ltd. v. Republic of Argentina* (2d Cir. Dec. 28, 2012) (No. 12-105-cv(L))

Brief of Republic of Argentina and Banco Central de la Republica Argentina, *Republic of Argentina v. Weltover, Inc.* (U.S. Feb. 11, 1992) (No. 91–763)

Joint Response Brief of Plaintiffs-Appellees NML Capital, Ltd. and Olifant Fund, Ltd., *NML Capital, Ltd. v. Republic of Argentina* (2d Cir. Jan. 25, 2013) (No. 12-105-cv(L))

Motion of the Euro Bondholders for Leave to Intervene as Interested Non-Parties, *NML Capital, Ltd. v. Republic of Argentina* (2d Cir. Dec. 4, 2012) (No. 12-105-cv(L))

Order, *NML Capital, Ltd. v. Republic of Argentina* (S.D.N.Y. Dec. 7, 2011) (No. 08 Civ. 6978 (TPG))

Order, *NML Capital, Ltd. v. Republic of Argentina* (S.D.N.Y. Feb. 23, 2012) (No. 08 Civ. 6978 (TPG))

Petition for a Writ of Certiorari to the United States Court of Appeals for the Second Circuit, *Comisaria General de Abastecimientos y Transportes v. Victory Transport, Inc.* (U.S. Jan. 7, 1965) (No. 815)

Petition for a Writ of Certiorari, *Exchange Bondholder Group v. NML Capital, Ltd.* (U.S. Feb. 18, 2014) (No. 13-991)

Petition for Panel Rehearing and Rehearing En Banc of Defendant-Appellant the Republic of Argentina, *NML Capital, Ltd. v. Republic of Argentina* (2d Circ. Nov. 13, 2012) (No. 12-105-cv(L))

Plaintiff's Memorandum of Law, *Banco Nacional de Cuba v. Manufacturers Trust Company* (Apr. 9, 1975) (S.D.N.Y. 61 Civ. 569)

Reply Brief of Plaintiffs in Response to the Remand from the Court of Appeals, *NML Capital, Ltd. v. Republic of Argentina* (S.D.N.Y. Nov. 19, 2012) (No. 08 Civ. 6978 (TPG))

Stipulation, *Berizzi Bros. Co. v. S.S. Pesaro* (Mar. 13, 1925) (S.D.N.Y. 78–248)

Transcript of Oral Argument, *NML Capital, Ltd. v. Republic of Argentina* (S.D.N.Y. Jun. 27, 2014) (No. 08 Civ. 6978 (TPG))

Transcript of Oral Argument, *Republic of Argentina v. NML Capital, Ltd.* (U.S. Apr. 21, 2014) (No. 12–842)

NOTES

INTRODUCTION

1   Order, NML *Capital, Ltd. v. Republic of Argentina* (S.D.N.Y. Feb. 23, 2012)
(No. 08 Civ. 6978 (TPG)); Amended February 23, 2012 Order, NML
Capital, Ltd. v. Republic of Argentina (S.D.N.Y. Nov. 21, 2012) (No. 08 Civ.
6978 (TPG)).

2   *Republic of Argentina v.* NML *Capital, Ltd.*, 134 S. Ct. 2819 (2014) (cert.
denied).

3   See, among many other sources on the Argentine default, restructuring,
and litigation, Cantamutto and Ozarow, "Serial Payers, Serial Losers?";
Potts, "(Re-)Writing Markets"; Roos, *Why Not Default?*; Guzman,
"Analysis"; López and Nahón, "Growth of Debt."

4   Schumacher, Trebesch, and Enderlein, "Sovereign Defaults in Court."

5   See, e.g., Hudson, "Vulture Funds Trump Argentinian Sovereignty"; Sassen, "Short History of Vultures"; Guzman, "Wall Street's Worst."

6   See, e.g., Transcript of Oral Argument, *Republic of Argentina v.* NML *Capital, Ltd.* (U.S. Apr. 21, 2014) (No. 12–842).

7   See, e.g., *Pravin Banker Assocs., Ltd. v. Banco Popular del Peru,* 109 F.3d
850 (2d Cir. 1997).

8   This was even more pronounced in a related Supreme Court decision (*Republic of Argentina v.* NML *Capital, Ltd.*, 573 U.S. 134) issued on the same
day on which the Supreme Court declined to review the better-known
case described here. See chapter 5 for an extended analysis of both cases.

9   See, e.g., Allen et al., *Oxford Handbook of Jurisdiction*; Berman, "Globalization of Jurisdiction"; Slot and Bulterman, *Globalisation and
Jurisdiction.*

10 I follow scholars in the Third World Approaches to International Law
(TWAIL) tradition in using the term *Third World* not to suggest homoge-
neity across a radically diverse set of countries, but rather to call attention to a shared history of subjection to colonialism and the "structures
and processes of global capitalism." Chimni, "Third World Approaches,"
4. See also Achiume and Bâli, "Race and Empire." This is not intended to
obscure violence perpetrated by postcolonial governments themselves.
TWAIL scholars eschew "simplistic visions of an innocent third world,
and a colonizing and dominating first world," while arguing that modern

forms of domination cannot be separated from their imperial origins. Gathii, "TWAIL," 34.

11   Blomley, *Law, Space.*

12   For a basic overview, see Shaw, "International Law."

13   Sparke, *Introducing Globalization,* 182.

14   Sparke, *Introducing Globalization,* 183.

15   Dezalay and Garth, *Internationalization of Palace Wars*; Panitch and Gindin, *Making of Global Capitalism.*

16   Kohl, "Territoriality and Globalization."

17   For an overview of recent attempts to pin down the definition of transnational law, see Cotterrell, "What Is Transnational Law?" For comprehensive treatments of transnational commercial law, see Heidemann, *Transnational Commercial Law*; Goode, Kronke, and McKendrick, *Transnational Commercial Law*. And for contested definitions, issues, and debates in transnational law beyond commercial topics, see Zumbansen, *Oxford Handbook of Transnational Law.*

18   Goode, Kronke, and McKendrick, *Transnational Commercial Law,* lxv.

19   Anghie, *Imperialism.*

20   Pistor, *Code of Capital,* 18.

21   See also Kahraman, Kalyanpur, and Newman, "Domestic Courts."

22   Raustiala, *Does the Constitution Follow the Flag?*

23   Potts, "Reterritorializing Economic Governance."

24   Foreign Sovereign Immunities Act, 28 U.S.C. §1602 et seq. (1976).

25   For a detailed comparative history of US and foreign sovereign immunity rules, see Fox and Webb, *Law of State Immunity.*

26   For a general history of the act of state doctrine, see Patterson, "Act of State Doctrine."

27   Kohl, "Territoriality and Globalization," 306.

28   An explanation commonly provided to the supposed puzzle of why foreign states obey US and other powerful courts is that the reputational costs of failing to do so can cause economic difficulties. This is a depoliticized way of saying that current economic and legal structures force countries to choose between obeying foreign rulings or risking economic damage. See Roos, *Why Not Default?* for an excellent overview and critique of the way the "enforcement problem" is usually understood in relation to sovereign debt.

29   On the traditional "triangular" relationship between jurisdiction, sovereignty, and territory, and the turn toward more fluid and flexible bases of jurisdiction in the face of contemporary challenges, see Allen et al., *Oxford Handbook of Jurisdiction*; Berman, "Globalization of Jurisdiction"; Gerber, *Global Competition*; Slot and Bulterman, *Globalisation and Jurisdiction*; Raustiala, *Does the Constitution Follow the Flag?*; Buxbaum, "Territory, Territoriality." Note that the growing complexity of jurisdictional rules does not mean that the *idea* of a congruence between physical

territory, jurisdiction, and sovereignty is now irrelevant. This Westphalian conception remains central to many imaginaries of and debates about (inter)national law and sovereignty. Basaran, "Journey Through Law's Landscapes."

30 See, e.g., Whytock, "Domestic Courts and Global Governance"; Quintanilla and Whytock, "New Multipolarity in Transnational Litigation"; Putnam, *Courts without Borders*, 2016; Kahraman, Kalyanpur, and Newman, "Domestic Courts."

31 See, e.g., Goode, Kronke, and McKendrick, *Transnational Commercial Law,* though see also Kahraman, Kalyanpur, and Newman, "Domestic Courts"; Quintanilla and Whytock, "New Multipolarity in Transnational Litigation" for work that is less caught up in this narrative.

32 See, e.g., Goode, Kronke, and McKendrick, *Transnational Commercial Law*; Heidemann, *Transnational Commercial Law;* Mills, *Party Autonomy.*

33 I cannot do justice to the huge literature on this topic here, but for key examples, see Berman on the "Globalization of Jurisdiction" and the more recent compilation in Allen et al.'s *Oxford Handbook of Jurisdiction.*

34 Although reconceptualizing jurisdiction is not their primary analytical focus, Gerber and Raustiala are important exceptions to this tendency. Gerber, *Global Competition;* Raustiala, *Does the Constitution Follow the Flag?* Gerber, who uses the term *unilateral jurisdictionalism* to refer to the US imposition of competition law beyond US borders, is especially frank in his descriptions of the arrogance and parochialism of US views on the topic and of the resentments of other (European) countries regarding this extraterritorial overreach.

35 Pasternak, "Jurisdiction," 178.

36 Valverde, "Jurisdiction and Scale"; Valverde, "Deepening the Conversation between Socio-Legal Theory and Legal Scholarship about Jurisdiction."

37 In contrast to the well-documented tendency toward "methodological nationalism" in popular and academic analyses, this is a good example of "methodological globalism," or "the tendency for social scientists to prioritize the analysis of globalization processes over and above knowledge of the variety of socio-spatial structures, processes and practices that shape state forms and functions at various territorial scales." Moisio et al., *Changing Geographies of the State,* 14.

38 See Agnew, "Sovereignty Regimes"; Barkan, "Sovereignty"; Benton, *Search for Sovereignty;* Burbank and Cooper, *Empires in World History*; Mountz, "Political Geography I"; Sparke, "Globalizing Capitalism"; Ong, "Graduated Sovereignty in South-East Asia" for critiques of the myth of a clear progression from Westphalian to modern territoriality and the idea that sovereignty ever implied total, neatly demarcated control over a given area.

39 Kamminga, "Extraterritoriality." The term is also used to refer to earlier "consular courts" in places like nineteenth-century China or the Ottoman

empire, in which Western imperial subjects would be tried not by Chinese or Ottoman law, but by the laws of their own home states. Benton, *Law and Colonial Cultures*; Burbank and Cooper, *Empires in World History*; Kayaoğlu, *Legal Imperialism*; Raustiala, *Does the Constitution Follow the Flag?* The United States now has similar deals with countries in which its military bases are located.

40 Parrish, "Reclaiming International Law," 820.

41 Putnam, for example, rejects "political" as well as economic explanations for US extraterritorial law, instead arguing that US courts selectively assert extraterritorial jurisdiction in order to support "the integrity or operation" of domestic *US* law or to prosecute violations of "a short list of rights at the core of American political identity." Putnam, *Courts without Borders,* 2016, 4. Raustiala's study of US extraterritoriality is more ambivalent. While he notes that US extraterritorial law relies on and promotes US economic dominance, and while he refers variously to US empire and US hegemony, he nonetheless argues that the primary function of US extraterritorial law is to "manage and minimize legal difference." Raustiala, *Does the Constitution Follow the Flag?*, 21. In contrast, Parrish emphasizes the dangers extraterritorial law poses to democratic accountability, while Mattei and Lena identify US extraterritorial practices as a form of "legal imperialism." Parrish, "Reclaiming International Law"; Mattei and Lena, "U.S. Jurisdiction," 382.

42 Though see Colangelo's "What Is Extraterritorial Jurisdiction?" for an important exception.

43 The term is also often used defensively to criticize what one state sees as the *over*extension of another's jurisdiction. Buxbaum, "Territory, Territoriality."

44 As Basaran writes in a different context, complex, interscalar, and overlapping legal spaces show "how law's territory is distinct from physical territory, how inside and outside are susceptible to changes, and how borders shift through law." Basaran, "Journey Through Law's Landscapes," 24. Note that the extension of judicial territory occurs alongside strategic *suspensions* of or *limits* to US judicial reach—for example, with respect to offshore financial centers or Guantánamo Bay. Yet, these exclusions, too, remain territorial in that they are precisely about strategically (re)defining boundaries between American and non-American legal spaces. "Offshore" spaces are never defined as "nowheres," but rather as particular "elsewheres." Appel, *Licit Life of Capitalism*; Maurer, "Cyberspatial Sovereignties"; Palan, *Offshore World;* Potts, "Offshore."

45 A few legal scholars have embraced these concepts as well. While Hannah Buxbaum emphasizes the concept of territori*ality,* she sees territory as a static "factual input" that is no longer as relevant as it once was. Buxbaum, "Territory, Territoriality," 635. Other legal scholars, in contrast, define territory too in more relational ways and thus, like me, argue for

its continued salience. See, e.g., Brighenti, "On Territory as Relationship"; Kohl, "Territoriality and Globalization."

46 Sack, "Human Territoriality."

47 Brenner and Elden, "Henri Lefebvre." See also Painter, "Rethinking Territory," and compare Mitchell, "Society, Economy"; Koch, "'Spatial Socialization'"; Moisio et al., *Changing Geographies of the State* on the "state effect."

48 Ford, "Law's Territory"; Agnew, "Still Trapped in Territory?"; Agnew, "Territorial Trap."

49 Agnew, *Globalization and Sovereignty*; Brenner and Elden, "Henri Lefebvre."

50 Elden, "Land, Terrain, Territory"; Elden, "How Should We Do the History of Territory?"; Elden, *The Birth of Territory.*

51 Deakin et al., "Legal Institutionalism," 190. See also Knuth and Potts, "Legal Geographies of Finance"; Potts, "Beyond (De)Regulation."

52 Moisio et al., *Changing Geographies of the State,* 5.

53 Sparke cautions against the widespread tendency to see geopolitics and geoeconomics as dominant in discontinuous eras or in "distinct spaces of statecraft." Sparke, "Globalizing Capitalism," 485. Rather, he argues, they are best understood as dialectically entangled and as reflecting the underlying tensions of uneven development within capitalism. This dialectical relationship is inseparable from the production of territory today. The two domains are not associated with opposing territorial tendencies, as is sometimes assumed—rather, "territorial logics, either territorial fixity or fluidity, are products of geopolitical and geoeconomic processes . . ." Lee, Wainwright, and Glassman, "Geopolitical Economy," 421.

54 Think, for example, of US government authority over Indian reservations or overseas territories like Puerto Rico and Guantánamo Bay and see, also, Benton, *Search for Sovereignty,* for a detailed examination of the peculiar geographies of colonial Spanish and Portuguese territorial claims. Note also significant resonances with widespread practices of "border externalization," through which powerful Western states project migration control policies far beyond their own official borders, into both ocean spaces and foreign territories. Mountz, "Enforcement Archipelago"; Mountz, *The Death of Asylum;* Casas-Cortes, Cobarrubias, and Pickles, "'Good Neighbours Make Good Fences'"; Miller, *Empire of Borders.* All these spaces call to mind Boaventura de Sousa Santos' classic concept of "interlegality." de Sousa Santos, "Law."

55 For examples regarding foreign sovereign immunity, see Fox and Webb, *Law of State Immunity*; Bradley and Helfer, "International Law"; Damrosch, "Changing the International Law"; Goode, Kronke, and McKendrick, *Transnational Commercial Law.* For examples regarding the act of state doctrine, see Patterson, "Act of State Doctrine"; Schlossbach, "Arguably Commercial, Ergo Adjudicable"; Hoagland, "Act of State Doctrine";

Ireland-Piper, "Outdated and Unhelpful." Though see Diaz, "Territoriality Inquiry."

56 Hart, "Why Did It Take So Long?," 242.

57 See also Hart, "D/Developments after the Meltdown."

58 Panitch and Gindin, *Making of Global Capitalism*; Gowan, *Global Gamble*; Hart, "Why Did It Take So Long?"

59 Panitch and Gindin, "Finance and American Empire," 47.

60 Hart, "Why Did It Take So Long?"

61 See also Potts, "Law as Geopolitics." As Delaney puts it, law "constitutes much of modern reality through its relentless, if inconsistent, reiterations of divisions between 'the public and private,' 'the domestic and foreign,' 'the domestic and international,' 'subjects and objects' . . . and so on." Delaney, "Legal Geography I," 98.

62 The public/private, politics/economics, and law/politics distinctions have been the object of particular critique by critical legal scholars. See, e.g., Anghie, *Imperialism*; Horwitz, "History of the Public/Private Distinction"; Horwitz, *Transformation of American Law, 1870–1960*; Horwitz, *Transformation of American Law, 1780–1860*; Unger, "Critical Legal Studies Movement"; Ehrenreich, *The Reproductive Rights Reader*; Boyd, *Challenging the Public/Private Divide*. Geographers have contributed further insights into the spatial constitution of such legal dichotomies. See, e.g., Blomley, Delaney, and Ford, *Legal Geographies Reader*; Blomley, *Law, Space*; Blomley and Bakan, "Spacing Out"; Christophers and Niedt, "Resisting Devaluation"; Potts, "Law as Geopolitics"; Blomley, "Flowers in the Bathtub"; Cuomo and Brickell, "Feminist Legal Geographies."

63 Appel, *Licit Life of Capitalism*.

64 Judicialization refers more specifically to the increasing subjection of "political" issues to judicial oversight or to the growing power of judiciaries over other branches of government. Tate and Vallinder, *Global Expansion of Judicial Power*; Hirschl, "Judicialization of Politics"; Hirschl, "New Constitutionalism." The "political question doctrine" refers to a longstanding legal theory preventing US courts from intervening in issues over which the Constitution or another authority has relegated power to the executive. Tushnet, "Law and Prudence"; Barkow, "More Supreme than Court?"

65 For critics of growing judicial power, see, e.g., Tushnet, *Taking the Constitution Away*; Hirschl, "Judicialization of Mega-Politics"; Hirschl, "New Constitutionalism." For proponents, see, e.g., Thornhill, "Mutation of International Law." While judicial review can be used for either liberal or conservative ends, the rightward shift in US courts in the past few decades means it is often associated with the latter. Tribe, "Politicians in Robes"; Tribe and Lewin, "Rightwing US Supreme Court"; Greenhouse, *Justice on the Brink*.

66 Even those critical of growing judicial power have accepted a definition of the political that excludes economic questions a priori (foreground-

ing instead things like citizenship, voting rights, or electoral outcomes). Thus, even in the very occasional analyses that do consider these concepts transnationally (see, e.g., Cohen, "A Politics-Reinforcing Political Question Doctrine"), the types of "economic" cases analyzed in this book are excluded—thus missing the ways in which such issues are *made* nonpolitical.

67 Polanyi, *Great Transformation,* 74. See also, Block and Somers, *Power of Market Fundamentalism.*

68 MacKenzie, Muniesa, and Siu, *Do Economists Make Markets?*

69 Polanyi, *Great Transformation.* As Greta Krippner persuasively argues, while the concept of "disembeddedness" is more widely used, Polanyi's "own preferred terminology of 'institutional separation'" is more powerful. Krippner, "Polanyi for the Age of Trump," 249.

70 On the power of such a bounded conception of the economy, as well as the analytical and political importance of a "processual and relational understanding [that] refuses to take as given discrete objects, identities, places and events," see Hart, "Geography and Development," 98. While the impossibility of actually separating states from markets means neoliberalism can only ever be "impure," this very unattainability gives the *pursuit* of market purity significant power. Peck, *Constructions of Neoliberal Reason,* 22.

71 Among the most comprehensive and powerful treatments of neoliberalism are Brown, *Walled States, Waning Sovereignty;* Peck, *Constructions of Neoliberal Reason;* Foucault, *Birth of Biopolitics;* Slobodian, *Globalists;* Harvey, *Brief History of Neoliberalism.* On the co-constitution of law and neoliberalism, see also Britton-Purdy et al., "Building"; Grewal and Purdy, "Introduction."

72 In *Globalists,* Slobodian makes a major contribution to debates about neoliberalism by showing how concerns about decolonization fueled the development of neoliberal ideas.

73 See, especially, Harvey, *Limits to Capital;* Smith, *Uneven Development;* Sheppard, "Globalizing Capitalism's Raggedy Fringes"; Sheppard, "Thinking Geographically"; Sparke, *Introducing Globalization.*

74 On the co-constitution of the micro (including the intimate and embodied) and the macro, see, especially, feminist scholars like Hoang, *Dealing in Desire;* Klinger, *Rare Earth Frontiers;* McGranahan, "Empire Out of Bounds"; Lutz, "Empire Is in the Details"; Greenburg, *At War with Women;* Appel, *Licit Life of Capitalism;* Brickell and Cuomo, "Feminist Geolegality"; Hyndman, "Towards a Feminist Geopolitics."

75 Agnew, "Low Geopolitics"; Agnew, *Hidden Geopolitics.*

76 Putnam, "Courts without Borders," 2009, 483.

77 This phrase was popularized by Mnookin and Kornhauser, "Bargaining." Whytock extends it to transnational law, arguing that "the global governance functions of domestic courts matter not only because of

their direct impact on litigants, but also—and perhaps even more importantly—because of their influence beyond borders and beyond the parties to particular lawsuits." Whytock, "Domestic Courts and Global Governance," 72.

78   Potts, "Law's place in economic geography."

79   Potts, "Law as Geopolitics."

80   It is Third World governments (through their lawyers), and not Third World societies, that are directly involved in contesting US transnational law. These governments themselves are, of course, always the product of internal and often conflicting social and political pressures, but such dynamics are largely invisible during litigation. In this way, litigation contributes to producing the appearance or "effect" of a coherent, unitary state. See Appel, *Licit Life of Capitalism;* Mitchell, "Society, Economy, and the State Effect."

81   Pistor, *Code of Capital;* Coates, *Legalist Empire;* Dezalay and Garth, *Internationalization of Palace Wars.*

82   Federal courts include the US Supreme Court, as well as 13 US Courts of Appeals, and 94 US District Courts.

83   For key examples, see Blomley, *Law, Space;* Delaney, *Race, Place, and the Law, 1836–1948;* Ford, "Law's Territory." By the early twenty-first century, legal geography had become an established subfield, resulting, for example in important edited volumes like Blomley, Delaney, and Ford, *Legal Geographies Reader;* Holder and Harrison, "Law and Geography"; Braverman et al., *Expanding Spaces of Law.*

84   See, e.g., Brighenti, "On Territory"; Butler, "Critical Legal Studies"; Raustiala, "Geography of Justice"; Valverde, "Jurisdiction and Scale"; Valverde, "Analyzing the Governance of Security."

85   As Delaney explains, "'To legally constitute some entity X' (space, the home, the corporation, appropriate sex, persons, events) means much more than to shape or influence it. In the strongest sense it is to call it into being or modify its social significance through the distinctive practices of naming, classifying, ruling, governing, or ordering associated with law most broadly conceived." Delaney, "Legal Geography I," 98.

86   Hart, "Relational Comparison Revisited."

87   Blomley and Bakan, "Spacing Out," 688. Baxi, relatedly, argues that "No error in the doing of comparative legal studies is more egregious than that which remains complicit with the politics of organized amnesia of law as a form of conquest." Baxi, "Colonialist Heritage," 59.

88   Blomley, *Law, Space.*

89   Sheppard, "Globalizing Capitalism's Raggedy Fringes."

90   Throughout the book, I sometimes use the terms *North* and *South* as shorthand to refer, respectively, to the Global North and the Global South.

ONE. LAW, CAPITAL, AND THE GEOGRAPHIES OF EMPIRE

1   *Plessy v. Ferguson*, 163 U.S. 537 (1896)

2   *Downes v. Bidwell*, 182 U.S. 244 (1901)

3   *Downes v. Bidwell*, 182 U.S. 244, 287 (1901)

4   *Downes v. Bidwell*, 182 U.S. 244, 341 (1901)

5   *Cherokee Nation v. Georgia*, 30 U.S. 1, 17 (1831). See Jodi Byrd's spatial analysis of Marshall's ruling in *Transit of Empire*. Benton and Bender each usefully compare *Downes* to *Cherokee Nation*, while Immerwahr and Fonseca each connect *Downes* with *Plessy*. Benton, *Search for Sovereignty*; Bender, *Nation among Nations*; Immerwahr, *How to Hide an Empire*; Fonseca, "Beyond Colonial Entrapment."

6   *Brown v. Board of Education*, 347 U.S. 483 (1954).

7   See, among many others, Bhandar, *Colonial Lives of Property*; Biolsi, "Imagined Geographies"; Byrd, *Transit of Empire*; Harjo, *Spiral to the Stars*.

8   Burnett, "Untied States," 813.

9   *Underhill v. Hernandez*, 168 U.S. 250 (1897).

10   *Underhill v. Hernandez*, 168 U.S. 250, 252 (1897).

11   See, e.g., Fox, "Re-examining"; Chow, "Rethinking"; Patterson, "Act of State Doctrine"; Diaz, "Territoriality Inquiry"; Wight, "Evaluation."

12   "Redress of grievances by reason of such acts must be obtained through the means open to be availed of by sovereign powers as between themselves" (*Underhill v. Hernandez*, 168 U.S. 250, 252 (1897)).

13   My conception of empire draws heavily on historians Jane Burbank and Frederick Cooper, who understand empires as large political units driven by logics of enrichment and expansion, which "maintain distinction and hierarchy as they incorporate new people." Burbank and Cooper, *Empires in World History*, 8. Stoler and McGranahan, similarly, see empires as dynamic and complex economic, political, cultural, and ideological entities characterized by "inequitable treatment, hierarchical relations, and unequal rule." Stoler, McGranahan, and Perdue, *Imperial Formations*, 11.

14   Stoler, McGranahan, and Perdue, *Imperial Formations*.

15   Overly state-centric definitions of empire emphasizing the centralization of power in and coherence of imperial projects overlook a wealth of nuanced historical work on previous empires that has emerged in the past few decades. Such definitions impede recognition of key continuities between these past empires and certain powerful states today, whether or not one accepts the imperial label for the latter.

16   Bender, *Nation among Nations*; Benton, *Search for Sovereignty*; Burbank and Cooper, *Empires in World History*; Moore, *Empire's Labor*; Stoler, McGranahan, and Perdue, *Imperial Formations*.

17   Appel, *Licit Life of Capitalism*.

NOTES TO CHAPTER ONE · 207

18 Gibson-Graham, *Postcapitalist Politics*; Sheppard, "Globalizing Capital-ism's Raggedy Fringes."

19 Harvey, *New Imperialism*; Marx, *Capital*; Moore, *Capitalism in the Web of Life*; Walker, "Value and Nature." Capitalist dynamics also played a fundamental role in the (re)territorialization of state spaces within Europe. Indeed, Schoenberger argues that markets themselves evolved to facilitate "the state-building tasks of territorial conquest and control." Schoenberger, "Origins of the Market Economy," 663.

20 For the canonical text on racial capitalism, see Robinson, *Black Marxism*. For more recent work on the ways that racialized and gendered differ-ences are constitutive of capitalism, see, among many others, Appel, *Licit Life of Capitalism*; Federici, *Caliban and the Witch*; Gilmore, *Abolition Geography*; Hoang, *Dealing in Desire*; Hudson, *Bankers and Empire*.

21 Blaut, *Colonizer's Model of the World*; Sheppard, "Thinking Geographically."

22 Luxemburg, *Accumulation of Capital*; Marx, *Capital*; Moore, *Capitalism in the Web of Life*. Marxist accounts of empire have undoubtedly been too reductionist at times in their focus on accumulation as *the* driver of imperialism. Much of the most interesting recent work on empire has instead emphasized the diversity of imperial agents and motivations, among which capitalists and capitalist logics comprise only a subset (see, e.g., Benton, *Search for Sovereignty*; Burbank and Cooper, *Empires in World History*; Stoler, *Imperial Debris*; Stoler, McGranahan, and Perdue, *Imperial Formations*). Yet, such work has sometimes swung too far in the opposite direction, often mentioning capitalism as one factor in imperialism with-out sustained analyses of capitalist accumulation. Much work remains to be done to integrate empirically and theoretically rich studies of variegated imperial formations with equally nuanced analyses of intersecting capitalist dynamics. Fruitful work in this direction includes that by Fernando Coronil in "After Empire" and Peter J. Hudson in *Bankers and Empire*.

23 For a good overview, see Hobsbawm, *Age of Empire*. See also Burbank and Cooper, *Empires in World History*.

24 In "Imperialism, the Highest Stage of Capitalism," Lenin famously argued that the high age of intensified imperial expansion in the late nineteenth and early twentieth centuries was driven in large part by the need for profitable investment opportunities abroad in the context of a growing overaccumulation crisis in the metropole. Historians have since cast doubt on aspects of this analysis. (See, e.g., Burbank and Cooper, *Empires in World History*; Hobsbawm, *Age of Empire*). Yet, updated ver-sions of Lenin's argument remain powerful both for explaining certain contemporary capitalist tendencies (see, e.g., Amin, "Towards the Fifth International?"; Harvey, *New Imperialism*), and for analyzing the linked development of capitalist and territorial expansion within Europe in earlier periods (see Arrighi, *Long Twentieth Century*).

25   See, among many others, Amin, "Unequal Development"; Patnaik and
     Patnaik, *Theory of Imperialism*; Rodney, *How Europe Underdeveloped
     Africa*; Sanyal, *Rethinking Capitalist Development*.

26   The idea that American imperialism was limited to a brief period of over-
     seas expansion at the end of the nineteenth century depends on natural-
     izing the current continental borders of the United States and accepting
     exceptionalist discourses about the supposed uniqueness of American
     history. In fact, the United States was neither uniquely anti-imperialist,
     nor uniquely imperialist. Rather, it was "an empire among empires," and
     American expansion was always shaped by the broader imperial milieu
     within which it occurred. Bender, *Nation among Nations*, 182.

27   Bender, *Nation among Nations*, 187.

28   Bender, *Nation among Nations*, 245.

29   Grewal, "Laws of Capitalism," 652.

30   On property rights, see Blomley, "Law, Property"; Blomley, "Territory of
     Property"; Blomley, *Territory*. On mediating the distribution of value,
     see Ashton, "Evolving Juridical Space of Harm/Value"; Christophers and
     Niedt, "Resisting Devaluation"; Potts, "(Re-)Writing Markets." On in-
     stitutionalizing cultural norms, see Poon, Pollard, and Chow, "Resetting
     Neoliberal Values," 1442. On transforming things into assets, see Pistor,
     Code of Capital.

31   Brett Christophers's work on the performative role of law in bounding
     particular markets is especially innovative. Christophers, "Competition";
     Christophers, "Law's Markets"; Christophers, *Great Leveler*. Focusing on
     competition and antitrust law, he uses the concept of the "law's markets"
     to examine how, in attempting to describe markets, law actually defines
     and enacts them: "In its struggle to re-present markets that do not exist,
     the law, ironically, produces and reproduces *real* markets; not the precise
     markets envisioned by the law, but markets nonetheless." Christophers,
     "Law's Markets," 140 (emphasis in original).

32   Barkan, *Corporate Sovereignty*, 88 (emphasis in original).

33   On law and corporate sovereignty, see Barkan, *Corporate Sovereignty*. On the
     offshore and the enclave, see Appel, *Licit Life of Capitalism*; Clark, Lai, and
     Wójcik, "Editorial Introduction"; Maurer, "Cyberspatial Sovereignties."

34   Anghie, *Imperialism*; Bhandar, *Colonial Lives of Property*; Burbank,
     "Rights of Difference."

35   Benton, *Search for Sovereignty*; Burbank and Cooper, "Rules of Law, Poli-
     tics of Empire."

36   Benton, *Law and Colonial Cultures*; Benton, *Search for Sovereignty*; Ben-
     ton and Ross, *Legal Pluralism and Empires, 1500–1850*.

37   Anghie, *Imperialism*; Chimni, "Third World Approaches to International
     Law"; Gathii, "TWAIL."

38   See, among many others, Hall, *The West and the Rest*; Robinson, *Black
     Marxism*; Said, *Orientalism*.

39   See, e.g., Anghie, *Imperialism*; Baxi, "Colonialist Heritage"; Bhandar, *Colonial Lives of Property*; El-Enany, *(B)ordering Britain*; Rana, *Two Faces of American Freedom*. There has been a recent surge of interest in the intersection of law, race, and empire, emerging in part out of renewed efforts to connect the traditions of Third World Approaches to International Law (TWAIL), long focused on international law and empire, and Critical Race Theory (CRT), traditionally focused on domestic US law. This initiative gained considerable impetus from a 2020 symposium bringing TWAIL and CRT scholars together at the University of California, Los Angeles. For an overview of these conversations, see the introduction to a special issue that emerged out of this symposium: Achiume and Bâli, "Race and Empire."

40   Anghie, *Imperialism*. See also Koskenniemi, Rech, and Fonseca, *International Law and Empire* for a probing collection of essays on "international law's 'imperial ambivalence,'" 4.

41   For a recent insightful analysis, see Byrd, *Transit of Empire*.

42   Park, "Money."

43   Bhandar, *Colonial Lives of Property*, 5. Bhandar (4) argues more fully that:

> the evolution of modern property laws and justifications for private property ownership were articulated through the attribution of value to the lives of those defined as having the capacity, will, and technology to appropriate, which in turn was contingent on prevailing concepts of race and racial difference. The colonial encounter produced a racial regime of ownership that persists into the present, creating a conceptual apparatus in which justifications for private property ownership remain bound to a concept of the human that is thoroughly racial in its makeup.

Bhandar draws on and extends Cheryl Harris's classic text "Whiteness as Property." See also, Moreton-Robinson, *The White Possessive*. These conversations on race, property, and empire intersect with a growing, broader conversation on race and property in geography and other disciplines (for an overview, see Bonds, "Race and Ethnicity I").

44   See, especially, Horwitz, *Transformation of American Law, 1780–1860*; Horwitz, *Transformation of American Law, 1870–1960*; Pistor, *Code of Capital*.

45   Bender, *Nation among Nations*; Burbank and Cooper, *Empires in World History*; Bâli and Rana, "Constitutionalism."

46   See, generally, Ayala and Bernabe, *Puerto Rico in the American Century*; Burnett, "Untied States"; Burnett and Marshall, *Foreign in a Domestic Sense*; Fonseca, "Beyond Colonial Entrapment"; Meléndez, "Citizenship"; Raustiala, *Does the Constitution Follow the Flag?*

47   Bender, *Nation among Nations*.

48   Hudson, *Bankers and Empire*.

49   Coronil, "After Empire."

50   Hudson, *Bankers and Empire.*

51   Coates, *Legalist Empire*, 7.

52   Coates, *Legalist Empire*, 3.

53   Coates, *Legalist Empire*, 10. See also Dezalay and Garth, "Law, Lawyers, and Empire."

54   In addition to *Underhill*, see, e.g., *Shapleigh et al. v. Mier*, 299 U.S. 468, 471 (1937): "The question is not here whether the proceeding was so conducted as to be a wrong to our nationals under the doctrines of international law, though valid under the law of the situs of the land. For wrongs of that order the remedy to be followed is along the channels of diplomacy."

55   Panitch and Gindin, *Making of Global Capitalism*, vii.

56   On postwar US empire, see generally Camp and Greenburg, "Counterinsurgency Reexamined"; Coronil, "After Empire"; Gowan, *Global Gamble*; Greenburg, *At War with Women*; Hart, "Why Did It Take So Long?"; Immerwahr, *How to Hide an Empire*; Lutz, "Empire Is in the Details"; Mamdani, *Good Muslim, Bad Muslim*; Moore, *Empire's Labor*; Panitch and Gindin, *Making of Global Capitalism*.

57   McGranahan, "Empire Out of Bounds," 175. See also Lutz, "Empire Is in the Details."

58   See, among many others, Coronil, "After Empire"; Panitch and Gindin, *Making of Global Capitalism*; Mamdani, *Good Muslim, Bad Muslim*; Toussaint and Millet, *Debt, the IMF, and the World Bank*.

59   See, especially, Harvey, *Limits to Capital*; Sheppard, "Thinking Geographically"; Sheppard, "Globalizing Capitalism's Raggedy Fringes"; Smith, *Uneven Development*; Sparke, *Introducing Globalization*.

60   Amin, "Towards the Fifth International?"; Bond, *Looting Africa*; Bond and Garcia, BRICS; Patnaik and Patnaik, *Theory of Imperialism*.

61   Barkan, "Law"; Brown, *Undoing the Demos*; Bryan, Rafferty, and Wigan, "From Time–Space Compression to Spatial Spreads"; Foucault, *Birth of Biopolitics*; Peck and Tickell, "Neoliberalizing Space"; Peck, *Constructions of Neoliberal Reason*; Krippner, *Capitalizing on Crisis*; Slobodian, *Globalists*.

62   This is true both in what Peck calls the "roll-back" phase of neoliberalism, characterized by familiar policies like trade and capital liberalization, spending cuts, privatization, and so on, and in the "roll-out" phase of neoliberalism, when the disruptions of the previous phase are ameliorated through various state interventions of a "market conforming" variety. Peck, *Constructions of Neoliberal Reason*, 38. Neither phase fits a cookie-cutter model. Neoliberalism is better understood as a process of neoliberal*ization* that is always uneven and differentiated and grounded in particular places, policies, and institutions. Peck and Theodore, "Reanimating Neoliberalism." As Peck puts it, neoliberalism contains

"institutional promiscuity and ideological sprawl." Peck, *Constructions of Neoliberal Reason*, 47.

63   Panitch and Gindin, *Making of Global Capitalism*, 3.

64   Panitch and Gindin, *Making of Global Capitalism*, 223.

65   Anghie, *Imperialism*; Appel, *Licit Life of Capitalism*; Schneiderman, *Constitutionalizing Economic Globalization*.

66   Schneiderman, *Constitutionalizing Economic Globalization*; Panitch and Gindin, *Making of Global Capitalism*. US rules on due process, corporate legal personality, and the "takings doctrine" have been especially influential.

67   Dezalay and Garth, *Internationalization of Palace Wars*.

68   Dezalay and Garth, "Law, Lawyers, and Empire."

69   Dezalay and Garth, "Law, Lawyers, and Empire," 756.

70   Chimni, "Third World Approaches to International Law," 4, 5. On this point, see also Anghie, *Imperialism*; Gathii, "TWAIL"; Bâli and Rana, "Constitutionalism."

71   Although the consent or complicity of Third World elites is important to US judicial power today, this is a consent born at least partly out of the failure of years of concerted resistance, as well as the spread of technocratic expertise from North to South and the successful reengineering of the internal social relations of Third World states in the neoliberal era. Dezalay and Garth, *Internationalization of Palace Wars*; Gowan, *Global Gamble*; Roos, *Why Not Default?*

72   See, e.g., Buzan, *The United States and the Great Powers*; Clark, *Hegemony in International Society*; Ikenberry, *After Victory*; Ikenberry, *America Unrivaled*. For a useful overview of such approaches to hegemony, see Anderson, *H-Word*.

73   Agnew, for instance, argues that *hegemony*, which involves a mix of "convincing, cajoling, and coercing," is a better term than *empire* for illuminating the current configuration of US power. Agnew, *Hegemony*, 2. Specifically, he uses the concept to emphasize not only the centralized agency of the US government but also the far more diffuse power of nonstate, corporate, and intergovernmental institutions and of the social and cultural, as well as economic norms of market society. Moreover, he sees "American hegemony slowly giving way to a hegemony without a hegemon, or hegemony exercised increasingly through global markets and international institutions by a growing transnational class of business people and bureaucrats" (26). Arrighi likewise uses the concept of "world hegemony" to break with classical theories of imperialism, which he sees as ill-suited to capturing the specificity of post–World War II American power. Emphasizing contestation over and struggles to forge consent, his concept is meant to capture "the power associated with dominance expanded by the exercise of 'intellectual and moral leadership'" and the ability to "place all the issues around which conflict rages on a 'universal'

plane." Although the "claim of the dominant group to represent the general interest is always more or less fraudulent . . . we shall speak of hegemony only when the claim is at least partly true and adds something to the power of the dominant group." Arrighi, *Long Twentieth Century*, 29, 30.

74 See, e.g., Burbank, "Rights of Difference"; Burbank and Cooper, *Empires in World History*; Lutz, "Empire Is in the Details." As Anderson suggests, the line between hegemony and imperialism has often been blurry, both analytically and empirically, and all efforts to sharply distinguish the two inevitably run into difficulties. Anderson, *H-Word*.

75 Agnew, *Hegemony*, 20, 2.

76 Greenburg argues that the concept of imperialism also helps "to signify new, violent, and expansionary dimensions of US financial and military power and continuities of colonial ideologies of race imported into the present through military trainings." Greenburg, *At War with Women*, 15. See also Hart, "Why Did It Take So Long?"

77 See, among many others, Coates, *Legalist Empire*; Panitch and Gindin, *Making of Global Capitalism*; Panitch and Gindin, "Finance and American Empire"; Gowan, *Calculus of Power*; Go, *Patterns of Empire*.

78 Burbank and Cooper, *Empires in World History*.

79 Potts, "Reterritorializing Economic Governance."

80 On the concept of variegation, see Peck and Theodore, "Variegated Capitalism."

81 Benton, *Search for Sovereignty*; Burbank and Cooper, *Empires in World History*; Stoler, McGranahan, and Perdue, *Imperial Formations*.

82 Benton, *Search for Sovereignty*, xii. Benton discusses and critiques this tendency at length.

83 Goswami, "Rethinking the Modular Nation Form."

84 Burbank and Cooper, *Empires in World History*; Cooper, "Provincializing France." These authors show, furthermore, that many debates about rights and citizenship commonly associated with the rise of the nation-state actually emerged in imperial, not purely national contexts.

85 Stoler, McGranahan, and Perdue, *Imperial Formations*, 10.

86 Burbank and Cooper, *Empires in World History*, 17.

87 Benton, *Search for Sovereignty*, 103.

88 Benton, *Search for Sovereignty*, 102, 103, 108.

89 Benton, *Search for Sovereignty*; Benton, *Law and Colonial Cultures*; Benton and Ross, *Legal Pluralism and Empires, 1500–1850*.

90 Benton, *Search for Sovereignty*, 280.

91 On graduated sovereignty in other contexts, see Biolsi, "Imagined Geographies"; Ong, "Graduated Sovereignty in South-East Asia." For other examples of complex, non-Cartesian, and contorted sovereignties, see Billé, *Voluminous States*.

92 See the introduction.

93 See, e.g., Benton, *Search for Sovereignty*; Burbank and Cooper, *Empires in World History*; Lutz, "Empire Is in the Details"; Moore, *Empire's Labor*.

94 See, among many others, Bâli and Rana, "Constitutionalism"; Baxi, "Colonialist Heritage"; Chimni, "Third World Approaches"; Anderson, *American Foreign Policy*; Gowan, *Global Gamble*; Panitch and Gindin, *Making of Global Capitalism*.

95 Barkan, "Law."

96 Barkan, *Corporate Sovereignty*, 43.

97 Potts, "Deep Finance."

98 Hart, "Why Did It Take So Long?"

99 Anderson, *H-Word*, 31.

100 Potts, "Law as Geopolitics."

101 Brown, *Undoing the Demos*; Mitchell, *Rule of Experts*; Peck, *Constructions of Neoliberal Reason*; Polanyi, *Great Transformation*; Slobodian, *Globalists*.

102 Roberts, Secor, and Sparke, "Neoliberal Geopolitics," 433.

TWO. THE POLITICS OF THE PRIVATE

1 Brief for the Appellant, *Berizzi Bros. Co. v. S.S. Pesaro* (U.S. Apr. 10, 1926) (No. 334); Stipulation, *Berizzi Bros. Co. v. S.S. Pesaro* (Mar. 13, 1925) (S.D.N.Y. 78–248).

2 Brief for the Appellant at 6, *Berizzi Bros. Co. v. S.S. Pesaro* (U.S. Apr. 10, 1926) (No. 334).

3 Brief for the "Pesaro" and for her Claimant, the Royal Italian Ambassador at 18, *Berizzi Bros. Co. v. S.S. Pesaro* (U.S. 1925) (No. 334).

4 *Berizzi Bros. Co. v. S.S. Pesaro*, 271 U.S. 562, 574 (1926) (my emphasis).

5 Foreign Sovereign Immunities Act, 28 U.S.C. 1602 et seq. (1976).

6 Lauterpacht, "Problem"; Fox and Webb, *Law of State Immunity*; Goode, Kronke, and McKendrick, *Transnational Commercial Law*.

7 Fox and Webb, *Law of State Immunity*, 33.

8 See, e.g., Fox and Webb, *Law of State Immunity*; Dellapenna, "Interpreting"; Goode, Kronke, and McKendrick, *Transnational Commercial Law*. Verdier and Voeten reflect many of these general tendencies but are more geographically nuanced in their account of the diffusion of the restrictive approach. Verdier and Voeten, "How Does Customary International Law Change?"

9 Fox and Webb, *Law of State Immunity*, 98.

10 Lauterpacht, "Problem of Jurisdictional Immunities of Foreign States," 231.

11 Lauterpacht, "Problem of Jurisdictional Immunities of Foreign States," 220, 221.

12 Lauterpacht, "Problem of Jurisdictional Immunities of Foreign States," 226.

13 Lauterpacht, "Problem of Jurisdictional Immunities of Foreign States," 226.

14 See, e.g., Fox and Webb, *Law of State Immunity*; Wuerth, "Symposium Epilog."

15   Polanyi, *Great Transformation*, 74.

16   Panitch and Gindin, *Making of Global Capitalism*, 3.

17   Coronil, "After Empire," 262.

18   Polanyi, *Great Transformation*; Block, "Karl Polanyi"; Krippner, "Polanyi for the Age of Trump."

19   On the continued power of this discourse, even as its accuracy diminishes more than ever, see Peck, "On Capitalism's Cusp."

20   Mann, "Race Between Economics and Politics," A1.

21   Mitchell suggests this is better understood as frontier than boundary. Mitchell, "Properties of Markets."

22   Horwitz, *Transformation of American Law, 1870–1960*; Barkan, *Corporate Sovereignty*.

23   Horwitz, *Transformation of American Law, 1870–1960*, 207.

24   Horwitz, *Transformation of American Law, 1870–1960*.

25   Slobodian, *Globalists*.

26   Slobodian, *Globalists*, 212.

27   Quoted in Slobodian, *Globalists*, 240.

28   Peck and Tickell, "Neoliberalizing Space"; Peck, *Constructions of Neoliberal Reason*; Slobodian, *Globalists*; Barkan, "Law."

29   Krippner, "Polanyi for the Age of Trump"; Krippner, *Capitalizing on Crisis*.

30   Krippner, *Capitalizing on Crisis*.

31   Britton-Purdy et al., "Building a Law-and-Political-Economy Framework."

32   Britton-Purdy et al., "Building a Law-and-Political-Economy Framework"; Grewal and Purdy, "Introduction."

33   Britton-Purdy et al., "Building a Law-and-Political-Economy Framework," 1791.

34   For exceptions, see Slobodian, *Globalists*; Sheppard and Leitner, "Quo Vadis Neoliberalism?"

35   Prashad, *Darker Nations*.

36   Getachew, *Worldmaking after Empire*.

37   Getachew, *Worldmaking after Empire*; Prashad, *Darker Nations*; Rajagopal, *International Law from Below*.

38   Getachew, *Worldmaking after Empire*, 145.

39   Getachew, *Worldmaking after Empire*; Rajagopal, *International Law from Below*.

40   Declaration on the Establishment of a New International Economic Order, G. A. Res. 3201, Sixth Spec. Sess. GAOR, Supp 1, U. N. Doc. A/9559 (1974); Charter of Economic Rights and Duties of States, G. A. Res. 3281, 29 GAOR, Supp. 30, U. N. Doc. A/9030 (1974).

41   Amin, "Towards the Fifth International?"

42   See generally Rajagopal, *International Law from Below*; Getachew, *Worldmaking after Empire*; Prashad, *Darker Nations*.

43   Slobodian, *Globalists*.

44   Anghie, *Imperialism*; Getachew, *Worldmaking after Empire*.

45   Mann, "Race Between Economics and Politics," A2.

46   See, among many others, Chimni, "Third World Approaches to International Law"; Gowan, *Calculus of Power*; Mitchell, *Rule of Experts*.

47   Anghie, *Imperialism,* 230.

48   Anghie, *Imperialism,* 239.

49   Buxbaum, "Role of Public International Law," 16:9.

50   *The Schooner Exchange v. McFaddon*, 11 U.S. 116 (1812).

51   See, e.g., Bradley and Helfer, "International Law"; Goode, Kronke, and McKendrick, *Transnational Commercial Law*; Verdier and Voeten, "How Does Customary International Law Change?"; Chilton and Whytock, "Foreign Sovereign Immunity"; Fox and Webb, *Law of State Immunity*.

52   *The Schooner Exchange v. McFaddon*, 11 U.S. 116 (1812).

53   See, e.g., *Briggs v. Light-Boat Upper Cedar Point*, 93 Mass. 157 (1865) (which concerned the US government's immunity in its own courts but which drew on, and later influenced, foreign sovereign immunity cases); *Long v. The Tampico*, 16 F. 491 (S.D.N.Y. 1883) (immunity denied on other grounds). US courts also considered whether immunity *claims* were made by someone with sovereign status (see, e.g., *The Anne*, 16 U.S. 435 (1818); *The Maipo*, 252 F. 627 (S.D.N.Y. 1918); *The Sao Vicente*, 260 U.S. 151 (1922)).

54   See, e.g., *The Schooner Exchange v. McFaddon*, 11 U.S. 116 (1812); *Briggs v. Light-Boat Upper Cedar Point*, 93 Mass. 157 (1865); *Mason v. Intercolonial Railroad of Canada*, 197 Mass. 349 (1908). For a similar equation of private and personal in a different context see *The Paquete Habana*, 175 U.S. 677 (1900). Commercial activity was already widely defined as private in domestic US law, including in some cases regarding the immunity of US *states*. That this was not extended to foreign sovereigns may have been partly due to the infrequency of state involvement in transnational economic activity in the nineteenth century. Some judges, however, distinguished explicitly between domestic and transnational sovereign immunity in relation to the public/private distinction (see, e.g., *United States v. Wilder*, 28 F. Cas. 601, 604 (C.C.D. Mass. 1838)).

55   See, e.g., *The Pesaro*, 277 F. 473 (S.D.N.Y. 1921) (decision later vacated); *The Gul Djemal*, 264 U.S. 90 (1924) (case decided on different grounds). Those objecting to immunity for foreign state-owned merchant ships frequently cited the 1916 and 1920 Shipping Acts, which already limited immunity for *US* state-owned merchant ships in US courts.

56   During the early phases of *Berizzi*, the Department noted that it would not intervene, but that it believed "government-owned merchant vessels . . . should not be regarded as entitled to the immunities accorded public vessels of war" (*The Pesaro*, 277 F. 473, 479 (S.D.N.Y. 1921)). This was also a period of international debate about the issue.

57   *The Maipo*, 252 F. 627 (S.D.N.Y. 1918); *The Maipo*, 259 F. 367 (S.D.N.Y. 1919); *The Carlo Poma*, 259 F. 369 (2d Cir. 1919); *The Pesaro*, 13 F.2d 468 (2d Cir. 1926).

58   See, e.g., *The Maipo*, 259 F. 367, 368 (S.D.N.Y. 1919): "If the Republic of Chile considers it a governmental function to go into the carrying trade, as would appear to be the case here, that is the business of the Republic of Chile; and if we do not approve of it, if we do not like it, if we do not wish any longer to accord that respect to the property so engaged, which has hitherto been accorded to government property, then we must say so through diplomatic channels, and not through the judiciary."

59   *Berizzi Bros. Co. v. S.S. Pesaro*, 271 U.S. 562, 574 (1926).

60   See, e.g., *Republic of Mexico v. Hoffman*, 324 U.S. 30 (1945) (majority and concurring opinions); *Flota Maritima Browning de Cuba, Sociadad Anonima v. Motor Vessel Ciudad de la Habana*, 335 F.2d 619 (4th Cir. 1964).

61   Tate, "Tate Letter."

62   Jarvis, "Tate Letter."

63   Tate, "Tate Letter."

64   Tate offered no explicit definition of private in the letter, but his comments make clear that he considered merchant vessels, state trading activity, and generally the "increasing practice on the part of governments of engaging in commercial activities" to be in that category. Tate, "Tate Letter." Only because the equation of commercial and private has since become so entrenched has the anachronistic projection of this equation onto earlier periods been accepted so easily by later scholars.

65   *United States of Mexico v. Rask*, 118 Cal. App. 21 (Cal. Ct. App. 1931); *The Navemar*, 90 F.2d 673 (2d Cir. 1937); *Ex Parte Republic of Peru*, 318 U.S. 578 (1943); *Republic of Mexico v. Hoffman*, 324 U.S. 30 (1945) (immunity denied on other grounds).

66   Coates, *Legalist Empire*; Dezalay and Garth, "Law, Lawyers, and Empire."

67   *Ex Parte Republic of Peru*, 318 U.S. 578 (1943); *Republic of Mexico v. Hoffman*, 324 U.S. 30 (1945).

68   For an extended discussion of the relationship between the Tate Letter and *Berizzi* see *Flota Maritima Browning de Cuba, Sociadad Anonima v. Motor Vessel Ciudad de la Habana*, 335 F.2d 619 (4th Cir. 1964).

69   Tate, "Tate Letter." See also Tate's 1954 speech to the Association of the Bar of the City of New York, reprinted in Jarvis, "Tate Letter."

70   Verdier and Voeten, "How Does Customary International Law Change?" See also Fox and Webb, *Law of State Immunity* for a detailed timeline of the adoption of the restrictive approach by various countries.

71   Tate, "Tate Letter."

72   See also Department of State legal adviser Monroe Leigh's statement at a 1976 Congressional hearing on foreign sovereign immunity: "Naturally, all of the socialist countries which carry on their international commerce

through state trading corporations would like to be able to use the defense of sovereign immunity when they are sued in the courts of a foreign country . . . indeed, there are those who say that one of the motivations for the development of the restrictive theory of sovereign immunity was the fact that the Soviet Union in the 1920's was acting through state trading corporations which claimed immunity." U.S. Congress. House. Subcommittee on Administrative Law and Governmental Relations of the Committee on the Judiciary, "Jurisdiction of U.S. Courts in Suits Against Foreign States," 56. See also *Flota Maritima Browning de Cuba, Sociadad Anonima v. Motor Vessel Ciudad de la Habana*, 335 F.2d 619 (4th Cir. 1964); *In re Grand Jury Investigation of Shipping Industry*, 186 F. Supp. 298 (D.D.C. 1960).

73   Tate himself worked in various New Deal programs (https://www .trumanlibrary.gov/library/personal-papers/jack-b-tate-papers). As a Department of State official from the time later explained, "I'm sure that all of us who felt that we came in with the New Deal did have a free trade approach to it rather than protectionists; very much so. This became very much the policy of the whole State Department" (Oral History Interview with Michael H. Cardozo, https://www.trumanlibrary.gov/library/oral -histories/cardozom). See also Dezalay and Garth, "Law, Lawyers, and Empire."

74   "Sovereign Immunity Decisions of the Department of State."

75   *Victory Transport, Inc. v. Comisaria General de Abastecimientos y Transportes*, 336 F.2d 354, 359 (2d Cir. 1964) (my emphasis).

76   *United States of Mexico v. Rask*, 118 Cal. App. 21 (Cal. Ct. App. 1931); *The Navemar*, 90 F.2d 673 (2d Cir. 1937); *Ex Parte Republic of Peru*, 318 U.S. 578 (1943); *Republic of Mexico v. Hoffman*, 324 U.S. 30 (1945) (immunity denied on other grounds).

77   "Sovereign Immunity Decisions of the Department of State."

78   *Mason v. Intercolonial Railroad of Canada*, 197 Mass. 349 (1908) (see Barkan, *Corporate Sovereignty*, for an analysis of this case in relation to the public/private divide); *Oliver American Trading Co. v. Mexico*, 5 F.2d 659 (2d Cir. 1924); *Dexter & Carpenter, Inc. v. Kunglig Jarnvagsstyrelsen*, 43 F.2d 705 (2d Cir. 1930) (immunity denied on other grounds).

79   *In re Investigation of World Arrangements, etc.*, 13 F.R.D. 280, 289 (D.D.C. 1952).

80   "Sovereign Immunity Decisions of the Department of State."

81   "Sovereign Immunity Decisions of the Department of State."

82   "Sovereign Immunity Decisions of the Department of State."

83   *Ex Parte United States*, 257 U.S. 419, 430 (1922).

84   *New York & Cuba Mail S.S. Co. v. Republic of Korea*, 132 F. Supp. 684, 685 (S.D.N.Y. 1955).

85   *New York & Cuba Mail S.S. Co. v. Republic of Korea*, 132 F. Supp. 684, 686 (S.D.N.Y. 1955).

86　*New York & Cuba Mail S.S. Co. v. Republic of Korea,* 132 F. Supp. 684 (S.D.N.Y. 1955); "Sovereign Immunity Decisions of the Department of State," 1028–29.

87　The Agricultural Trade Development and Assistance Act of 1954 (Pub. L. 480, enacted July 10, 1954).

88　By underselling farmers in many low-income nations, the program also devastated their agricultural sectors, leaving many countries even more vulnerable when PL-480 was suspended a few years later. Gupta, *Postcolonial Developments.*

89　"Sovereign Immunity Decisions of the Department of State."

90　Petition for a Writ of Certiorari to the United States Court of Appeals for the Second Circuit at 8, *Comisaria General de Abastecimientos y Transportes v. Victory Transport, Inc.* (U.S. Jan. 7, 1965) (No. 815).

91　*Victory Transport, Inc. v. Comisaria General de Abastecimientos y Transportes,* 336 F.2d 354, 360 (2d Cir. 1964).

92　*Victory Transport, Inc. v. Comisaria General de Abastecimientos y Transportes,* 336 F.2d 354, 360 (2d Cir. 1964). The political/legal distinction elaborated in the 1940s continued to underpin the public/private distinction during the Tate period.

93　Citation history available from LexisNexis Academic: Nexis Uni°: https://advance.lexis.com.

94　For a decision holding that countries must determine for themselves what counts as public, see, e.g., *The Maipo,* 259 F. 367, 368 (S.D.N.Y. 1919). See also, *Frazier v. Hanover Bank* (Sup. Ct., N.Y. 1953), discussed in "Sovereign Immunity Decisions of the Department of State."

95　See, e.g., *Briggs v. Light-Boat Upper Cedar Point,* 93 Mass. 157 (1865); *Long v. The Tampico,* 16 F. 491 (S.D.N.Y. 1883); *The Roseric,* 254 F. 154 (D.N.J. 1918).

96　*Berizzi Bros. Co. v. S.S. Pesaro,* 271 U.S. 562, 574 (1926).

97　"Sovereign Immunity Decisions of the Department of State," 1038.

98　"Sovereign Immunity Decisions of the Department of State," 1046.

99　In practice, the nature/purpose distinction was applied inconsistently throughout the Tate Period, but the tendency was to move in this direction. "Sovereign Immunity Decisions of the Department of State."

100　*Morrison, Inc. v. Servicio Autonomo Nacional de Acueductos y Alcantarillados,* Civil No. 5092 (N.D. Ind. 1969). See also *Pruitt v. M/V Patignies* (E.D. Mich. 1968): the Canadian Department of Transport's piloting of boats was a commercial act, since private pilots also perform this activity; *Cole v. Heidtman* (S.D.N.Y. 1968): the British West Indies Central Labour Organization's arrangement of employment for Jamaican nationals in the United States was a commercial activity since these activities "are very much akin to those that might be conducted by a labor union or by a private employment agency." Discussed in "Sovereign Immunity Decisions of the Department of State," 1061–64.

101 Blomley, Delaney, and Ford, *Legal Geographies Reader*; Christophers, "Law's Markets."

102 For example, in a case involving an Argentine state bank's role in mediating payments for the construction of a privately owned aluminum complex and a state-owned hydroelectric plant, the Department of State identified the underlying activity not as economic development or providing electricity, but rather as "extending credits to private persons." "Sovereign Immunity Decisions of the Department of State," 1046.

103 *Victory Transport, Inc. v. Comisaria General de Abastecimientos y Transportes*, 336 F.2d 354 (2d Cir. 1964).

104 *French v. Banco Nacional de Cuba*, 23 N.Y.2d 46, 51 (N.Y. 1968).

105 See, e.g., *Cargo & Tankship Management Corp. v. India Supply Mission*, 336 F.2d 416, 420 (2d Cir. 1964) (defendants' argument "ignores the real cause of the loss by respondents of their right to reimbursement under their separate contract with the United States"); *Petrol Shipping Corp. v. Kingdom of Greece, Ministry of Commerce, etc.*, 360 F.2d 103 (2d Cir. 1966) (defining relevant transaction as the voyage charter and arbitration clause); *Venore Transportation Co. v. President of India*, 67 Civ. 2578, 68 Civ. 1134–1139 (S.D.N.Y. 1967 and 1968): the Department of State suggested that "plaintiff's claim in each of the present cases is based on a commercial contract"; *Ocean Transport Co. v. Government of Republic of Ivory Coast*, 269 F. Supp. 703 (E.D. La. 1967): the Department of State stated that "the contract out of which the present action . . . arises . . . is of a private nature." "Sovereign Immunity Decisions of the Department of State," 1067, 1058.

106 *Pan American Tankers Corp. v. Republic of Vietnam*, 296 F. Supp. 361 (S.D.N.Y. 1969).

107 28 U.S.C. 1602 et seq.

108 Monroe Leigh, for instance, who served as Legal Adviser to the Department of State from 1975 to 1977 and was particularly active in promoting the final versions of the FSIA, also represented investors whose property had been expropriated after the Cuban Revolution. He was a member of the prominent DC firm Steptoe and Johnson, which was active in this kind of litigation. Dezalay and Garth, "Law, Lawyers, and Empire"; "Monroe Leigh Dies."

109 Executive communication from the Departments of State and Justice (Oct. 31, 1975), reprinted in U.S. Congress. House. Subcommittee on Administrative Law and Governmental Relations of the Committee on the Judiciary, "Jurisdiction of U.S. Courts in Suits Against Foreign States," 45.

110 Leigh, for example, noted that the bill "would eliminate our peculiar and, in my view, outdated practice of having a political institution, namely, the State Department, decide many of these questions of law." Bruno Ristau from the Department of Justice likewise stated that "the bill is designed to depoliticize the area of sovereign immunity by placing the responsibility for determining questions of immunity in the courts." U.S.

Congress. House. Subcommittee on Administrative Law and Governmental Relations of the Committee on the Judiciary, 25, 31. See also U.S. Congress. House. Subcommittee on Claims and Governmental Relations of the Committee on the Judiciary, "Immunities of Foreign States."

111 U.S. Congress. House. Subcommittee on Administrative Law and Governmental Relations of the Committee on the Judiciary, "Jurisdiction of U.S. Courts in Suits Against Foreign States," 80.

112 U.S. Congress. House. Subcommittee on Claims and Governmental Relations of the Committee on the Judiciary, "Immunities of Foreign States"; U.S. Congress. House. Committee on the Judiciary, "Jurisdiction of U.S. Courts in Suits Against Foreign States."

113 U.S. Congress. House. Subcommittee on Administrative Law and Governmental Relations of the Committee on the Judiciary, "Jurisdiction of U.S. Courts in Suits Against Foreign States," 29.

114 U.S. Congress. House. Subcommittee on Administrative Law and Governmental Relations of the Committee on the Judiciary, "Jurisdiction of U.S. Courts in Suits Against Foreign States"; U.S. Congress. House. Subcommittee on Claims and Governmental Relations of the Committee on the Judiciary, "Immunities of Foreign States"; U.S. Congress. House. Committee on the Judiciary, "Jurisdiction of U.S. Courts in Suits Against Foreign States."

115 U.S. Congress. House. Subcommittee on Administrative Law and Governmental Relations of the Committee on the Judiciary, "Jurisdiction of U.S. Courts in Suits Against Foreign States," 71. The Rule of Law Committee similarly identified shipping, mineral resources, and agriculture, as well as banking, as areas giving rise or likely to give rise to litigation involving state-owned enterprises (83).

116 U.S. Congress. House. Subcommittee on Administrative Law and Governmental Relations of the Committee on the Judiciary, 93–94, 96.

117 U.S. Congress. House. Committee on the Judiciary, "Jurisdiction of U.S. Courts in Suits Against Foreign States," 16.

118 The FSIA's drafters were also concerned about expropriations, as I discuss in chapter 3.

119 Most nineteenth-century foreign sovereign immunity cases involved foreign ships, which had either been involved in some incident within US waters or had been seized or salvaged on the high seas and then brought within US waters.

120 Lauterpacht, "Problem of Jurisdictional Immunities of Foreign States," 229.

121 Foreign Sovereign Immunities Act, 28 U.S.C. 1602 et seq. (1976), §1602(2) (my emphasis).

122 Previously, would-be plaintiffs usually established jurisdiction by "attaching" some foreign state property located within the United States. The FSIA banned such attachments, while making it easier to establish jurisdiction in other ways. Its drafters argued that this simply ensured that the "jurisdictional standard is the same for the activities of a foreign state

as for the activities of a foreign private enterprise." U.S. Congress. House. Subcommittee on Claims and Governmental Relations of the Committee on the Judiciary, "Immunities of Foreign States," 41. Indeed, all transnational commercial cases at the time required some connection between the transaction in question and the United States. Yet, the spread of governing law clauses would soon eradicate this requirement for major commercial transactions. Today, some lawyers thus complain that the FSIA unfairly *limits* jurisdiction over transnational economic relations in comparison to wholly private transactions (see, e.g., Valentine, Feinberg, and Fabiilli, "Foreign Sovereign Immunities Act's Crippling Effect on United States Businesses").

123 Lauterpacht, "Problem"; Fox and Webb, *Law of State Immunity*.

124 Compare, for example, *The Schooner Exchange v. McFaddon*, 11 U.S. 116 (1812), *Long v. The Tampico,* 16 F. 491 (S.D.N.Y. 1883), *Mason v. Intercolonial Railroad of Canada*, 197 Mass. 349 (1908), or *The Roseric*, 254 F. 154 (D.N.J. 1918) to *The Maipo*, 259 F. 367 (S.D.N.Y. 1919), *Republic of Mexico v. Hoffman*, 324 U.S. 30 (1945), or *National City Bank v. Republic of China*, 348 U.S. 356 (1955).

125 Fox and Webb, *Law of State Immunity*. The US did add a terrorism exception to the FSIA in 1996, updated in 1998 and 2008.

126 Fox and Webb, *Law of State Immunity*, 86–87 (my emphasis).

127 The Committee on Maritime Legislation noted, for example, that, "considering that the United States is virtually the world's supermarket, the instances where a foreign state has no property here at all are probably very rare." U.S. Congress. House. Subcommittee on Administrative Law and Governmental Relations of the Committee on the Judiciary, "Jurisdiction of U.S. Courts in Suits Against Foreign States," 99.

128 Verdier and Voeten, "How Does Customary International Law Change?"

129 "Convention on the Jurisdictional immunities of States and Their Property," adopted by the United Nations General Assembly on December 2, 2004. As of November 2023, only twenty-eight countries had signed it, and only twenty-three had ratified it. (https://treaties.un.org/Pages/ViewDetails .aspx?src=TREATY&mtdsg_no=III-13&chapter=3&clang=_en).

130 Fox and Webb, *Law of State Immunity*; Kamminga, "Extraterritoriality"; Damrosch, "Changing the International Law of Sovereign Immunity."

THREE. REVOLUTION AND COUNTERREVOLUTION

1 Law No. 851, cited in *Banco Nacional de Cuba v. Sabbatino*, 376 U.S. 398, 401 (1964).

2 *Banco Nacional de Cuba v. Sabbatino*, 376 U.S. 398 (1964).

3 *Banco Nacional de Cuba v. Sabbatino*, 193 F. Supp. 375 (S.D.N.Y. 1961); *Banco Nacional de Cuba v. Sabbatino*, 307 F.2d 845 (2d Cir. 1962).

4   *Banco Nacional de Cuba v. Sabbatino*, 376 U.S. 398 (1964).

5   Codified at 22 U.S.C. § 2370(e)(2). This law is known as the "Hicken-looper Amendment"; I discuss it later in the chapter.

6   The distinction between nationalizations and expropriations is somewhat fluid. The former term is often reserved for more sweeping seizures and for those motivated by "ideological" reasons, while the latter can refer to any state seizure of private property. See, e.g., Francioni, "Compensation for Nationalisation of Foreign Property"; Kobrin, "Expropriation."

7   Franklin, *Cuba and the U.S. Empire*.

8   See, e.g., Patterson, "Act of State Doctrine."

9   Patterson, "Act of State Doctrine," 120.

10   See, e.g., *Republic of Cuba v. Arcade Bldg. of Savannah*, 104 Ga. App. 848 (Ga. Ct. App. 1961); *Republic of Cuba v. Dixie Paint & Varnish Co.*, 104 Ga. App. 854 (Ga. Ct. App. 1961); *State ex rel. National Institute of Agrarian Reform v. Dekle*, 137 So. 2d 581 (Fla. Ct. App. 1962).

11   28 U.S.C. §1610(2).

12   Statement for the Rule of Law Committee (of which FSIA drafter Monroe Leigh was a founder). U.S. Congress. House. Subcommittee on Administrative Law and Governmental Relations of the Committee on the Judiciary, "Jurisdiction of U.S. Courts in Suits Against Foreign States," 82.

13   Feldman, "A Drafter's Interpretation of the FSIA," 2–3.

14   See de Quadros and Dingfelder Stone, "Act of State Doctrine" for a basic overview.

15   *Underhill v. Hernandez*, 168 U.S. 250, 252 (1897).

16   Fox, "Reexamining the Act of State Doctrine"; Chow, "Rethinking"; Patterson, "Act of State Doctrine"; Diaz, "Territoriality Inquiry."

17   *Plessy v. Ferguson*, 163 U.S. 537 (1896); *Downes v. Bidwell*, 182 U.S. 244 (1901); *Underhill v. Hernandez*, 168 U.S. 250 (1897).

18   *The Schooner Exchange v. McFaddon*, 11 U.S. 116 (1812).

19   *The Schooner Exchange v. McFaddon*, 11 U.S. 116, 136, 137 (1812).

20   This approach is distinctive even among Western countries, most of which continue to see foreign sovereign immunity as merited by the inherent sovereignty of the *foreign* state. Fox and Webb, *Law of State Immunity*.

21   By the 1880s, US businesses were heavily invested in Cuba, and 83 percent of Cuban exports went to the United States, while a mere 6 percent went to Spain. Baklanoff, *Expropriation of U.S. Investments*. US economic penetration into Cuba increased in the twentieth century as US investors bought up sugar plantations and other businesses across the island. Hudson, *Bankers and Empire*.

22   Bender, *Nation among Nations*; Hudson, *Bankers and Empire*. The Amendment also gave the United States the right to lease land for naval stations from Cuba, leading to the establishment of Guantánamo Bay in 1903.

23   Baklanoff, *Expropriation of U.S. Investments*.

24   "UN General Assembly: Fifteenth Session, 872nd Plenary Meeting, Official Records" (official UN translation). At 269 minutes long, this is apparently the longest speech ever delivered at the United Nations (https://ask .un.org/faq/37127).

25   "UN General Assembly: Fifteenth Session, 872nd Plenary Meeting, Official Records."

26   Anghie, *Imperialism*; Getachew, *Worldmaking after Empire*.

27   Mexico's post-Revolution land redistribution programs and its nationalization of foreign oil companies in 1938 are important exceptions.

28   Kobrin, "Expropriation."

29   Francioni, "Compensation for Nationalisation of Foreign Property."

30   Permanent Sovereignty Over Natural Resources, G. A. Res. 1803, 17 GAOR, Supp. 17, U. N. Doc. A/5217.

31   Charter of Economic Rights and Duties of States, G. A. Res. 3281, 29 GAOR, Supp. 30, U. N. Doc. A/9030 (1974).

32   Hull, "Letter from Secretary of State, July 21, 1938."

33   Hay, "Letter from Mexican Minister for Foreign Affairs, August 3, 1938."

34   Hull, "Letter from Secretary of State, August 22, 1938."

35   Rabinowitz, *Unrepentant Leftist*.

36   Bravo, "Las Nacionalizaciones Cubanas, Los Tribunales Norteamericano y La Enmienda Hickenlooper," 8. In the original: "En Miami, la actitud judicial era muy virulenta y admonitoria. En Nueva York, la actitud era más sobria."

37   *Victory Transport, Inc. v. Comisaria General de Abastecimientos y Transportes*, 336 F.2d 354, 360 (2d Cir. 1964).

38   The cases that did reach US courts led to numerous but contradictory judicial opinions. As one US Supreme Court Justice put it in 1942: "One cannot read this body of judicial opinions . . . and not be left with the conviction that they are the product largely of casuistry, confusion, and indecision" (concurring opinion in *United States v. Pink*, 315 U.S. 203, 235 (1942)). Courts and the executive branch sometimes butted heads over how these cases should be handled, with courts usually, though not always, bowing to the Department of State's authority (see, e.g., *United States v. Belmont*, 301 U.S. 324 (1937) and *Weilamann v. Chase Manhattan Bank*, 21 Misc. 2d 1086 (N.Y. App. Div. 1959), but see also *Guaranty Trust Co. v. United States*, 304 U.S. 126 (1938) and *Stephen v. Zivnostenska Banka, Nat'l Corp.*, 12 N.Y.2d 781 (1962).

39   See, e.g., *Ricaud v. American Metal Co.*, 246 U.S. 304 (1918); *Oetjen v. Central Leather Company*, 246 U.S. 297 (1918); *Shapleigh et al. v. Mier*, 299 U.S. 468 (1937). The exception was a 1954 case involving Nazi seizures of Jewish property in Germany: *Bernstein v. N.V. Nederlandsche-Amerikaansche Stoomvaart-Maatschappij*, 210 F.2d 375 (2d Cir. 1954). This case, however, did not have significant lasting effects on the way the act of state doctrine was eventually transformed.

40 See, e.g., *Underhill v. Hernandez*, 168 U.S. 250 (1897); *Oetjen v. Central Leather Company*, 246 U.S. 297 (1918); *Ricaud v. American Metal Co.*, 246 U.S. 304 (1918).

41 347 U.S. 483 (1954). See Horwitz, "Warren Court and the Pursuit of Justice."

42 Rabinowitz, *Unrepentant Leftist*, 232.

43 *Banco Nacional de Cuba v. Sabbatino*, 376 U.S. 398, 421 (1964).

44 *Banco Nacional de Cuba v. Sabbatino*, 376 U.S. 398, 428 (1964).

45 *Banco Nacional de Cuba v. Sabbatino*, 376 U.S. 398, 423 and 427–428 (1964).

46 *Banco Nacional de Cuba v. Sabbatino*, 376 U.S. 398, 432 (1964) (my emphasis).

47 Brief for the United States as Amicus Curiae, *Banco Nacional de Cuba v. Sabbatino* (U.S. Sep. 10, 1963) (No. 16).

48 Brief for the United States as Amicus Curiae at 2, *Banco Nacional de Cuba v. Sabbatino* (U.S. Sep. 10, 1963) (No. 16).

49 Brief for the United States as Amicus Curiae at 3, *Banco Nacional de Cuba v. Sabbatino* (U.S. Sep. 10, 1963) (No. 16).

50 Brief for the United States as Amicus Curiae at 3, *Banco Nacional de Cuba v. Sabbatino* (U.S. Sep. 10, 1963) (No. 16).

51 Lastra and Buchheit, *Sovereign Debt Management*.

52 "We have learned of no case involving the effect on the rights of litigants of a federal statute, inconsistent with a Supreme Court mandate, which became law after the Supreme Court had remanded a case to the trial court but before the trial court had acted upon the merits after the remand." *Banco Nacional de Cuba v. Farr*, 383 F.2d 166, 178 (2d Cir. 1967).

53 PL 88–633 § 301(d)(4), amending the Foreign Assistance Act of 1961, now codified at 22 U.S.C. § 2370(e)(2). Also known as the Second Hickenlooper Amendment or the Sabbatino Amendment. It became a permanent part of the Foreign Assistance Act in 1965 (PL 89–171§ 301(d)(2)).

54 Cited at 965 in *Banco Nacional de Cuba v. Farr*, 243 F. Supp 957 (S.D.N.Y. 1965).

55 As described by Judge Bryan in *Banco Nacional de Cuba v. Farr*, 243 F. Supp 957, 965 (S.D.N.Y. 1965).

56 U.S. Code Cong. and Adm. News 1964, p. 3852, cited at 963 in *Banco Nacional de Cuba v. Farr*, 243 F. Supp 957 (S.D.N.Y. 1965).

57 110 Cong. Rec. 18936 (daily ed. Aug. 14, 1964), cited at 969 in *Banco Nacional de Cuba v. Farr*, 243 F. Supp 957 (S.D.N.Y. 1965).

58 *Banco Nacional de Cuba v. Farr*, 243 F. Supp 957, 969 (S.D.N.Y. 1965).

59 *Banco Nacional de Cuba v. Farr*, 243 F. Supp 957, 980 (S.D.N.Y. 1965).

60 *Banco Nacional de Cuba v. Farr*, 272 F. Supp 836 (S.D.N.Y. 1965).

61 *Banco Nacional de Cuba v. Farr*, 383 F.2d 166 (2d Cir. 1967).

62 Bravo, "Las Nacionalizaciones Cubanas, Los Tribunales Norteamericano y La Enmienda Hickenlooper," 29. In the original: "[la legislación] revocó

el principio de la Doctrina del Acto de Estado Soberano y de un plumazo echó por tierra el efímero triunfo de la justicia."

63   Foreign Assistance Act of 1961 (PL 87–195) § 620(e)(1)(c), now codified at 22 U.S.C. § 2370(e)(1)(c).

64   *Banco Nacional de Cuba v. Sabbatino*, 193 F. Supp. 375 (S.D.N.Y. 1961); *Banco Nacional de Cuba v. Sabbatino*, 307 F.2d 845 (2d Cir. 1962).

65   *Banco Nacional de Cuba v. Sabbatino*, 193 F. Supp. 375, 381 (S.D.N.Y. 1961).

66   *Banco Nacional de Cuba v. Sabbatino*, 193 F. Supp. 375, 384 (S.D.N.Y. 1961).

67   *Banco Nacional de Cuba v. Sabbatino*, 193 F. Supp. 375, 384, 385 (S.D.N.Y. 1961).

68   Anghie, *Imperialism*; Schneiderman, "Global Regime of Investor Rights."

69   *Banco Nacional de Cuba v. Sabbatino*, 307 F.2d 845, 864 (2d Cir. 1962).

70   *Banco Nacional de Cuba v. Sabbatino*, 307 F.2d 845, 866 (2d Cir. 1962).

71   Bâli and Rana, "Constitutionalism"; Chimni, "Third World Approaches to International Law"; Schneiderman, *Constitutionalizing Economic Globalization*.

72   See, e.g., *Shapleigh et al. v. Mier*, 299 U.S. 468, 471 (1937). Chief Justice Harlan acknowledged this in the Supreme Court decision striking down Dimock's: "the plain implication of all these opinions . . . is that the act of state doctrine is applicable even if international law has been violated" *Banco Nacional de Cuba v. Sabbatino*, 376 U.S. 398, 431 (1964).

73   *Banco Nacional de Cuba v. Sabbatino*, 307 F.2d 845, 861 (2d Cir. 1962).

74   *Banco Nacional de Cuba v. Sabbatino*, 376 U.S. 398, 422 (1964).

75   *Banco Nacional de Cuba v. Sabbatino*, 376 U.S. 398, 428 (1964). This passage has since been referenced in support of a treaty exception to the act of state doctrine. Patterson, "Act of State Doctrine."

76   *Banco Nacional de Cuba v. Sabbatino*, 376 U.S. 398, 403 (1964).

77   *Banco Nacional de Cuba v. Sabbatino*, 376 U.S. 398, 429–430 (1964).

78   A point Cuba's lawyers were well aware of. See, for instance, Plaintiff's Memorandum of Law at 33, *Banco Nacional de Cuba v. Manufacturers Trust Company* (Apr. 9, 1975) (S.D.N.Y. 61 Civ. 569).

79   *Banco Nacional de Cuba v. Sabbatino*, 376 U.S. 398, 430 (1964).

80   Brief for the United States as Amicus Curiae at 10, *Banco Nacional de Cuba v. Sabbatino* (U.S. Sep. 10, 1963) (No. 16).

81   See especially the struggle over the Hickenlooper Amendment in *First National City Bank v. Banco Nacional de Cuba*, 406 U.S. 759 (1972). See Dellapenna, "Deciphering the Act of State Doctrine" for an extended discussion of the amendment's legacy.

82   Britton-Purdy et al., "Building."

83   *Banco Nacional de Cuba v. First National City Bank of New York*, 442 F.2d 530 (2d Cir. 1971).

84   *First National City Bank v. Banco Nacional de Cuba*, 406 U.S. 759 (1972).

85   *First National City Bank v. Banco Nacional de Cuba*, 406 U.S. 759, 773 (1972).

86   *First National City Bank v. Banco Nacional de Cuba*, 406 U.S. 759, 790–792 (1972).

87   *Alfred Dunhill of London, Inc. v. Cuba*, 425 U.S. 682 (1976).

88   *Menendez v. Faber, Coe & Gregg, Inc.*, 345 F. Supp. 527 (S.D.N.Y. 1972).

89   *Menendez v. Saks & Co.*, 485 F.2d 1355 (2d Cir. 1973).

90   *Alfred Dunhill of London, Inc. v. Cuba*, 425 U.S. 682 (1976).

91   *Alfred Dunhill of London, Inc. v. Cuba*, 425 U.S. 682, 693 (1976).

92   Thus, in *Underhill*, the Supreme Court held that the Venezuelan com-
        mander's actions were public because they were done for the "benefit
        of the community and the revolutionary forces" and not on account of
        "malice or any personal or private motive." *Underhill v. Hernandez*, 168
        U.S. 250, 254 (1897). *Oetjen v. Central Leather Company*, 246 U.S. 297
        (1918), *Ricaud v. American Metal Co.*, 246 U.S. 304 (1918), and *Shapleigh
        et al. v. Mier*, 299 U.S. 468 (1937) all involved state seizures of private
        property deemed to be public acts. The question of whether the seizures
        were commercial was not raised in these opinions at all.

93   The lower *Sabbatino* courts had classified Cuba's nationalizations as pri-
        vate, not by characterizing them as commercial, but rather as retaliatory
        and discriminatory—a definition of private much closer to the "malice"
        cited in classic foreign sovereign immunity and act of state cases. In the
        Hickenlooper Amendment, Congress did frame nationalizations as
        within the aegis of Congress under the Commerce Clause of the US Con-
        stitution, and the District Court that applied the Amendment to reverse
        Sabbatino picked up on this theme. *Banco Nacional de Cuba v. Farr*, 243 F.
        Supp 957, 972 (S.D.N.Y. 1965). Yet, over the following decade, no serious
        arguments for a commercial exception were made.

94   *Alfred Dunhill of London, Inc. v. Cuba*, 425 U.S. 682, 695 (1976).

95   *Alfred Dunhill of London, Inc. v. Cuba*, 425 U.S. 682, 697 n. 11 (1976) (my
        emphasis).

96   *Banco Nacional de Cuba v. Sabbatino*, 376 U.S. 398, 466 n. 24 (1964)
        (quoting the Association of the Bar of the City of New York).

97   *Alfred Dunhill of London, Inc. v. Cuba*, 425 U.S. 682, 704 (1976).

98   *Alfred Dunhill of London, Inc. v. Cuba*, 425 U.S. 682, 706 n. 18 (1976).

99   The Department of State's legal adviser Monroe Leigh, a key player in
        drafting the FSIA, wrote that "we do not believe that the *Dunhill* case
        raises an act of state question because the case involves an act which
        is commercial, and not public, in nature" and that "adjudications of
        commercial liability against foreign states do not impede the conduct of
        foreign relations" (cited in *Alfred Dunhill of London, Inc. v. Cuba*, 425 U.S.
        682, 707 (1976)). Similarly, the Solicitor General argued in an *amicus*
        brief written by a young Antonin Scalia, that "repudiations by a foreign
        sovereign of its commercial debts should not be considered to be acts
        of state beyond legal question in our courts" (as summarized in *Alfred
        Dunhill of London, Inc. v. Cuba*, 425 U.S. 682, 696 (1976)).

100 *Alfred Dunhill of London, Inc. v. Cuba*, 425 U.S. 682, 704 (1976).

101 *Alfred Dunhill of London, Inc. v. Cuba*, 425 U.S. 682, 729 (1976). Justice Marshall, who authored the dissent, argued that "under any realistic view of the facts of this case, the interventors' retention of and refusal to return funds paid to them by Dunhill constitute an act of state." *Alfred Dunhill of London, Inc. v. Cuba*, 425 U.S. 682, 716 (1976).

102 Schlossbach, "Arguably Commercial, Ergo Adjudicable," 160. Schlossbach (153) explains further that "because Second Circuit cases account for a disproportionately large percentage of the total number of Act of State Doctrine decisions . . . a surprisingly high percentage of Act of State cases, which might not otherwise be adjudicated, would be adjudicated by the Second Circuit on commercial activity grounds."

103 *Alfred Dunhill of London, Inc. v. Cuba*, 425 U.S. 682, 698 et al. (1976).

104 See, especially, *Republic of Argentina v. Weltover, Inc.*, 504 U.S. 607 (1992).

105 Kobrin, "Expropriation"; Panitch and Gindin, *Making of Global Capitalism*.

106 Kobrin, "Expropriation."

107 However, the number of BITs signed between two low-income countries actually surpassed that of those signed between wealthy and low-income countries in the late 1990s. Weiss, "U.S. Bilateral Investment Treaty Program."

108 U.S. Department of State, United States Bilateral Investment Treaties, https://www.state.gov/investment-affairs/bilateral-investment-treaties -and-related-agreements/united-states-bilateral-investment-treaties/, accessed November 30, 2023.

109 Weiss, "U.S. Bilateral Investment Treaty Program," 11.

110 Sparke, *Introducing Globalization*, 193.

111 Anghie, *Imperialism*; Khalili, *Sinews of War and Trade*.

112 After receiving around three thousand requests for arbitration in the fifty-three years from 1923 to 1976, the International Chamber of Commerce received its next three thousand arbitration requests in just eleven years. Dezalay and Garth, *Internationalization of Palace Wars*; Dezalay and Garth, "Law, Lawyers, and Empire."

113 Anghie, *Imperialism*. The case in question involved the Libyan nationalization of Texaco's property.

114 Schwebel, "BIT about ICSID"; Lowenfeld, "ICSID Convention." Panitch and Gindin suggest that the *Sabbatino* decision itself spurred the establishment of ICSID, but I have not been able to verify this independently. Panitch and Gindin, *Making of Global Capitalism*.

115 Panitch and Gindin make this point specifically in relation to ICSID, which they see as designed to "depoliticize" and "delocalize" investment related disputes. Panitch and Gindin, *Making of Global Capitalism*, 117.

116 For some discussion of continued act of state litigation related to expropriations see Dellapenna, "Deciphering the Act of State Doctrine"; Patterson, "Act of State Doctrine."

117   Schneiderman, *Constitutionalizing Economic Globalization.*
118   See Francioni, "Compensation," for a useful discussion of this strategy
       and its inherent logical flaws.
119   Other exceptions include a "counterclaim" exception and a torture excep-
       tion. The act of state doctrine was further weakened by a 1990 Supreme
       Court decision that construed it very narrowly (*W. S. Kirkpatrick & Co.
       v. Environmental Tectonics Corp., Int'l*, 493 U.S. 400 (1990), discussed in
       Patterson, "Act of State Doctrine"). Despite these successive restrictions,
       many legal scholars today criticize the doctrine for being incoherent,
       and/or for disadvantaging private investors by continuing to limit US
       judicial authority over foreign governments. Several scholars support
       abandoning it altogether. See, e.g., Hoagland, "Act of State Doctrine";
       Ireland-Piper, "Outdated and Unhelpful." Patterson, in contrast, argues
       that courts have actually been fairly consistent, but that they are applying
       a factor-balancing rather than a rules-based approach. Patterson, "Act of
       State Doctrine."

FOUR. DEBT, DEFAULT, AND JUDICIAL DISCIPLINE

1   These terms are, of course, shorthand for various complex processes,
       whose definitions have been hotly debated. On neoliberalization, see
       the introduction and chapter 2. On financialization, see Christophers,
       "Limits to Financialization"; Christopherson, Martin, and Pollard,
       "Financialisation"; French, Leyshon, and Wainwright, "Financializing
       Space, Spacing Financialization"; Ioannou and Wójcik, "On Financializa-
       tion and Its Future"; Krippner, *Capitalizing on Crisis*; Pike and Pollard,
       "Economic Geographies of Financialization."
2   See, e.g., Amin, "Towards the Fifth International?"; Prashad, *Darker Na-
       tions*; Getachew, *Worldmaking after Empire.*
3   See, among many others, Chang, *23 Things*; George, *Fate Worse Than
       Debt*; Roddick, *Dance of the Millions*; Soederberg, "Transnational Debt
       Architecture"; Toussaint and Millet, *Debt.*
4   Anderson, *American Foreign Policy and Its Thinkers*; Chimni, "Third
       World Approaches to International Law"; Gowan, *Global Gamble.*
5   There is a vast literature on these topics. I draw especially from Anderson,
       American Foreign Policy; Gowan, *Global Gamble*; Panitch and Gindin,
       Making of Global Capitalism.
6   More precisely, this reconfiguration cemented the position of a New
       York–London financial nexus—but one definitively weighted toward
       American geopolitical economic interests. Gowan, *Global Gamble*;
       Wójcik, "The Dark Side of NY–LON."
7   It also ushered in a new era of high unemployment among Black
       Americans and other people of color and fueled the War on Drugs and

a transformation of carceral geographies across the United States. Stein, *Fearing Inflation, Inflating Fears.*

8   Anderson, *American Foreign Policy*; Gowan, *Global Gamble*; Panitch and Gindin, *Making of Global Capitalism.* Panitch and Gindin argue that this was not so much about sidelining US manufacturing in favor of finance as it was about recentering the US economy around legal and financial services, technology, and globally integrated production chains that remained headquartered in the United States.

9   This does not mean that the NIEO had no lasting effects. Amin sees these efforts to reorganize the world system as leading to important real advances for the Third World. Rajagopal sees the NIEO as influencing international laws and institutions, though his assessment of the effects of this is more ambivalent. Amin, "Towards the Fifth International?"; Rajagopal, *International Law from Below.*

10   Toussaint and Millet, *Debt.*

11   See, e.g., Corbridge, *Debt and Development*; Gowan, *Global Gamble*; Helleiner, *States*; Kapstein, *Governing the Global Economy*; Toussaint and Millet, *Debt.*

12   Corbridge, *Debt and Development*; Roddick, *Dance of the Millions*; Strange, *Casino Capitalism*; Toussaint and Millet, *Debt.* Figures include bilateral, multilateral, and commercial loans.

13   South Asia and most of sub-Saharan Africa continued to rely mostly on official credit from other countries and international financial institutions. They were thus not immediately targets of private holdout litigation, although they were subjected to brutal structural adjustment policies. Bond, *Looting Africa*; Chang, *23 Things*; Corbridge, *Debt and Development.*

14   Hudson, *Bankers and Empire.*

15   Gowan, *Global Gamble.*

16   Though it accelerated in the 1980s, this process began in the early 1970s. Panitch and Gindin, *Making of Global Capitalism.*

17   Anghie, *Imperialism*; Getachew, *Worldmaking after Empire.*

18   Gowan, *Global Gamble*; Roos, *Why Not Default?*; Soederberg, "Transnational."

19   Fried and Trezise, *Third World Debt.*

20   According to World Bank President Barber Conable, for example, "Debt reduction based on unchanged debtor country policies is a waste of time." Similarly, the Chairman of the Bank of Tokyo stated that "resolution of the debt issue depends more than anything else on the will and efforts of the debtor countries to come to grips with the need for structural adjustments to revitalize their economies." Fried and Trezise, *Third World Debt,* 21, 50. Out of roughly 250 people listed as attending this conference, only a handful were representatives of debtor countries.

21   Fried and Trezise, *Third World Debt,* 24, 81. See also Sachs, "Making the Brady Plan Work."

22   Fried and Trezise, *Third World Debt*, 5.

23   *Allied Bank Int'l v. Banco Credito Agricola de Cartago*, 566 F. Supp. 1440 (S.D.N.Y. 1983); *Allied Bank Int'l v. Banco Credito Agricola de Cartago*, 733 F.2d 23 (2d Cir. 1984); *Allied Bank Int'l v. Banco Credito Agricola de Cartago*, 757 F.2d 516 (2d Cir. 1985).

24   Before *Allied*, a simple failure to pay a loan was not always enough to give creditors legal cause for accelerating a debt, especially when the debtor was making good faith efforts to address the problem. Gathii, "Sanctity of Sovereign Loan Contracts."

25   Gathii, "Sanctity of Sovereign Loan Contracts," 301.

26   *Allied Bank Int'l v. Banco Credito Agricola de Cartago*, 566 F. Supp. 1440, 1443 (S.D.N.Y. 1983).

27   *Allied Bank Int'l v. Banco Credito Agricola de Cartago*, 566 F. Supp. 1440, 1444 (S.D.N.Y. 1983).

28   Griesa simultaneously rejected Costa Rica's foreign sovereign immunity claims. He held that *payment* of a loan, in contrast to the government's prevention of that payment, was a commercial activity within the meaning of the FSIA with "a direct effect" on the United States. *Allied Bank Int'l v. Banco Credito Agricola de Cartago*, 566 F. Supp. 1440, 1443 (S.D.N.Y. 1983).

29   *Allied Bank Int'l v. Banco Credito Agricola de Cartago*, 733 F.2d 23 (2d Cir. 1984).

30   *Allied Bank Int'l v. Banco Credito Agricola de Cartago*, 733 F.2d 23, 27 (2d Cir. 1984).

31   Rendell, "Allied Bank Case," 823. See also Gathii, "Sanctity of Sovereign Loan Contracts."

32   Brief for the United States as Amicus Curiae at 2, *Allied Bank Int'l v. Banco Credito Agricola De Cartago* (2d Cir. 1985) (No. 83–7714).

33   This emphasis on voluntary creditor participation would be echoed a few years later in the design of the Brady Plan and during all sovereign debt crises since. Potts, "Displaced Sovereignty"; Potts, "Debt in the Time of COVID-19."

34   Brief for the United States as Amicus Curiae at 12, 13 n. 9, *Allied Bank Int'l v. Banco Credito Agricola De Cartago* (2d Cir. 1985) (No. 83–7714).

35   Brief for the United States as Amicus Curiae at 10 n. 6, *Allied Bank Int'l v. Banco Credito Agricola De Cartago* (2d Cir. 1985) (No. 83–7714).

36   Brief for the United States as Amicus Curiae at 15, *Allied Bank Int'l v. Banco Credito Agricola De Cartago* (2d Cir. 1985) (No. 83–7714).

37   Brief for the United States as Amicus Curiae at 18, *Allied Bank Int'l v. Banco Credito Agricola De Cartago* (2d Cir. 1985) (No. 83–7714).

38   As paraphrased in Clark Jr, "Resolution of Act of State Disputes Involving Indefinitely Situated Property," 912. As two later proponents of the litigation strategy put it, "The Clearing House's position was seemingly motivated by a desire to establish unambiguous legal precedent for

enforcing the rights of commercial banks and other creditors against sovereign debtors. A judicial decision favorable to the claim . . . would provide bank advisory committees (and other commercial banks) with additional leverage in negotiating agreements with sovereign debtors and in developing restructuring plans in future crises." Fisch and Gentile, "Vultures or Vanguards?," 1084.

39   Clark Jr, "Resolution," 912.

40   Bank of America weighed in on the case as part of the Rule of Law Committee (which had previously lobbied on behalf of the FSIA). Gathii, "Sanctity of Sovereign Loan Contracts."

41   Harvey, *Brief History of Neoliberalism*; Foucault, *Birth of Biopolitics*; Slobodian, *Globalists*.

42   Bratton and Gulati, "Sovereign Debt Reform"; Sturzenegger and Zettelmeyer, *Debt Defaults*.

43   *Allied Bank Int'l v. Banco Credito Agricola de Cartago*, 757 F.2d 516 (2d Cir. 1985).

44   *Allied Bank Int'l v. Banco Credito Agricola de Cartago*, 757 F.2d 516, 519 (2d Cir. 1985).

45   *Allied Bank Int'l v. Banco Credito Agricola de Cartago*, 757 F.2d 516, 522 (2d Cir. 1985).

46   Quale Jr., "Allied Bank's Effect," 26. The 1985 *Allied* decision was "generally viewed as the lesser of two evils." Quale Jr., "Allied Bank's Effect," 30. Yet, many analysts remained dissatisfied with the decision for not going far enough. See, e.g., Bazyler, "Abolishing the Act of State Doctrine"; Gruson, "Act of State Doctrine"; Hoagland, "Act of State Doctrine."

47   One New York judge held, for instance, that, despite potentially having a "devastating financial impact" on Jamaica and its ongoing debt restructurings, *Allied* had established that creditors' contracts "remain valid and enforceable." *A.I. Credit Corp. v. Government of Jamaica*, 666 F. Supp. 629, 633 (S.D.N.Y. 1987). Another held that, whatever the effect on the Congo's debt restructuring, refusing to enforce a holdout creditor's claim "would have the effect of depriving a creditor of its *right to choose*" and "would be contrary to United States policy as articulated in *Allied Bank*" (my emphasis). *National Union Fire Ins. Co. v. People's Republic of Congo*, 729 F. Supp. 936, 944 (S.D.N.Y. 1989). See also *Turkmani v. Republic of Bol.*, 193 F. Supp. 2d 165 (D.D.C. 2002); *Lloyds Bank PLC v. Republic of Ecuador*, 1998 U.S. Dist. LEXIS 3065 (S.D.N.Y. 1998); *Pravin Banker Assocs., Ltd. v. Banco Popular del Peru*, 109 F.3d 850 (2d Cir. 1997). In *Commercial Bank of Kuwait v. Rafidain Bank*, 15 F.3d 238 (2d Cir. 1994), "the Second Circuit went even further than *Allied II* in holding that a default occasioned by war, economic sanctions, and the freezing of its assets, thus making it impossible to obtain foreign currency to repay its debts, did not preclude the finding that Iraq had willfully defaulted." Gathii, "Sanctity of Sovereign Loan Contracts," 302.

48   *Pravin Banker Assocs., Ltd. v. Banco Popular del Peru*, 165 B.R. 379, 382
      (S.D.N.Y. 1994).

49   *Pravin Banker Assocs., Ltd. v. Banco Popular del Peru*, 109 F.3d 850, 855
      (2d Cir. 1997).

50   *Pravin Banker Assocs., Ltd. v. Banco Popular del Peru*, 109 F.3d 850 (2d
      Cir. 1997).

51   Fisch and Gentile, "Vultures or Vanguards?," 1051.

52   During its recent debt crisis, this threat was enough to make Greece forgo
      several billion in debt relief by continuing to pay all its foreign-law bonds
      in full, rather than risk litigation by attempting to restructure them along
      with its domestic law bonds. Schumacher, Trebesch, and Enderlein, "Sover-
      eign Defaults in Court"; Fisch and Gentile, "Vultures or Vanguards?," 1051.
      The fear of messy and protracted litigation led European policymakers,
      with the exception of the 2012 Greek restructuring, "to repay, in full and
      on time, all of the private sector creditors of Eurozone countries receiving
      bailouts." Gulati, Buchheit, and Tirado, "Problem of Holdout Creditors," 1.

53   Hartman and Kear, "Critical Financial Geography," 318.

54   *Allied Bank Int'l v. Banco Credito Agricola de Cartago*, 757 F.2d 516 (2d
      Cir. 1985).

55   *Alfred Dunhill of London, Inc. v. Cuba*, 425 U.S. 682 (1976).

56   *Menendez v. Faber, Coe & Gregg, Inc.*, 345 F. Supp. 527, 538 (S.D.N.Y. 1972).
      See also *Republic of Iraq v. First National City Bank*, 353 F.2d 47 (2d Cir.
      1965), cert. denied, 382 U.S. 1027 (1966); *Tabacalera Severiano Jorge, S.A. v.
      Standard Cigar Co.*, 392 F.2d 706 (5th Cir. 1968). This statement was itself
      an oversimplification, but the point is that this strong claim was made in
      the nationalization context in order to protect US interests.

57   Although payments were to be made in New York in US dollars, the Costa
      Rican banks did not have offices or employees in New York, nor did they
      "conduct banking business there," and most of the contract negotiations
      had "occurred outside the US." (*Allied Bank Int'l v. Banco Credito Agricola
      de Cartago*, 733 F.2d 23, 27 (2d Cir. 1984)). The District Court's 1983 deci-
      sion did not explicitly focus on the situs of the debt at all (*Allied Bank Int'l
      v. Banco Credito Agricola de Cartago*, 566 F. Supp. 1440 (S.D.N.Y. 1983)).

58   The court cemented the analogy to nationalization cases by defining the
      Costa Rican exchange decrees as "taking" private property. *Allied Bank Int'l
      v. Banco Credito Agricola de Cartago*, 757 F.2d 516, 521 n. 3 (2d Cir. 1985).

59   *Tabacalera Severiano Jorge, S.A. v. Standard Cigar Co.*, 392 F.2d 706
      (5th Cir. 1968).

60   For an overview of situs rules in relation to debt see, e.g., Rogerson, "Situs
      of Debts"; Goldthwaite, "Recent Approaches."

61   *Tabacalera Severiano Jorge, S.A. v. Standard Cigar Co.*, 392 F.2d 706, 715
      (5th Cir. 1968).

62   *Tabacalera Severiano Jorge, S.A. v. Standard Cigar Co.*, 392 F.2d 706, 715
      (5th Cir. 1968) (emphasis added). The court projected this reasoning

anachronistically onto the whole history of the act of state doctrine, suggesting that courts were never fundamentally concerned with territorial sovereignty or protecting the executive branch. Rather, early act of state decisions were based on the "common-sense" fact that "in most situations there was nothing the United States courts could do about it in any event" (*Tabacalera Severiano Jorge, S.A. v. Standard Cigar Co.*, 392 F.2d 706, 715 (5th Cir. 1968)). The unstated implication is that, as the United States became more powerful, it no longer needed to respect the territorial integrity of other countries.

63   *Allied Bank Int'l v. Banco Credito Agricola de Cartago*, 757 F.2d 516, 521 (2d Cir. 1985).

64   *Allied Bank Int'l v. Banco Credito Agricola de Cartago*, 757 F.2d 516, 521–522 (2d Cir. 1985).

65   Goldthwaite, "Recent Approaches," 152 (my emphasis).

66   Johnson, "Act of State," 125. Most legal scholars complained only that the Court's new situs decision was still was not flexible enough. See, e.g., Hoffman Jr. and Deming, "Role of the U.S. Courts"; Miller, "Debt Situs"; Tahyar, "Act of State Doctrine."

67   The growing reliance on New York governing law clauses has cemented this shift. Potts, "Reterritorializing Economic Governance."

68   Number based on the LexisNexis Shepardize® function. LexisNexis Academic: Nexis Uni®, https://advance.lexis.com, retrieved November 30, 2023. On the lasting influence of *Allied*, see Lastra and Buchheit, *Sovereign Debt Management*.

69   See, e.g., Brief for the United States as Amicus Curiae at 12, *Allied Bank Int'l v. Banco Credito Agricola De Cartago* (2d Cir. 1985) (No. 83–7714).

70   Gathii, "Sanctity of Sovereign Loan Contracts," 307.

71   *Republic of Argentina v. Weltover, Inc.*, 504 U.S. 607 (1992).

72   Fox and Webb, *Law of State Immunity*.

73   *Victory Transport, Inc. v. Comisaria General de Abastecimientos y Transportes*, 336 F.2d 354, 360 (2d Cir. 1964).

74   These early drafts made an exception for contracts that included explicit immunity waivers. U.S. Congress. House. Subcommittee on Claims and Governmental Relations of the Committee on the Judiciary, "Immunities of Foreign States," 6.

75   See, e.g., comments by Charles Brower, Acting Legal Adviser to the Department of State, in U.S. Congress. House. Subcommittee on Claims and Governmental Relations of the Committee on the Judiciary, 22.

76   Statement for the Committee on International Law of the Association of the Bar of the City of New York. U.S. Congress. House. Subcommittee on Administrative Law and Governmental Relations of the Committee on the Judiciary, "Jurisdiction of U.S. Courts in Suits Against Foreign States," 75.

77   U.S. Congress. House. Committee on the Judiciary, "Jurisdiction of U.S. Courts in Suits Against Foreign States."

78 Much of the "sovereign" debt in crisis in the 1980s came from governments taking over the debts of private businesses. Roddick, *Dance of the Millions*. In Argentina's case, much of the government's own debt had been accumulated under the military dictatorship that governed Argentina from 1976 to 1983, with the support of the IMF and the United States. Toussaint and Millet, *Debt*.

79 Brief of Republic of Argentina and Banco Central de la Republica Argentina at 10, *Republic of Argentina v. Weltover, Inc.* (U.S. Feb. 11, 1992) (No. 91–763).

80 *Weltover, Inc. v. Republic of Argentina*, 753 F. Supp. 1201 (S.D.N.Y. 1991); *Weltover, Inc. v. Republic of Argentina*, 941 F.2d 145 (2d Cir. 1991); *Republic of Argentina v. Weltover, Inc.*, 504 U.S. 607 (1992).

81 28 U.S.C. §1605(2).

82 Brief for the United States as Amicus Curiae Supporting Respondents at 1–2, *Republic of Argentina v. Weltover, Inc.* (U.S. Mar. 5, 1992) (No. 91–763). The executive itself (at 21 n. 15) cited *Allied* as evidence that the United States "favors enforcement of contracts in accordance with their terms in the context of sovereign debt restructurings."

83 *Republic of Argentina v. Weltover, Inc.*, 504 U.S. 607, 612 (1992).

84 *Republic of Argentina v. Weltover, Inc.*, 504 U.S. 607, 614 (1992). In *Dunhill* itself, ironically, Justice White had based his commercial exception argument in large part on the increasing restriction of foreign sovereign immunity under the Tate Letter.

85 *Republic of Argentina v. Weltover, Inc.*, 504 U.S. 607, 614 (1992) (emphasis in original).

86 *Republic of Argentina v. Weltover, Inc.*, 504 U.S. 607, 617 (1992) (emphasis in original).

87 *Republic of Argentina v. Weltover, Inc.*, 504 U.S. 607, 615 (1992).

88 *Republic of Argentina v. Weltover, Inc.*, 504 U.S. 607, 617 (1992) (emphasis in original).

89 Fox and Webb, *Law of State Immunity*, 260.

90 Slobodian, *Globalists*.

91 Brief of Republic of Argentina and Banco Central de la Republica Argentina, *Republic of Argentina v. Weltover, Inc.* (U.S. Feb. 11, 1992) (No. 91–763).

92 Brief of Republic of Argentina and Banco Central de la Republica Argentina at 8, *Republic of Argentina v. Weltover, Inc.* (U.S. Feb. 11, 1992) (No. 91–763).

93 Brief of Republic of Argentina and Banco Central de la Republica Argentina at 20, *Republic of Argentina v. Weltover, Inc.* (U.S. Feb. 11, 1992) (No. 91–763) (my emphasis).

94 *Republic of Argentina v. Weltover, Inc.*, 504 U.S. 607, 609 (1992) (my emphasis).

95 *Weltover, Inc. v. Republic of Argentina*, 941 F.2d 145, 150 (2d Cir. 1991). Quoted in Brief for the United States as Amicus Curiae Supporting Respondents at 9, *Republic of Argentina v. Weltover, Inc.* (U.S. Mar. 5, 1992) (No. 91–763).

96   *Weltover, Inc. v. Republic of Argentina*, 941 F.2d 145, 150 (2d Cir. 1991) (my emphasis).

97   See Fox and Webb, *Law of State Immunity*, on the continued ambiguity surrounding the nature/purpose distinction and efforts to "individuate" events in order to identify the relevant act.

98   Moreover, in the neoliberal era, governments in both North and South have operated through so-called market-like mechanisms as much as possible. See, e.g., Greider, *Secrets of the Temple*; Krippner, *Capitalizing on Crisis*; Ashton and Christophers, "On Arbitration."

99   Greener, "Commercial Exception"; Hess, "International Law Commission's Draft Convention"; Bankas, *State Immunity Controversy*.

100   Leacock, "Joy of Access," 83, 121.

101   The most recent version of the "Convention on Jurisdictional Immunities of States and Their Property" states: "In determining whether a contract or transaction is a 'commercial transaction' . . . reference should be made primarily to the nature of the contract or transaction, but its purpose should also be taken into account if the parties to the contract or transaction have so agreed, or if, in the practice of the State of the forum, that purpose is relevant to determining the non-commercial character of the contract or transaction." "Convention on the Jurisdictional immunities of States and Their Property," Article 2(2) (https://treaties.un.org/Pages /ViewDetails.aspx?src=TREATY&mtdsg_no=III-13&chapter=3&clang= _en, accessed December 16, 2023).

102   Greener, "Commercial Exception," 198.

103   Bankas, *State Immunity Controversy*.

104   *Republic of Argentina v. Weltover, Inc.*, 504 U.S. 607, 618 (1992).

105   *Republic of Argentina v. Weltover, Inc.*, 504 U.S. 607, 618 (1992).

106   Leacock, "Joy of Access."

107   Fox and Webb, *Law of State Immunity*, 262.

108   "The United States has a substantial interest in maintaining New York's status as an international financial center" (*Weltover, Inc. v. Republic of Argentina*, 753 F. Supp. 1201, 1207 (S.D.N.Y. 1991)); "Public policy should make American courts available to foreign plaintiffs if this will preserve or even enhance New York's status as a world financial leader" (*Weltover, Inc. v. Republic of Argentina*, 941 F.2d 145, 153 (2d Cir. 1991)). Both courts cited *Allied* in support of this point.

109   *Republic of Argentina v. Weltover, Inc.*, 504 U.S. 607, 618 (1992).

110   Number based on the LexisNexis Shepardize® function. LexisNexis Academic: Nexis Uni®, https://advance.lexis.com, accessed November 30, 2023.

111   Lew, "*Republic of Argentina v. Weltover, Inc.*," 758.

112   Sweet, "Foreign Sovereign Immunities Act," 375.

113   Laufer and Spiguel, "Intervencionismo En El Mundo 'Globalizado,'" 18. In the original: "rechazando la inmunidad soberana del Estado argentino para reprogramar el pago de bonos de deuda externa pública."

114 Laufer and Spiguel, "Intervencionismo En El Mundo 'Globalizado,'" 18. In the original: "establecer un criterio de extraterritorialidad de la legislación estadounidense que aspira a consagrar la supremacía del interés nacional de esa potencia por sobre la normatividad internacional."

115 Baker, "Whither Weltover"; McGuire, "Direct Effect Jurisdiction in the 90's"; Pizzurro, "*Republic of Argentina v. Weltover, Inc.*"; Schano, "Scattered Remains."

116 Ruccolo, "Foreign Sovereign Immunities Act," 520.

117 Leacock, "Joy of Access," 121, 110.

118 Leacock, "Joy of Access," 82.

119 Fox and Webb, *Law of State Immunity.*

120 Roos, *Why Not Default?*

121 Potts, "Deep Finance"; Potts, "Displaced Sovereignty."

122 Schoenberger, "Creating the Corporate World," 377.

123 See, e.g., Schumacher, Trebesch, and Enderlein, "Sovereign Defaults in Court"; Buchheit et al., "How to Restructure Sovereign Debt."

124 Krueger and Hagan, "Sovereign Workouts."

125 Potts, "Deep Finance"; Potts, "Debt in the Time of COVID-19."

126 For a summary of such debates, see Guzman, Ocampo, and Stiglitz, *Too Little, Too Late.*

127 Soederberg, "Transnational."

128 This includes the IMF's own 2001 attempt to create a Sovereign Debt Restructuring Mechanism, as well as the UN General Assembly's 2014 effort to establish a debt restructuring system at the United Nations. Deforge and Lemoine, "Faillite d'État et Fragilité Juridique"; Helleiner, "Mystery of the Missing Sovereign Debt Restructuring Mechanism"; Potts, "Debt in the Time of COVID-19"; Soederberg, "Transnational."

129 Potts, "Deep Finance."

130 Potts, "Beyond (De)Regulation." See also Riles, "Managing Regulatory Arbitrage," 98–99: "In the absence of clear scientific answers to epistemological questions like 'where is a security?' lawyers have been busy inventing creative answers rooted in the pragmatics of the implications of those answers for their clients, and for the most part, these are answers that serve the interests of the financial industry."

131 Roos, *Why Not Default?*; Lienau, *Rethinking Sovereign Debt.*

FIVE. SOVEREIGN DISOBEDIENCE

1 I use this title as shorthand to refer to a handful of linked cases, represented most importantly by Docket No. 08 Civ. 6978 (TPG) at the District Court for the Southern District of New York and Docket No. 12–105-cv(L) at the Second Circuit Court of Appeals.

2   For some of the most authoritative legal scholarship on this much-discussed case, see, e.g., Sgard and Weidemaier, "Global Market for Sovereign Debt"; Weidemaier and Gelpern, "Injunctions"; Buchheit and Gulati, "Restructuring Sovereign Debt"; Gelpern, "Courts and Sovereigns."

3   Roos, *Why Not Default?*

4   See Order, NML *Capital, Ltd. v. Republic of Argentina* (S.D.N.Y. Feb. 23, 2012) (No. 08 Civ. 6978 (TPG)).

5   See NML *Capital, Ltd. v. Republic of Argentina*, 727 F.3d 230 (2d. Cir 2013).

6   *Republic of Argentina v.* NML *Capital, Ltd.*, 134 S. Ct. 2819 (2014) (cert. denied).

7   *Republic of Argentina v.* NML *Capital, Ltd.*, 573 U.S. 134.

8   This shift accelerated even more under President Donald Trump, whose three new appointees (Gorsuch, Kavanaugh, and Barrett) gave the Supreme Court's conservative members a supermajority of six to three.

9   Purdy, "Neoliberal Constitutionalism"; Shanor, "New Lochner"; Ehrenreich, "Cluster Introduction"; Kapczynski, "Lochnerized First Amendment."

10   *Citizens United v. Federal Election Commission*, 558 U.S. 310 (2010).

11   Gulati and Scott, *Three and a Half Minute Transaction*.

12   See, generally, Docket No. 12–105-cv(L) at the Second Circuit and Supreme Court Docket No. 13–00990.

13   Kapczynski, "Lochnerized First Amendment."

14   Alba-TCP, "Alba-TCP Emite Declaración Exigiendo a Obama 'Cese de Inmediato El Hostigamiento' Contra Venezuela y Derogar La Orden Ejecutiva"; "Parlasur Respalda a Argentina En Su Batalla Contra Los Fondos Buitre"; CEPAL, "CEPAL Se Refiere a las Implicancias de los Holdouts Para el Sistema Financiero Internacional"; OAS, "Meeting of Consultation."

15   OAS, "Meeting of Consultation."

16   General Assembly Resolution 68/304, *Towards the Establishment of a Multilateral Legal Framework for Sovereign Debt Restructuring Processes*, A/RES/68/304 (September 9, 2014), available from http://undocs.org /A/RES/68/304. The resolution passed by an overwhelming majority of 124 votes to 11, with 41 abstentions, but failed to materialize in any meaningful changes due to opposition from every major Western country. Deforge and Lemoine, "Faillite d'État et Fragilité Juridique"; Potts, "Displaced Sovereignty."

17   Wolf, "Defend Argentina from the Vultures."

18   See, e.g., *Economist*, "Argentine Bonds: Argy-Bargy"; Cotterill, "Poker"; Gelpern, "Pari Passu Whiplash"; Gulati and Scott, *Three and a Half Minute Transaction*; Weidemaier and Gelpern, "Injunctions."

19   See, e.g., Hudson, "Vulture Funds Trump Argentinian Sovereignty"; Sassen, "Short History of Vultures"; Stiglitz and Guzman, "Argentina Default?"; Toussaint, "How to Resist?"

20　Not everyone was critical of Griesa's decisions, of course. Those who celebrated the decisions as a triumph for contract rights and the rule of law did so in terms just as emotionally and morally charged as those of Griesa's harshest critics. Judges, vulture funds, and many financial journalists cast Argentina, in tones ranging from bemused to outraged, as a "recidivist deadbeat," full of "teenage narcissism," characterized by "bloody-mindedness," breathing "hellfire," a "scofflaw," a "serial defaulter," and a "recalcitrant debtor." *Wall Street Journal*, "Rule of Law 3, Argentina 0"; *Economist*, "Luis Suarez of International Finance"; Cotterill, "Around the World?"; Cotterill, "Fairytale of New York"; Dugan, "Argentine Lobby Mystifies 'Members'"; Newman, "We Holdouts Are Open"; Norris, "Ruling on Argentina." The unifying justification for all these accusations was Argentina's dual refusal to make good on its debt contracts with the holdouts and to obey US court orders.

21　Cotterill, "Poker with Judge Griesa, Part Two"; Monaghan and Goni, "Argentina's Government Blames 'Conspiracy' for Defaulting on Debt"; *MercoPress*, "Argentina Prepared"; Pritchard, "Argentina Accuses US."

22　Potts, "Deep Finance."

23　On the longstanding crisis of overaccumulation since the 1970s, see Harvey, *New Imperialism*; Brenner, *Economics of Global Turbulence*; Arrighi, *Long Twentieth Century*.

24　Potts, "Deep Finance"; Schumacher, Trebesch, and Enderlein, "Sovereign Defaults in Court"; Fisch and Gentile, "Vultures or Vanguards?"

25　In a 1990 advertisement, for example, Salomon Brothers identified the fact that "bondholders could take legal enforcement action more easily than bank lenders" as a selling point in favor of sovereign bonds (cited in Buckley, "Facilitation of the Brady Plan," 1852).

26　The history of Singer, Straus, and Newman described here is taken from *Elliott Assocs., L.P. v. Republic of Peru*, 12 F. Supp. 2d 328 (S.D.N.Y. 1998).

27　Outside *Elliott v. Peru*, there is strikingly little information available on the company. The cases cited by Judge Sweet do not come up on Nexis Uni® or Bloomberg Law. Pacer.gov shows that multiple documents in these cases have been "sealed" and that several were "dismissed without prejudice" in 1994 and 1995.

28　*Elliott Assocs., L.P. v. Republic of Peru*, 12 F. Supp. 2d 328, 335 (S.D.N.Y. 1998).

29　*Elliott Assocs., L.P. v. Republic of Peru*, 12 F. Supp. 2d 328 (S.D.N.Y. 1998). The champerty doctrine had been partly undermined earlier in the decade including in *CIBC Bank and Trust Co. (Cayman) Ltd. v. Banco Central do Brasil*, 886 F. Supp. 1105 (S.D.N.Y. 1995); *Elliott Assocs., L.P. v. Republic of Panama*, 975 F. Supp. 332 (S.D.N.Y. 1997); *Pravin Banker Assocs., Ltd. v. Banco Popular del Peru*, 109 F.3d 850 (2d Cir. 1997); and *Banque de Gestion Privee-SIB v. La Republica de Paraguay*, 787 F. Supp 53 (S.D.N.Y. 1992).

30　*Elliott Assocs., L.P. v. Republic of Peru*, 194 F.3d 363 (2d Cir. 1999).

31   *Elliott Assocs., L.P. v. Republic of Peru*, 194 F.3d 363, 378 (2d Cir. 1999).

32   *Elliott Assocs., L.P. v. Republic of Peru*, 194 F.3d 363, 379 (2d Cir. 1999). During the same case, Elliott successfully lobbied to make collecting compound interest on debts issued before 1989 legal (described in *Elliott Assocs., L.P. v. Republic of Peru*, 194 F.R.D. 116 (S.D.N.Y. 2000)).

33   The bill jacket "indicates that the Legislature acted out of concern that distressed debt investors' 'ability to collect on these claims without fear of champerty litigation is essential to the fluidity of commerce in New York.'" N.Y. State Assembly, Mem. in Support of Legislation, Bill No. A7244C, at 1 (July 20, 2004) (cited in Skadden, Arps, Slate, Meagher & Flom LLP & Affiliates, "Current Issues," 15).

34   Blackman and Mukhi, "Evolution"; Guzman, "Analysis."

35   Schumacher, Trebesch, and Enderlein, "Sovereign Defaults in Court." The authors exclude cases by retail investors and merge multiple claims by the same creditor against a single debtor.

36   Schumacher, Trebesch, and Enderlein, "Sovereign Defaults in Court."

37   Schumacher, Trebesch, and Enderlein, "Sovereign Defaults in Court."

38   Cantamutto and Ozarow argue that, given the prices at which these bonds were purchased and the extended maturities of the new bonds, many investors actually profited from this deal. Cantamutto and Ozarow, "Serial Payers, Serial Losers?"

39   For detailed analyses of the default and restructurings see, among others, Guzman, "Analysis"; Cantamutto and Ozarow, "Serial Payers, Serial Losers?"; Roos, *Why Not Default?*

40   *Abaclat and Others (formerly Giovanna A. Beccara and Others) v. Argentine Republic* (ICSID Case No. ARB/07/5).

41   Schumacher, Trebesch, and Enderlein, "Sovereign Defaults in Court."

42   See, e.g., NML *Capital, Ltd. v. Republic of Argentina*, 2009 U.S. Dist. LEXIS 19046 (S.D.N.Y. 2009).

43   Lienau, *Rethinking Sovereign Debt*; Roos, *Why Not Default?*; Guzman, Ocampo, and Stiglitz, *Too Little, Too Late.*

44   Cantamutto and Ozarow, "Serial Payers, Serial Losers?"; Wylde, "Post-Neoliberal Developmental Regimes in Latin America."

45   Just how anti-neoliberal the Kirchners actually were is hotly debated. Some use the term *neodesarollismo* to suggest a combination of neoliberal and developmental approaches. Wylde, "State, Society and Markets."

46   Based on amounts listed in NML *Capital, Ltd. v. Republic of Argentina*, 2011 U.S. Dist. LEXIS 110811 (S.D.N.Y. 2011).

47   Fiscal Agency Agreement Between the Republic of Argentina and Bankers Trust Co., 1994 (copy in Appendix of NML *Capital, Ltd. v. Republic of Argentina*, 699 F.3d 246 (2d. Cir 2012)).

48   In *Three and a Half Minute Transaction*, Gulati and Scott call pari passu a "chameleon" clause, because it is so vague as to admit of all manner of interpretation.

49   Order, *NML Capital, Ltd. v. Republic of Argentina* (S.D.N.Y. Dec. 7, 2011)
      (No. 08 Civ. 6978 (TPG)).

50   Peru caved shortly after and paid Elliott the amount demanded. Fisch
      and Gentile, "Vulturae or Vanguards?"; Schumacher, Trebesch, and
      Enderlein, "Sovereign Defaults in Court."

51   Gulati and Scott, *Three and a Half Minute Transaction.* The Belgian case,
      in combination with Argentina's dramatic default, was part of what
      spurred the IMF to propose a binding Sovereign Debt Restructuring
      Mechanism in the early 2000s. International Monetary Fund, *Current
      Developments in Monetary and Financial Law.*

52   Gelpern, "Sovereign Damage Control."

53   Order, *NML Capital, Ltd. v. Republic of Argentina* (S.D.N.Y. Dec. 7, 2011)
      (No. 08 Civ. 6978 (TPG)); Order, *NML Capital, Ltd. v. Republic of Argen-
      tina* (S.D.N.Y. Feb. 23, 2012) (No. 08 Civ. 6978 (TPG)).

54   *NML Capital, Ltd. v. Republic of Argentina*, 727 F.3d 230 (2d. Cir 2013).
      The court affirmed the ruling in October 2012 (*NML Capital, Ltd. v.
      Republic of Argentina*, 699 F.3d 246 (2d. Cir 2012)) but sent the decision
      back to Griesa to determine how much Argentina should pay the vulture
      funds—the same absolute amount of money they paid to the exchange
      bondholders, or the same *proportion* of what was owed to each creditor
      (i.e., 100 percent). Griesa followed the vulture funds in choosing the
      latter option (Amended February 23, 2012 Order, *NML Capital, Ltd. v.
      Republic of Argentina* (S.D.N.Y. Nov. 21, 2012) (No. 08 Civ. 6978 (TPG)).

55   *Republic of Argentina v. NML Capital, Ltd.*, 134 S. Ct. 2819 (2014) (cert.
      denied).

56   Order, *NML Capital, Ltd. v. Republic of Argentina* (S.D.N.Y. Feb. 23, 2012)
      (No. 08 Civ. 6978 (TPG)); Amended February 23, 2012 Order, *NML
      Capital, Ltd. v. Republic of Argentina* (S.D.N.Y. Nov. 21, 2012) (No. 08 Civ.
      6978 (TPG)).

57   Weidemaier and Gelpern, "Injunctions."

58   Order at 4, *NML Capital, Ltd. v. Republic of Argentina* (S.D.N.Y. Feb. 23,
      2012) (No. 08 Civ. 6978 (TPG)).

59   Order, *NML Capital, Ltd. v. Republic of Argentina* (S.D.N.Y. Feb. 23, 2012)
      (No. 08 Civ. 6978 (TPG)).

60   Motion of the Euro Bondholders for Leave to Intervene as Interested
      Non-Parties, *NML Capital, Ltd. v. Republic of Argentina* (2d Cir. Dec. 4,
      2012) (No. 12–105-cv(L)).

61   Brief of Amicus Curiae Euroclear Bank SA/NV in Support of Petitioner
      at 8, *Republic of Argentina v. NML Capital, Ltd.* (U.S. Mar. 24, 2014)
      (No. 13–990). For a detailed discussion of these payment geographies and
      the legal debates surrounding them, see Potts, "(Re-)Writing Markets."

62   Petition for Panel Rehearing and Rehearing En Banc of Defendant-
      Appellant the Republic of Argentina at iv, *NML Capital Ltd. v. Republic of
      Argentina* (2d Circ. Nov. 13, 2012) (No. 12–105-cv(L)).

63 Petition for Panel Rehearing and Rehearing En Banc of Defendant-Appellant the Republic of Argentina at 7, *NML Capital Ltd. v. Republic of Argentina* (2d Circ. Nov. 13, 2012) (No. 12–105-cv(L)).

64 Order, *NML Capital, Ltd. v. Republic of Argentina* (S.D.N.Y. Feb. 23, 2012) (No. 08 Civ. 6978 (TPG)); *NML Capital, Ltd. v. Republic of Argentina*, 727 F.3d 230 (2d. Cir 2013).

65 Brief of Amicus Curiae Euroclear Bank SA/NV in Support of Petitioner at 4, *Republic of Argentina v. NML Capital, Ltd.* (U.S. Mar. 24, 2014) (No. 13–990).

66 Amended February 23, 2012 Order at 4, *NML Capital, Ltd. v. Republic of Argentina*, (S.D.N.Y. Nov. 21, 2012) (No. 08 Civ. 6978 (TPG)).

67 *NML Capital, Ltd. v. Republic of Argentina*, 727 F.3d 230, 243 (2d. Cir 2013).

68 See, e.g., Joint Response Brief of Plaintiffs-Appellees NML Capital, Ltd. and Olifant Fund, Ltd., *NML Capital Ltd. v. Republic of Argentina* (2d Cir. Jan. 25, 2013) (No. 12–105-cv(L)).

69 Argentina reminded the Court that courts "may not grant, by injunction, relief which they may not provide by attachment." Brief of Defendant-Appellant the Republic of Argentina at 21, *NML Capital Ltd. v. Republic of Argentina* (2d Cir. Dec. 28, 2012) (No. 12–105-cv(L)), quoting *S&S Mach. Co. v. Masinexportimport*, 706 F.2d 411, 418 (2d Cir. 1983).

70 "If ICE Canyon and the Euro Bondholders are correct in stating that the payment process for their securities takes place entirely outside the United States, then the district court misstated that. . . . But this possible misstatement is of no moment because, again, the amended injunctions enjoin no one but Argentina, a party that has voluntarily submitted to the jurisdiction of the district court." *NML Capital, Ltd. v. Republic of Argentina*, 727 F.3d 230, 244 (2d. Cir 2013).

71 Transcript of Oral Argument, *NML Capital, Ltd. v. Republic of Argentina* (S.D.N.Y. Jun. 27, 2014) (No. 08 Civ. 6978 (TPG)).

72 This was widely referred to as a technical default to distinguish it from defaults caused by underlying economic factors.

73 This figure is for citations of the Second Circuit's decision to uphold Griesa's order and injunction (*NML Capital, Ltd. v. Republic of Argentina*, 727 F.3d 230 (2d. Cir 2013)) as given via the LexisNexis Shepardize® function. LexisNexis Academic: Nexis Uni®, https://advance.lexis.com, retrieved November 30, 2023.

74 Although officially denied by Argentina's lawyers, NML et al. cited various reports suggesting that the country was attempting to find a way to reroute payments outside the United States. See, e.g., Reply Brief of Plaintiffs in Response to the Remand from the Court of Appeals at 26, *NML Capital Ltd. v. Republic of Argentina* (S.D.N.Y. Nov. 19, 2012) (No. 08 Civ. 6978 (TPG)).

75 Petition for a Writ of Certiorari at 11, *Exchange Bondholder Group v. NML Capital, Ltd.* (U.S. Feb. 18, 2014) (No. 13-991).

76 Brief for the United States of America as Amicus Curiae in Support of Reversal, *NML Capital, Ltd. v. Republic of Argentina* (2d Cir. Apr. 4, 2012) (No. 12–105-cv(L)); Brief for the United States of America as Amicus Curiae in Support of the Republic of Argentina's Petition for Panel Rehearing and Rehearing En Banc, *NML Capital, Ltd. v. Republic of Argentina* (2d Cir. Dec. 28, 2012) (No. 12–105-cv(L)). The US executive and the IMF initially planned to file briefs at the Supreme Court level too, but suddenly changed their minds in July 2013. Gelpern, "Pari Passu Whiplash."

77 Brief for the United States of America as Amicus Curiae in Support of Reversal at 22–23, *NML Capital, Ltd. v. Republic of Argentina* (2d Cir. Apr. 4, 2012) (No. 12–105-cv(L)).

78 Brief for the United States of America as Amicus Curiae in Support of Reversal at 29, *NML Capital, Ltd. v. Republic of Argentina* (2d Cir. Apr. 4, 2012) (No. 12–105-cv(L)).

79 Brief for the United States of America as Amicus Curiae in Support of Reversal at 29, *NML Capital, Ltd. v. Republic of Argentina* (2d Cir. Apr. 4, 2012) (No. 12–105-cv(L)) (my emphasis).

80 Brief for the United States of America as Amicus Curiae in Support of Reversal at 6, *NML Capital, Ltd. v. Republic of Argentina* (2d Cir. Apr. 4, 2012) (No. 12–105-cv(L)).

81 Brief for the United States of America as Amicus Curiae in Support of the Republic of Argentina's Petition for Panel Rehearing and Rehearing En Banc at 5, *NML Capital, Ltd. v. Republic of Argentina* (2d Cir. Dec. 28, 2012) (No. 12–105-cv(L)).

82 *Republic of Argentina v. NML Capital, Ltd.*, 573 U.S. 134.

83 *Republic of Argentina v. NML Capital, Ltd.*, 573 U.S. 134, 145.

84 Number based on the LexisNexis Shepardize® function. LexisNexis Academic: Nexis Uni®, https://advance.lexis.com, retrieved November 30, 2023.

85 28 U.S.C. §1610(a).

86 Transcript of Oral Argument, *Republic of Argentina v. NML Capital, Ltd.* (U.S. Apr. 21, 2014) (No. 12–842).

87 Transcript of Oral Argument, *Republic of Argentina v. NML Capital, Ltd.* (U.S. Apr. 21, 2014) (No. 12–842).

88 Brief for the United States as Amicus Curiae, *Republic of Argentina v. NML Capital, Ltd.* (U.S. Dec. 4, 2013) (No. 12–842); Brief for the United States as Amicus Curiae in Support of Petitioner, *Republic of Argentina v. NML Capital, Ltd.* (U.S. Mar. 3, 2014) (No. 12–842).

89 Brief for the United States as Amicus Curiae at 15, *Republic of Argentina v. NML Capital, Ltd.* (U.S. Dec. 4, 2013) (No. 12–842).

90 *Republic of Argentina v. NML Capital, Ltd.*, 573 U.S. 134, 141.

91   Brief for the United States as Amicus Curiae in Support of Petitioner at 25, *Republic of Argentina v. NML Capital, Ltd.* (U.S. Mar. 3, 2014) (No. 12–842).

92   Transcript of Oral Argument, *Republic of Argentina v. NML Capital, Ltd.* (U.S. Apr. 21, 2014) (No. 12–842).

93   Transcript of Oral Argument at 11, *Republic of Argentina v. NML Capital, Ltd.* (U.S. Apr. 21, 2014) (No. 12–842).

94   Transcript of Oral Argument, *Republic of Argentina v. NML Capital, Ltd.* (U.S. Apr. 21, 2014) (No. 12–842); Brief for the United States as Amicus Curiae, *Republic of Argentina v. NML Capital, Ltd.* (U.S. Dec. 4, 2013) (No. 12–842); Brief for the United States as Amicus Curiae in Support of Petitioner, *Republic of Argentina v. NML Capital, Ltd.* (U.S. Mar. 3, 2014) (No. 12–842).

95   *Bush v. Gore*, 531 U.S. 98 (2000); *Citizens United v. Federal Election Commission*, 558 U.S. 310 (2010).

96   Transcript of Oral Argument at 33, *Republic of Argentina v. NML Capital, Ltd.* (U.S. Apr. 21, 2014) (No. 12–842).

97   "Well, that makes it a lot harder for me because I thought you just looked to the Foreign Sovereign Immunities Act. And anything that is executable in this country under that, you can get information on to try to execute abroad. But you are saying, oh, no, it's more than that, it's stuff that you couldn't execute on in this country, but that some foreign countries will let you execute on." Transcript of Oral Argument at 38–39, *Republic of Argentina v. NML Capital, Ltd.* (U.S. Apr. 21, 2014) (No. 12–842).

98   Transcript of Oral Argument at 34, *Republic of Argentina v. NML Capital, Ltd.* (U.S. Apr. 21, 2014) (No. 12–842).

99   *Republic of Argentina v. NML Capital, Ltd.*, 573 U.S. 134, 145.

100 *Republic of Argentina v. NML Capital, Ltd.*, 573 U.S. 134, 148. Justice Sotomayor took no part in the decision.

101 Transcript of Oral Argument at 25, 21, *Republic of Argentina v. NML Capital, Ltd.*, (U.S. Apr. 21, 2014) (No. 12–842).

102 Brief for the United States as Amicus Curiae at 22, *Republic of Argentina v. NML Capital, Ltd.* (U.S. Dec. 4, 2013) (No. 12–842).

103 Brief for the United States as Amicus Curiae in Support of Petitioner at 10, *Republic of Argentina v. NML Capital, Ltd.* (U.S. Mar. 3, 2014) (No. 12–842).

104 Brief for the United States as Amicus Curiae in Support of Petitioner at 20, *Republic of Argentina v. NML Capital, Ltd.* (U.S. Mar. 3, 2014) (No. 12–842).

105 Transcript of Oral Argument at 17, 22, *Republic of Argentina v. NML Capital, Ltd.* (U.S. Apr. 21, 2014) (No. 12–842).

106 *Republic of Argentina v. NML Capital, Ltd.*, 573 U.S. 134, 146 (citations omitted, brackets in original).

107 Allen, "Argentina on Brink"; Phelan, "Argentina in Latest Debt Default Crisis."

108 Blitzer, "Good Week for Vulture Funds."

109 Guzman, "Analysis," 726. Guzman also served as Minister of Economy of the Republic of Argentina from December 2019 to July 2022, under the Kirchnerist government that succeeded Macri's.

110 Cantamutto and Ozarow, "Serial Payers, Serial Losers?"; López and Nahón, "Growth of Debt"; Wylde, "Post-Neoliberal Developmental Regimes."

111 Mihanovich and Kelly, "Is Argentina's Debt Saga Nearing Its End?"

112 Levine, "Argentina's New Attitude Pays Off"; Stevenson, "How Argentina Settled."

113 Schumacher, Trebesch, and Enderlein, "Sovereign Defaults in Court." Guzman calculates NML Capital's return as approximately 1270 percent. He also reports that Argentina was required to pay the vulture funds $325 million to cover the legal fees they incurred during the trial. Guzman, "Analysis of Argentina's 2001 Default Resolution."

114 Agnew, "Elliott's Former $2.4bn Argentina Man."

115 Wernau and Cui, "Argentina Returns to Global Debt Markets." Investors' sudden willingness to snatch up Argentine debt after 15 years of its "rogue" behavior is telling. What draws such investors is not long-term calculations, but high-interest payments and immediate outlets for surplus capital. The point is that investors are "looking for higher yields in a period of low interest rates." Wernau and Cui, "Argentina's New Debt Offering." Interest on Argentina's new bonds ranged from 6.25 to almost 8 percent—significantly higher than on US or European bonds.

116 Brief for the United States of America as Amicus Curiae at 17, *Aurelius Capital Master, Ltd., et al., v. Republic of Argentina* (2d Cir. Mar. 23, 2016) (No. 16–628(L)).

117 Stott and Mander, "Argentina's Economic Woes"; Torres, "In Argentina, Fernández"; Porzecanski, "Argentina Fiasco"; Gallagher, "Argentina's Creditors Must Face Up."

118 Mander and Smith, "Argentina Clinches Near-Unanimous Backing"; Mander, "Argentina Averts Default"; Portes, "Argentina's Ruling Peronists Suffer"; Elliott, "Argentina's Congress Approves $45bn."

119 Gelpern and Gulati, "Wonder-Clause."

120 Schumacher, Trebesch, and Enderlein, "Sovereign Defaults in Court," 3.

121 The phrase was popularized in Mnookin and Kornhauser, "Bargaining."

122 Gelpern hinted at this in 2013 when she observed that Griesa's "goal had become to give creditors leverage—any leverage, it seems—and to recapture some dignity for the court itself, now feeling slighted and ignored." Gelpern, "Contract Hope and Sovereign Redemption," 139.

1   Appel, *Licit Life of Capitalism.*

2   See, e.g., *Pravin Banker Assocs., Ltd. v. Banco Popular del Peru,* 109 F.3d
    850 (2d Cir. 1997).

3   *Dobbs v. Jackson Women's Health Organization,* 597 U.S. ___ (2022); *New
    York State Rifle & Pistol Association, Inc. v. Bruen,* 597 U.S. ___ (2022);
    West Virginia v. Environmental Protection Agency, 597 U.S. ___ (2022).

4   See discussion in chapter 5. Sotomayor recused herself from the final
    decision.

5   See, e.g., Brief for the United States of America as Amicus Curiae in
    Support of the Republic of Argentina's Petition for Panel Rehearing and
    Rehearing En Banc at 3, *NML Capital, Ltd. v. Republic of Argentina* (2d
    Cir. Dec. 28, 2012) (No. 12-105-cv(L)).

6   Panitch and Gindin, *Making of Global Capitalism.*

7   Anderson, *American Foreign Policy;* Gowan, *Global Gamble.* Panitch and
    Gindin, furthermore, argued in 2012 that China did not yet have the
    capacity to take over the superintendency of the capitalist system as a
    whole. Panitch and Gindin, *Making of Global Capitalism.*

8   For economic geographical analyses of the rise of interconnected East
    Asian financial centers, see, e.g., Fang, Pan, and Lai, "Brokerage Role";
    Lai, "Singapore"; Lai et al., "New Financial Geographies of Asia." I
    switch to the term *legal territory* rather than the more specific *judicial
    territory* here because countries have different legal and governance
    systems, and there is no guarantee that judiciaries will play the same role
    in the transnational extension of non-US legal spaces as they have in the
    US context.

9   Putnam, *Courts without Borders,* 2016.

10 "Final Report of the Task Force on New York Law in International
    Matters."

11 Potts, "Debt."

12 Fox and Webb, *Law of State Immunity.*

13 As Hung argues, "The China boom has been dependent on the global
    neoliberal order, which is based on expanding, unfettered transnational
    flow of goods and capital, and it is in China's vested interest to maintain
    the status quo, though China might seek to change the balance of power
    within this arrangement." Hung, *China Boom,* 5. See also Hopewell,
    Breaking the WTO; Matisoff, "Multilateralism."

14 This is true despite the fact that, as Geoff Mann has pointed out, the
    politics/economics distinction is more important to *liberalism* than it is
    to *capitalism,* and that China and other countries have successfully em-
    braced illiberal forms of the latter in many ways. Mann, "Race Between
    Economics and Politics." A key difference may be the scale of analysis.

China may well reinforce the public/private and political/economic divides *transnationally,* while being far less invested in these distinctions at the domestic scale.

15 For broader discussion of the complex geographical formations of contemporary sovereignty, see Agnew, "Sovereignty Regimes"; Barkan, "Sovereignty"; Billé, *Voluminous States;* Ong, "Graduated Sovereignty."

BIBLIOGRAPHY

Achiume, E. Tendayi, and Asli Bâli. "Race and Empire: Legal Theory Within, Through, and Across National Borders." *UCLA Law Review* 67 (2021): 1386–1431.

Agnew, Harriet. "Elliott's Former $2.4bn Argentina Man Comes after India." *Financial Times,* October 4, 2021. https://www.ft.com/content/d085241d -efa0-4fe7-9dee-b563354b1734.

Agnew, John. *Globalization and Sovereignty: Beyond the Territorial Trap.* Lanham, MD: Rowman and Littlefield, 2018.

Agnew, John. *Hegemony: The New Shape of Global Power.* Philadelphia: Temple University Press, 2005.

Agnew, John. *Hidden Geopolitics: Governance in a Globalized World.* London: Rowman and Littlefield, 2022.

Agnew, John. "Low Geopolitics: Credit-Rating Agencies, the Privatization of Authority and the New Sovereignty." *Geopolitica(s)* 3 no. 2 (2012): 171–83.

Agnew, John. "Sovereignty Regimes: Territoriality and State Authority in Contemporary World Politics." *Annals of the American Association of Geographers* 95, no. 2 (2005): 437–61. doi:10.1111/j.1467-8306.2005.00468.x.

Agnew, John. "Still Trapped in Territory?" *Geopolitics* 15, no. 4 (2010): 779–84. doi:10.1080/14650041003717558.

Agnew, John. "The Territorial Trap: The Geographical Assumptions of International Relations Theory." *Review of International Political Economy* 1, no. 1 (1994): 53–80. doi:10.1080/09692299408434268.

Alba-TCP. "Alba-TCP Emite Declaración Exigiendo a Obama 'Cese de Inmediato El Hostigamiento' Contra Venezuela y Derogar La Orden Ejecutiva." *Alba Ciudad 96.3 FM* (blog), March 18, 2015. http://albaciudad.org/2015 /03/alba-tcp-emite-declaracion-exigiendo-a-obama-cese-de-inmediato -el-hostigamiento-contra-venezuela-y-derogar-la-orden-ejecutiva/.

Allen, Katie. "Argentina on Brink of Second Debt Default in 12 Years." *The Guardian,* July 29, 2014, sec. Business. https://www.theguardian.com /business/2014/jul/29/argentina-brink-second-debt-default-12-years.

Allen, Stephen, Daniel Costelloe, Malgosia Fitzmaurice, Paul Gragl, and Edward Guntrip, eds. *The Oxford Handbook of Jurisdiction in International Law.* Oxford: Oxford University Press, 2019.

Amin, Samir. "Towards the Fifth International?" In *BRICS and the New American Imperialism: Global Rivalry and Resistance,* edited by Vishwas Satgar, 148–66. Johannesburg: Wits University Press, 2020.

Amin, Samir. "Unequal Development: An Essay on the Social Formations of Peripheral Capitalism," *Science and Society,* 42, no. 2 1978.

Anderson, Perry. *American Foreign Policy and Its Thinkers.* Brooklyn: Verso, 2015.

Anderson, Perry. *The H-Word: The Peripeteia of Hegemony.* Brooklyn: Verso, 2017.

Anghie, Antony. *Imperialism, Sovereignty and the Making of International Law.* Cambridge: Cambridge University Press, 2007.

Appel, Hannah. *The Licit Life of Capitalism: U.S. Oil in Equatorial Guinea.* Durham, NC: Duke University Press, 2019.

Arrighi, Giovanni. *The Long Twentieth Century: Money, Power, and the Origins of Our Times.* London: Verso, 2010.

Ashton, Philip. "The Evolving Juridical Space of Harm/Value: Remedial Powers in the Subprime Mortgage Crisis." *Journal of Economic Issues* 48, no. 4 (2014): 959–79. doi:10.2753/JEI0021–3624480405.

Ashton, Philip, and Brett Christophers. "On Arbitration, Arbitrage and Arbitrariness in Financial Markets and Their Governance: Unpacking LIBOR and the LIBOR Scandal." *Economy and Society* 44, no. 2 (2015): 188–217. doi:10.1080/03085147.2015.1013352.

Ayala, César J., and Rafael Bernabe. *Puerto Rico in the American Century: A History since 1898.* Chapel Hill: University of North Carolina Press, 2009.

Baker, Mark B. "Whither Weltover: Has the U.S. Supreme Court Clarified or Confused the Exceptions Enumerated in the Foreign Sovereign Immunities Act?" *Temple International and Comparative Law Journal* 9, no. 1 (1995): 1–26.

Baklanoff, Eric N. *Expropriation of U.S. Investments in Cuba, Mexico, and Chile.* New York: Praeger, 1975.

Bâli, Aslı, and Aziz Rana. "Constitutionalism and the American Imperial Imagination." *University of Chicago Law Review* 85, no. 2 (2018): 257–92.

Bankas, Ernest K. *The State Immunity Controversy in International Law: Private Suits against Sovereign States in Domestic Courts.* Berlin: Springer, 2005.

Barkan, Joshua. *Corporate Sovereignty: Law and Government under Capitalism.* Minneapolis: University of Minnesota Press, 2013.

Barkan, Joshua. "Law and the Geographic Analysis of Economic Globalization." *Progress in Human Geography* 35, no. 5 (2011): 589–607. doi:10.1177/0309132510389221.

Barkan, Joshua. "Sovereignty." In *The Wiley Blackwell Companion to Political Geography,* edited by John A. Agnew, Virginie Mamadouh, Anna Secor, and Joanne Sharp, 48–60. West Sussex, UK: John Wiley and Sons, 2017.

Barkow, Rachel E. "More Supreme than Court? The Fall of the Political Question Doctrine and the Rise of Judicial Supremacy." *Columbia Law Review* 102, no. 2 (2002): 237–336.

Basaran, Tugba. "A Journey Through Law's Landscapes: Close Encounters of the Scalar Kind." In *Landscapes of Law: Practicing Sovereignty in Transnational Terrain,* edited by Carol J. Greenhouse and Christina L. Davis, 23–36. Philadelphia: University of Pennsylvania Press, 2020.

Baxi, Upendra. "The Colonialist Heritage." In *Comparative Legal Studies: Traditions and Transitions,* edited by Pierre Legrand and Roderick J.C. Munday, 46–75. Cambridge: Cambridge University Press, 2003.

Bazyler, Michael J. "Abolishing the Act of State Doctrine." *University of Pennsylvania Law Review* 134, no. 2 (1986): 325–98. doi:10.2307/3312072.

Bender, Thomas. *A Nation among Nations: America's Place in World History.* New York: Hill and Wang, 2006.

Benton, Lauren. *A Search for Sovereignty: Law and Geography in European Empires, 1400–1900.* Cambridge: Cambridge University Press, 2009.

Benton, Lauren. *Law and Colonial Cultures: Legal Regimes in World History, 1400–1900.* Cambridge: Cambridge University Press, 2002.

Benton, Lauren, and Richard J. Ross. *Legal Pluralism and Empires, 1500–1850.* New York: NYU Press, 2013.

Berman, Paul S. "The Globalization of Jurisdiction." *University of Pennsylvania Law Review* 151, no. 2 (2002): 311–545. doi:10.2307/3312952.

Bhandar, Brenna. *Colonial Lives of Property: Law, Land, and Racial Regimes of Ownership.* Durham, NC: Duke University Press, 2018.

Billé, Franck, ed. *Voluminous States: Sovereignty, Materiality, and the Territorial Imagination.* Durham, NC: Duke University Press, 2020.

Biolsi, Thomas. "Imagined Geographies: Sovereignty, Indigenous Space, and American Indian Struggle." *American Ethnologist* 32, no. 2 (2005): 239–59. doi:10.1525/ae.2005.32.2.239.

Blackman, Jonathan I., and Rahul Mukhi. "The Evolution of Modern Sovereign Debt Litigation: Vultures, Alter Egos, and Other Legal Fauna." *Law and Contemporary Problems* 73, no. 4 (2010): 47–61.

Blaut, James. *The Colonizer's Model of the World: Geographical Diffusionism and Eurocentric History.* New York: Guilford Press, 1993.

Blitzer, Jonathan. "A Good Week for Vulture Funds." *The New Yorker,* March 5, 2016. http://www.newyorker.com/business/currency/a-good-week-for-vulture-funds.

Block, Fred. "Karl Polanyi and the Writing of the *Great Transformation*." *Theory and Society* 32, no. 3 (2003): 275–306. doi:10.1023/A:1024420102334.

Block, Fred, and Margaret R. Somers. *The Power of Market Fundamentalism.* Cambridge, MA: Harvard University Press, 2014.

Blomley, Nicholas. "Flowers in the Bathtub: Boundary Crossings at the Public–Private Divide." *Geoforum* 36, no. 3 (2005): 281–96. doi:10.1016/j.geoforum.2004.08.005.

Blomley, Nicholas. "Law, Property, and the Geography of Violence: The Frontier, the Survey, and the Grid." *Annals of the Association of American Geographers* 93, no. 1 (2003): 121–41. doi:10.1111/1467-8306.93109.

Blomley, Nicholas. *Law, Space, and the Geographies of Power.* New York: Guilford Press, 1994.

Blomley, Nicholas. *Territory: New Trajectories in Law.* London: Routledge, 2022.

Blomley, Nicholas. "The Territory of Property." *Progress in Human Geography* 40, no. 5 (2016): 593–609. doi:10.1177/0309132515596380.

Blomley, Nicholas, and Joel C. Bakan. "Spacing out: Towards a Critical Geography of Law." *Osgoode Hall Law Journal* 30, no. 3 (1992): 661–90.

Blomley, Nicholas, David Delaney, and Richard T. Ford, eds. *The Legal Geographies Reader: Law, Power and Space.* Oxford: Blackwell Publishers, 2001.

Bond, Patrick. *Looting Africa: The Economics of Exploitation.* Scottsville, South Africa: University of KwaZulu-Natal Press, 2006.

Bond, Patrick, and Ana Garcia, eds. *BRICS: An Anti-Capitalist Critique.* London: Pluto Press, 2015.

Bonds, Anne. "Race and Ethnicity I: Property, Race, and the Carceral State." *Progress in Human Geography* 43, no. 3 (2019): 574–83. doi:10.1177/0309132517751297.

Boyd, Susan B., ed. *Challenging the Public/Private Divide: Feminism, Law, and Public Policy.* Toronto; Buffalo, NY: University of Toronto Press, 1997.

Bradley, Curtis A., and Laurence R. Helfer. "International Law and the U.S. Common Law of Foreign Official Immunity." *The Supreme Court Review* 2010, no. 1 (2011): 213–73.

Bratton, William W., and Mitu Gulati. "Sovereign Debt Reform and the Best Interest of Creditors." *Vanderbilt Law Review* 57, no. 1 (2004): 1–80.

Braverman, Irus, Nicholas Blomley, David Delaney, and Alexandre Kedar, eds. *The Expanding Spaces of Law: A Timely Legal Geography.* Stanford, CA: Stanford University Press, 2014.

Bravo, Olga Miranda. "Las Nacionalizaciones Cubanas, Los Tribunales Norteamericano y La Enmienda Hickenlooper." *Revista Cubana de Derecho* 2 (1972): 5–36.

Brenner, Neil, and Stuart Elden. "Henri Lefebvre on State, Space, Territory." *International Political Sociology* 3, no. 4 (2009): 353–77. doi:10.1111/j.1749-5687.2009.00081.x.

Brenner, Robert. *The Economics of Global Turbulence: The Advanced Capitalist Economies from Long Boom to Long Downturn, 1945–2005.* London: Verso, 2006.

Brickell, Katherine, and Dana Cuomo. "Feminist Geolegality." *Progress in Human Geography* 43, no. 1 (2019): 104–22. doi:10.1177/0309132517735706.

Brighenti, Andrea. "On Territory as Relationship and Law as Territory." *Canadian Journal of Law and Society* 21, no. 2 (2006): 65–86. doi:10.1017/S0829320100008954.

Britton-Purdy, Jedediah, David Singh Grewal, Amy Kapczynski, and K. Sabeel Rahman. "Building a Law-and-Political-Economy Framework: Beyond the Twentieth-Century Synthesis." *Yale Law Journal* 129, no. 6 (2020): 1784–1835.

Brown, Wendy. *Undoing the Demos: Neoliberalism's Stealth Revolution.* New York: Zone Books, 2015.

Brown, Wendy. *Walled States, Waning Sovereignty.* New York: Zone Books, 2010.

Bryan, Dick, Michael Rafferty, and Duncan Wigan. "From Time–Space Compression to Spatial Spreads: Situating Nationality in Global Financial Liquidity." In *Money and Finance After the Crisis: Critical Thinking for Uncertain Times,* edited by Brett Christophers, Andrew Leyshon, and Geoff Mann, 41–67. Chichester, UK: John Wiley and Sons, 2017.

Buchheit, Lee C., Guillaume Chabert, Chanda DeLong, and Jeromin Zettelmeyer. "How to Restructure Sovereign Debt: Lessons from Four Decades." Working Papers. Peterson Institute for International Economics, 2019. http://dx.doi.org/10.2139/ssrn.3387455.

Buchheit, Lee C., and G. Mitu Gulati. "Restructuring Sovereign Debt After NML v. Argentina." *Capital Markets Law Journal* 12, no. 2 (2017): 224–38. doi:10.1093/cmlj/kmx018.

Buckley, Ross P. "The Facilitation of the Brady Plan: Emerging Markets Debt Trading from 1989 to 1993." *Fordham International Law Journal* 21, no. 5 (1997): 1802–89.

Burbank, Jane. "The Rights of Difference: Law and Citizenship in the Russian Empire." In *Imperial Formations,* edited by Ann Laura Stoler, Carole McGranahan, and Peter C. Perdue, 77–111. Santa Fe, NM: School for Advanced Research Press, 2007.

Burbank, Jane, and Frederick Cooper. *Empires in World History: Power and the Politics of Difference.* Princeton, NJ: Princeton University Press, 2010.

Burbank, Jane, and Frederick Cooper. "Rules of Law, Politics of Empire." In *Legal Pluralism and Empires, 1500–1850,* edited by Lauren Benton and Richard J. Ross, 279–93. New York: NYU Press, 2013.

Burnett, Christina D. "Untied States: American Expansion and Territorial Deannexation." *University of Chicago Law Review* 72, no. 3 (2005): 797–879.

Burnett, Christina Duffy, and Burke Marshall, eds. *Foreign in a Domestic Sense: Puerto Rico, American Expansion, and the Constitution.* Durham, NC: Duke University Press, 2001. doi:10.2307/j.ctv1134g0r.

Butler, C. "Critical Legal Studies and the Politics of Space." *Social and Legal Studies* 18, no. 3 (2009): 313–32.

Buxbaum, Hannah L. "Territory, Territoriality, and the Resolution of Jurisdictional Conflict." *The American Journal of Comparative Law* 57, no. 3 (2009): 631–76. doi:10.5131/ajcl.2008.0018.

Buxbaum, Richard M. "The Role of Public International Law in International Business Transactions." In *Public International Law and the Future World Order: Liber Amicorum in Honor of A.J. Thomas, Jr,* edited by Joseph J. Norton, Ch. 16. Littleton, CO: Rothman, 1987.

Buzan, Barry. *The United States and the Great Powers: World Politics in the Twenty-First Century.* Cambridge, MA: Polity, 2004.

Byrd, Jodi A. *The Transit of Empire: Indigenous Critiques of Colonialism.* Minneapolis: University of Minnesota Press, 2011.

Camp, Jordan T., and Jennifer Greenburg. "Counterinsurgency Reexamined: Racism, Capitalism, and U.S. Military Doctrine." *Antipode* 52, no. 2 (2020): 430–51. doi:10.1111/anti.12592.

Cantamutto, Francisco J., and Daniel Ozarow. "Serial Payers, Serial Losers? The Political Economy of Argentina's Public Debt." *Economy and Society* 45, no. 1 (2016): 123–47. doi:10.1080/03085147.2016.1161118.

Casas-Cortes, Maribel, Sebastian Cobarrubias, and John Pickles. "'Good Neighbours Make Good Fences': Seahorse Operations, Border Externalization and Extra-Territoriality." *European Urban and Regional Studies* 23, no. 3 (2016): 231–51. doi:10.1177/0969776414541136.

CEPAL. "CEPAL Se Refiere a las Implicancias de los Holdouts Para el Sistema Financiero Internacional," June 26, 2014. http://www.cepal.org/en /pressreleases/eclac-refers-implications-holdouts-international-financial -system.

Chang, Ha-Joon. *23 Things They Don't Tell You About Capitalism.* New York: Bloomsbury Press, 2011.

Chilton, Adam S., and Christopher A. Whytock. "Foreign Sovereign Immunity and Comparative Institutional Competence." *University of Pennsylvania Law Review* 163, no. 2 (2015): 411–86.

Chimni, B. S. "Third World Approaches to International Law: A Manifesto." *International Community Law Review* 8, no. 1 (2006): 3–27. doi.org/10 .1163/187197306779173220.

Chow, Daniel C. K. "Rethinking the Act of State Doctrine: An Analysis in Terms of Jurisdiction to Prescribe." *Washington Law Review* 62, no. 3 (1987): 397–478.

Christophers, Brett. "Competition, Law, and the Power of (Imagined) Geography: Market Definition and the Emergence of Too-Big-to-Fail Banking in the United States." *Economic Geography* 90, no. 4 (2014): 429–50. doi:10.1111/ecge.12062.

Christophers, Brett. *The Great Leveler: Capitalism and Competition in the Court of Law.* Cambridge, MA: Harvard University Press, 2016.

Christophers, Brett. "The Law's Markets." *Journal of Cultural Economy* 8, no. 2 (2015): 125–43. doi:10.1080/17530350.2013.781533.

Christophers, Brett. "The Limits to Financialization." *Dialogues in Human Geography* 5, no. 2 (July 2015): 183–200. doi:10.1177/2043820615588153.

Christophers, Brett, and Christopher Niedt. "Resisting Devaluation: Foreclosure, Eminent Domain Law, and the Geographical Political Economy of Risk." *Environment and Planning A: Economy and Space* 48, no. 3 (2016): 485–503. doi:10.1177/0308518X15610579.

Christopherson, Susan, Ron Martin, and Jane Pollard. "Financialisation: Roots and Repercussions." *Cambridge Journal of Regions, Economy and Society* 6, no. 3 (November 1, 2013): 351–57. doi:10.1093/cjres/rst023.

Clark, Gordon L., Karen P. Y. Lai, and Dariusz Wójcik. "Editorial Introduction to the Special Section: Deconstructing Offshore Finance." *Economic Geography* 91, no. 3 (2015): 237–49. doi:10.1111/ecge.12098.

Clark, Ian. *Hegemony in International Society.* Oxford: Oxford University Press, 2011.

Clark Jr, Jonathan M. "The Resolution of Act of State Disputes Involving Indefinitely Situated Property." *Virginia Journal of International Law* 25, no. 4 (1984): 901–38.

Coates, Benjamin Allen. *Legalist Empire: International Law and American Foreign Relations in the Early Twentieth Century.* New York: Oxford University Press, 2016.

Cohen, Harlan Grant. "A Politics-Reinforcing Political Question Doctrine." *Arizona State Law Journal* 49 (2017): 1–60.

Colangelo, Anthony J. "What Is Extraterritorial Jurisdiction?" *Cornell Law Review* 99, no. 6 (2014): 1303–52.

Cooper, Frederick. "Provincializing France." In *Imperial Formations,* edited by Ann Laura Stoler, Carole McGranahan, and Peter C. Perdue, 341–77. Santa Fe, NM: School for Advanced Research Press, 2007.

Corbridge, Stuart. *Debt and Development.* Oxford: Blackwell, 1993.

Coronil, Fernando. "After Empire: Reflections on Imperialism from the Américas." In *Imperial Formations,* edited by Ann Laura Stoler, Carole McGranahan, and Peter C. Perdue, 241–71. Santa Fe, NM: School for Advanced Research Press, 2007.

Cotterill, Joseph. "Around the World in Argentine Bond Payments?" *Financial Times,* October 31, 2012. https://ftalphaville.ft.com/2012/10/31/1240281/around-the-world-in-argentine-bond-payments/?ft_site=falcon&desktop=true.

Cotterill, Joseph. "Fairytale of New York—in Pari Passu, Anyway." *Financial Times,* January 3, 2013. https://ftalphaville.ft.com/2013/01/03/1317513/fairytale-of-new-york-in-pari-passu-anyway/?ft_site=falcon&desktop=true.

Cotterill, Joseph. "Poker with Judge Griesa, Part Two." *Financial Times,* November 22, 2012. https://ftalphaville.ft.com/2012/11/23/1276923/poker-with-judge-griesa-part-two/.

Cotterrell, Roger. "What Is Transnational Law?" *Law and Social Inquiry* 37, no. 2 (2012): 500–524. doi:10.1111/j.1747-4469.2012.01306.x.

Cuomo, Dana, and Katherine Brickell. "Feminist Legal Geographies." *Environment and Planning A: Economy and Space* 51, no. 5 (2019): 1043–49. http://dx.doi.org/10.1177/0308518X19856527.

Damrosch, Lori Fisler. "Changing the International Law of Sovereign Immunity Through National Decisions." *Vanderbilt Journal of Transnational Law* 44, no. 5 (2011): 1185–1200.

Deakin, Simon, David Gindis, Geoffrey M. Hodgson, Kainan Huang, and
Katharina Pistor. "Legal Institutionalism: Capitalism and the Constitutive Role of Law." *Journal of Comparative Economics* 45, no. 1 (2017):
188–200. doi:10.1016/j.jce.2016.04.005.

Deforge, Quentin, and Benjamin Lemoine. "Faillite d'État et Fragilité Juridique. L'Argentine Face à l'ordre Financier International." *Actes de La
Recherche En Sciences Sociales* 221–22, no. 1–2 (2018): 38–63. doi:10.3917/
arss.221.0038.

Delaney, David. "Legal Geography I: Constitutivities, Complexities, and
Contingencies." *Progress in Human Geography* 39, no. 1 (2015): 96–102.
doi:10.1177/0309132514527035.

Delaney, David. *Race, Place, and the Law, 1836–1948.* Austin: University of Texas
Press, 1998.

Dellapenna, Joseph W. "Deciphering the Act of State Doctrine." *Villanova Law
Review* 35, no. 1 (1990): 1–130.

Dellapenna, Joseph W. "Interpreting the Foreign Sovereign Immunities Act:
Reading or Construing the Text?" *Lewis and Clark Law Review* 15, no. 3
(2011): 555–88.

Dezalay, Yves, and Bryant G. Garth. *The Internationalization of Palace Wars:
Lawyers, Economists, and the Contest to Transform Latin American States.*
Chicago: University of Chicago Press, 2002.

Dezalay, Yves, and Bryant G. Garth. "Law, Lawyers, and Empire." In *The
Cambridge History of Law in America,* edited by Michael Grossberg and
Christopher Tomlins, 718–58. Cambridge: Cambridge University Press,
2008.

Diaz, Ariel Oscar. "The Territoriality Inquiry under the Act of State Doctrine:
Continuing the Search for an Appropriate Application of Situs of Debt
Rules in International Debt Disputes." *ILSA Journal of International and
Comparative Law* 10, no. 2 (2004): 525–48.

Dugan, Ianthe Jeanne. "Argentine Lobby Mystifies 'Members.'" *The Wall Street
Journal,* October 15, 2012. https://www.wsj.com/articles/SB1000087239
63904446578045780509237964991176.

Ehrenreich, Nancy. "Cluster Introduction: The Great Recession and the Politics
of Economics: Lochner Redux." *Berkeley La Raza Law Journal* 22, no. 1
(2012): 15–20.

Ehrenreich, Nancy, ed. *The Reproductive Rights Reader: Law, Medicine, and the
Construction of Motherhood.* New York: NYU Press, 2008.

Elden, Stuart. *The Birth of Territory.* Chicago: University of Chicago Press, 2013.

Elden, Stuart. "How Should We Do the History of Territory?" *Territory, Politics,
Governance* 1, no. 1 (2013): 5–20. doi:10.1080/21622671.2012.733317.

Elden, Stuart. "Land, Terrain, Territory." *Progress in Human Geography* 34, no. 6
(2010): 799–817. doi:10.1177/0309132510362603.

El-Enany, Nadine. *(B)ordering Britain: Law, Race and Empire.* Manchester, UK:
Manchester University Press, 2020.

Elliott, Lucinda. "Argentina's Congress Approves $45bn Debt Deal with IMF." *Financial Times,* March 11, 2022. https://www.ft.com/content/4a59f631 -7a86-49f2-9081-0b08d0407243.

Fang, Cheng, Fenghua Pan, and Karen P. Y. Lai. "The Brokerage Role of Hong Kong in Global Financial Networks: The Case of Mainland Chinese Companies' US Listings." *Regional Studies* 57, no. 2 (2023): 317–29.

Federici, Silvia. *Caliban and the Witch.* New York: Autonomedia, 2004.

Feldman, Mark B. "A Drafter's Interpretation of the FSIA." *Art and Cultural Heritage Law Newsletter, American Bar Association Section of International Law,* 2018.

"Final Report of the Task Force on New York Law in International Matters." New York State Bar Association, 2011. https://nysba.org/NYSBA /Sections/Dispute%20Resolution/Dispute%20Resolution%20PDFs /Task%20Force%20on%20New%20York%20Law%20in%20 International%20Matters.pdf.

Fisch, Jill E., and Caroline M. Gentile. "Vultures or Vanguards?: The Role of Litigation in Sovereign Debt Restructuring." *Emory Law Journal* 53 (2004): 1043–1114.

Fonseca, Melody. "Beyond Colonial Entrapment: The Challenges of Puerto Rican 'National Consciousness' in Times of Promesa." *Interventions* 21, no. 5 (2019): 747–65. doi:10.1080/1369801X.2019.1585917.

Ford, Richard T. "Law's Territory (A History of Jurisdiction)." *Michigan Law Review* 97, no. 4 (1999): 843–930.

Foucault, Michel. *The Birth of Biopolitics: Lectures at the Collège de France, 1978– 79.* Edited by Michel Senellart. New York: Palgrave Macmillan, 2008.

Fox, Gregory H. "Re-Examining the Act of State Doctrine: An Integrated Conflicts Analysis." *Harvard International Law Journal* 33, no. 2 (1992): 521–69.

Fox, Hazel, and Philippa Webb. *The Law of State Immunity.* 3rd ed. Oxford: Oxford University Press, 2013.

Francioni, Francesco. "Compensation for Nationalisation of Foreign Property: The Borderland between Law and Equity." *International and Comparative Law Quarterly* 24, no. 2 (1975): 255–83. doi:10.1093/iclqaj/24.2.255.

Franklin, Jane. *Cuba and the U.S. Empire: A Chronological History.* New York: Monthly Review Press, 2016.

French, Shaun, Andrew Leyshon, and Thomas Wainwright. "Financializing Space, Spacing Financialization." *Progress in Human Geography* 35, no. 6 (2011): 798–819.

Fried, Edward R., and Philip H. Trezise, eds. *Third World Debt: The Next Phase.* Report of a Conference Held in Washington, D.C., on March 10, 1989. Washington, DC: Brookings Institution, 1989.

Gallagher, Kevin. "Argentina's Creditors Must Face Up to the Coronavirus Challenge." *Financial Times,* April 20, 2020. https://www.ft.com/content /e4c731df-bb09-428f-a90a-1c31035f0763.

Gathii, James Thuo. "The Sanctity of Sovereign Loan Contracts and Its Origins in Enforcement Litigation." *George Washington International Law Review* 38, no. 2 (2006): 251–326.

Gathii, James Thuo. "TWAIL: A Brief History of Its Origins, Its Decentralized Network, and a Tentative Bibliography." *Trade, Law and Development* 3, no. 1 (2011): 26–64.

Gelpern, Anna. "Contract Hope and Sovereign Redemption." *Capital Markets Law Journal* 8, no. 2 (2013): 132–48. doi:10.1093/cmlj/kmt005.

Gelpern, Anna. "Courts and Sovereigns in the Pari Passu Goldmines." *Capital Markets Law Journal* 11, no. 2 (2016): 251–77. doi:10.1093/cmlj/kmw008.

Gelpern, Anna. "Pari Passu Whiplash." *Credit Slips: A Discussion on Credit, Finance, and Bankruptcy* (blog), July 24, 2013. http://www.creditslips.org/creditslips/2013/07/pari-passu-whiplash.html.

Gelpern, Anna. "Sovereign Damage Control." Policy Briefs. Peterson Institute for International Economics, May 2013. https://www.piie.com/publications/policy-briefs/sovereign-damage-control.

Gelpern, Anna, and Mitu Gulati. "The Wonder-Clause." *Journal of Comparative Economics,* Law in Finance, 41, no. 2 (May 1, 2013): 367–85. doi:10.1016/j.jce.2013.03.009.

George, Susan. *A Fate Worse Than Debt.* New York: Grove Press, 1990.

Gerber, David J. *Global Competition: Law, Markets and Globalization.* Oxford: Oxford University Press, 2010.

Getachew, Adom. *Worldmaking after Empire: The Rise and Fall of Self-Determination.* Princeton, NJ: Princeton University Press, 2019.

Gibson-Graham, Julie Katherine. *A Postcapitalist Politics.* Minneapolis: University of Minnesota Press, 2006.

Gilmore, Ruth Wilson. *Abolition Geography: Essays Towards Liberation.* New York: Verso Books, 2022.

Go, Julian. *Patterns of Empire: The British and American Empires, 1688 to the Present.* Cambridge: Cambridge University Press, 2011.

Goldthwaite, Karen L. "Recent Approaches to Situs of Debt in Act of State Decisions." *Connecticut Journal of International Law* 1 (1985): 151–84.

Goode, Roy, Herbert Kronke, and Ewan McKendrick, eds. *Transnational Commercial Law: Text, Cases, and Materials.* 2nd ed. Oxford: Oxford University Press, 2015.

Goswami, Manu. "Rethinking the Modular Nation Form: Toward a Sociohistorical Conception of Nationalism." *Comparative Studies in Society and History* 44, no. 4 (2002): 770–99. doi:10.1017/S001041750200035X.

Gowan, Peter. *A Calculus of Power: Grand Strategy in the Twenty-First Century.* London: Verso, 2010.

Gowan, Peter. *The Global Gamble: Washington's Faustian Bid for World Dominance.* London: Verso, 1999.

Greenburg, Jennifer. *At War with Women: Military Humanitarianism and Imperial Feminism in an Era of Permanent War.* Ithaca, NY: Cornell University Press, 2023.

Greener, Gary Jay. "The Commercial Exception to Foreign Sovereign Immunity: To Be Immune or Not to Be Immune? That Is the Question—A Look at the International Law Commission's Draft Articles on Jurisdictional Immunities of States and Their Property." *Loyola of Los Angeles International and Comparative Law Review* 15, no. 1 (1992): 173–202.

Greenhouse, Linda. *Justice on the Brink: The Death of Ruth Bader Ginsburg, the Rise of Amy Coney Barrett, and Twelve Months That Transformed the Supreme Court.* New York: Random House, 2021.

Greider, William. *Secrets of the Temple: How the Federal Reserve Runs the Country.* New York: Simon and Schuster, 1987.

Grewal, David Singh. "The Laws of Capitalism." *Harvard Law Review* 128, no. 2 (2014): 626–67.

Grewal, David Singh, and Jedediah Purdy. "Introduction: Law and Neoliberalism." *Law and Contemporary Problems* 77, no. 4 (2014): 1–23.

Gruson, Michael. "The Act of State Doctrine in Contract Cases as a Conflict-of-Laws Rule." *University of Illinois Law Review* 1988 (1988): 519–62.

Gulati, Mitu, Lee C. Buchheit, and Ignacio Tirado. "The Problem of Holdout Creditors in Eurozone Sovereign Debt Restructuring." SSRN, 2013. https://ssrn.com/abstract=2205704.

Gulati, Mitu, and Robert E. Scott. *The Three and a Half Minute Transaction: Boilerplate and the Limits of Contract Design.* Chicago: University of Chicago Press, 2013.

Gupta, Akhil. *Postcolonial Developments: Agriculture in the Making of Modern India.* Durham, NC: Duke University Press, 1998.

Guzman, Martin. "An Analysis of Argentina's 2001 Default Resolution." *Comparative Economic Studies* 62, no. 4 (2020): 701–38. doi:10.1057/s41294-020-00124-1.

Guzman, Martin. "Wall Street's Worst Vulture Hedge Funds Are Making a Killing by Undermining the Global Economy." Quartz, June 17, 2016. https://qz.com/707165/wall-streets-vulture-hedge-funds-are-making-a-killing-by-undermining-the-global-economy/.

Guzman, Martin, José Antonio Ocampo, and Joseph E. Stiglitz, eds. *Too Little, Too Late: The Quest to Resolve Sovereign Debt Crises.* New York: Columbia University Press, 2016.

Hall, Stuart. "The West and the Rest: Discourse and Power." In *The Formations of Modernity,* edited by Bram Gieben and Stuart Hall, 275–331. Cambridge, UK: Polity Press, 1992.

Harjo, Laura. *Spiral to the Stars: Mvskoke Tools of Futurity.* Critical Issues in Indigenous Studies. Tucson: The University of Arizona Press, 2019.

Harris, Cheryl I. "Whiteness as Property." *Harvard Law Review* 106 no. 8 (1993), 1707–91.

Hart, Gillian. "D/Developments after the Meltdown." *Antipode* 41, no. S1 (2010): 117–41. doi:10.1111/j.1467-8330.2009.00719.x.

Hart, Gillian. "Geography and Development: Critical Ethnographies." *Progress in Human Geography* 28, no. 1 (2004): 91–100. doi:10.1191/0309132504ph472pr.

Hart, Gillian. "Relational Comparison Revisited: Marxist Postcolonial Geographies in Practice." *Progress in Human Geography* 42, no. 3 (2018): 371–94. doi:10.1177/0309132516681388.

Hart, Gillian. "Why Did It Take So Long? Trump-Bannonism in a Global Conjunctural Frame." *Geografiska Annaler: Series B, Human Geography* 102, no. 3 (2020): 239–66. doi:10.1080/04353684.2020.1780791.

Hartman, Julian, and Mark Kear. "Critical Financial Geography." In *The Routledge Handbook of Critical Finance Studies,* edited by Christian Borch and Robert Wosnitzer, 317–42. London: Routledge, 2020.

Harvey, David. *A Brief History of Neoliberalism.* Oxford: Oxford University Press, 2007.

Harvey, David. *The Limits to Capital.* London: Verso, 2006.

Harvey, David. *The New Imperialism.* Oxford: Oxford University Press, 2003.

Hay, Eduardo. "Letter from the Mexican Minister for Foreign Affairs (Hay) to the American Ambassador (Daniels)." Foreign Relations of the United States Diplomatic Papers, 1938, The American Republics, Volume V, Doc. 663, August 3, 1938. https://history.state.gov/historicaldocuments/frus1938v05/d663.

Heidemann, Maren. *Transnational Commercial Law.* London: Bloomsbury Publishing, 2018.

Helleiner, Eric. "The Mystery of the Missing Sovereign Debt Restructuring Mechanism." *Contributions to Political Economy* 27, no. 1 (2008): 91–113. doi:10.1093/cpe/bzn003.

Helleiner, Eric. *States and the Reemergence of Global Finance: From Bretton Woods to the 1990s.* Ithaca, NY: Cornell University Press, 1994.

Hess, Burkhard. "The International Law Commission's Draft Convention on the Jurisdictional Immunities of States and Their Property." *European Journal of International Law* 4, no. 2 (1993): 269–82. doi:10.1093/oxfordjournals.ejil.a035830.

Hirschl, Ran. "The Judicialization of Mega-Politics and the Rise of Political Courts." *Annual Review of Political Science* 11, no. 1 (2008): 93–118. doi:10.1146/annurev.polisci.11.053006.183906.

Hirschl, Ran. "The Judicialization of Politics." In *The Oxford Handbook of Law and Politics,* 119–41. Oxford: Oxford University Press, 2008. http://www.oxfordhandbooks.com/view/10.1093/oxfordhb/9780199208425.001.0001/oxfordhb-9780199208425-e-8.

Hirschl, Ran. "The New Constitutionalism and the Judicialization of Pure Politics Worldwide." *Fordham Law Review* 75, no. 2 (2006): 721–54.

Hoagland, Donald W. "The Act of State Doctrine: Abandon It." *Denver Journal of International Law and Policy* 14 (1985): 317–42.

Hoang, Kimberly Kay. *Dealing in Desire: Asian Ascendancy, Western Decline, and the Hidden Currencies of Global Sex Work.* Oakland: University of California Press, 2015.

Hobsbawm, Eric. *Age of Empire: 1875–1914.* New York: Vintage Books, 1989.

Hoffman Jr., John E., and Rachel E. Deming. "The Role of the U.S. Courts in the Transnational Flow of Funds." *New York University Journal of International Law and Politics* 17, no. 3 (1985): 493–510.

Holder, Jane, and Carolyn Harrison, eds. *Law and Geography.* Oxford: Oxford University Press, 2003.

Hopewell, Kristen. *Breaking the WTO: How Emerging Powers Disrupted the Neoliberal Project.* Stanford, CA: Stanford University Press, 2016.

Horwitz, Morton J. "The History of the Public/Private Distinction." *University of Pennsylvania Law Review* 130, no. 6 (1982): 1423–28. doi:10.2307/3311976.

Horwitz, Morton J. *The Transformation of American Law, 1780–1860.* Cambridge, MA: Harvard University Press, 1977.

Horwitz, Morton J. *The Transformation of American Law, 1870–1960: The Crisis of Legal Orthodoxy.* Oxford: Oxford University Press, 1992.

Horwitz, Morton J. "The Warren Court and the Pursuit of Justice." *Washington and Lee Law Review* 50, no. 1 (1993): 5–13.

Hudson, Michael. "Vulture Funds Trump Argentinian Sovereignty." *Michael Hudson on Finance, Real Estate and the Powers of Neoliberalism* (blog), July 24, 2014. http://michael-hudson.com/2014/07/vulture-funds-trump-argentinian-sovereignty/.

Hudson, Peter James. *Bankers and Empire: How Wall Street Colonized the Caribbean.* Chicago: University of Chicago Press, 2017.

Hull, Cordell. "Letter from Secretary of State (Cordell Hull) to the Mexican Ambassador (Castillo Nájera)." Foreign Relations of the United States Diplomatic Papers, 1938, The American Republics, Volume V, Doc. 662, July 21, 1938. https://history.state.gov/historicaldocuments/frus1938v05/d662.

Hull, Cordell. "Letter from Secretary of State (Cordell Hull) to the Mexican Ambassador (Castillo Nájera)." Foreign Relations of the United States Diplomatic Papers, 1938, The American Republics, Volume V, Doc. 665, August 22, 1938. https://history.state.gov/historicaldocuments/frus1938v05/d665.

Hung, Ho-fung. *The China Boom: Why China Will Not Rule the World.* New York: Columbia University Press, 2015.

Hyndman, Jennifer. "Towards a Feminist Geopolitics." *Canadian Geographer/Le Géographe Canadien* 45, no. 2 (2001): 210–22. doi:10.1111/j.1541-0064.2001.tb01484.x.

Ikenberry, G. John. *After Victory: Institutions, Strategic Restraint, and the Re-building of Order after Major Wars.* Princeton, NJ: Princeton University Press, 2001.

Ikenberry, G. John. *America Unrivaled: The Future of the Balance of Power.* Ithaca, NY: Cornell University Press, 2002.

Immerwahr, Daniel. *How to Hide an Empire: A Short History of the Greater United States.* New York: Random House, 2019.

International Monetary Fund. *Current Developments in Monetary and Financial Law.* Vol. 4. Seminar Volumes. Washington, DC: International Monetary Fund, 2008. https://www.elibrary.imf.org/display/book /9781589065079/9781589065079.xml.

Ioannou, Stefanos, and Dariusz Wójcik. "On Financialization and Its Future." *Environment and Planning A: Economy and Space* 51, no. 1 (2019): 263–71. doi:10.1177/0308518X18820912.

Ireland-Piper, Danielle. "Outdated and Unhelpful: The Problem With the Co-mity Principle and Act of State Doctrine." *Australian International Law Journal* 24 (2018): 15–34.

Jarvis, Robert M. "The Tate Letter: Some Words Regarding Its Authorship." *American Journal of Legal History* 55, no. 4 (2015): 465–72. doi:10.1093 /ajlh/55.4.465.

Johnson, James A. "Act of State: The Fundamental Inquiry of Situs Determination for Expropriated Intangible Property: Braka v. Bancomer, S.N.C." *North Carolina Journal of International Law and Commercial Regulation* 11 (1986): 121–30.

Kahraman, Filiz, Nikhil Kalyanpur, and Abraham L. Newman. "Domestic Courts, Transnational Law, and International Order." *European Journal of International Relations* 26, no. S1 (2020): 184–208. doi:10.1177/1354066120938843.

Kamminga, Menno T. "Extraterritoriality." In *Max Planck Encyclopedia of Public International Law*, online database. Oxford: Oxford University Press, 2012. https://opil.ouplaw.com/display/10.1093/law:epil/9780199231690 /law-9780199231690-e1040?rskey=GpI8WM&result=3&prd=OPIL.

Kapczynski, Amy. "The Lochnerized First Amendment and the FDA: Toward a More Democratic Political Economy." *Columbia Law Review* 118, no. 7 (2018): 179–206.

Kapstein, Ethan B. *Governing the Global Economy: International Finance and the State.* Cambridge, MA: Harvard University Press, 1994.

Kayaoğlu, Turan. *Legal Imperialism: Sovereignty and Extraterritoriality in Japan, the Ottoman Empire, and China.* Cambridge: Cambridge University Press, 2010.

Khalili, Laleh. *Sinews of War and Trade: Shipping and Capitalism in the Arabian Peninsula.* London: Verso, 2020.

Klinger, Julie Michelle. *Rare Earth Frontiers: From Terrestrial Subsoils to Lunar Landscapes.* Ithaca, NY: Cornell University Press, 2018.

Knuth, Sarah, and Shaina Potts. "Legal Geographies of Finance: Editors' Introduction." *Environment and Planning A: Economy and Space* 48, no. 3 (2016): 458–64. doi:10.1177/0308518X15613356.

Kobrin, Stephen J. "Expropriation as an Attempt to Control Foreign Firms in LDCs: Trends from 1960 to 1979." *International Studies Quarterly* 28, no. 3 (1984): 329–48. doi:10.2307/2600634.

Koch, Natalie. "'Spatial Socialization': Understanding the State Effect Geographically." *Nordia Geographical Publications* 44, no. 4 (2015): 29–35.

Kohl, Uta. "Territoriality and Globalization." In *The Oxford Handbook of Jurisdiction in International Law,* edited by Stephen Allen, Daniel Costelloe, Malgosia Fitzmaurice, Paul Gragl, and Edward Guntrip, 300–29. Oxford: Oxford University Press, 2019.

Koskenniemi, Martti, Walter Rech, and Manuel Jiménez Fonseca, eds. *International Law and Empire: Historical Explorations.* Oxford: Oxford University Press, 2017.

Krippner, Greta R. *Capitalizing on Crisis: The Political Origins of the Rise of Finance.* Cambridge, MA: Harvard University Press, 2011.

Krippner, Greta R. "Polanyi for the Age of Trump." *Critical Historical Studies* 4, no. 2 (2017): 243–54. doi:10.1086/693902.

Krueger, Anne O., and Sean Hagan. "Sovereign Workouts: An IMF Perspective." *Chicago Journal of International Law* 6, no. 1 (2005): 203–18.

La República. "Parlasur Respalda a Argentina En Su Batalla Contra Los Fondos Buitre." July 7, 2014. https://www.larepublica.ec/blog/2014/07/07/parlasur-argentina-litigio-fondos-buitre/.

Lai, Karen P.Y. "Singapore: Connecting Asian Markets with Global Finance." In *International Financial Centres after the Global Financial Crisis and Brexit,* edited by Youssef Cassis and Dariusz Wójcik, 154–81. Oxford: Oxford University Press, 2018.

Lai, Karen P.Y., Fenghua Pan, Martin Sokol, and Dariusz Wójcik. "New Financial Geographies of Asia." *Regional Studies* 54, no. 2 (2020): 143–48. doi:10.1080/00343404.2019.1689549.

Lastra, Rosa María, and Lee C. Buchheit. *Sovereign Debt Management.* Oxford: Oxford University Press, 2014.

Laufer, Rubén, and Claudio Spiguel. "Intervencionismo En El Mundo 'Globalizado': ¿Ruptura o Continuidad Del Viejo Orden?" *Globalización e Historia,* Buenos Aires: Cámara de Diputados de la Nación, 1998. https://rubenlaufer.com/wp-content/uploads/2020/11/1996-Intervencionismo-en-el-mundo-globalizado.pdf.

Lauterpacht, Hersch. "The Problem of Jurisdictional Immunities of Foreign States." *British Year Book of International Law* 28 (1951): 220–72.

Leacock, Stephen J. "The Joy of Access to the Zone of Inhibition: Republic of Argentina v. Weltover, Inc. and the Commercial Activity Exception Under the Foreign Sovereign Immunities Act of 1976." *Minnesota Journal of Global Trade* 5, no. 1 (1996): 81–122.

Lee, Seung-Ook, Joel Wainwright, and Jim Glassman. "Geopolitical Economy and the Production of Territory: The Case of US–China Geopolitical-Economic Competition in Asia." *Environment and Planning A: Economy and Space* 50, no. 2 (2018): 416–36. doi:10.1177/0308518X17701727.

Lenin, Vladimir Ilyich. "Imperialism, the Highest Stage of Capitalism." In *Selected Works*, 1:667–766. Moscow: Progress Publishers, 1963.

Levine, Matt. "Argentina's New Attitude Pays Off in Bond Fight." *Bloomberg,* February 22, 2016, sec. Opinion. https://www.bloombergview.com /articles/2016-02-22/argentina-s-new-attitude-pays-off-in-bond-fight.

Lew, Avi. "Republic of Argentina v. Weltover, Inc.: Interpreting the Foreign Sovereign Immunity Act's Commercial Activity Exception to Jurisdictional Immunity." *Fordham International Law Journal* 17, no. 3 (1994): 726–75.

Lienau, Odette. *Rethinking Sovereign Debt: Politics, Reputation, and Legitimacy in Modern Finance.* Cambridge, MA: Harvard University Press, 2014.

López, Pablo J., and Cecilia Nahón. "The Growth of Debt and the Debt of Growth: Lessons from the Case of Argentina." *Journal of Law and Society* 44, no. 1 (2017): 99–122. doi:10.1111/jols.12016.

Lowenfeld, Andreas F. "The ICSID Convention: Origins and Transformation." *Georgia Journal of International and Comparative Law* 38, no. 1 (2009): 47–61.

Lutz, Catherine. "Empire Is in the Details." *American Ethnologist* 33, no. 4 (2006): 593–611. doi:10.1525/ae.2006.33.4.593.

Luxemburg, Rosa. *The Accumulation of Capital.* New York: Routledge and Kegan Paul, 1951.

MacKenzie, Donald A., Fabian Muniesa, and Lucia Siu. *Do Economists Make Markets? On the Performativity of Economics.* Princeton, NJ: Princeton University Press, 2007.

Mamdani, Mahmood. *Good Muslim, Bad Muslim: America, the Cold War, and the Roots of Terror.* New York: Three Leaves Press, 2005.

Mander, Benedict. "Argentina Averts Default in Debt Deal with Paris Club." *Financial Times,* June 22, 2021. https://www.ft.com/content/36392153 -c1d1-40ce-82d9-840b05881bbc.

Mander, Benedict, and Colby Smith. "Argentina Clinches Near-Unanimous Backing for Debt Restructuring." *Financial Times,* August 31, 2020. https://www.ft.com/content/e3e8b783-9455-46f3-946f-15c31a29778b.

Mann, Geoff. "A Race Between Economics and Politics, or, a Liberal Theory of Crisis?" *Geoforum* 50 (2013): A1–3. doi:10.1016/j.geoforum.2013.07.011.

Marx, Karl. *Capital: A Critique of Political Economy.* Vol. 1. New York: Penguin Classics, 1992.

Matisoff, Adina. "Multilateralism with Chinese Characteristics: The Emergence of the Asian Infrastructure Investment Bank and Its Place in the International Economic Order." PhD diss., University of California at Los Angeles, 2022.

Mattei, Ugo, and Jeffrey Lena. "U.S. Jurisdiction Over Conflicts Arising Outside of the United States: Some Hegemonic Implications." *Hastings International and Comparative Law Review* 24, no. 3 (2001): 381–400.

Maurer, Bill. "Cyberspatial Sovereignties: Offshore Finance, Digital Cash, and the Limits of Liberalism." *Indiana Journal of Global Legal Studies* 5, no. 2 (1998): 493–520.

McGranahan, Carole. "Empire Out of Bounds: Tibet in the Era of Decolonization." In *Imperial Formations,* edited by Ann Laura Stoler, Carole McGranahan, and Peter C. Perdue, 241–71. Santa Fe, NM: School for Advanced Research Press, 2007.

McGuire, Matthew Patrick. "Direct Effect Jurisdiction in the 90's: Weltover, Inc. v. Republic of Argentina and a Broad Interpretation of the Foreign Sovereign Immunities Act of 1976." *North Carolina Journal of International Law and Commercial Regulation* 17, no. 2 (1992): 383–400.

Meléndez, Edgardo. "Citizenship and the Alien Exclusion in the Insular Cases: Puerto Ricans in the Periphery of American Empire." *Centro Journal* 25, no. 1 (2013): 106–45.

MercoPress. "Argentina Prepared to Reopen Bonds' Swap Under Certain Conditions." November 27, 2012. https://en.mercopress.com/2012/11/27/argentina-prepared-to-reopen-bonds-swap-under-certain-conditions.

Mihanovich, Marcelo Etchebarne, and Cabanellas Etchebarne Kelly. "Is Argentina's Debt Saga Nearing Its End? Not So Fast." *Financial Times,* December 14, 2015. https://www.ft.com/content/0d5323f0-e320-364d-8dfd-c0e5725fe641.

Miller, Kenneth L. "Debt Situs and the Act of State Doctrine: A Proposal for a More Flexible Standard." *Albany Law Review* 49, no. 3 (1985): 647–80.

Miller, Todd. *Empire of Borders: The Expansion of the U.S. Border around the World.* New York: Verso, 2019.

Mills, Alex. *Party Autonomy in Private International Law.* Cambridge University Press, 2018.

Mitchell, Timothy. "The Properties of Markets." In *Do Economists Make Markets?: On the Performativity of Economics,* edited by Donald A. MacKenzie, Fabian Muniesa, and Lucia Siu, 244–75. Princeton, NJ: Princeton University Press, 2007.

Mitchell, Timothy. *Rule of Experts: Egypt, Techno-Politics, Modernity.* Berkeley: University of California Press, 2002.

Mitchell, Timothy. "Society, Economy, and the State Effect." In *State/Culture: State-Formation after the Cultural Turn,* edited by George Steinmetz, 76–97. Ithaca, NY: Cornell University Press, 1999.

Mnookin, Robert H., and Lewis Kornhauser. "Bargaining in the Shadow of the Law: The Case of Divorce." *The Yale Law Journal* 88, no. 5 (1979): 950–97. doi:10.2307/795824.

Moisio, Sami, Andrew EG Jonas, Natalie Koch, Christopher Lizotte, and Juho Luukkonen, eds. *Handbook on the Changing Geographies of the State:*

New Spaces of Geopolitics. Cheltenham, UK: Edward Elgar Publishing, 2020.

Monaghan, Angela, and Uki Goni. "Argentina's Government Blames 'Conspiracy' for Defaulting on Debt." *The Guardian,* July 31, 2014, sec. World news. https://www.theguardian.com/world/2014/jul/31/argentina-government-defiant-debt-default-axel-kicillof.

Moore, Adam. *Empire's Labor: The Global Army That Supports U.S. Wars.* Ithaca, NY: Cornell University Press, 2019.

Moore, Jason. *Capitalism in the Web of Life: Ecology and the Accumulation of Capital.* Verso Books, 2015.

Moreton-Robinson, Aileen. *The White Possessive: Property, Power, and Indigenous Sovereignty.* Minneapolis: University of Minnesota Press, 2015.

Mountz, Alison. *The Death of Asylum: Hidden Geographies of the Enforcement Archipelago.* Minneapolis: University of Minnesota Press, 2020.

Mountz, Alison. "The Enforcement Archipelago: Detention, Haunting, and Asylum on Islands." *Political Geography* 30, no. 3 (2011): 118–28. doi:10.1016/j.polgeo.2011.01.005.

Mountz, Alison. "Political Geography I: Reconfiguring Geographies of Sovereignty." *Progress in Human Geography* 37, no. 6 (2013): 829–41. doi:10.1177/0309132513479076.

Newman, Jay. "We Holdouts Are Open to Compromise But Argentina Has to Talk." *Financial Times,* July 7, 2014. https://www.ft.com/content/63cf7454-05be-11e4-8b94-00144feab7de.

Norris, Floyd. "Ruling on Argentina Gives Investors an Upper Hand." *The New York Times,* June 19, 2014. http://www.nytimes.com/2014/06/20/business/economy/ruling-on-argentina-gives-investors-an-upper-hand.html.

OAS. "Meeting of Consultation of Ministers of Foreign Affairs of the OAS Supports Argentina in the Restructuring of Its Sovereign Debt," July 3, 2014. http://www.oas.org/en/media_center/press_release.asp?sCodigo=E-286/14.

Ong, Aihwa. "Graduated Sovereignty in South-East Asia." *Theory, Culture and Society* 17, no. 4 (2000): 55–75. doi:10.1177/02632760022051310.

Painter, Joe. "Rethinking Territory." *Antipode* 42, no. 5 (2010): 1090–1118. doi:10.1111/j.1467-8330.2010.00795.x.

Palan, Ronen. *The Offshore World: Sovereign Markets, Virtual Places, and Nomad Millionaires.* Ithaca, NY: Cornell University Press, 2003.

Panitch, Leo, and Sam Gindin. "Finance and American Empire." In *American Empire and the Political Economy of Global Finance,* edited by Leo Panitch and Martijn Konings, 17–47. Basingstoke, UK: Palgrave Macmillan, 2008.

Panitch, Leo, and Sam Gindin. *The Making of Global Capitalism: The Political Economy of American Empire.* London: Verso, 2012.

Park, K-Sue. "Money, Mortgages, and the Conquest of America." *Law and Social Inquiry* 41, no. 4 (2016): 1006–35. doi:10.1111/lsi.12222.

Parrish, Austen L. "Reclaiming International Law from Extraterritoriality." *Minnesota Law Review* 93, no. 3 (2009): 815–74.

Pasternak, Shiri. "Jurisdiction." In *The Routledge Handbook of Law and Society,* edited by Mariana Valverde, Kamari M. Clarke, Eve Darian Smith, and Prabha Kotiswaran, 178–81. London: Routledge, 2021.

Patnaik, Utsa, and Prabhat Patnaik. *A Theory of Imperialism.* New York: Columbia University Press, 2016.

Patterson, Andrew D. "The Act of State Doctrine Is Alive and Well: Why Critics of the Doctrine Are Wrong." *U.C. Davis Journal of International Law and Policy* 15, no. 1 (2008): 111–56.

Peck, Jamie. *Constructions of Neoliberal Reason.* Oxford: Oxford University Press, 2010.

Peck, Jamie. "On Capitalism's Cusp." *Area Development and Policy* 6, no. 1 (2021): 1–30. doi:10.1080/23792949.2020.1866996.

Peck, Jamie, and Nik Theodore. "Reanimating Neoliberalism: Process Geographies of Neoliberalisation." *Social Anthropology* 20, no. 2 (2012): 177–85. doi:10.1111/j.1469-8676.2012.00194.x.

Peck, Jamie, and Nik Theodore. "Variegated Capitalism." *Progress in Human Geography* 31, no. 6 (2007): 731–72. doi:10.1177/0309132507083505.

Peck, Jamie, and Adam Tickell. "Neoliberalizing Space." *Antipode* 34, no. 3 (2002): 380–404. doi:10.1111/1467-8330.00247.

Phelan, Stephen. "Argentina in Latest Debt Default Crisis Pits 'Motherland' Against 'Vultures.'" *The Guardian,* August 20, 2014, sec. World news. https://www.theguardian.com/world/2014/aug/20/argentina-kirchner-debts-crisis-bond-holders-economics.

Pike, A., and J. Pollard. "Economic Geographies of Financialization." *Economic Geography* 86, no. 1 (2010): 29–51.

Pistor, Katharina. *The Code of Capital: How the Law Creates Wealth and Inequality.* Princeton, NJ: Princeton University Press, 2019.

Pizzurro, Joseph D. "Republic of Argentina v. Weltover, Inc." *American Journal of International Law* 86, no. 4 (1992): 820–24. doi:10.2307/2203797.

Polanyi, Karl. *The Great Transformation: The Political and Economic Origins of Our Time.* 2nd ed. Boston: Beacon Press, 2001.

Poon, Jessie PH, Jane Pollard, and Yew Wah Chow. "Resetting Neoliberal Values: Lawmaking in Malaysia's Islamic Finance." *Annals of the American Association of Geographers* 108, no. 5 (2018): 1442–56.

Portes, Ignacio. "Argentina's Ruling Peronists Suffer Heavy Defeat in Midterm Primaries." *Financial Times,* September 13, 2021. https://www.ft.com/content/64d12108-887a-45f4-abf1-17703b387dab.

Porzecanski, Arturo. "Argentina Fiasco Should Prompt Reflection at the IMF." *Financial Times,* October 17, 2019. https://www.ft.com/content/b90e9fdd-d8ae-421f-9a40-380305ed811a.

Potts, Shaina. "Beyond (De)Regulation: Law and the Production of Financial Geographies." In *The Routledge Handbook of Financial Geography,* edited by Janelle Knox-Hayes and Dariusz Wójcik, 103–21. New York: Routledge, 2020.

Potts, Shaina. "Debt in the Time of COVID-19: Creditor Choice and the Failures of Sovereign Debt Governance." *Area Development and Policy* 8, no. 2 (2023): 126–41. doi:10.1080/23792949.2023.2174887.

Potts, Shaina. "Deep Finance: Sovereign Debt Crises and the Secondary Market 'Fix.'" *Economy and Society* 46, no. 3–4 (2017): 452–75. doi:10.1080/0308 5147.2017.1408215.

Potts, Shaina. "Displaced Sovereignty: U.S. Law and the Transformation of International Financial Space." PhD diss., University of California at Berkeley, 2017.

Potts, Shaina. "Law's place in economic geography: Time, space, and methods." *Environment and Planning A: Economy and Space* (2023).

Potts, Shaina. "Law as Geopolitics: Judicial Territory, Transnational Economic Governance, and American Power." *Annals of the American Association of Geographers* 110, no. 4 (2020): 1192–1207. doi:10.1080/24694452.2019.1 670041.

Potts, Shaina. "Offshore." In *Keywords in Radical Geography: Antipode at 50,* 198–201. West Sussex, UK: John Wiley and Sons, 2019. doi:10.1002/9781119558071.ch36.

Potts, Shaina. "Reterritorializing Economic Governance: Contracts, Space, and Law in Transborder Economic Geographies." *Environment and Planning A: Economy and Space* 48, no. 3 (2016): 523–39. doi:10.1177/0308518X15607468.

Potts, Shaina. "(Re-)Writing Markets: Law and Contested Payment Geographies." *Environment and Planning A: Economy and Space* 52, no. 1 (2020): 46–65. doi:10.1177/0308518X18768286.

Prashad, Vijay. *The Darker Nations: A People's History of the Third World*. New York: New Press, 2008.

Pritchard, Ambrose Evans. "Argentina Accuses US of Judicial Malpractice for Triggering Needless Default." *The Telegraph*, July 31, 2014. https://www .telegraph.co.uk/finance/financialcrisis/11004486/Argentina-accuses -US-of-judicial-malpractice-for-triggering-needless-default.html.

Purdy, Jedediah. "Neoliberal Constitutionalism: Lochnerism for a New Economy." *Law and Contemporary Problems* 77, no. 4 (2014): 195–213.

Putnam, Tonya L. "Courts without Borders: Domestic Sources of U.S. Extraterritoriality in the Regulatory Sphere." *International Organization* 63, no. 3 (2009): 459–90. doi:10.1017/S002081830909016X.

Putnam, Tonya L. *Courts without Borders: Law, Politics, and US Extraterritoriality*. Cambridge: Cambridge University Press, 2016.

Quadros, Fausto de, and John H. Dingfelder Stone. "Act of State Doctrine." In *Max Planck Encyclopedia of Public International Law*, online encyclopedia. Oxford: Oxford University Press, 2012. https://opil.ouplaw.com /view/10.1093/law:epil/9780199231690/law-9780199231690-e1374.

Quale Jr., Andrew C. "Allied Bank's Effect on International Lending." *International Financial Law Review* 4, no. 8 (1985): 26–31.

Quintanilla, Marcus S., and Christopher A. Whytock. "The New Multipolarity in Transnational Litigation: Foreign Courts, Foreign Judgments, and Foreign Law." *Southwestern Journal of International Law* 18 (2011): 31–49. doi.org/10.2139/ssrn.1874370.

Rabinowitz, Victor. *Unrepentant Leftist: A Lawyer's Memoir.* Urbana: University of Illinois Press, 1996.

Rajagopal, Balakrishnan. *International Law from Below: Development, Social Movements and Third World Resistance.* Cambridge: Cambridge University Press, 2003.

Rana, Aziz. *The Two Faces of American Freedom.* Cambridge, MA: Harvard University Press, 2014.

Raustiala, Kal. *Does the Constitution Follow the Flag?: The Evolution of Territoriality in American Law.* Oxford: Oxford University Press, 2009.

Raustiala, Kal. "The Geography of Justice." *Fordham Law Review* 73, no. 6 (2004): 2501–60.

Rendell, Robert S. "The Allied Bank Case and Its Aftermath." *The International Lawyer* 20, no. 3 (1986): 819–28.

Riles, Annelise. "Managing Regulatory Arbitrage: A Conflict of Laws Approach." *Cornell International Law Journal* 47, no. 1 (2014): 63–120. doi:10.2139/ssrn.2335338.

Roberts, Susan. "Neoliberal Geopolitics." In *The Handbook of Neoliberalism,* edited by Simon Springer, Kean Birch, and Julie MacLeavy, 433–43. London: Routledge, 2016.

Roberts, Susan, Anna Secor, and Matthew Sparke. "Neoliberal Geopolitics." *Antipode* 35, no. 5 (2003): 886–97. doi:10.1111/j.1467-8330.2003.00363.x.

Robinson, Cedric J. *Black Marxism: The Making of the Black Radical Tradition.* Chapel Hill: University of North Carolina Press, 2000.

Roddick, Jacqueline. *The Dance of the Millions: Latin America and the Debt Crisis.* London: Latin America Bureau, 1988.

Rodney, Walter. *How Europe Underdeveloped Africa.* New York: Verso Books, 2018.

Rogerson, P. J. "The Situs of Debts in the Conflict of Laws—Illogical, Unnecessary and Misleading." *The Cambridge Law Journal* 49, no. 3 (1990): 441–60. doi:10.1017/S0008197300122317.

Roos, Jerome E. *Why Not Default?: The Political Economy of Sovereign Debt.* Princeton, NJ: Princeton University Press, 2019.

Ruccolo, Sharon D. "The Foreign Sovereign Immunities Act: Encouraging Foreign Plaintiffs to Sue Foreign Sovereigns in American Courts." *Rutgers Law Journal* 25, no. 2 (1994): 517–56.

Sachs, Jeffrey. "Making the Brady Plan Work." *Foreign Affairs* 68, no. 3 (1989): 87–104.

Sack, R. D. "Human Territoriality: A Theory." *Annals of the Association of American Geographers* 73, no. 1 (1983): 55–74.

Said, Edward. *Orientalism*. New York: Vintage Books, 1979.

Sanyal, Kalyan. *Rethinking Capitalist Development: Primitive Accumulation, Governmentality and Post-Colonial Capitalism*. London: Routledge, 2014.

Sassen, Saskia. "A Short History of Vultures." *Foreign Policy,* August 3, 2014. http://foreignpolicy.com/2014/08/03/a-short-history-of-vultures/.

Schano, Sarah K. "The Scattered Remains of Sovereign Immunity for Foreign States after Republic of Argentina v. Weltover, Inc.—Due Process Protection or Nothing." *Vanderbilt Journal of Transnational Law* 27, no. 3 (1994): 673–718.

Schlossbach, Russ. "Arguably Commercial, Ergo Adjudicable: The Validity of a Commercial Activity Exception to the Act of State Doctrine." *Boston University International Law Journal* 18, no. 1 (2000): 139–62.

Schneiderman, David. *Constitutionalizing Economic Globalization: Investment Rules and Democracy's Promise*. Cambridge: Cambridge University Press, 2008.

Schneiderman, David. "The Global Regime of Investor Rights: Return to the Standards of Civilised Justice?" *Transnational Legal Theory* 5, no. 1 (2014): 60–80. doi:10.5235/20414005.5.1.60.

Schoenberger, Erica. "Creating the Corporate World: Strategy and Culture, Time and Space." In *A Companion to Economic Geography,* edited by Eric Sheppard and Trevor Barnes, 377–91. Malden, MA: Blackwell Publishing, 2000.

Schoenberger, Erica. "The Origins of the Market Economy: State Power, Territorial Control, and Modes of War Fighting." *Comparative Studies in Society and History* 50, no. 3 (2008): 663–91. doi:10.1017/S0010417508000297.

Schumacher, Julian, Christoph Trebesch, and Henrik Enderlein. "Sovereign Defaults in Court." *Journal of International Economics* 131 (2021): 1–75. doi:10.1016/j.jinteco.2020.103388.

Schwebel, Stephen M. "A BIT about ICSID." ICSID *Review* 23, no. 1 (2008): 1–9. doi:10.1093/icsidreview/23.1.1.

Sgard, Jérôme, and Mark Weidemaier. "Global Market for Sovereign Debt: Argentina v. NML Capital, Ltd." In *Global Private International Law,* edited by Horatio Muir Watt, Lucia Bíziková, Agatha Brandão de Oliveira, and Diego P. Fernandez Arroyo, 255–70. Cheltenham, UK: Edward Elgar Publishing, 2019.

Shanor, Amanda. "The New Lochner." *Wisconsin Law Review* 2016, no. 1 (2016): 133–208. doi:10.2139/ssrn.2652762.

Shaw, Malcolm. "International Law." In *Encyclopedia Britannica*. Accessed July 1, 2022. https://www.britannica.com/topic/international-law.

Sheppard, Eric. "Globalizing Capitalism's Raggedy Fringes: Thinking Through Jakarta." *Area Development and Policy* 4, no. 1 (2019): 1–27. doi:10.1080/23792949.2018.1523682.

Sheppard, Eric. "Thinking Geographically: Globalizing Capitalism and Beyond." *Annals of the Association of American Geographers* 105, no. 6 (2015): 1113–34. doi:10.1080/00045608.2015.1064513.

Sheppard, Eric, and Helga Leitner. "Quo Vadis Neoliberalism? The Remaking of Global Capitalist Governance After the Washington Consensus." *Geoforum* 41, no. 2 (2010): 185–94. doi:10.1016/j.geoforum.2009.09.009.

Skadden, Arps, Slate, Meagher & Flom LLP & Affiliates. "Current Issues in Complex Commercial Real Estate Litigation." Memorandum, May 19, 2010. https://www.skadden.com/insights/current-issues-complex -commercial-real-estate-litigation.

Slobodian, Quinn. *Globalists: The End of Empire and the Birth of Neoliberalism.* Cambridge, MA: Harvard University Press, 2018.

Slot, Pieter J., and Mielle K. Bulterman, eds. *Globalisation and Jurisdiction.* The Hague: Kluwer Law International, 2004.

Smith, Neil. *Uneven Development: Nature, Capital, and the Production of Space.* 3rd edition. Athens: University of Georgia Press, 2010.

Soederberg, Susanne. "The Transnational Debt Architecture and Emerging Markets: The Politics of Paradoxes and Punishment." *Third World Quarterly* 26, no. 6 (2005): 927–49. doi:10.1080/01436590500089257.

Sousa Santos, Boaventura de. "Law: A Map of Misreading. Toward a Postmodern Conception of Law." *Journal of Law and Society*, 1987, 279–302.

"Sovereign Immunity Decisions of the Department of State—May 1952 to January 1977." *Digest of United States Practice in International Law.* Department of State, 1977.

Sparke, Matthew. "Globalizing Capitalism and the Dialectics of Geopolitics and Geoeconomics." *Environment and Planning A: Economy and Space* 50, no. 2 (2018): 484–89. doi:10.1177/0308518X17735926.

Sparke, Matthew. *Introducing Globalization: Ties, Tensions, and Uneven Integration.* West Sussex, UK: Wiley-Blackwell, 2013.

Stein, David. *Fearing Inflation, Inflating Fears: The End of Full Employment and the Rise of the Carceral State.* Order No. 3643181. University of Southern California, 2014. https://www.proquest.com/dissertations-theses /fearing-inflation-inflating-fears-end-full/docview/1622414677/se-2.

Stevenson, Alexandra. "How Argentina Settled a Billion-Dollar Debt Dispute with Hedge Funds." *The New York Times,* April 25, 2016, sec. Business and Policy. https://www.nytimes.com/2016/04/25/business/dealbook/how -argentina-settled-a-billion-dollar-debt-dispute-with-hedge-funds.html.

Stiglitz, Joseph E., and Martin Guzman. "Argentina Default? Griesafault Is Much More Accurate." *The Guardian,* August 7, 2014, sec. Business. https://www.theguardian.com/business/2014/aug/07/argentina-default -griesafault-more-accurate.

Stoler, Ann Laura, ed. *Imperial Debris: On Ruins and Ruination.* Durham, NC: Duke University Press, 2013.

Stoler, Ann Laura, Carole McGranahan, and Peter C. Perdue, eds. *Imperial Formations*. Santa Fe, NM: School for Advanced Research Press, 2007.

Stott, Michael, and Benedict Mander. "Argentina's Economic Woes Spell Doom for Macri's Election Prospects." *Financial Times,* October 13, 2019. https://www.ft.com/content/59e751c0-e8f6-11e9-a240 -3b065ef5fc55.

Strange, Susan. *Casino Capitalism*. Manchester, UK: Manchester University Press, 1997.

Sturzenegger, Federico, and Jeromin Zettelmeyer. *Debt Defaults and Lessons from a Decade of Crises*. Cambridge, MA: MIT Press, 2006.

Sweet, Lisa Naomi. "Foreign Sovereign Immunities Act Before and After Republic of Argentina v. Weltover." *Wisconsin International Law Journal* 12, no. 2 (1993): 375–400.

Tahyar, Margaret E. "The Act of State Doctrine: Resolving Debt Situs Confusion." *Columbia Law Review* 86, no. 3 (1986): 594–617. doi:10.2307/1122638.

Tate, C. Neal, and Torbjörn Vallinder, eds. *The Global Expansion of Judicial Power*. New York: NYU Press, 1995.

Tate, Jack. "Letter from Jack B. Tate, Acting Legal Adviser, Department of State, to Acting Attorney General Philip B. Perlman." 26 DEPT ST. BULL., May 19, 1952.

The Economist. "Argentine Bonds: Argy-Bargy." December 1, 2012. http://www .economist.com/news/finance-and-economics/21567386-argy-bargy.

The Economist. "The Luis Suarez of International Finance." July 5, 2014. https:// www.economist.com/the-americas/2014/07/05/the-luis-suarez-of -international-finance.

Thornhill, Chris. "The Mutation of International Law in Contemporary Constitutions: Thinking Sociologically about Political Constitutionalism." *The Modern Law Review* 79, no. 2 (2016): 207–47.

Torres, Hector. "In Argentina, Fernández Will Have to Clear Up Macri's Mess." *Financial Times,* December 8, 2019. https://www.ft.com/content /ef710a3c-174b-11ea-b869-0971bffac109.

Toussaint, Eric. "How to Resist Vulture Funds and Financial Imperialism?" Committee for the Abolition of Illegitimate Debt, October 1, 2014. http://www.cadtm.org/How-to-resist-vulture-funds-and.

Toussaint, Eric, and Damien Millet. *Debt, the IMF, and the World Bank: Sixty Questions, Sixty Answers*. New York: Monthly Review Press, 2010.

Tribe, Laurence H. "Politicians in Robes." *The New York Review of Books,* March 10, 2022. https://www.nybooks.com/articles/2022/03/10 /politicians-in-robes-justice-breyer-tribe/.

Tribe, Laurence, and Jeremy Lewin. "The Rightwing US Supreme Court Has Climate Protection in Its Sights." *The Guardian,* February 28, 2022. https://amp.theguardian.com/commentisfree/2022/feb/28/us-supreme -court-rightwing-climate-crisis.

Tushnet, Mark. "Law and Prudence in the Law of Justiciability: The Transformation and Disappearance of the Political Question Doctrine." *North Carolina
Law Review* 80, no. 4 (2002): 1203–36. doi:10.2139/ssrn.283464.

Tushnet, Mark. *Taking the Constitution Away from the Courts.* Princeton, NJ:
Princeton University Press, 2000. doi:10.1515/9781400822973.

"UN General Assembly: Fifteenth Session, 872nd Plenary Meeting, Official Records." United Nations, September 26, 1960. https://digitallibrary.un.org
/record/740821?ln=en.

Unger, Roberto Mangabeira. "The Critical Legal Studies Movement." *Harvard
Law Review* 96, no. 3 (1983): 561–675.

U.S. Congress. House. Committee on the Judiciary. "Jurisdiction of U.S. Courts
in Suits Against Foreign States." H. Rep. 94–1487. 94th Cong., 2d Sess.,
June 2, 1976.

U.S. Congress. House. Subcommittee on Administrative Law and Governmental
Relations of the Committee on the Judiciary. "Jurisdiction of U.S. Courts
in Suits Against Foreign States: Hearings before the Subcommittee on
Administrative Law and Governmental Relations of the Committee on
the Judiciary." Serial No. 47. 94th Cong., 2d Sess., June 2, 1976.

U.S. Congress. House. Subcommittee on Claims and Governmental Relations of
the Committee on the Judiciary. "Immunities of Foreign States: Hearing before the Subcommittee on Claims and Governmental Relations of the Committee on the Judiciary." Serial No. 10. 93rd Cong., 1st Sess., June 7, 1973.

Valentine, Victoria A., Shelli Barish Feinberg, and Simone R. Fabiilli. "The
Foreign Sovereign Immunities Act's Crippling Effect on United States Businesses." *Michigan State International Law Review* 24, no. 3 (2016): 625–66.

Valverde, Mariana. "Analyzing the Governance of Security: Jurisdiction
and Scale." *Behemoth: A Journal on Civilisation* 1, no. 1 (2008): 3–15.
doi:10.6094/behemoth.2008.1.1.748.

Valverde, Mariana. "Deepening the Conversation between Socio-Legal Theory
and Legal Scholarship about Jurisdiction." In *The Oxford Handbook of Jurisdiction in International Law,* edited by Stephen Allen, Daniel Costelloe,
Malgosia Fitzmaurice, Paul Gragl, and Edward Guntrip, 161–81. Oxford:
Oxford University Press, 2019.

Valverde, Mariana. "Jurisdiction and Scale: Legal Technicalities' as Resources for Theory." *Social and Legal Studies* 18, no. 2 (2009): 139–57.
doi:0.1177/0964663909103622.

Verdier, Pierre-Hugues, and Erik Voeten. "How Does Customary International
Law Change? The Case of State Immunity." *International Studies Quarterly* 59, no. 2 (2015): 209–22. doi:10.1111/isqu.12155.

Walker, Richard. "Value and Nature: Rethinking Capitalist Exploitation and Expansion." *Capitalism Nature Socialism* 28, no. 1 (2017): 53–61. http://dx
.doi.org/10.1080/10455752.2016.1263674.

Wall Street Journal. "Rule of Law 3, Argentina 0: A Deadbeat Nation Can't
Discriminate Among Its Creditors." November 8, 2012, sec. Opinion.

https://www.wsj.com/articles/SB10001424052970204712904578091023801581636.

Washington Post. "Monroe Leigh Dies." December 1, 2001. https://www.washingtonpost.com/archive/local/2001/12/01/monroe-leigh-dies/16ba1ee6-3ffc-4478-a01f-1ea2a67a26ba/.

Weidemaier, W. Mark C., and Anna Gelpern. "Injunctions in Sovereign Debt Litigation." *Yale Journal on Regulation* 31, no. 1 (2014): 189–218.

Weiss, Martin A. "The U.S. Bilateral Investment Treaty Program: An Overview." CRS Report for Congress. Congressional Research Service, April 24, 2007.

Wernau, Julie, and Carolyn Cui. "Argentina Returns to Global Debt Markets with $16.5 Billion Bond Sale." *Wall Street Journal,* April 20, 2016, sec. Markets. http://www.wsj.com/articles/argentina-returns-to-global-debt-markets-with-16-5-billion-bond-sale-1461078033.

Wernau, Julie, and Carolyn Cui. "Argentina's New Debt Offering Drawing Strong Demand." *Wall Street Journal,* April 18, 2016, sec. Markets. http://www.wsj.com/articles/argentinas-new-debt-offering-drawing-strong-demand-1461003618.

Whytock, Christopher A. "Domestic Courts and Global Governance." *Tulane Law Review* 84, no. 1 (2009): 67–124.

Wight, Jonathan M. "An Evaluation of the Commercial Activities Exception to the Act of State Doctrine." *University of Dayton Law Review* 19, no. 3 (1993): 1265–1303.

Wójcik, Dariusz. "The Dark Side of NY–LON: Financial Centres and the Global Financial Crisis." *Urban Studies* 50, no. 13 (2013): 2736–52. doi:10.1177/0042098012474513.

Wolf, Martin. "Defend Argentina from the Vultures." *Financial Times,* June 24, 2014, sec. Opinion. https://www.ft.com/content/2bfc9a52-f8a3-11e3-befc-00144feabdco#axzz3wyEMxGgn.

Wuerth, Ingrid. "Symposium Epilog: Foreign Sovereign Immunity at Home and Abroad." *Vanderbilt Journal of Transnational Law* 44, no. 5 (2011): 1233–38.

Wylde, Christopher. "Post-Neoliberal Developmental Regimes in Latin America: Argentina Under Cristina Fernandez de Kirchner." *New Political Economy* 21, no. 3 (2016): 322–41. doi:10.1080/13563467.2016.1113949.

Wylde, Christopher. "State, Society and Markets in Argentina: The Political Economy of Neodesarrollismo under Néstor Kirchner, 2003–2007." *Bulletin of Latin American Research* 30, no. 4 (2011): 436–52. doi:10.1111/j.1470-9856.2011.00527.x.

Zumbansen, Peer, ed. *The Oxford Handbook of Transnational Law.* Oxford: Oxford University Press, 2021.

INDEX

absolute theory, of foreign sovereign
immunity, 57, 71, 84–85, 176, 185;
Department of State relation to, 69;
restrictive theory compared to, 59,
66–67

act of state doctrine, 11, 90–91, 107,
176–77, 185, 187; *Allied Bank Int'l
v. Banco Credito Agricola de Cartago*
and, 125–29; commercial exception
to, 46, 108–11, 133–34, 188; Cuban
Revolution and, 25, 88–89, 97–98,
114–15; debt crises relation to, 26;
foreign/domestic dichotomy and,
100; foreign policy and, 7–8; foreign
sovereign immunity and, 12, 13, 15,
22, 111; international law relation
to, 104; judicial authority and, 6–7;
litigation for, 172; nationalizations/
expropriations and, 113–14, 173,
228n116; Second Circuit Court of
Appeals and, 228n102; separation of
powers and, 99; sovereign debt relation to, 131–32; Supreme Court and,
229n119; treaty exception to, 226n75;
Underhill v. Hernandez and, 30, 91–
92, 97, 185. See also *Alfred Dunhill of
London, Inc. v. Cuba*; Banco Nacional
de Cuba v. Sabbatino

Agnew, John, 20

Agrarian Reform Law (1959), 90

Agricultural Trade Development and
Assistance Act (1954), 75, 76, 78,
219n88

Alfred Dunhill of London, Inc. v. Cuba,
107–9, 111, 134, 188, 227n99; international law and, 110

*Allied Bank Int'l v. Banco Credito Agric-
ola de Cartago*, 124–28, 132, 141, 143,
189; legal geography and, 129–31

American Bar Association, 79

American Indians, 29, 30, 203n54;
dispossession and, 37

Americanization, 5, 43, 50, 85, 182

Anderson, Perry, 52

Anghie, Antony, 64–65

Appel, Hannah, 16–17, 33

arbitration, 64–65, 113–14

Argentina, 26–27, 123, 143; Bonods of,
133–38; debt crises in, 166, 174, 189;
foreign sovereign immunity and,
220n102; FSIA and, 157; government
assets of, 160–63; holdout litigation
against, 124–25; neoliberalism in,
165–67; sovereign debt of, 145–46,
153, 235n78; sovereignty of, 1–2, 139,
169; vulture funds and, 1, 3, 13, 145–
50, 154–55, 174, 239n20, 241n54,
245n113. See also *NML Capital v.
Argentina*; *Republic of Argentina v.
Weltover*

attachment, 160–62, 221n122

Banco Nacional de Cuba v. Sabbatino,
87–88, 98–100, 187; Hickenlooper
Amendment relation to, 101–3;
international law and, 104, 110;

Cold War, 13–15, 40–41; Communism and, 24–25; Cuba relation to, 93; foreign sovereign immunity relation to, 57; restrictive theory relation to, 71

Cold War Era (CWE), 14–15

colonialism, 172, 210n43; capitalism and, 199n10; NIEO relation to, 62–63

commercial exception, to act of state doctrine, 108–11, 133–34, 188

commercial exception, to foreign sovereign immunity, 7–8, 25, 46, 55–58, 65, 72–73; act of state doctrine compared to, 88; case precedent for, 173–74; Cold War relation to, 71; Department of State relation to, 69; FSIA and, 77, 80–81, 85, 133, 188; international law and, 70; litigation and, 146; nature/purpose dichotomy in, 134; public/private dichotomy and, 79, 216n54; purpose test and, 77; SOEs and, 76; Tate Letter and, 186; Third World states and, 84; World War I relation to, 185

common law, 7–8, 18, 24, 31, 51; act of state doctrine and, 25, 89; case precedent and, 21–22, 23, 53, 77; debt crises and, 123; foreign governments relation to, 20; foreign sovereign immunity and, 58–59; imperialism relation to, 50; litigation relation to, 12, 21, 53; neoliberalism in, 118; US empire relation to, 52, 66

Communism, 15; capitalism relation to, 62; Cold War and, 24–25; nationalizations/expropriations and, 94, 105; restrictive theory and, 80; SOEs and, 73

Communist Revolution, 93

compensation, for nationalizations/expropriations, 91, 95–96, 111

Conable, Barber, 230n20

Congo, 232n47

Congress, US: *Banco Nacional de Cuba v. Sabbatino* and, 88, 100; FSIA and, 79–81; international law and, 102

constitutionalism, 43, 44

Cooper, Frederick, 47

Coronil, Fernando, 60

Costa Rica, 123, 143, 233n57; Griesa and, 231n28; holdout litigation against, 124–31

COVID-19 pandemic, 166

Cox, Archibald, 99

critical legal studies, 23, 204n62

Critical Race Theory (CRT), 210n39

Cuba, 74, 78, 115; act of state doctrine and, 108–10; *Alfred Dunhill of London, Inc. v.*, 107–8; executive branch relation to, 99; foreign sovereign immunity relation to, 71; Hickenlooper Amendment and, 101–2, 227n93; US and, 90, 93, 130, 223n22

Cuban Assets Control Regulations program, 99

Cuban Revolution, 15, 87; act of state doctrine relation to, 25, 88–89, 97–98, 114–15; nationalizations/expropriations and, 89–90, 93–94, 96–104, 172–73, 186–88, 220n108

CWE (Cold War Era), 14–15

DC Bar Association, 79

debt crises, 63; in Argentina, 166, 174, 189; common law and, 123; extraction and, 141; in Greece, 233n52; intangible property and, 142; neoliberalization during, 146–47; NIEO relation to, 117, 139–40; of Third World states, 16, 26, 117–18, 120, 132–33, 188–89; Volcker Shock relation to, 121 debt restructuring, 122, 124, 180, 231n38, 232n47, 237n128; for Argentina, 145, 166; boutique investors relation to, 150–51; of Costa Rica, 125, 127; holdout litigation relation to, 123, 126, 127–28, 140–41; IMF and, 15–16, 133; UN and, 238n16

decolonization, 64–65, 72, 177, 186

Department of Justice, 161

Department of State, 14–15, 39–40, 75, 161, 220n108, 227n99; foreign sovereign immunity relation to, 69–72, 79; nationalizations/expropriations and, 96

depoliticization, 58, 64, 171, 228n115; dichotomies and, 24, 25, 52; FSIA and, 79–81, 220n110; neoliberalism and, 19, 61, 142

development contracts, 2, 74–76

Dezalay, Yves, 43

dichotomies, 17, 58, 204nn61–62; common law and, 21; foreign/domestic, 16, 26, 97, 123, 138, 147, 162, 168, 175–76; nature/purpose, 134, 136–37, 182, 219n99, 236n97; political/legal, 97–98, 100–101, 107, 159, 168, 175–76, 182, 219n92. See also public/private dichotomy

Dimock, Edward (Judge), 103–4

direct effects, foreign sovereign immunity and, 132, 138, 140, 231n28

discovery, 160–64, 169

disembeddedness, 205n69

dispossession, 36–37, 39

District Court for the Southern District of New York, 1, 22, 108, 179; *Allied Bank Int'l v. Banco Credito Agricola de Cartago* in, 124; *Banco Nacional de Cuba v. Sabbatino* in, 87–88; *Elliott Assocs., L.P. v. Republic of Peru* in, 152; international law relation to, 104; *NML Capital v. Argentina* in, 145

District of Columbia Bar, 133

domestic law, 174, 183; BITs and, 114; CRT and, 210n39; extraterritoriality compared to, 11; imperialism relation to, 46; international law compared to, 39–40; international law relation to, 103–6; transnational law relation to, 6, 205n77

Downes v. Bidwell, 29–30, 38, 207n5

economic crises: of US, 119–20. *See also* debt crises

economic nationalism, 62

economic power: extraterritoriality relation to, 202n41; judicial authority relation to, 174, 182–83; of New York state, 8, 22, 131–32, 181, 229n6; of US, 8, 13, 84–85, 142–43, 158–59, 169–70, 233n62

economic sovereignty, 176–77; act of state doctrine relation to, 89; of foreign governments, 73, 165; judicial authority and, 150; nationalizations/expropriations and, 93–94, 111–12; political sovereignty relation to, 58, 64, 66, 172–73; of Third World states, 3, 65, 76, 139–40. *See also* sovereignty

Elliott Assocs., L.P. v. Republic of Peru, 151, 152

Elliott Management, 151, 154, 165–66, 240n32; Peru relation to, 156, 241n50

enforcement problem, 145, 155, 200n28

English courts, 6, 9

English law bonds, 157

Euroclear, 148, 157

Europe: capitalism and, 208n19; imperialism of, 33–34, 36; nationalism in, 47; social welfare programs in, 18–19

execution/attachment, foreign sovereign immunity from, 72, 90, 162 executive branch: depoliticization and, 80; foreign governments relation to, 7, 16; foreign policy and, 59; foreign sovereign immunity relation to, 69–70, 82; FSIA and, 161–64; geopolitics relation to, 25; Hickenlooper Amendment and, 101–2; international law relation to, 40, 104; interventions of, 30–31; judiciary relation to, 2, 15–17, 27, 46, 67, 99, 107, 125, 159–60, 178–81, 187

Export Import Bank, 133

expropriations. *See* nationalizations/expropriations

extraction: capitalism and, 33, 34; debt crises and, 141; from Global South, 53, 171; imperialism and, 32, 52; legal practices relation to, 36

extraterritoriality, 4, 9, 11, 201n39; economic power relation to, 202n41; transnational law and, 20

Feldman, Mark, 91

Fernandez, Alberto, 166

Fidelity Union Trust Company of New Jersey, 125–26

Fifth Circuit Court of Appeals, 130

financialization, 117, 132, 187

First National City Bank v. Banco Nacional de Cuba, 107

food aid: FSIA relation to, 80; public/private dichotomy and, 75–76

Foreign Assistance Act (1964), 100–102, 225n53

foreign debts. *See specific topics*

foreign/domestic dichotomy, 16, 138, 147, 162, 168, 175–76; act of state doctrine and, 100; intangible property and, 26, 123; in *Underhill v. Hernandez*, 97

foreign governments, 223n20; common law relation to, 20; economic

sovereignty of, 73, 165; executive branch relation to, 7, 16; judicial authority and, 6–7, 31, 46, 171, 229n119; judicial power over, 12, 46, 58; judiciary relation to, 17–18, 52–53; political/legal dichotomy and, 159; private corporations and, 58, 171–72; public ships of, 55–56, 68–69; restrictive theory and, 83; US relation to, 13–14, 200n28

foreign policy, 16, 43, 91; act of state doctrine and, 7–8; Department of State relation to, 69–70; executive branch and, 59; judiciary and, 2, 51, 105; political/legal dichotomy and, 98; separation of powers and, 114–15; socialist states and, 102; sovereign debt and, 178–79

Foreign Sovereign Immunities Act (FSIA), 7, 56, 58, 76, 172; *Alfred Dunhill of London, Inc. v. Cuba* and, 111; Argentina and, 157; attachment and, 221n122; commercial exception and, 77, 80–81, 85, 133, 188; depoliticization and, 79–80; executive branch and, 161–64; international law and, 90–91; nature/purpose dichotomy in, 134; *Republic of Argentina v. nml Capital, ltd.* and, 244n97; Scalia and, 137–38; SOEs relation to, 80–81; spatial rules and, 81–82, 155, 160–61, 189

foreign sovereign immunity, 4, 6, 11, 223n20; absolute theory of, 57, 59, 66–67, 69, 71, 84–85, 176, 185; act of state doctrine and, 12, 13, 15, 22, 111; act of state doctrine compared to, 90–91; Argentina and, 220n102; boundaries and, 78; common law and, 58–59; debt crises relation to, 26; Department of State relation to, 69–72, 79; direct effects and, 132, foreign sovereign immunity (*continued*) 138, 140, 231n28; from execution/attachment, 72, 90, 162; executive branch relation to, 69–70, 82; jurisdiction and, 92; litigation for, 72–73, 172; nationalizations/expropriations and, 113–14, 173; socialist states relation to, 58, 65–66, 217n72; SOEs and, 96; spatial rules for, 81–82, 142; Third World states relation to, 71–72; UN relation to, 85–86. *See also* absolute theory, of foreign sovereign immunity; commercial exception, to foreign sovereign immunity; restrictive theory, of foreign sovereign immunity

Foucault, Michel, 51

Fox, Hazel, 57, 84, 135, 138

Friedman, Milton, 119

FSIA. *See* Foreign Sovereign Immunities Act

Fuller, Melville (Chief Justice), 30

Garth, Bryant G., 43

Gathii, James, 124, 131–32

geoeconomics, 203n53

geopolitics, 17, 20; capitalism and, 203n53; judicial authority and, 50; neoliberalism and, 52; of sovereignty, 25

Getachew, Adom, 62

Gindin, Sam, 15, 41, 42, 59–60

Ginsburg, Ruth Bader (Justice), 163, 179

globalization, 19, 41, 176, 183, 201n37; capitalism relation to, 50; extraterritoriality relation to, 11; judicial authority and, 175; neoliberal, 42, 61; neoliberalism and, 3, 18, 171; public/private dichotomy and, 84; Westphalian sovereignty relation to, 49

Global South, 44, 206n90; anticapitalist economic practices in, 120, 172; extraction from, 53, 171; US relation to, 178

governing law clauses, 6; extraterritoriality and, 11; of New York state, 234n67

Gramsci, 44

The Great Transformation (Polanyi), 59

Greece, 233n52

Grewal, David Singh, 35

Griesa, Thomas (Judge), 1–2, 124–25, 239n20, 245n122; Costa Rica and, 231n28; injunctions of, 156–59; *NML Capital v. Argentina* and, 145, 149, 167, 241n54

Guantánamo Bay, 202n44, 203n54, 223n22

Guzmán, Martín, 165, 245n109

Harlan, John Marshall (Justice), 98, 104–5

Hart, Gillian, 14

Hay, Eduardo, 95–96

Hayek, Friedrich, 61

Heavily Indebted Poor Countries (HIPC), 152

hegemony: coercion, consent and, 44, 52; common law relation to, 52; CWE, 14–15; imperialism relation to, 212n73, 213n74; of US, 44, 64, 186, 202n41, 212n73; of US dollar, 174, 177–78; Wall Street and, 119–20, 127

Hickenlooper Amendment, 103–5, 187, 225n53; Cuba and, 101–2, 227n93; international law and, 107, 110

hierarchy, 43, 207n13; capitalism and, 33; imperialism and, 32; racial, 36, 39

HIPC (Heavily Indebted Poor Countries), 152

holdout creditors, 123, 159, 165, 232n47; *Allied Bank Int'l v. Banco*

International Monetary Fund (IMF)
(*continued*)
structural adjustment programs of,
117–18, 121–22, 188–89; Third World
states relation to, 63
Iraq, 232n47

Jamaica, 219n100, 232n47
Jefferson, Thomas, 34, 35
Jim Crow laws, 29
Johnson (President), 101
judicial authority, 51, 141, 149;
over debt relations, 118–19, 124;
economic power relation to, 174,
182–83; economic sovereignty and,
150; foreign governments and, 6–7,
31, 46, 171, 229n119; FSIA and, 81;
geopolitics and, 50; globalization
and, 175; imperialism and, 45;
international law relation to, 104;
nationalizations/expropriations
and, 87–88, 96–97, 102, 106–7, 115;
nature/purpose dichotomy and,
136–37; public/private dichotomy
and, 77; spatial control and, 92, 162,
168–69
judicialization, 17, 204n64
judicial power, 16, 51, 174, 204nn65–
66; boundaries of, 8, 109, 169; executive branch and, 178; over foreign
governments, 12, 46, 58; Wall Street
and, 128
judicial review, 204n65
judicial territory. *See specific topics*
judiciary: domestic law and, 40; executive branch relation to, 2, 15–17, 27,
46, 67, 99, 107, 125, 159–60, 178–81,
187; foreign governments relation
to, 17–18, 52–53; foreign policy and,
2, 51, 105; geopolitics relation to, 25;
international law and, 102; neoliberalism of, 146–47

jure gestionis (private acts), 67–69
jure imperii (public acts), 67–69
jurisdiction, 4, 201n34; boundaries
and, 49; extraterritoriality and, 13;
foreign sovereign immunity and, 92;
sovereignty, territory and, 9–11

Kagan, Elena (Justice), 163, 179
Kapczynski, Amy, 148
Kirchner, Cristina Fernandez de, 149,
154–55, 165, 240n45
Kirchner, Nestor, 154–55, 240n45
Kneedler, Edwin, 163–64
Korea, 75
Krippner, Greta R., 61

labor unions, 119, 219n100
Latin America, 93–94, 120; IMF relation to, 122–23
Lauterpacht, Hersch, 57, 81, 85
law of nations, 39, 42
legal geography: discipline of, 23,
206n83
Legalist Empire (Coates), 39
Legal Realists, 60–61, 98
Leigh, Monroe, 217n72, 220n108,
220n110, 227n99
liberalism, 41, 42, 246n14; binaries
and, 59–60
litigation, 14, 146; common law relation to, 12, 21, 53; enforcement of,
145; for foreign sovereign immunity,
72–73, 172; of public/private dichotomy, 66; of public ships, 68–69;
of SOEs, 221n115; Third World
states and, 206n80. *See also* holdout
litigation
Lochner era, 60, 147
Louisiana Purchase, 37

Macri, Mauricio, 165–66
Manley, Michael, 63

Mann, Geoff, 60, 63–64

Maritime Law Association, 79

Marshall, John (Chief Justice), 29, 67–68, 92

Marshall, Thurgood (Justice), 228n101

Marxism, 208n22

McGranahan, Carole, 32, 41, 47

Mexican-American War, 37

Mexico, 74, 95–96, 120

Milei, Javier, 166–67

militarism, of US, 38, 41

modernization, 84

Monroe, James (President), 38

Napoleonic Wars, 66–67

nationalism, 201n37; economic, 62; in Europe, 47

nationalizations/expropriations, 25–26, 63, 223n6; act of state doctrine and, 113–14, 173, 228n116; *Alfred Dunhill of London, Inc. v. Cuba* and, 107–8; BITs and, 112–14, 173; compensation for, 91, 95–96, 111; Cuban Revolution and, 89–90, 93–94, 96–104, 172–73, 186–88, 220n108; international law and, 105; judicial authority and, 87–88, 96–97, 102, 106–7, 115; Russian Revolution and, 185; situs of debt and, 129; *Tabacalera Severiano Jorge, S.A. v. Standard Cigar Co.* and, 130; Third World states and, 94–95, 111–12. See also *Banco Nacional de Cuba v. Sabbatino*

nature/purpose dichotomy, 134, 136–37, 182, 219n99, 236n97

neoliberal counterrevolution, 63, 127, 141; IMF relation to, 118; NIEO and, 112; *Republic of Argentina v. Weltover* and, 135–36

neoliberalism, 18–19, 131, 205n70, 240n45; anti-colonialism relation to, 62; in Argentina, 165–67; China

and, 246n13; in common law, 118; economy relation to, 141–42, 176; free markets and, 42; geopolitics and, 52; globalization and, 3, 18, 42, 61, 171; of IMF, 26; of judiciary, 146–47; nature/purpose dichotomy and, 136–37; sovereignty relation to, 16; in structural adjustment programs, 121–22, 188–89

neoliberalization, 117, 187; during debt crises, 146–47

New Deal, 60–62, 71; Tate relation to, 218n73

New International Economic Order (NIEO), 26, 110; BITs relation to, 113; debt crises relation to, 117, 139–40; economic equality and, 15; nationalizations/expropriations and, 94; neoliberal counterrevolution and, 112; structural adjustment programs relation to, 122; Third World states and, 25, 62–63, 172–73, 188, 230n9; transnational law relation to, 64–65; UN Declaration on the Establishment of, 63, 188

Newman, Jay, 151–52

New York City, 126–27, 152, 236n108

New York City Bar Association, 133

New York Clearing House Association, 126

New York state, 6, 27, 96; economic power of, 8, 22, 131–32, 181, 229n6; governing law clauses and, 234n67; Third World states relation to, 143; transnational law and, 9. *See also* District Court for the Southern District of New York

NIEO. *See* New International Economic Order

Nixon (President), 119, 187

NML Capital, 151, 153–56, 245n113; government assets and, 160, 163

NML *Capital v. Argentina*, 146, 148, 150, 159, 169; economic sovereignty and, 165; executive branch and, 178, 180; Griesa and, 145, 149, 167, 241n54; injunctions, 156–57; pari passu in, 155–56; public/private dichotomy in, 157–58, 162–63, 168

Nyerere, Julius, 63

Obama, Barack, 163

Obama Administration, 3, 148–49, 166, 179, 180

Olson, Theodore, 163

Organization of the Petroleum Exporting Companies (OPEC), 119, 120

Panitch, Leo, 15, 41, 42, 59–60

pari passu, 147, 158, 168, 189, 240n48; bonds and, 155–56

Park, K-Sue, 37

Patterson, Andrew D., 90

Peru, 151–53; Elliott Management relation to, 156, 241n50; IMF relation to, 128

The Pesaro (steamship), 55–56

Pistor, Katharina, 6

PL-480. *See* Agricultural Trade Development and Assistance Act

Platt Amendment, 93

Plessy v. Ferguson, 29–30

Polanyi, Karl, 59

political/legal dichotomy, 97–98, 168, 175–76; BRICs relation to, 182; foreign governments and, 159; Hickenlooper Amendment and, 100–101; nationalizations/expropriations and, 107; public/private dichotomy relation to, 16–17, 70, 79, 98, 219n92

political question doctrine, 17, 204n64

political sovereignty, economic sovereignty relation to, 58, 64, 66, 172–73

politics/economics dichotomy, 18–19, 70; liberalism and, 59–64, 246n14

post-colonial governments, 64–66, 76, 172; anticapitalist economic practices of, 71; restrictive theory relation to, 74, 83–84. *See also* Third World states

private acts (*jure gestionis*), 67–69

property law, 37

property rights, 3, 33, 35, 37, 210n43

public acts (*jure imperii*), 67–69

public/private dichotomy, 11, 18, 59, 67–68, 97, 147, 204n61, 246n14; act of state and, 227n92; *Berizzi Bros. Co. v. S.S. Pesaro* and, 186; BRICs relation to, 182; capitalism relation to, 135, 175–76; commercial exception and, 79, 216n54; food aid and, 75–76; FSIA and, 155; globalization and, 84; judicial authority and, 77; litigation of, 66; nationalizations/expropriations and, 103, 107–8; neoliberalism relation to, 141–42; in NML *Capital v. Argentina*, 157–58, 162–63, 168; political/legal dichotomy relation to, 16–17, 70, 79, 98, 219n92; Second Circuit Court of Appeals and, 73; in *Underhill v. Hernandez*, 185; in *Victory Transport, Inc. v. Comisaria General de Abastecimientos y Transportes*, 187

public ships, 55–56, 68–69, 73–74, 185, 216n55, 216nn55–56, 217n58

Puerto Rico, 29, 30, 37, 203n54

purpose test, 77

Putnam, Tonya, 20

Rabinowitz, Victor, 98

racial capitalism, 38

racial hierarchies, 36; legal practices for, 39

racialized logics, 34, 110; legal practices and, 36–37

railways, foreign sovereign immunity and, 74

Reagan Administration, 125–27

Rehnquist, William (Justice), 106–7

Rehnquist Court, 146

Republic of Argentina v. NML Capital, LTD., 189, 199n8, 244n97

Republic of Argentina v. Weltover, 132–34, 137–39, 141, 143, 189; neoliberal counterrevolution and, 135–36

Resolution on Permanent Sovereignty over Natural Resources, of UN General Assembly, 95, 186–87

restrictive theory, of foreign sovereign immunity, 7, 24–25, 57–58, 82, 85; absolute theory compared to, 59, 66–67; Cold War relation to, 71; Communism and, 80; Department of State relation to, 69; post-colonial governments relation to, 74, 83–84; purpose test and, 77; Tate Letter relation to, 72

Roberts, John (Chief Justice), 163

Roberts, Susan, 52

Roberts Court, 146–47

Roosevelt, Franklin Delano, 95

rule of law, 42, 43, 51; foreign sovereign immunity relation to, 57

Rule of Law Committee, 79, 232n40

Russia, 178, 181; absolute theory and, 85

Russian Revolution, 60; nationalizations/expropriations in, 185

Sabbatino, Peter, 87

Sabbatino Amendment. *See* Hickenlooper Amendment

Salomon Brothers, 239n25

Scalia, Antonin (Justice), 134–38, 146, 161–64, 179, 227n99

The Schooner Exchange, 66–68, 92, 185

Schumacher, Julian, 152, 167

Second Circuit Court of Appeals, 22, 187; act of state doctrine and, 228n102; *Allied Bank Int'l v. Banco Credito Agricola de Cartago* in, 124–25, 127–31, 189; *Banco Nacional de Cuba v. Sabbatino* and, 101–3; *Elliott Assocs., L.P. v. Republic of Peru* in, 152; international law relation to, 104; on nationalizations/expropriations, 96; *NML Capital v. Argentina* in, 145, 149, 156; public/private dichotomy and, 73; *Republic of Argentina v. Weltover* in, 136; *Victory Transport* and, 76, 132–33

Secor, Anna, 52

separation of powers, 17, 31, 178, 187; act of state doctrine and, 99; *Banco Nacional de Cuba v. Sabbatino* and, 106, 109; *First National City Bank v. Banco Nacional de Cuba* and, 107; foreign policy and, 114–15; Supreme Court and, 88

Shipping Acts, 216n55

Singer, Paul, 151–52

situs of debt, 124, 140, 233n57; Costa Rica and, 129; intangible property and, 130; in US, 131–32

Slobodian, Quinn, 61

Snow, Conrad, 69

socialist states: foreign policy and, 102; foreign sovereign immunity relation to, 58, 65–66, 217n72; private corporations relation to, 14

SOEs. *See* state-owned enterprises

Sotomayor, Sonia (Justice), 179, 244n100, 246n4

sovereign debt, 2, 117–18, 120–29, 189; of Argentina, 145–46, 153, 235n78; bonds relation to, 150–51; *Elliott Assocs., L.P. v. Republic of Peru* and,

sovereign debt (*continued*)
152; enforcement and, 154; foreign
policy and, 178–79; UN General Assembly relation to, 148; US relation
to, 131–35, 137–38, 140–41. *See also*
debt restructuring
Sovereign Debt Restructuring Mechanism, of IMF, 237n128, 241n51
sovereignty, 40; of American Indians, 29; of Argentina, 1–2, 139,
169; boundaries and, 48; economic equality relation to, 62–63;
geopolitics of, 25; international law
relation to, 103–6; jurisdiction and,
9–11; neoliberalism relation to, 16;
political, 58, 64, 66, 172–73; territoriality relation to, 31, 46, 48–50;
transnational law and, 14, 174–75,
183; Westphalian, 10, 24, 30–31, 47,
49, 92, 174–75, 183
Soviet Union, 14–15, 40–41; anticapitalist economic practices of, 71; foreign sovereign immunity and, 56–57
SpaceX, 160
Spain, 76
Spanish-American War, 37, 93
Sparke, Matthew, 5, 52, 113
spatial control: judicial authority and,
92, 162, 168–69; territoriality relation to, 11–12
spatial rules, 142; FSIA and, 81–82, 155,
160–61, 189
state-owned enterprises (SOEs), 2, 56,
73–74; commercial exception and,
76; foreign sovereign immunity and,
96; FSIA relation to, 80–81; litigation of, 221n115
Stiglitz, Joseph, 165
Stoler, Ann Laura, 32, 47
Straus, Michael, 151–52
structural adjustment programs, 117,
174; neoliberal counterrevolution

and, 141; neoliberalism in, 121–22,
188–89; US empire and, 118, 123
Supreme Court, US, 1, 22, 179, 185–89;
act of state doctrine and, 229n119;
Alfred Dunhill of London, Inc. v. Cuba
in, 108; *Banco Nacional de Cuba v.
Sabbatino* and, 88, 98–100, 101–4;
Berizzi Bros. Co. v. S.S. Pesaro in, 55–
56, 68–69; *First National City Bank
v. Banco Nacional de Cuba* in, 107;
foreign sovereign immunity relation
to, 70; Hickenlooper Amendment
and, 100–101; holdout creditors
relation to, 145–46; Insular Cases
in, 38; *NML Capital v. Argentina* in,
148–49, 156; *Plessy v. Ferguson* in,
29–30; *Republic of Argentina v. NML
Capital, LTD.* in, 199n8; *Republic
of Argentina v. Weltover* in, 132–33;
Trump relation to, 238n8; *Underhill
v. Hernandez* in, 91; vulture funds
relation to, 160–61, 165
Sweet, Robert (Judge), 152

*Tabacalera Severiano Jorge, S.A. v. Stan-
dard Cigar Co.*, 130
Tate, Jack B., 69–71, 85, 217n64; New
Deal relation to, 218n73
Tate Letter, 69–75, 79, 172, 186,
217n64, 235n84; FSIA compared
to, 81
territoriality, 3, 10, 92, 142, 168–69,
202n45; act of state doctrine and,
98–99; direct effects and, 139; imperialism relation to, 46–49; judicial
territory relation to, 40, 84, 174–75;
situs of debt and, 130–31; sovereignty relation to, 31, 46, 48–50;
spatial control relation to, 11–12.
See also Westphalian territorial
sovereignty
Tet Offensive, 78

Third World Approaches to International Law (TWAIL), 199n10, 210n39

Third World states, 14, 113, 212n71; BITS and, 114; capitalism in, 19; debt crises of, 16, 26, 117–18, 120, 132–33, 188–89; economic sovereignty of, 3, 65, 76, 139–40; elites of, 212n71; foreign sovereign immunity relation to, 71–72; Hickenlooper Amendment and, 103–4; litigation and, 206n80; nationalizations/expropriations and, 94–95, 111–12; New York state relation to, 143; NIEO and, 25, 62–63, 172–73, 188, 230n9; private corporations relation to, 82; restrictive theory and, 80; UN General Assembly and, 91; US empire relation to, 15; US relation to, 65

Timerman, Héctor, 148

transnational law, 9, 66; BITS and, 114; domestic law relation to, 6, 205n77; economic power relation to, 8; extraterritoriality and, 20; NIEO relation to, 64–65; politics and, 51; sovereignty and, 14, 174–75, 183; spatio-legal operations of, 16

treaty exception, to act of state doctrine, 226n75

Trump, Donald, 238n8

TWAIL (Third World Approaches to International Law), 199n10, 210n39

UN. See United Nations

UN Charter of Economic Rights and Duties of States, 63, 95, 188

UN Convention on Jurisdictional Immunities, 182, 222n29, 236n101

UN Declaration on the Establishment of a New International Economic Order, 63, 188

Underhill v. Hernandez, 30–31, 91, 97, 185, 227n92; Westphalian sovereignty and, 92

UN General Assembly, 63, 105; Castro at, 93–94; Resolution on Permanent Sovereignty over Natural Resources of, 95, 186–87; sovereign debt relation to, 148, 237n128; Third World states and, 91

United Nations (UN), 42–43; debt restructuring and, 238 n16; Declaration on the Establishment of a New International Economic Order of, 63; foreign sovereign immunity relation to, 85–86; International Law Commission of, 137; nationalizations/expropriations and, 113

United States (US): annexation by, 37–38; BITS and, 112; China relation to, 180–82; Cuba and, 90, 93, 130, 223n22; debt crises relation to, 121; economic crises of, 119–20; economic power of, 8, 13, 84–85, 142–43, 158–59, 169–70, 233n62; economy of, 230n8; extraterritoriality and, 11; foreign governments relation to, 13–14, 200n28; Global South relation to, 178; hegemony of, 44, 64, 186, 202n41, 212n73; interventions of, 30–31; Napoleonic Wars relation to, 66–67; situs of debt in, 131–32; social welfare programs in, 18–19; sovereign debt relation to, 131–35, 137–38, 140–41; Third World states relation to, 65; UN Charter of Economic Rights and Duties of States and, 95. *See also* Supreme Court, US; US empire

US. See United States

USAID, 75, 78; FSIA relation to, 80

US dollar, 119–20, 173, 187; hegemony of, 174, 177–78. *See also* economic power

US empire, 209n26, 213n76; common law relation to, 52, 66; economic interests of, 18; foreign governments relation to, 17; free markets and, 34–35; global capitalism and, 4, 41–44; IFIs relation to, 121; judicial territory and, 13, 27, 171, 177–78; juridical empires compared to, 45; structural adjustment programs and, 118, 123; Third World states relation to, 15; Wall Street relation to, 16, 173, 187; after World War II, 31–32, 40–41, 48

Valverde, Mariana, 10

Venezuela, 30, 31

Victory Transport, 76, 78, 132–33, 187

Vietnam War, 119

Volcker, Paul, 119

Volcker Shock, 119, 121, 188

vulture funds, 167–68; Argentina and, 1, 3, 13, 145–50, 154–55, 174, 239n20, 241n54, 245n113; holdout creditors and, 152–53; Supreme Court relation to, 160–61, 165. *See also* holdout creditors

Wall Street, 117; hegemony and, 119–20, 127; judicial power and, 128; US empire relation to, 16, 173, 187

War on Drugs, 229n7

War on Terror, 16

Warren, Earl (Chief Justice), 98

Warren Court, 98, 146

Washington Legal Foundation, 148

Waterman, Sterry (Judge), 103–4

Water Street, 151

Webb, Philippa, 57, 84, 135, 138

Westphalian territorial sovereignty, 10, 24, 174–75, 183, 200n29; globalization relation to, 49; imperialism and, 47; *Underhill v. Hernandez* and, 30–31, 92

White, Byron (Justice), 29, 106, 108–11, 134, 188, 235n84

white supremacy, 36

Wolf, Martin, 148

World Bank, 42–43, 230n20; ICSID of, 113, 153–54; structural adjustment programs of, 117–18, 121–22, 188–89

World Trade Organization (WTO), 42–43, 63

World War I, 60, 185

World War II, 14, 186; US empire after, 31–32, 40–41, 48

WTO (World Trade Organization), 42–43, 63